WRITING CAPTIVITY IN THE EARLY MODERN ATLANTIC

Published for the

Omohundro Institute of

Early American History and Culture,

Williamsburg, Virginia,

by the

University of North Carolina Press,

Chapel Hill

WRITING CAPTIVITY IN THE EARLY MODERN ATLANTIC

Circulations of Knowledge and Authority in the Iberian and English Imperial Worlds

LISA VOIGT

The Omohundro Institute of
Early American History and Culture is
sponsored jointly by the College of William and Mary
and the Colonial Williamsburg Foundation.
On November 15, 1996, the Institute adopted the
present name in honor of a bequest from
Malvern H. Omohundro, Jr.

Set in Monticello by Tseng Information Systems, Inc.
Manufactured in the United States of America

Library of Congress Cataloging-in-Publication Data
Voigt, Lisa.
Writing captivity in the early modern Atlantic : circulations of knowledge and authority in the Iberian and English imperial worlds / Lisa Voigt.
p. cm.
Includes bibliographical references and index.
ISBN 978-0-8078-3199-1 (cloth : alk. paper) —
ISBN 978-0-8078-5944-5 (pbk. : alk. paper)
1. America—Ethnic relations—History—To 1500—Historiography. 2. America—Ethnic relations—History—16th century—Historiography. 3. America—Church history—Historiography. 4. Captivity narratives—America. 5. Europeans—Ethnic identity—America—Historiography. 6. Intercultural communication—America—Historiography. 7. Authority in literature. 8. Spain—Colonies—America—Historiography. 9. Portugal—Colonies—America—Historiography. 10. Great Britain—Colonies—America—Historiography. I. Omohundro Institute of Early American History & Culture. II. Title.
E29.A1V65 2009
305.80097—dc22 2008023202

Publication of this book was aided by grants from the University of Chicago as well as the Program for Cultural Cooperation between Spain's Ministry of Culture and United States Universities.

This book was written with the support of a National Endowment for the Humanities Fellowship at the Newberry Library. Any views, findings, conclusions, or recommendations expressed in this essay do not necessarily represent those of the National Endowment for the Humanities.

The paper in this book meets the guidelines for permanence and durability of the Committee on Production Guidelines for Book Longevity of the Council on Library Resources.
The University of North Carolina Press has been a member of the Green Press Initiative since 2003.

cloth 13 12 11 10 09 5 4 3 2 1
paper 13 12 11 10 09 5 4 3 2 1

To Pedro and Benvindo

[Acknowledgments]

My long captivity to this project has been a happy one only because I have enjoyed the supportive company of so many family members, friends, colleagues, and mentors along the way. Two individuals stand out for their role in shaping this book at the very beginning and the end of its writing: Stephanie Merrim, my dissertation director at Brown University, and Fredrika Teute, my editor at the Omohundro Institute of Early American History and Culture. Their meticulous readings and suggestions improved this project immeasurably at those two critical stages, and I am certainly a better writer for working with both of them. Fredrika's encouragement and advice pushed me to expand the book's argument and archive far beyond my original goals. Stephanie, an exemplary teacher, advisor, scholar, and friend, has been an invaluable source of support over the years. I am deeply grateful for all that I have learned from them about reading and writing about the early modern Atlantic world as well as for their sustained enthusiasm for this project.

Two fellowships allowed me to complete essential research and revisions, and I am thankful for not only the financial support but also the opportunities they provided to meet and interact with a wonderful and diverse group of scholars. I greatly benefited from the camaraderie and feedback of my fellow fellows while on a National Endowment of the Humanities Fellowship at the Newberry Library in 2002–2003; I am grateful to the librarians and staff, and especially to Jim Grossman and Sara Austin of the Office of Research and Education, for making it such a pleasant and productive environment in which to work. The Andrew W. Mellon Postdoctoral Research Fellowship at the Omohundro Institute of Early American History and Culture in 2005–2006 allowed me to research and write Chapter 5 as well as to reshape the book as a whole. I was moved by the cordial reception that the people of the Institute (Ron Hoffman, Sally Mason, Mendy Gladden, fellows Patrick Erben and Alec Haskell, among many others) extended to me and my work—they demonstrated, far better than any argument I make in the book, that traditional boundaries between fields of study can and should be traversed through conversation and dialogue. Many thanks to David Boruchoff for participating in the colloquium at the Institute that proved so helpful in shaping the final chapter. Thanks also to Anna Turner and Anna Brickhouse for providing useful feedback on early drafts of that chapter.

I am indebted to many other readers and audience members for their responses to different portions of this book. At the University of Chicago, presentations at the Renaissance Seminar and the Franke Institute for the Humanities were helpful in revising Chapter 1, and participants in the New Americas Studies Faculty Working Group (especially Kelly Austin, Raúl Coronado, and Eric Slauter) and the Renaissance Workshop (especially Bradin Cormack, Carla Mazzio, Carmen Nocentelli, Josh Scodel, and Richard Strier) gave insightful suggestions for Chapter 5. I am particularly grateful to the following individuals for invitations to present my work at other venues: Diogo Ramada Curto (European University Institute, Florence), Lúcia Helena Costigan (The Ohio State University), Karen Kupperman (The Atlantic World Workshop, New York University), Neil Whitehead (University of Wisconsin–Madison), and Eyda Merediz (Latin American Studies Association 2007). Other scholars and friends who have offered vital encouragement at different stages of my writing of this book include Nelson H. Vieira, Isabel Ferreira Gould, Raquel Chang-Rodríguez, Mariselle Meléndez, Josiah Blackmore, and Diana Robin.

More informal opportunities for sharing my work among friends have been at least as beneficial to me as talks and workshops. The participants in the Summer 2006 Think Tank in Chicago—Ryan Giles, Richard Gordon, Patrick Hajovsky, Nicolle Jordan, and Yarí Pérez-Marín—read final drafts of several chapters and made it possible for me to meet my submission deadline. The members of my writing group (Daisy Delogu, Cecily Hilsdale, Nicole Lassahn, Lucy Pick, and Rebecca Zorach) have patiently read many versions of chapters, and their comments and suggestions—as well as their good humor and moral support—are always much appreciated. Both of these groups have amply demonstrated that collaboration yields far better results (and is infinitely more fun) than working in isolation. My work has benefited from the support of many friends in the academic community, but none more than Richard Gordon, who has accompanied this project since its inception. He has been a constant source of energy and encouragement, and I am eternally grateful for his readiness to offer detailed feedback on any piece of writing at a moment's notice.

I published a portion of Chapter 1 in "Naufrágio, cativeiro e relações ibéricas: A *História trágico-marítima* num contexto comparativo," *Varia história,* XXXIX, no. 1 (January–June 2008), and an early, abbreviated version of Chapter 2 appeared as "Captivity, Exile, and Interpretation in *La Florida del Inca," Colonial Latin American Review,* XI, no. 2 (December 2002), 251–273. I thank both journals for their permission to reprint that material here.

Several individuals played key roles in the final stages of bringing this book to light. Ralph Bauer and Barbara Fuchs served as ideal readers of the manuscript, and their pointed suggestions and questions pushed me to think about the book's argument more comprehensively and ambitiously. I value their feedback on this as on many other occasions. Special thanks to Kimberly Borchard for assisting me with the bibliography and footnotes as I prepared the manuscript for final submission; directing her dissertation has contributed to my own work in many ways, and she is a terrific friend and (future) colleague. Finally, it was a privilege to have Kathy Burdette hone my writing as she guided the manuscript through the Institute's rigorous editorial process.

I owe a tremendous debt of gratitude to my parents, James and Margaret Voigt, for their boundless love, encouragement, and assistance through all stages of my education and career. I am incredibly grateful to have spent the last eight years working on this book in proximity to them, to my brother Jason, and to my sister Megan and her family. My Portuguese family is always near to my heart, despite our physical distance, and their invitation of an Anglo-American stranger into their home in 1993 has had an indelible impact on my life—and surely has influenced my sensitivity to the stories of individuals who embrace members of other cultures. Without the love and support of my husband, Pedro Pereira, I would never have completed this project; just as important, he has always reminded and helped me not be too captive to it. I dedicate this book to him and to our son, Benvindo Pereira. Benvindo's luminous presence in our life is so, so, so welcome.

contents

Illustrations

Introduction

In the early modern period, European publics were captivated by tales of Christians held prisoner by religious and political adversaries. Imperial expansion, spearheaded by Portugal and Spain in the fifteenth and sixteenth centuries, increased the geographical range in which subjects could fall into enemy hands as well as the forms that narratives of captivity could take. Imperial administrators heard survivors' oral reports. Pirates and privateers interrogated captured enemy pilots, who, in turn, presented accounts to their own sovereigns upon their release. Inquisition officials evaluated depositions attesting to ransomed captives' religious integrity. Audiences witnessed theatrical representations of captivity as well as sermons and public processions of ex-captives seeking to raise alms for ransom. Armchair travelers perused "true histories" of shipwreck and captivity published in book as well as pamphlet form. This study explores the role of captivity in the production of knowledge, identity, and authority in the early modern imperial world by examining texts written by and about European and Euro-American captives in a variety of languages and genres.

The practice of captivity, of course, attests to the violence that infused relations between people of different faiths and cultures in an age of extraordinary religious divisiveness and imperial ambitions within and without Europe. Yet far from simply exploiting tales of captivity to emphasize oppositions and hostilities, early modern writers frequently assert the value of the captive's cross-cultural experience and the expertise derived from it. This book focuses on both the use of the captive's knowledge and the use of the authority derived from such knowledge, particularly in works describing European exploration and colonization in the Americas. The production and circulation of captivity accounts in new and exotic locales responds, on one hand, to a desire for eyewitness information about cultures and lands where Europeans hoped to extend commercial and territorial dominion. But narrators also emphasize the pleasure that their accounts offer readers by presenting an experience both novel and familiar, in literature and in life. Early modern representations and uses of captivity thus point to epistemological as well as generic transformations that predate and prefigure those associated with what would come to be known as the Scientific Revolution

and the "rise of the novel": the privileging of experiential authority and the proliferation of prose fiction claiming to be both true and entertaining.

Iberia was not only at the forefront of the overseas exploration that resulted in new sites of captivity for Europeans but also in the vanguard of these epistemological and generic transformations. The role of the sixteenth-century Spanish Empire in the production of knowledge about the natural world and the development of scientific practices has been increasingly (albeit far from universally) acknowledged in the English-speaking world, in large part owing to the work of such scholars as Jorge Cañizares-Esguerra and Antonio Barrera-Osorio. But Portugal's even earlier pursuit of empirical knowledge about navigational routes and foreign lands in its pursuit of empire is rarely recognized outside of Portuguese scholarship. The fourth viceroy of India and cosmographer dom João de Castro (1500–1548) expresses a common Portuguese claim about the superiority of experiential knowledge when he asserts, in his *Tratado da esfera* (ca. 1538), that the erroneous opinions of the "ancients" can be corrected through "[a] muita experiencia dos modernos, e principalmente a muita navegação de Portugal" [the vast experience of the moderns, and especially the extensive navigation of the Portuguese]. Castro offers an early articulation of the link between experience, navigation, and the surpassing of classical knowledge, which in the following century would be rendered in the famous frontispiece of Francis Bacon's *Instauratio magna* (1620) as a ship sailing through the pillars of Hercules, with the biblical motto "Multi pertransibunt et augebitur scientia" [Many shall pass through and knowledge shall be increased]. Bacon probably derived the frontispiece from a Spanish treatise, Andrés García de Céspedes's *Regimiento de navegación* (1606), but his debt to Iberian precedents is also evident in his comparison of his own project with that of Columbus, in terms of their shared conviction that new knowledge remained to be discovered by experience.[1]

1. [João de Castro], *Tratado da esfera por perguntas e respostas,* in Armando Cortesão and Luís de Albuquerque, eds., *Obras completas de D. João de Castro,* 4 vols. (Coimbra, 1968–1982), I, 23–114, esp. 50 (hereafter cited as Castro, *Obras completas*). Translations throughout this book are my own unless otherwise noted. I have modernized my citations from pre-twentieth-century editions of Spanish and Portuguese texts only with respect to accent marks, the letters *f/s, b/v, y/i, g/j,* and *h,* and word division; English sources have been modernized with respect to *f/s* and *u/v.* Bacon refers to how Columbus's "reasons, though rejected at first, were afterwards made good by experience" in his *Novum organum,* in James Spedding, Robert Leslie Ellis, and Douglas Denon Heath, eds., *The Works of Francis Bacon,* 14 vols. (London, 1857–1874 [orig. publ. London, 1620]), IV, 38–248, esp. 91. On the role of the Span-

Bacon elsewhere employs another, more specific travel metaphor that also has concrete antecedents in Iberian expansion. To illustrate the difference between the Aristotelian use of sense experience and the one that he promoted for the proper interpretation of nature, Bacon explains in *Novum organum,* "Both ways set out from the senses and particulars, and rest in the highest generalities; but the difference between them is infinite. For the one just glances at experiment and particulars in passing, the other dwells duly and orderly among them." In contrast to the Aristotelian tendency to "[fly] from the senses and particulars to the most general axioms," Bacon's inductive method requires detainment in the realm of experience in the effort to produce new discoveries rather than explanations of what is commonly perceived. Bacon's correlation of scientific and navigational discovery, empiricism and imperialism is not exclusively metaphorical, as scholars like Mary

———

ish Empire in an "early scientific revolution," see Jorge Cañizares-Esguerra, "Iberian Science in the Renaissance: Ignored How Much Longer?" *Perspectives on Science,* XII (2004), 86–124 (rpt. in Cañizares-Esguerra, *Nature, Empire, and Nation: Explorations of the History of Science in the Iberian World* [Stanford, Calif., 2006], 14–45); and Antonio Barrera-Osorio, *Experiencing Nature: The Spanish American Empire and the Early Scientific Revolution* (Austin, Tex., 2006). Ralph Bauer discusses the Spanish and English Empires' contribution to a modern, "mercantilist" system of knowledge production in Bauer, *The Cultural Geography of Colonial American Literatures: Empire, Travel, Modernity* (Cambridge, 2003); for a different argument about colonial British America's contribution to natural history and modern science, stressing instead a "polycentric" empirical enterprise that depended on Euro-Americans as well as Amerindians and Africans, see Susan Scott Parrish, *American Curiosity: Cultures of Natural History in the Colonial British Atlantic World* (Chapel Hill, N.C., 2006), 315. On the Portuguese contribution to modern science, see Francisco Contente Domingues, "Science and Technology in Portuguese Navigation: The Idea of Experience in the Sixteenth Century," in Francisco Bethencourt and Diogo Ramada Curto, *Portuguese Oceanic Expansion, 1400–1800* (Cambridge, 2007), 460–479; Onésimo T. Almeida, "Portugal and the Dawn of Modern Science," in George D. Winius, ed., *Portugal, the Pathfinder: Journeys from the Medieval toward the Modern World, 1300–ca. 1600* (Madison, Wis., 1995), 341–361; and R. Hookyas, "Science in Manueline Style: The Historical Context of D. João de Castro's Works," in Castro, *Obras completas,* IV, 231–426; Hookyas addresses Renaissance notions of experience on 322–349. See also Brian W. Ogilvie, *The Science of Describing: Natural History in Renaissance Europe* (Chicago, 2006), 17–21. Ogilvie notes the lack of explicit theorization of the concept among Renaissance natural historians but stresses the importance of firsthand observation, evident in Castro's use of the term. Unfortunately, Ogilvie excludes Iberian natural history from his account based

Baine Campbell and Timothy J. Reiss have argued. But the Portuguese had long been aware of the importance of "dwelling among them," in a literal sense, for the acquisition of experiential knowledge that would serve the goals of imperial expansion. In the fifteenth century, Portuguese commercial interests in Africa were facilitated by the mediation and interpretation of *lançados,* sailors who "threw themselves" into the native societies of newly explored territories. Timothy J. Coates has described how the Crown's initial policy of encouraging lançados was replaced in the early sixteenth century with the more controlled use of *degredados* [penal exiles], whose role as involuntary colonizers was necessitated by Portugal's small demographic base and wide-ranging imperial ambitions. Vasco da Gama brought along several such degredados in his voyage to India in 1497–1499, and Pedro Álvares Cabral's follow-up expedition to Calicut in 1500 left two of them in Brazil. Pero Vaz de Caminha's letter to King Manuel describing Cabral's landfall in South America claims that the decision to leave the convicts there rather than take indigenous hostages to Portugal would get "muito melhor informação da terra" ["far better information about the land"] as well as "mais os amansar e apacificar" ["tame and pacify (the natives) all the more"].[2]

---

on an unfounded assumption about Iberians' lack of participation in "the broader European community" (24). On Bacon's debt to Spanish models and sources, particularly García de Céspedes's *Regimiento de navigación,* see Cañizares-Esguerra, "Iberian Science," *Perspectives on Science,* XII (2004), 89–93; and Bauer, *Cultural Geography of Colonial American Literatures,* 19–22; the connection between the two frontispieces has previously been made by Juan Pimentel, "The Iberian Vision: Science and Empire in the Framework of a Universal Monarchy, 1500–1800," *Osiris,* XV (2000), 17–30, esp. 24.

2. Bacon, *Novum organum,* in Spedding, Ellis, and Heath, eds., *Works of Francis Bacon,* IV, 50; Pero Vaz de Caminha, *A carta de Pero Vaz de Caminha,* ed. Jaime Cortesão (Rio de Janeiro, 1943), 217; "Letter of Pedro Vaz de Caminha to King Manuel," in William Brooks Greenlee, trans. and ed., *The Voyage of Pedro Álvares Cabral to Brazil and India from Contemporary Documents and Narratives* (London, 1938), 3–33, esp. 19. Caminha's letter was first published in Manuel Aires de Casal's *Corografia brasílica* (Rio de Janeiro, 1817), I, 12–34. See [Álvaro Velho], *Journal of the First Voyage of Vasco da Gama, 1497–1499,* trans. and ed. E. G. Ravenstein (London, 1898), 178–179, for the names of five of the degredados accompanying Gama's expedition. On Baconian empirical and imperial discourse, see Mary Baine Campbell, *Wonder and Science: Imagining Worlds in Early Modern Europe* (Ithaca, N.Y., 1999), 74–75; and Timothy J. Reiss, "'Seated between the Old World and the New': Geopolitics, Natural Philosophy, and Proficient Method," in Julie Robin Solomon and Catherine

The Portuguese Crown and chroniclers began to take advantage of the experience and expertise of those who had "dwelt among" foreigners—whether voluntarily or involuntarily—during the first exploratory and commercial voyages to Africa, sponsored by the Infante dom Henrique (Prince Henry "the Navigator") in the 1440s. In 1444, a Portuguese squire named João Fernandes willingly left the expedition of Antão Gonçalves to stay among the Muslim Berbers of Rio do Ouro in the western Sahara. Although he is often described as the first lançado, Fernandes did not intend to adopt permanent residence there. According to a contemporary chronicler, Gomes Eanes da Zurara, Fernandes stayed behind "somente pola ver e trazer novas ao Infante, quando quer que se acertasse de tornar" [only to see (the land) and to bring news to the prince, whenever he managed to return]. Indeed, Fernandes was able to return to Portugal seven months later when Prince Henry, always

---

Gimelli Martin, eds., *Francis Bacon and the Refiguring of Early Modern Thought* (Aldershot, Eng., 2005), 223–246. Reiss's argument about Bacon's association of the acquisition of knowledge to the imperial project importantly acknowledges Spanish and Portuguese antecedents (224, 231). Reiss also discusses the connection between experimental discourse and the outward voyage—a halting, repetitive journey that involves detainment and confinement before proceeding—in *The New Atlantis* (in which both the mariners and Bensalem's inhabitants speak Spanish), in Reiss, *The Discourse of Modernism* (Ithaca, N.Y., 1982), 180–197. On Portuguese Crown policies toward lançados and degredados, see Timothy J. Coates, *Convicts and Orphans: Forced and State-Sponsored Colonizers in the Portuguese Empire, 1550–1755* (Stanford, Calif., 2001), esp. 86–88. Coates characterizes lançados as renegades and points out Portuguese fears that such individuals would not only abandon their faith but serve a foreign (Moorish or Mogul) army. Other historians, however, emphasize the utility of lançados, and their mixed-race descendants, as commercial and cultural mediators for the Portuguese in Africa, Asia, and South America; see T. H. Elkiss, "On Service to the Crown—Portuguese Overseas Expansion: A Neglected Aspect," *The Journal of the American Portuguese Society*, X (1976), 44–53; Jorge Couto, "A Contribuição dos 'lançados' para os descobrimentos," *Vértice*, II (1988), 31–34; and Alida Metcalf, *Go-betweens and the Colonization of Brazil, 1500–1600* (Austin, Tex., 2005), esp. 17–35. This book corroborates and extends beyond the Portuguese Empire Metcalf's argument about the important role of go-betweens (in her terms, "physical" and "transactional" go-betweens, like captives, as well as "representational" go-betweens, like authors) in the colonization of Brazil. George E. Brooks describes the reception and integration of lançados and their Luso-African descendants into West African communities in Brooks, *Landlords and Strangers: Ecology, Society, and Trade in West Africa, 1000–1630* (Boulder, Colo., 1993), 137, 188–196. The Portuguese reliance on lançados and degredados has been attributed to Portugal's small population and lack

eager to learn about trading prospects in the region, sent Antão Gonçalves back to look for him. Prince Henry and his navigators frequently relied on captured natives to serve as interpreters and informants as they explored the West African coastline in the 1440s, but Fernandes surely knew that his report would be valorized over those of potentially duplicitous foreign captives.[3]

Indeed, the chronicler Zurara declared the "serviço especial" [special service] that Fernandes had performed for Prince Henry to be "digno de memoria, no qual não posso tantas vezes considerar que me não maravilhe mais que assaz" [worthy of remembrance, and extraordinarily marvelous each time I consider it]. A century later, the renowned historian of the Portuguese Empire João de Barros described Prince Henry's favorable reaction to the gold and slaves brought back by Gonçalves as "pouco em comparação de ver

---

of sufficient manpower for colonization; aside from the aforementioned historians, see also A. J. R. Russell-Wood, *A World on the Move: The Portuguese in Africa, Asia, and America, 1415–1808* (Manchester, 1992), 106.

3. On João Fernandes, see Gomes Eanes da Zurara, *Crónica de Guiné* (ca. 1453), ed. José de Bragança, 2d ed. (Oporto, 1973 [orig. publ. Paris, 1841]), 140, 149–150, 157–159, 325–329 (quotation on 140); and João de Barros, *Da Ásia de João de Barros e de Diogo de Couto* (Lisbon, 1778; rpt. Lisbon, 1973 [orig. publ. Lisbon, 1552]), 75–83. For an English translation of Zurara's work, see Zurara, *The Chronicle of the Discovery and Conquest of Guinea,* trans. Charles Raymond Beazley and Edgar Prestage, 2 vols. (London, 1896 and 1899). Fernandes's experience is described and contextualized in Metcalf, *Go-betweens,* 26–27; and Peter Russell, *Prince Henry "the Navigator": A Life* (New Haven, Conn., 2000), 203–206. Russell asserts that the "novelty and importance of what he did has not received in modern times the recognition it merits, perhaps because of the emphasis historians of the Portuguese discoveries have always put on seaborne exploits" (203). On the use of foreign captives as interpreters, see Jeanne Hein, "Portuguese Communication with Africans on the Searoute to India," *Terra Incognitae,* XXV (1993), 41–52. Hein cites a 1436 directive from Prince Henry ordering his captain to seize an individual in the most distant land explored in order to serve as an interpreter on future voyages. Caminha's "Letter to King Manuel" acknowledges the common practice of taking hostages as interpreters but asserts the greater utility of degredados: "Acordaram que não era necessário tomar por fôrça homens, porque era geral costume dos que assim levavam por fôrça para alguma parte dizerem que há alí de tudo quanto lhes preguntam; e que melhor e muito melhor informação da terra dariam dois homens dêstes degredados que aquí deixassem, do que êles dariam se os levassem, por ser gente que ninguém entende. Nem êles tão cêdo aprenderiam a falar para o saberem tão bem dizer que muito melhor estoutros o não digam, quando Vossa Alteza cá mandar" ["They agreed that it was not

ante si João Fernandes são, e salvo, e cheio de tanta novidade, e estranheza de terra" [little in comparison to seeing João Fernandes before him, healthy and safe, and full of such novelty and strangeness of the land]. For their part, Zurara and Barros seem to marvel at not only Fernandes's geographic and ethnographic information about an exotic land but also the narrative intrigue of his tale: the seizure of his clothes and belongings by his Berber captors, the hardships he was willing to suffer among "uma gente pouco menos de selvagem" [a people little less than savage], the kindness and affection with which he is eventually treated, and his surprisingly plump, Berber-looking appearance upon his return. In Zurara's and Barros's hands, Fernandes's tale becomes an exemplary and dramatic narrative of captivity and redemption, however voluntary his sojourn and benevolent his treatment. Fernandes's value to the chroniclers certainly overlapped with his value to Prince Henry, for they both relay his information about the societies and trading practices of the interior of the western Sahara. But their indulgence in narrative detail, and Zurara's frequent exclamations regarding Fernandes's exemplarity, suggest other ways in which the tales of ex-captives, and not simply their knowledge of foreign lands and peoples, could be used to delight and instruct audiences.[4]

Prince Henry and the authors Zurara and Barros all instrumentalized Fernandes's cross-cultural experience. Yet Fernandes's sojourn in West Africa was also motivated by self-interest, as he hoped to be rewarded for service

---

necessary to take men by force, since it was general custom that those taken away by force to another place said that everything about which they were asked was there; and that these two convicts whom we should leave would give better and far better information about the land than would be given by those carried away by us, because they are people whom no one understands nor would they learn [Portuguese] quickly enough to be able to tell it as well as those others when Your Highness sends here"]; see Caminha, *A carta,* ed. Cortesão, 216–217; "Letter," in Greenlee, trans. and ed., *Voyage of Pedro Álvares Cabral,* 19.

4. Zurara, *Crónica de Guiné,* ed. Bragança, 149 (first and third quotations); Barros, *Da Ásia,* 79 (second quotation). Barros implies Fernandes's status as a captive when he recounts how the Moors "levaram pela terra dentro" [took him inland] and stripped him of his clothes and food, in contrast to the warm reception that Prince Henry offered to the Moor taken to Portugal, among whose relatives Fernandes remained. Zurara extols the exemplary suffering of Fernandes, whom he calls a "homem de boa consciencia e assaz católico cristão" [man of good conscience and a very Catholic Christian] (158–159). On Fernandes's transformed but contented appearance on his return, see Barros, *Da Ásia,* 83.

rendered to the prince. In fact, Fernandes was himself instrumentalizing a prior experience of captivity, for Zurara tells us that he made the decision to stay in Rio do Ouro because he had previously been a "cativo entre os Mouros, em esta parte maior do mar Medioterreno, onde houvera conhecimento da linguagem; mas não sei se lhe prestaria entre aqueles" [captive among the Moors, in this larger part of the Mediterranean Sea, where he gained a knowledge of the language; but I don't know if it helped him among those people]. Zurara later confirms that Fernandes's Berber hosts spoke a different language than the Arabic that Fernandes had presumably acquired among his Moorish captors. Former captives in North Africa would, in fact, occasionally serve as interpreters on Portuguese voyages, but Fernandes sought to use his linguistic expertise acquired in captivity to immerse himself in another culture and thus position himself as an even more useful intermediary. According to Zurara, Fernandes viewed his former captivity as an opportunity to undertake a key role in the discovery and transmission of new knowledge about unfamiliar lands. The experience of individuals like Fernandes could profit not only figures of authority (and authors like Zurara and Barros) but also the ex-captives themselves.[5]

Fernandes's dual captivities point to the connections between the fifteenth-century Mediterranean world, where Christendom was confronting a growing Islamic empire under the Ottoman Turks, and the new territories abroad where the Portuguese—soon to be followed by the Spaniards and other Europeans—were seeking to extend their own commercial and imperial reach. As Fernandes's itinerary illustrates, captivity among Muslims was an experience familiar to Iberians long before they embarked on overseas exploration. Religious orders dedicated to the redemption of captives in Muslim territories of the Iberian peninsula were formed in 1198 and 1218, and the conflict between Christendom and Islam at the core of the practice is indicated in Alfonso X's mid-thirteenth-century legal definition of captives as "aquellos que caen en prisión de homes de otra creencia" [those that are imprisoned by men of another faith]. Captive-taking intensified in the century following the Reconquest owing to military conflicts with the Ottoman Empire and the rise of the North African–based piracy of the "Barbary corsairs." Algiers, in-

5. Zurara, *Crónica de Guiné,* 149, 326. One of Vasco da Gama's interpreters had also been a captive of Moors; see [Velho], *Journal of the First Voyage of Gama,* trans. and ed. Ravenstein, 23. See also Dejanirah Couto, "The Role of Interpreters, or *Linguas,* in the Portuguese Empire during the 16th Century," *E-Journal of Portuguese History,* I (2003), 1–10.

corporated into the Ottoman Empire in 1518, was the center of such a profitable economy of captive redemption that it became known as the "Indies" of the Turks, according to several seventeenth-century authors. In this context, accounts of captivity in a variety of official, learned, and popular genres both reflected and contributed to widespread anxiety in the Iberian peninsula about the possibility of capture and enslavement by Moors and Turks. Certainly Iberians' prior and greater familiarity with Muslim captors in the Mediterranean shaped how captivity in other locales would be interpreted and depicted. Yet Fernandes's career shows how the exploration of new lands also transformed and enhanced the uses that North African captivity could serve. As that exploration extended to a "New" World, a transatlantic (and, indeed, global) exchange ensued that was just as mutual. That is, models for representing captivity among non-Christians were not simply exported from the Mediterranean to the Americas; as argued in Chapter 1, accounts of Moorish and Turkish captivity also draw on New World sources for both specific content and, more broadly, rhetorical strategies.[6]

The Portuguese king João III, to whom João de Barros dedicated his *Décadas da Ásia* (1552), valued the experience of ex-captives like João Fernandes just as much as the Infante dom Henrique a century before him. Accompanying the first governor appointed to the Portuguese colony in Brazil, Tomé de Sousa, was a letter written by João III to one Diogo Álvares, a Portuguese sailor who had been shipwrecked in Bahia and captured by the Tupinambá Indians in the early sixteenth century. Historical accounts differ as to whether Álvares was saved from cannibalistic sacrifice because of the intervention of the chief's daughter or his own fortuitous use of a gun salvaged from the shipwreck. In any case, he subsequently rose in status

6. Alfonso X, *Las siete partidas del rey don Alfonso el Sabio* . . . (ca. 1263) (Madrid, 1807 [orig. publ. Seville, 1491]), II, 327. The Trinitarians and the Mercedarians, the two main orders devoted to the ransom of captives, were founded in 1198 and 1218, respectively; see Mercedes García Arenal and Miguel Ángel de Bunes, *Los españoles y el norte de África: Siglos XV–XVIII* (Madrid, 1992), 279. For references to Algiers as the Turkish "Indies," see Diego de Haedo, *Topografía e historia general de Argel* (Madrid, 1929 [orig. publ. Valladolid, 1612]), II, 88; and Francis Knight, *A Relation of Seaven Yeares Slaverie under the Turkes of Argeire, Suffered by an English Captive Merchant* . . . (London, 1640), 32, 55. On Spanish captives and redemptionist activity in North Africa, see Ellen G. Friedman, *Spanish Captives in North Africa in the Early Modern Age* (Madison, Wis., 1983). George Camamis demonstrates the prevalence of the theme of captivity in Spanish Golden Age literature in Camamis, *Estudios sobre el cautiverio en el Siglo de Oro* (Madrid, 1977).

among his captors and adopted an indigenous name, Caramuru. Álvares's successful integration with the Tupinambá was well known even to his distant sovereign, who viewed it as useful to the establishment of royal government in an area where previous private colonization efforts had failed. In the letter, dated November 19, 1548, the king praises Álvares's "muita práctica e experiência que tendes dessas terras, e da gente e costumes dellas" [much practice and experience that you have of these lands, and of the people and their customs], exhorting him to assist the new Portuguese arrivals and conciliate them with the natives. He commands Álvares to help Governor Sousa in every way possible, "porque fareis niso muito serviço" [because in this you will render much service]. This former captive's "much practice and experience" was even more highly valued than that of João Fernandes, not despite but because of his lengthier residence and more extensive assimilation, which included having children with an indigenous wife, Paraguaçu. Confirming Álvares's success at forging a powerful role out of his experience as a captive—a success already intimated in the letter from João III—is the legendary status that he acquired in later centuries, as a mediator and facilitator of the early Portuguese colony, as well as progenitor, with Paraguaçu, of a famous line of *mameluco* descendants.[7]

Mameluco, the Portuguese term for a person of mixed indigenous and European ancestry in Brazil, recalls the Mediterranean and North African coordinates that Iberians traditionally associated with captivity. *Mameluco* derives from the Arabic *mamluk* ("owned"), which refers to the captives (usually Christian) who converted to Islam and rendered military service to Muslim rulers beginning in the ninth century, similar to the Janissary Corps of the Ottoman Turks. Sometimes, like Diogo Álvares among the Tupinambá, these slave soldiers rose to power in their adoptive society, as in the Mamluk sultanate that ruled Egypt from 1250 to 1517. The Por-

7. "King João III to Diogo Álvares, 19 November 1548," in "Cartas Regias sobre Tomé de Sousa, 1548–1551," Arquivo Público do Estado da Bahia, cópias 627. I thank Alida Metcalf for generously sharing her transcription of this document. Antonio de Santa Maria Jaboatão identifies Diogo Álvares and Paraguaçu's numerous descendants (as well as the offspring of Álvares's children with other indigenous women) over two centuries in "Catálogo genealógico das principaes famílias que procederam de Albuquerques, e Cavalcantes em Pernambuco, e Caramurus na Bahia," *Revista trimensal de historia e geographia; ou, Jornal do Instituto Histórico e Geográfico Brasileiro,* LII (1889), 5–497, esp. 84–91, 138–140. As Metcalf explains, Álvares's twelve daughters married European men who became prominent figures in the colony, and three of Álvares's sons were granted nobility; see *Go-betweens,* 86.

tuguese use of the term to denote persons of mixed European and Amerindian descent suggests an assumption about the propensity of captives in the New World to procreate with their captors, an assumption fully realized by Diogo Álvares. The Spanish use of the word for janissary, *genízaro* (from the Turkish for "new soldier"), makes a similar association: the 1734 *Diccionario de autoridades* defines *genízaro* as "hijo de padres de diversa Nación: como de Español y Francesa; o al contrario" [child of parents of different nationalities: like a Spanish man and a French woman; or the reverse]. Despite this intra-European example, the entry also includes a citation from a seventeenth-century history of Chile, Alonso de Ovalle's *Historica relacion del reino de Chile* (1646): "Esta ha sido la causa de que estos *Genízaros* vivan como Gentiles, por haberse criado entre ellos" [This is the reason why these *janissaries* live like gentiles, for having been raised among them]. The genízaros to whom Ovalle refers are the mestizo children of Christian captives in southern Chile, whose upbringing among Araucanians renders them indistinguishable from their mother's or father's captors. In the New World use of *mameluco* and *genízaro,* biological *mestizaje* supplements the sense of enslavement and conversion that obtains in the terms' Arabic and Turkish roots.[8]

8. *Diccionario de la lengua castellana, en que se explica el verdadero sentido de las voces, su naturaleza y calidad, con las phrases o modos de hablar, los proverbios o refranes, y otras cosas convenientes al uso de la lengua [Diccionario de autoridades]* (Madrid, 1734), s.v. *genízaro;* Alonso de Ovalle, *Histórica relación del reino de Chile* (Santiago de Chile, 1969 [orig. publ. Rome, 1646]), 284. On captives in Chile, see Carlos Lázaro Ávila, "Los cautivos en la frontera araucana," *Revista española de antropología americana,* XXIV (1994), 191–207. Metcalf speculates on the connections between the Arabic *mamluk* and Portuguese *mameluco* in *Go-betweens,* 95; although she suspects that the association was made because many "mamelucos were the sons of Indian women who were servants and slaves," it may also result from the knowledge of white captives of Amerindians who had mixed-race children. *Mamluk* and *janissary* existed in English in the sixteenth century, but a closer (albeit rare) equivalent to the Spanish and Portuguese figurative use of these terms is one more familiar to us: *hybrid,* whose first appearance the *Oxford English Dictionary* dates to 1630, although it only began to be commonly used to denote human "cross-breeds" in the nineteenth century; see Robert J. C. Young, *Colonial Desire: Hybridity in Theory, Culture, and Race* (London, 1995), 6. Henry Cockeram's *English Dictionarie; or, An Interpreter of Hard English Words . . .* (London, 1623) defines "hybridan" in terms quite close to the *Diccionario de autoridades*'s "genízaro": "whose parents are of divers and sundry Nations."

It is just such a conflation of captivity and racial mixing that led some Europeans, in contrast to João III, to view captives with suspicion. In another seventeenth-century Chilean history, *Memorias de los sucesos de la guerra de Chile,* the ex-soldier Jerónimo de Quiroga claims, not the value, but the threat that Spanish captives and their mestizo offspring represent to the Spanish colony: "Hase reconocido con grandes experiencias que todos estos españoles o mestizos cautivos, criados o nacidos entre los indios, aman tanto sus vicios, costumbres y libertad, que son perjudiciales entre nosotros" [It has been recognized from much experience that all those Spanish and mestizo captives, born or raised among the Indians, love their vices, customs, and freedom so much that they are harmful among us]. In particular, adult Spanish captives are

> peores que los más fieros bárbaros, porque son bárbaros con discurso, y así fuera conveniente echar de la frontera a todos los que nacieron, se criaron o estuvieron muchos años cautivos, en especial si son hombres ruines, como lo son casi todos, menos los hombres principales, como no tengan nada de indio: que una pequeña raza los hace declinar de sus obligaciones, y he observado que en pasando diez años el cautiverio, en todos se hace naturaleza aquel trato continuado y vida suelta y viciosa, y son generalmente todos unos.

> worse than the fiercest barbarians, because they are barbarians with reason, and for this reason it would be best to expel from the frontier all those who were born, raised, or held captive for many years, especially if they are vile men, as most of them are, and except for the principal men, as long as they do not have anything Indian: for a little racial taint makes them decline in their obligations, and I have observed that after ten years of captivity, everyone naturalizes through continuous contact that free and vice-ridden life, and all generally become one.

The liberty that Quiroga attributes to the life of the captive would seem to contradict the state of captivity itself. However, it is precisely the freedom from Christian constraints and the resulting temptation to "go native" that make captives and mestizos such threatening figures. Whether biologically hybrid or transculturated captives, as "barbarians with reason," they obscure the clear demarcation of adversaries on a colonial frontier where Amerindians continued to resist Spanish domination until the nineteenth century. According to Quiroga, cultural contamination can extend even to those of higher status and pure blood after an extended period of time in captivity, for continuous contact tends to make them "all one."[9]

Quiroga's imputation of barbarism and moral degeneration to captives and mestizos alike resembles arguments that have been made by northern Europeans about the Spanish and Portuguese themselves. In 1899, R. S. Whiteway attributed to the Portuguese "an alacrity not found in other European nations, to mix their race with others differing entirely in status from themselves." He characterized the resulting "deterioration in the Portuguese race" as one of the "moral causes"—along with the "adoption of Oriental methods of diplomacy"—of the decline of the Portuguese Empire in the East Indies. Whiteway's reference to the 1493 papal bull dividing the unexplored globe between the "half-savage Spaniards and half-savage Portuguese" suggests a similar perspective on Iberian "mixing" with Moors and Jews before

9. Jerónimo de Quiroga, *Memorias de los sucesos de la guerra de Chile* (ca. 1690), ed. Sergio Fernández Larraín (Santiago, 1979), 229. García Arenal and Bunes describe similar perspectives in Iberia on the harm posed by captives returning from North Africa, as a result of their contact with Moors and Turks; see *Los españoles y el norte de África,* 249. In this book, I use "hybrid" to describe not only mixed-race individuals but also texts that are the product of diverse parentage (in terms of authorship as well as literary/cultural provenance). I use "transculturated" to characterize persons who selectively absorb elements of another culture and "transculturation" to describe this transformative process, whereas "intercultural" simply denotes an activity that occurs between different cultures (i.e., "intercultural mediators" mediate between cultures). Fernando Ortiz first proposed "transculturación" as an alternative to the anthropological concepts of *acculturation* and *deculturation* in Ortiz, *Contrapunteo cubano del tabaco y el azúcar (advertencia de sus contrastes agrarios, económicos, históricos, y sociales, su etnografía y su transculturación)* (Havana, 1940), translated as Ortiz, *Cuban Counterpoint: Tobacco and Sugar,* trans. Harriet de Onís (New York, 1947); see also Ángel Rama, *Transculturación narrativa en América Latina* (Mexico City, 1982); and Mary Louise Pratt, *Imperial Eyes: Travel Writing and Transculturation* (London, 1992). Román de la Campa summarizes the different perspectives on transculturation in Latin American criticism, from Ortiz's and Rama's use of the concept to explain the participation of subaltern ethnicities in modern national identities, to its critique as a "totalizing paradigm . . . , a will to cultural or racial synthesis all too willing to erase difference"; see "Of Border Artists and Transculturation: Toward a Politics of Transmodern Performances," in Campa, *Latin Americanism* (Minneapolis, 1999), 57–84, esp. 65. In this study, I examine how writers present transculturation as a potential form of service to imperialism, but I also highlight instances in their texts that denote a refusal or inability to "erase difference."

the period of expansion. Although the Black Legend of the Spanish Empire initially arose from depictions of a more military than sexual conquest, the explanations given for the savage cruelty of Spaniards in the New World have sometimes revolved around arguments about the "tropicalization of the white man"—moral degeneration as a result of contact with a barbarous environment—which are similar to those applied to the Portuguese.[10]

Beginning in the 1930s, the Brazilian sociologist Gilberto Freyre turned Whiteway's account of imperial decadence on its head by making Portuguese (and, to a lesser extent, Spanish) "alacrity" in miscegenation as well as in the adoption of indigenous customs the reasons for the distinctive superiority of Iberian colonialism. According to Freyre, centuries of contact and intermingling with Jews and Moors on the peninsula prepared the Iberians, and the Portuguese in particular, to engage in a more humane form of imperialism that involved integration and miscegenation with the native inhabitants of Asia, Africa, and the Americas. Freyre first developed the notion of Portuguese adaptability and racial tolerance with respect to master-slave relations in colonial Brazil in *Casa-grande e senzala* (1933), published in English as *The Masters and the Slaves* (1946). He extended the concept to all of the Portuguese colonies in *O mundo que o português criou* (1940) and

10. R. S. Whiteway, *The Rise of Portuguese Power in India, 1497–1550* (Westminster, 1899), 17, 21, 25. On the Spanish and Portuguese Black Legends, see William S. Maltby, *The Black Legend in England: The Development of Anti-Spanish Sentiment, 1558–1660* (Durham, N.C., 1971); and George Winius, *The Black Legend of Portuguese India* (New Delhi, 1985). Boaventura de Sousa Santos offers examples of the "'black legend' of Portugal and the Portuguese among the British" in his "Entre Prospero y Caliban: Colonialismo, pós-colonialismo e inter-identidade," in Maria Irene Ramalho and António Sousa Ribeiro, eds., *Entre ser e estar: Raízes, percursos e discursos da identidade* (Oporto, 2001), 23–85, esp. 49–52, published in English as Santos, "Between Prospero and Caliban: Colonialism, Postcolonialism, and Inter-identity," *Luso-Brazilian Review,* XXXIX, no. 2 (Winter 2002), 9–43, esp. 21–23; see also Carmen Nocentelli, "Discipline and Love: Linschoten and the *Estado da Índia,*" in Margaret R. Greer, Walter D. Mignolo, and Maureen Quilligan, *Rereading the Black Legend: The Discourses of Religious and Racial Difference in the Renaissance Empires* (Chicago, 2007), 205–224. On the "tropicalization of the white man," see Antonello Gerbi, *The Dispute of the New World: The History of a Polemic, 1750–1900,* trans. Jeremy Moyle, rev. enl. ed. (Pittsburgh, 1973 [orig. publ. Milan, 1955]), 571–576; Gerbi cites seventeenth- through twentieth-century arguments about Europeans' moral and physical transformation in the tropics, most frequently with negative qualifications.

introduced the term "Luso-Tropicalism" to describe the distinctive character of Portuguese imperialism in several lectures of the early 1950s as well as in the subsequent publications *Integração portuguesa nos trópicos* (1958) and *O luso e o trópico* (1961). In these volumes, Freyre describes not only a mode of civilization and colonization but a form of knowledge production—a "Lusotropicology" consisting in "saber de experiência feito" [knowledge of experience made], according to his frequent invocation of Camões:

> Não há exagero em dizer-se do Português que foi um dos iniciadores de um humanismo científico que opôs ao saber hieràticamente clássico o corajosamente indagador de novas realidades, uma vez alterada a situação de clima e de ambiente, quer físico, quer social, do Europeu: transferido o Europeu, não como transeunte, mas como residente, da Europa para os trópicos.
>
> It is not an exaggeration to speak of the Portuguese as having been one of the initiators of a scientific humanism that opposed to the hieratically classical knowledge another type of knowledge courageously inquiring into new realities, once having been altered both the physical and social situation of climate and environment of the European; the European having been transferred as a resident, and not as a passer-by, from Europe to the tropics.

For Freyre, as for Bacon, experiential knowledge required a "dwelling among" rather than a glance "in passing," a knowledge that the cultural and ethnic diversity of medieval Iberia made the Portuguese (and Spaniards) uniquely poised to acquire. In Freyre's Luso-Tropicalism, "tropicalization" was a sign of modern scientific inquiry rather than moral degradation.[11]

11. Gilberto Freyre, *Integração portuguesa nos trópicos / Portuguese Integration in the Tropics* (Lisbon, 1958), 34, 100–101; this is a bilingual edition. Luis de Camões's reference to "um saber só de experiências feito" [a knowledge only of experience made] appears in canto IV, stanza 94, of *Os Lusíadas* (Lisbon, 1931 [orig. publ. Lisbon, 1572]), 154. Freyre sometimes extends his claims to the Spanish Empire, referring to "Hispanotropical" civilization or symbiosis; see, for example, *Integração portuguesa nos trópicos,* 22, 88. Claúdia Castelo surveys the development of the notion of Luso-Tropicalism in Freyre's lectures and published works in Castelo, *"O modo português de estar no mundo": O luso-tropicalismo e a ideologia colonial portuguesa (1933–1961)* (Oporto, 1998), 17–43. In "The 'Kaffirs of Europe': A Comment on Portugal and the Historiography of European Expansion in Asia," *Studies in History,* IX

In a sense, the appropriation of the Brazilian sociologist's theories by the Portuguese Estado Novo in the 1950s and 1960s mirrors Prince Henry's and João III's valorization and use of the knowledge acquired by Luso-Tropical "residents" like João Fernandes and Diogo Álvares. Although similarly essentialist and exceptionalist notions of national and imperial identity already existed in Portugal, Freyre's benevolent interpretation of Portuguese colonialism was warmly received by a dictatorial regime anxious to hold on to its last remaining colonies, despite pressure from the international community and African liberation movements. In early 1961, Angola initiated its war of independence, soon to be followed by Portugal's other African colonies of Mozambique and Guinea Bissau; later that year, Goa, Daman, and Diu of the Portuguese Estado da Índia were annexed by the Indian Union. As if to counteract the real and impending loss of its overseas empire, in the same year, a government commission—formed to commemorate the quincentennial anniversary of the death of Henry the Navigator—sponsored the publication of *O luso e o trópico* (simultaneously in English, French, and Portuguese), Freyre's definitive articulation of Luso-Tropicalism. In *Race Relations in the Portuguese Colonial Empire,* published a few years later as a historical critique of Freyre's notion of inherent Portuguese tolerance, Charles Boxer cites the 1961 decree abolishing the racist "Statute of Portuguese Natives of the Provinces of Guiné, Angola, and Moçambique," which

(1992), 131–146, Sanjay Subrahmanyam describes how Luso-Tropicalism preserves, but inverts the hierarchy of, the distinction drawn by northern Europeans about Portuguese colonialism: "Rather than being a sign of weakness, miscegenation was portrayed as the great Portuguese strength, that which gave their tropical culture its resilience, and above all a sign of their humane attitude towards the colonised" (141). Subrahmanyam finds the contrast between northern European and Portuguese attitudes toward native peoples to be overstated, at least in the early modern period. Similar valorizations of mestizaje as an essential—and superior—quality of Latin American civilization have been made in other national contexts; José Vasconcelos describes the mestizo "Ibero American race" created by Spanish colonization as ushering in an era of universal hybridization in Vasconcelos, *The Cosmic Race/La raza cósmica,* trans. Didier T. Jaén (Baltimore, 1997 [orig. publ. Mexico City, 1925]). J. Jorge Klor de Alva discusses more recent examples of celebratory official discourse on mestizaje (as a synthesis culminating in "the embrace of the West") in "The Postcolonization of the (Latin) American Experience: A Reconsideration of 'Colonialism,' 'Postcolonialism,' and 'Mestizaje,'" in Gyan Prakash, ed., *After Colonialism: Imperial Histories and Postcolonial Displacements* (Princeton, N.J., 1995), 241–275, esp. 249–251.

well illustrates the convergence of Luso-Tropicalism and colonial state ideology:

> The heterogenous composition of the Portuguese People, their traditional community and patriarchal structure, and the Christian ideal of brotherhood which was always at the base of our overseas expansion early defined our reaction to other societies and cultures, and stamped it, from the beginning, with a marked respect for the manners and customs of the peoples we encountered.

As critics of Luso-Tropicalism like Boxer have long noted, such a characterization not only erases past and present violence and racism from the history of "our overseas expansion" but also casts the integration of individuals like João Fernandes and Diogo Álvares as motivated by an essential Portuguese cultural trait rather than pragmatism or necessity. Fernandes and Álvares, as much as Prince Henry and João III, recognized that dwelling among indigenous peoples produced knowledgeable intermediaries who could help to extend Portuguese power abroad. The role that Luso-Tropicalism itself would play in the ideological defense of the Portuguese Empire highlights the imperial interests served by the integration and knowledge acquisition that the theory celebrates.[12]

These interests were not lost on the author who most contributed to the legendary status of Diogo Álvares "Caramuru" in the Brazilian imagination of its colonial origins. In *Caramuru: Poema épico do descobrimento da Bahia* (1781), the Brazilian-born friar José de Santa Rita Durão cast Álvares as no less than the hero of the Portuguese colonization of Brazil. Durão's epic poem was composed a few decades after the members of a literary society in Bahia, the Academia Brasílica dos Renascidos, debated Álvares's primacy

12. C. R. Boxer, *Race Relations in the Portuguese Colonial Empire, 1415–1825* (Oxford, 1963), 2. On the reception of Freyre in Portugal as well as Portuguese antecedents to Luso-Tropicalism, see Miguel Vale de Almeida, *"Tristes Luso-Tropiques:* The Roots and Ramifications of Luso-Tropicalist Discourses," in Almeida, *An Earth-Colored Sea: "Race," Culture, and the Politics of Identity in the Postcolonial Portuguese-Speaking World* (New York, 2004), 45–64, a revised translation of Almeida, *Um mar da cor da terra: "Raça," cultura e política da identidade* (Oeiras, 2000). Castelo, *"O modo português de estar no mundo,"* 96–101, describes the appropriation of Freyre's theories for state propaganda in the 1950s and 1960s, from Salazar's invocations of Luso-Tropicalism in interviews in the foreign press to the commission, publication, and distribution of Freyre's work by governmental ministries.

in the "discovery" of Brazil and his role in the foundation of the colony. One member, who was composing an epic entitled *Brasileida,* denied Álvares's suitability as its protagonist because Álvares had been a "captivo dos Índios, ainda que depois passasse de servo a senhor" [captive of the Indians, even if he later went from servant to master]. In contrast, Durão presents Álvares's captivity as allowing him to acquire the linguistic skills, ethnographic knowledge, and indigenous alliances necessary to bring about the peaceful establishment of Portuguese rule and religion. Durão's portrayal of Diogo Álvares "Caramuru" thus imaginatively substantiates, three centuries later, João III's recognition of the captive's contribution to Portuguese colonization. Indeed, Durão portrays Álvares as a figure known to and honored by not only the Portuguese sovereign but also Charles V of Spain and the Holy Roman Empire and Henry II of France. Through his succor of a shipwrecked Spanish vessel and his report to the French king during a voyage to Paris (where his indigenous wife is baptized), Álvares shares his experiential knowledge and mediating abilities across national and linguistic borders.[13]

Yet Durão's motivation for writing *Caramuru* extends beyond recovering and revalorizing Álvares's service to João III (and other European sovereigns). In the "Reflections" that precede the poem, Durão announces the patriotic sentiment that inspired him to write *Caramuru,* referring to his "amor da Pátria" (love for [his] homeland). Durão's attachment to his native land of Brazil, despite leaving there at the age of nine, inspired him to emulate Luis de Camões's renowned epic celebrating Portuguese expansion in the East, *Os Lusíadas* (1572). Diogo Álvares's tale of captivity, romance, and rise to power in Brazil affords Durão an opportunity to extol his homeland and present it as an equally important part of the Portuguese Empire, even if it was not viewed as such in Álvares's time. Unlike Camões, Durão cannot present himself as a participant in some of the events depicted in the poem or invoke his "longa experiência" [long experience] in the imperial arena as a source of authority. Instead, Durão asserts his Brazilian birthplace, identifying himself as "natural da Cara-Preta nas Minas Gerais" [native of Cara-

13. José de Santa Rita Durão, *Caramuru: Poema épico do descobrimento da Bahia* (São Paulo, 1945 [orig. publ. Lisbon, 1781]); Domingos de Silva Teles, "Carta para o director perpetuo," in João Lúcio de Azevedo, "Academia dos Renascidos: A história. 'Desaggravos do Brasil' e o poema 'Brasileida,'" *Revista de língua portuguesa,* XIX (1922), 85–95, esp. 89–94. On the discussions about Diogo Álvares's role in the discovery of Brazil in the eighteenth-century Brazilian academies, see Carlos de Assis Pereira, *Fontes do "Caramuru" de Santa Rita Durão* (Assis, Brazil, 1971), 1–9.

Preta in Minas Gerais] on the title page of *Caramuru* (Plate 1). Durão's portrait of a Portuguese resident in Brazil as a knowledgeable and powerful intermediary reflects favorably on his self-presentation as a native of Brazil writing in Portugal. For Durão, Portugal's appreciation of its largest overseas colony depended on the mediation of authors like himself, as much as Portuguese sovereignty in Brazil relied on the negotiating abilities of ex-captives like Diogo Álvares.[14]

Durão's vindication of the epic grandeur of the "events of Brazil" participates in the intellectual defense of American homelands that increasingly preoccupied American-born writers in the eighteenth century. Antonello Gerbi has described the "dispute of the New World" instigated by naturalists and historians of the European Enlightenment like the comte de Buffon, Cornelius de Pauw, and William Robertson, who asserted the inferiority of the American climate and its deleterious effects on the flora, fauna, and inhabitants of the New World. Among the American responses to such allegations is a work completed in 1757 and aptly entitled *Desagravos do Brasil e glorias de Pernambuco* [Brazilian Retaliation and Glories of Pernambuco], with which the Brazilian friar Domingos de Loreto Couto sought to "refutar alguns erros, e calumnias, com que alguns Autores, que têm escrito do Brazil, mancharão a opinião dos nossos Índios, e de algumas pessoas beneméritas" [refute some of the errors and calumnies with which some authors, who have written about Brazil, have tarnished the image of our Indians, and of some worthy people]. As Couto insinuates, such "calumnies" were often directed at not only Amerindians but also Americans of European descent, who in the sixteenth century began to be ascribed with degeneration as a result of negative environmental and astrological influence. Juan López de Velasco's *Geografía y descripción universal de las Indias,* written between 1571 and 1574, asserts the detrimental consequences of the New World climate and constellations on the bodies of Spaniards who reside in the Indies, and especially on the *criollos* born there, in whom "las [calidades] del ánimo suelen seguir las del cuerpo, y mudando él se alteran también" [the qualities of the soul tend to follow those of the body, and when this changes they are altered too]. Arguments about climatic determinism impugned not just the bodies but the spiritual, moral, and intellectual capacities of American residents, as well.[15]

14. Durão, *Caramuru,* 13; Camões, *Os Lusíadas,* 374.

15. Domingos do Loreto Couto, *Desagravos do Brasil e glórias de Pernambuco* (Rio de Janeiro, 1904; rpt. Recife, 1981), 7; Juan López de Velasco, *Geografía y descripción*

CARAMURÚ.

POEMA EPICO

DO

DESCUBRIMENTO

DA

BAHIA,

COMPOSTO

POR

Fr. JOSÉ DE SANTA RITA

DURÃO,

Da Ordem dos Eremitas de Santo Agostinho, natural da Cata-Preta nas Minas Geraes.

LISBOA

NA REGIA OFFICINA TYPOGRAFICA.

ANNO M. DCC. LXXXI.

Com licença da Real Meza Censoria.

PLATE I. *Title page of José de Santa Rita Durão,* Caramurú *(Lisbon, 1781). Photo courtesy of Edward E. Ayer Collection, The Newberry Library, Chicago*

American-born writers of all ethnicities responded vigorously to allegations of intellectual inferiority. In the preface to a treatise of Thomist philosophy published in Rome in 1688, the Peruvian Juan de Espinosa Medrano—fluent in Quechua, and generally thought to be indigenous or mestizo—dedicates several pages to refuting European assertions of the barbarism of American-born intellectuals: "Los europeos sospechan seriamente que los estudios de los hombres del Nuevo Mundo son bárbaros . . . los peruanos no hemos nacido en rincones oscuros y despreciables del mundo ni bajo aires más torpes, sino en un lugar aventajado de la tierra, donde sonríe un cielo mejor" [Europeans seriously suspect that the studies of New World men are barbarous . . . we Peruvians have not been born in obscure and despicable corners of the world nor in a duller atmosphere, but in an advantageous place on the earth, underneath a better sky]. Espinosa Medrano demonstrates how the affirmation of the superiority of America's temperate climate and benign heavens in response to European theories of environmental determinism was not exclusive to criollo intellectuals. His reference in the same preface to "tantos y tan grandes hombres que sobresalen en el Perú en letras, en ingenio, en doctrina, en amenidad de costumbres, y en santidad" [so many and such great men in Peru that excel in letters, wit, learning, pleasant customs, and godliness] was surely meant to include himself—a published poet, playwright, translator, and author of works of the-

universal de las Indias . . . desde el año de 1571 al de 1574, ed. Justo Zaragoza (Madrid, 1894), 37–38. José Juan Arrom cites this passage as the first instance of the use of *criollo* to refer to a Spaniard born in the Indies ("Criollo: Definición y matices de un concepto," in Arrom, *Certidumbre de América: Estudios de letras, folklore, y cultura* [Havana, 1959], 9–26, esp. 10–12). As Arrom explains, the term initially also applied to those of African descent born in the Americas; this continues to be the predominant sense of the Portuguese *crioulo,* from which *criollo* derives. In this study, I use "creole" in the Spanish sense of "a descendant of Europeans born in the Americas." On the dispute over the inferiority of the New World and its residents, see Gerbi, *Dispute of the New World,* trans. Moyle; Jorge Cañizares-Esguerra, "New World, New Stars: Patriotic Astrology and the Invention of Amerindian and Creole Bodies in Colonial Spanish America, 1600–1650," in Cañizares-Esguerra, *Nature, Empire, and Nation,* 64–95 (orig. publ. in *American Historical Review,* CIV [1999], 33–68); Stuart B. Schwartz, "The Formation of a Colonial Identity in Brazil," in Nicholas Canny and Anthony Pagden, eds., *Colonial Identity in the Atlantic World, 1500–1800* (Princeton, N.J., 1987), 15–50, esp. 37, 41–42, 46–47; Anthony Pagden, "Identity Formation in Spanish America," ibid., 51–93, esp. 80–83; and in the Anglophone context, Parrish, *American Curiosity,* 77–102.

ology, philosophy, and literary criticism—even though he humbly disavows his authority to list these men by name.[16]

Jorge Cañizares-Esguerra has argued that the defense of a superior American climate and the emergence of a "patriotic astrology" among seventeenth-century criollos required the early development of a notion of racialized bodies, usually assumed to arise only in the eighteenth or nineteenth centuries. The creation of different corporeal categories would leave creole claims of Amerindian and African inferiority intact while explaining the greater European receptiveness to the beneficial influences of the American climate and its stars. Although Cañizares-Esguerra finds references to mestizaje absent from the works that he surveys, Gerónimo de Quiroga's late-seventeenth-century description of both Spanish and mestizo captives in Chile as "worse than the fiercest barbarians"—whether because of "racial taint" or "continuous contact" with Amerindians—suggests how cultural integration and miscegenation could play an even blunter role in theories of American "degeneration" than negative climatic and astrological influence. Quiroga decries the perverse transformation of captives as a result of their exposure to a distinct cultural, and not just natural, environment.[17]

Yet as we will see in Chapter 3, one of Quiroga's contemporaries, the Chilean creole Francisco Núñez de Pineda y Bascuñán, offers an altogether different argument about his own captivity among Araucanians in the early seventeenth century. According to Pineda, his exposure to Amerindian culture as a captive indeed led to his adoption of and participation in certain indigenous customs. However, his captivity also provided him with the experience and knowledge necessary to explain the reasons and to propose solutions for the Spanish failure to pacify the Chilean frontier, in a work

16. Juan de Espinosa Medrano, "Prefacio al lector de la *Lógica,*" in Augusto Tamayo Vargas, ed., *Apologético* (Caracas, 1982 [orig. publ. Rome, 1688]), 325–329, esp. 325–327. Espinosa Medrano refers to himself as a "criollo" in the preface to his *Apologético en favor de don Luís de Góngora . . .* (Lima, 1662), a treatise defending the Spanish Baroque poet Luís de Góngora from the critique of the Portuguese writer Manuel de Faria e Sousa; see Tamayo Vargas, ed., *Apologético,* 1–109, esp. 17. However, the editor of the volume, Augusto Tamayo Vargas, discusses Espinosa Medrano's probable indigenous or mestizo origins and suggests that he might have used "criollo" simply to denote his American birthplace; see "Lo barroco y 'el Lunarejo,'" ibid., ix–lviii.

17. Cañizares-Esguerra, "New World, New Stars," in Cañizares-Esguerra, *Nature, Empire, and Nation,* 92; Quiroga, *Memorias de los sucesos de la guerra de Chile,* ed. Larraín, 229.

addressed to the Spanish Crown entitled *Cautiverio feliz y razón individual de las guerras dilatadas del reino de Chile* [Happy Captivity and Individual Reason for the Prolonged Wars of Chile] (ca. 1663). Despite the generic distance between Pineda's autobiographical account and Durão's epic *Caramuru*—as well as their geographical and historical distance—both authors identify their American "locus of enunciation" with the site of a "happy captivity." That is, Pineda and Durão implicitly respond to allegations of the intellectual inferiority of New World writers by addressing suspicions about the moral and cultural degeneration of captives. Rather than insist on the captives' intransigence, they present the transformation that results from contact with native cultures, not as detrimental, but as beneficial, allowing the captive—and, by extension, the writer—to speak from a position of authority and knowledge. If captives were sometimes viewed, as Quiroga states at one point about a mestizo renegade, as individuals who "una vez se conforma[n] con lo indio y otras con lo español, sólo para lo malo" [sometimes conform to the Indian and sometimes to the Spanish, only for the bad], these texts transform the captive's (and the author's) ability to "conform" to both sides into a positive and productive quality that does not subvert, but rather serves, imperial goals.[18]

18. Cañizares-Esguerra, "New World, New Stars," in Cañizares-Esguerra, *Nature, Empire, and Nation,* 68; Quiroga, *Memorias de los sucesos de la guerra de Chile,* 228. In *How to Write the History of the New World: Histories, Epistemologies, and Identities in the Eighteenth-Century Atlantic World* (Stanford, Calif., 2001), Jorge Cañizares-Esguerra describes the eighteenth-century development of a "patriotic epistemology" that valorized the credibility of Amerindian and Creole elites over that of European natural historians and foreign travelers; authority to write about the New World was derived from "long periods of residence in America and close contact with the natives through mastery of their language" (248). Cañizares-Esguerra argues that, despite their approval of noble indigenous testimony, creole intellectuals continued to condemn mestizos as a source of dubious credibility (208–209). I draw on Walter Mignolo's use of the phrase "locus of enunciation" to describe the discursive attempt to legitimize "specifically American geocultural identities"; see Mignolo, "Afterword: Human Understanding and (Latin) American Interests—The Politics and Sensibilities of Geocultural Locations," *Poetics Today,* XVI (1995), 171–214, esp. 176. Although, like Mignolo, I occasionally invoke the term "identity" to describe this gesture, my examples thus far should indicate that I am more interested in processes of *identification*—especially self-identification and self-representation—than in the *identity* of writers and captives, whether this is understood in the "hard" sense of an essential, shared condition or the "soft" sense of a flexible, fragmentary, multiple

Such strategies of self-authorization, and the fluidity and permeability of cultural and ethnic categories that they entail, have perhaps been more "invisible in European consciousness" than the notion of "sharp racial typologies" that Cañizares-Esguerra identifies as an overlooked sign of colonial Spanish America's precocious modernity. Yet the valorization of the captive's authority and knowledge is not, in fact, a uniquely criollo gesture, nor even one that is exclusive to American-born writers more broadly defined (including mestizos like el Inca Garcilaso de la Vega, whom I discuss in Chapter 2). As we have seen, Prince Henry's and Gomes Eanes da Zurara's favorable responses to João Fernandes date to the mid-fifteenth century, before the discovery of the Americas. But Portugal's early and sustained recognition of the valuable role of captives and their narratives should also not be taken as a confirmation of Luso-Tropical exceptionalism. This study finds ample acknowledgment of the captive's key role in knowledge production and imperial expansion in Spanish and English texts, and the occasional German and Italian authors—and African and Asian settings—of the works under discussion suggest the even broader geographical dimensions of this paradigm.[19]

---

sense of self; see Frederick Cooper and Rogers Brubaker, "Identity," in Cooper, *Colonialism in Question: Theory, Knowledge, History* (Berkeley, Calif., 2005), 59–90. Cooper and Brubaker argue that the prevalence of the latter understanding of identity has obviated the usefulness of the term and propose several more specific alternatives (including identification, self-identification, and self-representation). In *Constructing the* Criollo *Archive: Subjects of Knowledge in the Bibliotheca Mexicana and the Rusticatio Mexicana* (West Lafayette, Ind., 2000), Antony Higgins examines specific cases of the construction of American loci of enunciation in eighteenth-century New Spain, where creole writers "[weave] between identifications with Western paradigms of culture and subjectivity, on the one hand, and with the available models of indigenous civilizations, on the other" (ix).

19. Cañizares-Esguerra, "New World, New Stars," in Cañizares-Esguerra, *Nature, Empire, and Nation,* 64–95, esp. 95. Historians have increasingly rendered the valorization of captives and their powerful mediating positions in different geocultural contexts more visible: see James F. Brooks, *Captives and Cousins: Slavery, Kinship, and Community in the Southwest Borderlands* (Chapel Hill, N.C., 2002); Linda Colley, *Captives: Britain, Empire, and the World, 1600–1850* (London, 2002); Carina Lee Johnson, "Negotiating the Exotic: Aztec and Ottoman Culture in Habsburg Europe, 1500–1590" (Ph.D. diss., University of California, Berkeley, 2000); Francis Xavier Luca, "Re-'interpreting' the Conquest: European and Amerindian Transla-

The greater visibility of the Portuguese reliance on captives, lançados, and degredados can, however, call attention to the function and representation of those who "dwell among" foreigners under other imperial banners—as when Francis Bacon explains, in the *New Atlantis,* Bensalem's method of acquiring information about foreign lands through mariners who "stay abroad" for no fewer than twelve years. The foregrounding of Portugal's foundational role in European imperial expansion thus has a somewhat different effect than the scholarly efforts to reincorporate the Spanish Empire into a narrative of modernity typically limited to Northern Europe. Whereas the comparison of Spain and England in the Americas may reinforce, as Ralph Bauer argues, the notion of a "geo-political dialectic between imperial consolidation and Creole resistance," the treatment of Portuguese ex-captives like João Fernandes and Diogo Álvares demonstrates how much imperial consolidation depended on transculturated individuals as well as how much those individuals were seeking to serve the project of imperial consolidation rather than to resist it.[20]

Indeed, an examination of the role of captivity, not in fomenting oppositions, but in producing and circulating knowledge and authority complicates narratives of the emergence of national as well as creole identities in the early modern period. Captives' experience and expertise were valorized across national borders, however greatly prevailing imperial ideologies may appear to differ (Portuguese "tropicalization," Spanish "conquest," English "commerce"). Furthermore, captivity contributed to the sharing of knowledge—whether through coercion or cooperation—across national, religious, and linguistic boundaries. Although the border crossing involved in captivity is at least initially involuntary, examples abound of captives who embrace,

---

tors and Go-betweens in the Colonization of the Americas, 1492–1675" (Ph.D. diss., Florida International University, 2004); and Metcalf, *Go-betweens.*

20. Francis Bacon, *New Atlantis and the Great Instauration,* ed. Jerry Weinberger, rev. ed. (Wheeling, Ill., 1989), 59; Bauer, *Cultural Geography of Colonial American Literatures,* 29; see also Barrera-Osorio, *Experiencing Nature;* the works of Jorge Cañizares-Esguerra cited above as well as his *Puritan Conquistadors: Iberianizing the Atlantic, 1550–1700* (Stanford, Calif., 2006); and Walter D. Mignolo, *The Darker Side of the Renaissance: Literacy, Territoriality, and Colonization,* 2d ed. (Ann Arbor, Mich., 1995). Like the majority of comparative American or "hemispheric" historical studies, J. H. Elliott focuses exclusively on the Spanish and English colonies in his otherwise masterful *Empires of the Atlantic World: Britain and Spain in America, 1492–1830* (New Haven, Conn., 2006).

sincerely or strategically, their ability to traverse and mediate cultural differences. Such captives problematize not only "sharp racial typologies" but also sharp national and imperial typologies. Claims of captive degeneration like Quiroga's can certainly be found in many imperial settings—and, as we have seen, similar notions were sometimes used to denigrate creoles, mestizos, and the Spanish or Portuguese themselves. Nevertheless, a more favorable and flexible discourse about captives persists alongside and confounds the imperial drive to differentiate and oppose.[21]

Many studies have, in fact, stressed ways in which colonial captivity narratives reinforce imperialist oppositions between civilized Europeans and barbarous "others." Critics of Anglo-American captivity narratives have long analyzed how accounts of the suffering of Puritan, often female, captives at the hands of brutal Amerindians bolstered notions of steadfast religious communities and civilized English identities in a "savage" environment. Taking landmark studies by Roy Harvey Pearce and Richard Slotkin as a point of departure, Pauline Turner Strong has outlined a "selective tradition of captivity" in Anglo-American culture, based on "oppositional typification" rather than "transformative identification" between captive and captor. Although no comparable generic tradition of colonial captivity narratives exists in Spanish or Portuguese, critics have sometimes made similar arguments about the function of captives' tales in Latin America, particularly in the context of nineteenth-century Argentina's state-sponsored extermination campaigns against Amerindians.[22]

21. In *Colonialism in Question,* Cooper defines *empire* as an expansionist political unit that "reproduces differentiation and inequality among people it incorporates," wherein the "balance between the poles of incorporation (the empire's claim that its subjects belonged within the empire) and differentiation (the empire's claim that different subjects should be governed differently) was a matter of dispute and shifting strategies" (154). The different evaluations of captives and American residents reviewed in this introduction suggest that variable and conflicting strategies of "incorporation" and "differentiation" also applied to individuals of European descent who were born or lived in colonial territories.

22. Pauline Turner Strong, *Captive Selves, Captivating Others: The Politics and Poetics of Colonial American Captivity Narratives* (Boulder, Colo., 1999), 203–204; Roy Harvey Pearce, "The Significances of the Captivity Narrative," *American Literature,* XIX (1947), 1–20; Richard Slotkin, *Regeneration through Violence: The Mythology of the American Frontier, 1600–1860* (Middletown, Conn., 1973). For similar readings of captivity in the Latin American context, see Pratt, *Imperial Eyes,* 185; David T. Haberly, "Captives and Infidels: The Figure of the Cautiva in Argentine

On the other hand, scholars have sought to explain the scarcity of firsthand captivity accounts in Spanish America compared to British America by asserting such narratives' threat to the Spanish imperial or the Argentine national project. In one of the few comprehensive historical studies of captivity in Spanish America, Fernando Operé argues that captives' accounts represented a clear challenge to imperial interests by testifying to "Spain's powerlessness to control all its territories." Similarly, Susana Rotker's examination of captivity in nineteenth-century Argentina points out the incompatibility of captive women, tainted by their contact with Amerindians, with a national imaginary based on the exclusion of all nonwhite elements. Other critics have taken the notion of the captive's incompatibility or threat with respect to imperial goals and rhetoric as their point of departure, interpreting captivity as a site where the conquest was inverted through the capture of European conquistadors who assimilated into Amerindian society. Garnering the most attention in this regard is Gonzalo Guerrero, a Spanish castaway captured by Mayans on the Yucatán Peninsula in 1511, who not only refused to rejoin Spanish society and serve Hernán Cortés as an interpreter but who might have also taken up arms against the Spaniards. Guerrero has been the object of several contemporary fictional re-creations and even a commemorative statue and has been praised by scholars as an exemplary "good captive" and a "model of cultural syncretism."[23]

Literature," *American Hispanist,* IV (1978), 7–16, esp. 9; Cristina Iglesia and Julio Schvartzman, *Cautivas y misioneros: Mitos blancos de la conquista* (Buenos Aires, 1987), 57; Efraín Kristal, "Captive in the Wilderness: An Argentine Adaptation of an Anglo-Saxon Image," in Armin Paul Frank and Helga Essmann, eds., *The Internationality of National Literatures in Either America: Transfer and Transformation* (Göttingen, 1999), 215–229, esp. 226–227. Despite the hegemonic tradition of "oppositional typification" in Anglo-American captivity narratives, critics have also acknowledged their fractured, hybrid dimensions; see Tara Fitzpatrick, "The Figure of Captivity: The Cultural Work of the Puritan Captivity Narrative," *American Literary History,* III (1991), 1–26, esp. 21; Michelle Burnham, *Captivity and Sentiment: Cultural Exchange in American Literature, 1682–1861* (Hanover, N.H., 1997), 3; Rebecca Blevins Faery, *Cartographies of Desire: Captivity, Race, and Sex in the Shaping of an American Nation* (Norman, Okla., 1999), 58–59; Strong, *Captive Selves, Captivating Others,* 204; and Colley, *Captives,* 15–16. Whereas these scholars primarily highlight transitory moments that may be uncovered by reading "against the grain" of the text, I examine works in a range of traditions that explicitly valorize the transculturation of captives.

23. Fernando Operé, *Historias de la frontera: El cautiverio en la América hispánica*

The presentation of Gonzalo Guerrero as a "counter model to the conquest" in both novels and scholarship depends, as Rolena Adorno has pointed out, upon the very lack of information about him in colonial accounts: "It is the unknown and the indeterminable of his case that foments the desire to give him body, life, and significance—significances relevant for us and not for the historical figure—through the act of narration." This book, in contrast, focuses on individuals' own acts of narrating their captivity after their return—and on the appropriation and retelling of their stories by other authors—in order to flesh out the significances of captivity for early modern readers and writers. Such an approach requires reading accounts of captivity in a transatlantic and (inter-)imperial context and not as the foundational texts of national identities and literatures or as "counter-narratives" to the conquest. The works examined here, in fact, demonstrate the degree to

(Buenos Aires, 2001), 27; Jaime Concha, "Requiem por el 'buen cautivo,'" *Hispamérica: Revista de literatura,* XV (1986), 3–15; Rolando J. Romero, "Texts, Pre-texts, Con-texts: Gonzalo Guerrero in the Chronicles of Indies," *Revista de estudios hispánicos,* XXVI (1992), 345–367, esp. 363. In *Captive Women: Oblivion and Memory in Argentina,* trans. Jennifer French (Minneapolis, 2002) (orig. publ. as Rotker, *Cautivas: Olvidos y memoria en la Argentina* [Buenos Aires, 1999]), Susana Rotker explains the lack of "memoirs, diaries, testimonies, or narratives of the captive women of Argentina, where there were apparently more captives than in the United States" by arguing that, in the Argentine context, such women represented a "threat that must be forgotten" (50–51). For other discussions of the dearth of primary materials on captivity in Spanish America, see Susan Migden Socolow, "Spanish Captives in Indian Societies: Cultural Contact along the Argentine Frontier, 1600–1835," *Hispanic American Historical Review,* LXXII (1992), 73–99; and Carlos Lázaro Ávila, "Los cautivos en la frontera araucana," *Revista española de antropología americana,* XXIV (1994), 191–207. Although Brooks finds "surprisingly rich" sources including "an extensive body of written and oral folk literature in both Indian and New Mexican communities," he also acknowledges that accounts of captivity "must be fretted from more familiar narratives where they have long lain hidden beneath epics of exploration and conquest"; see *Captives and Cousins,* 39–40. In contrast to both Rotker and Brooks, this book focuses on the central role of European male captives in a variety of genres, and even in works that have been described as "epics of exploration and conquest," like Garcilaso's *La Florida del Inca* and Durão's *Caramuru.* On Gonzalo Guerrero, see also Rolena Adorno, "La estatua de Gonzalo Guerrero en Akumal: Íconos culturales en la reactualización del pasado colonial," *Revista iberoamericana,* LXII (1996), 905–919 (trans. and rev. in "The Narrative Invention of Gonzalo the Warrior," *The Polemics of Possession in Spanish American Narrative* [New Haven, Conn., 2007]); and Roseanna Mueller, "Two Unofficial Captive Nar-

which tales of captivity could take a central role in works that support and defend the imperial enterprise.[24]

Nevertheless, the writing of captivity ultimately suggests more about tensions within imperial projects than about the seamless extension of metropolitan power, for it reveals ways in which ex-captives and American-born writers were able to appropriate the valorization of firsthand knowledge about other lands and cultures in order to authorize suspect, if not subaltern, voices. At the same time, the narrators' frequent assertions of their capacity to delight readers suggest that the transmission of cognitive pleasure, and not only factual information, constituted another viable avenue of authorization. The tensions of the early modern imperial world also include the fraught but not yet exclusionary relationship between "wonder and science," as Mary Baine Campbell argues in her book of the same name. As texts that flaunt both fictional and ethnographic sources and claims, early modern captivity narratives belong to a history of the novel as well as of science and point to the contribution of New World novelties to the histories of both. The authorial appeal to, in Campbell's words, the "value of a pleasurable emotion, or relation to knowing, that requires the suspension of mastery, certainty, knowingness itself" renders the reader's captivation with the story analogous to the protagonist's captivity, both involving a "suspension of mastery" that is not entirely recovered with the report of the captive's knowledge of another culture.[25]

---

ratives: Gonzalo Guerrero's *Memorias* and Cabeza de Vaca's *Naufragios,*" in Maria Elena de Valdés, Mario J. Valdés, and Richard A. Young, eds., *Latin America as Its Literature* (Whitestone, N.Y., 1995), 20–35. Mueller's reading of a modern novel (Mario Aguirre Rosas's *Gonzalo de Guerrero: Padre del mestizaje iberomexicano* [Mexico City, 1975]) as an autobiographical account comparable to Álvar Núñez Cabeza de Vaca's *Relación* (1542, 1555) reveals the contemporary appeal of colonial texts that, she claims, "contradict and subvert the official stories of the chronicles" (23). On the questionable authenticity of the different versions of Guerrero's supposed memoirs that have been "discovered" and published, see Adorno, "La estatua de Gonzalo Guerrero," *Revista iberoamericana,* LXII (1996), 911n. 6.

24. Romero, "Texts, Pre-texts, Con-texts," *Revista de estudios hispánicos,* XXVI (1992), 345–367, esp. 363; Adorno, "La estatua de Gonzalo Guerrero," *Revista iberoamericana,* LXII (1996), 911. Concha reflects on the modern-day significance of the imaginary figure of the "good captive" in "Requiem por el 'buen cautivo,'" *Hispamérica,* XV (1986), 3–15, esp. 14.

25. Mary Baine Campbell, *Wonder and Science: Imagining Worlds in Early Modern Europe* (Ithaca, N.Y., 1999), 3, 24. Campbell discusses "ethnographic pleasure"

Several aspects of my approach resonate with articulations of, as well as reactions to, postcolonial theory: reading captivity narratives as an index of ambiguities and contradictions, interrogating binary oppositions between colonizer and colonized or submission and subversion, invoking concepts such as hybridity and transculturation, and interpreting the relationship between metropole and colony as mutually determining and interdependent, albeit asymmetrical. Yet like many scholars, I have often found colonial texts to anticipate and illuminate the features and concepts usually assumed to emerge only in a postcolonial world. From this perspective, Frederick Cooper and Laura Ann Stoler have questioned the very opposition between colonial and postcolonial:

> Today's world is often said to be one of global movement, of fractured social relations, implicitly or explicitly contrasted to a colonial world of spatial and cultural confinement. But it may be that we have taken the categories of colonial archives—organized around specific colonial powers, their territorial units, and their maps of subject cultures—too literally, and our colonial historiography has missed much of the dynamics of colonial

---

in terms of the imaginative possession of an exotic "other" in travel narratives and voyage collections (26–50); however, the pleasure of captivity narratives, as we will see in Chapter 1, appears to derive more from reading about the European or Euro-American as a captive, in a position of subordination rather than mastery. On the "tensions of empire," see Ann Laura Stoler and Frederick Cooper, "Between Metropole and Colony: Rethinking a Research Agenda," in Cooper and Stoler, eds., *Tensions of Empire: Colonial Cultures in a Bourgeois World* (Berkeley, Calif., 1997), 1–56; Stoler and Cooper argue that scholars have traditionally granted imperial enterprises "more coherence than they warrant," for competing strategies and contested categories not only characterize indigenous resistance but also lie "at the heart of colonial politics" (6). With respect to the New World empires, specifically, J. H. Elliott argues for the importance of analyzing the voices of the "conquerors, colonists, and chroniclers" with the same attention and subtlety granted to the voices of subaltern "others": "In reality there are many voices, among the conquerors and the conquered alike. We may not like what some of those voices are saying, but, as historians, we have an obligation to give a hearing to each and every one. There is no more crying need at this moment than to observe the observers with that same sensibility to historical context and environment which we pride ourselves on possessing when we come to reconstruct the world of the observed"; see Elliott, "Final Reflections: The Old World and the New Revisited," in Karen Ordahl Kupperman, ed., *America in European Consciousness, 1493–1750* (Chapel Hill, N.C., 1995), 391–408, esp. 399.

history, including the circuits of ideas and people, colonizers and colonized, within and among empires. . . . Similarly, the current emphasis on the hybridities and fractured identities of the postcolonial moment looks far less distinctive when the interstitiality of colonial lives is brought into sharper relief.

Indeed, the intra- and interimperial circulation and transformation of subjects and texts that I trace in this book demonstrate that the early modern imperial world was hardly one of "spatial and cultural confinement" that obliterates the agency of its "captives." Such a perspective does not deny the violence and pervasiveness of binary oppositions in the course and discourse of imperial conquest, evangelization, and colonial rule. I have already referred to the imputations of barbarism directed at captives and renegades, creoles and mestizos, Amerindians and Africans, and such fictions entailed powerfully real, if dramatically diverse, effects on people's lives. Captives and American-born writers may resist some of the categories used to describe them, but they do not seek to dispute nor do they successfully undermine all national, religious, or cultural identifications and hierarchies.[26]

Tracing these authors' theoretical moves, instead of positing them as examples of postcolonial ones *avant la lettre,* is not only more historically and textually sound but also more revealing of the contradictory and complex ways in which colonial empires functioned. Furthermore, such an approach elicits a reconsideration of the transgressive potential frequently ascribed to hybridity and transculturation in postcolonial scholarship. In his discussion of the distinctiveness of Portuguese colonialism vis-à-vis its Anglo-Saxon counterpart—the way in which "ambiguity and hybridity between colonizer

26. Stoler and Cooper, "Between Metropole and Colony," in Cooper and Stoler, eds., *Tensions of Empire,* 33–34. Stoler and Cooper also make the important point that "colonial historiography has been so nationally bound that it has blinded us to those circuits of knowledge and communication that took other routes than those shaped by the metropole-colony axis alone" (28); I explore some of these circuits in Chapter 5. For other discussions of the colonial anticipation of postcolonial notions of hybridity and categorical instability, see Young, *Colonial Desire,* 27, and Homi K. Bhabha, *The Location of Culture* (London, 1994), 173. On Spanish colonialism, specifically, as a precursor and challenge to Anglophone postcolonial theory, see Sara Castro-Klaren, "Writing Subalterity: Guaman Poma and Garcilaso Inca," *Dispositio/n,* XIX (1994), 229–244, esp. 230; and José Rabasa, *Writing Violence on the Northern Frontier: The Historiography of Sixteenth-Century New Mexico and Florida and the Legacy of Conquest* (Durham, N.C., 2000), 16–20.

and colonized, far from being a postcolonial claim, was the experience of Portuguese colonialism for long periods of time"—Boaventura de Sousa Santos points out the need to distinguish between the types of hybridity that "reinforce the power inequalities of the colonial relation and those that minimize or even subvert them." He concludes that, although it is appropriate for Anglo-Saxon postcolonialism to focus its critique on "polarization," the Portuguese context calls for a "critique of ambivalence." Indeed, the knowledge of hybrid or transculturated figures like ex-captives often sought—and was usefully employed—to reinforce rather than undercut power inequalities. Just as we can find examples of the "ambiguity and hybridity" that Santos argues to be particular to the Portuguese Empire in early modern English and Spanish imperial discourse as well, so we must also approach claims of transculturation in other contexts (including a postcolonial one) with the same critical spirit. Nowhere is transculturation necessarily a process that subverts colonial discourse or deconstructs binary oppositions.[27]

This book's focus on narratives of European and Euro-American captives who "return"—for it is as a consequence of their return that they are able to write or be written about in European languages and genres—means that I have neglected what Joyce Chaplin calls "captivity without the narrative," the enslavement of Amerindians in British America. Chaplin argues that Amerindian captives are both without narratives, lacking the "critical body of written testimony that has drawn attention to white captives and black slaves," and outside of the narratives that have traditionally structured colonial Anglo-American and Atlantic history. In the context of the Iberian Atlantic, such absences apply not only to the Amerindians and Muslims enslaved through what were claimed to be just wars, but the Africans abducted through the transatlantic slave trade initiated by the Portuguese. Such captivities resulted in so few narratives that are available to us today

27. Santos, "Between Prospero and Caliban," *Luso-Brazilian Review,* XXXIX, no. 2 (Winter 2002), 16–17. Barbara Fuchs challenges postcolonial celebrations of "hybridity" through the analysis of a colonial text that underscores its negative effects on indigenous populations in Fuchs, "A Mirror across the Water: Mimetic Racism, Hybridity, and Cultural Survival," in Philip D. Beidler and Gary Taylor, *Writing Race across the Atlantic World: Medieval to Modern* (New York, 2005), 9–26, esp. 20–23. For other critiques of the celebratory use of transculturation in Latin American discourse, see John Beverley, *Subalternity and Representation: Arguments in Cultural Theory* (Durham, N.C., 1999), 41–64; and Gareth Williams, *The Other Side of the Popular: Neoliberalism and Subalternity in Latin America* (Durham, N.C., 2002), 26–29.

that Juan Francisco Manzano's *Autobiografía de un esclavo*—published in an English translation in 1840 and first printed in Spanish in 1937—is thought to be the "only autobiographical account written by a slave during slavery" in Spanish America. In several chapters, I highlight the incorporation of (or silence about) the captivity of Amerindians or Africans in the texts that I examine, but here it bears mentioning two narratives written by captives of Europeans that did circulate during and after their lifetimes.[28]

Hassan ibn Muhammad al-Wazzan al-Fasi, known in English as Leo Africanus, was a Moor from Granada who moved with his family to Morocco when the Catholic sovereigns conquered the city in 1492; he traveled widely in Africa as a diplomat until he was captured by Spanish corsairs in the Mediterranean in 1518 and presented as a gift to Pope Leo X in Rome. Hassan al-Wazzan converted to Christianity and spent nine years in Italy, where he became a prolific author and translator, before returning to North Africa. Among his works is a pioneering historical and geographical description of Africa, *Della descrittione dell'Africa et delle cose notabili che quivi sono, per*

28. Joyce E. Chaplin, "Enslavement of Indians in Early America: Captivity without the Narrative," in Elizabeth Mancke and Carole Shammas, eds., *The Creation of the British Atlantic World* (Baltimore, 2005), 45–70, esp. 46; Ivan A. Schulman, introduction, in Juan Francisco Manzano, *The Autobiography of a Slave/Autobiografía de un esclavo,* ed. Schulman, trans. Evelyn Picon Garfield (Detroit, Mich., 1996), 5–38, esp. 7. Juan Francisco Manzano's autobiography was first published in R. R. Madden, *Poems by a Slave in the Island of Cuba, Recently Liberated, . . . with the History of the Early Life of the Negro Poet, Written by Himself* (London, 1840); the many editorial interventions in the work's publication history lead Sylvia Molloy to argue that Manzano's autobiography is not only a text about dispossession but also a "dispossessed" text; see Molloy, "From Serf to Self: The Autobiography of Juan Francisco Manzano," in Molloy, *At Face Value: Autobiographical Writing in Spanish America* (Cambridge, 1991), 36–54, esp. 38. The enslavement of Amerindians—officially proscribed with the New Laws of 1542—and of Moors in peninsular Spain has been less widely studied than the infamous transatlantic slave trade; see Antonio Domínguez Ortiz, *La esclavitud en Castilla en la Edad Moderna y otros estudios de marginados* (Granada, 2003), 1–64. Esteban Mira Caballos estimates that at least 2,442 Amerindian slaves were brought to Spain between 1493 and 1550 but affirms that they left no written testimonies of their impressions of their captors' world; see Mira Caballos, *Indios y mestizos americanos en la España del siglo XVI* (Madrid, 2000), 68, 109. On shifting Spanish Crown policies toward Amerindian slavery, see Silvio Zavala, *New Viewpoints on the Spanish Colonization of America* (Philadelphia, 1943), 49–68; on the different policies and practices of slavery in the Portuguese Atlantic, see Metcalf, *Go-betweens,* 157–193.

Giovan Lioni Africano, published by Giovanni Battista Ramusio in the first volume of his collection *Delle navigationi et viaggi* in 1550, and subsequently a bestseller with multiple editions and translations published in various European cities. Although produced during his captivity rather than upon his return, Hassan al-Wazzan's *Description of Africa* exemplifies both the reception and the strategies of many of the European and Euro-American captives discussed here. First, his authorial success points to the increasing valorization of eyewitness testimony in the sixteenth century. In the preface to the English translation, *A Geographical Historie of Africa, Written in Arabicke and Italian by John Leo a More* (1600), John Pory defends the author's credibility—"albeit by birth a More, and by religion for many yeeres a Mahumetan"—by pointing to his status and education, but especially to his "diligence" as a traveler: "And so much the more credite and commendation deserveth this woorthy Historie of his; in that it is . . . nothing else but a large *Itinerarium* or *Journal* of his African voiages: neither describeth he almost anye one particular place, where himselfe had not sometime beene an eie-witnes." Of course, it was not only Hassan al-Wazzan's first-hand experience that earned him an authoritative reputation in sixteenth- and seventeenth-century Europe but the captivity that led to his conversion to Christianity and acquisition of Italian, thus making his knowledge accessible and credible to European publics. Yet however much European writers, editors, and translators might have appropriated the image and works of "Leo Africanus," Hassan al-Wazzan also demonstrates the advantages of self-fashioning for those who cross cultures, languages, and geographies. At the end of book one, he tells a parable of an amphibious bird who avoids tax collection by alternately posing as a bird and a fish and concludes, "For mine owne part, when I heare the Africans evill spoken of, I wil affirme my self to be one of Granada: and when I perceive the nation of Granada to be discommended, then will I professe my selfe to be an African." Hassan al-Wazzan—or Yuhanna al-Asad, the translation of his Christian name with which he signed after his baptism—illustrates the strategic value of variable and contradictory self-identifications, the ability to conform to both sides "for the good."[29]

29. [Hassan ibn Muhammad al-Wazzan al-Fasi, a.k.a. Leo Africanus], *The History and Description of Africa and of the Notable Things Therein Contained,* trans. John Pory (London, 1896 [orig. publ. London, 1600]), I, 4, 6–7, 190. Samuel Purchas anthologized John Pory's translation in Purchas, *Hakluytus Posthumus; or, Purchas His Pilgrimes* (London, 1625), and John Smith praises him as an "excel-

It is another captive of Spaniards in the Mediterranean who affirms the value of the indigenous knowledges with which Europeans came into contact in the New World. Juan Bautista Túpac Amaru—the stepbrother of José Gabriel Túpac Amaru, leader of the 1780 indigenous rebellion in Peru—was a political prisoner following the suppression of the uprising for some forty years in Ceuta, one of the last Spanish colonies in North Africa. In a memoir entitled "El dilatado cautiverio bajo del gobierno español," written shortly after his liberation and voyage to Buenos Aires in 1820, Juan Bautista sums up the Spanish conquest of the New World as depriving humanity of "conocimientos importantes a la ciencia social y natural" [knowledge important to social and natural science]. His footnote to "natural science" explains that, whereas Europe's first botanic garden was established in Padua in 1545, Cortés and other conquistadors encountered gardens with medicinal plants already in use in the New World: "por consiguiente fueron más antiguos que en Europa y se podría correr sobre todo el cuadro científico de Bacon con igual certidumbre para mostrar esta verdad si los límites de este papel lo permitiesen" [and thus they were more ancient there than in Europe, and one could go over Bacon's whole scientific table with equal certainty to demonstrate this fact, if the limits of this paper permitted it]. From Juan Bautista's perspective at the twilight of Spanish control over its American colonies, the Iberian encounter with indigenous culture in the New World was an opportunity lost, for the conquest deprived the world of expertise that preceded and exceeded the knowledge gained through the scientific reforms associated with Bacon and other European naturalists and philosophers. For the captives and authors discussed in this study, firsthand knowledge of indigenous cultures was an opportunity to be exploited, and in doing so they contributed to the shift toward empiricism that also antedates Bacon's

---

lent Statesman . . . who afterward turned Christian" when he borrows from his work in Smith, *The True Travels, Adventures, and Observations of Captaine John Smith* (1630); see Philip L. Barbour, ed., *The Complete Works of Captain John Smith (1580–1631)* (Chapel Hill, N.C., 1986), III, 207. For an exhaustive biography and analysis of Hassan al-Wazzan's works, see Natalie Zemon Davis, *Trickster Travels: A Sixteenth-Century Muslim between Worlds* (New York, 2006); Davis explores the Arabic and European sources of inspiration for the tale of the trickster bird (which al-Wazzan attributes to an invented Arabic story collection) and concludes, "He was building a bridge for himself, one that he could cross in either direction . . . he was also advising his Italian readers that the condition for his truth-telling was that he be not too tightly classified" (114).

famous defense of it. Nevertheless, the memoir of an Inca captive of Spaniards in North Africa reminds us that European imperial expansion did as much to destroy as it did to generate "knowledge important to social and natural science." European and Euro-American captives might have been most successful at transmitting information that enabled the domination of indigenous cultures, even as they derived authority from their knowledge of those cultures.[30]

This book is structured so that chapters addressing the valorization and instrumentalization of captives and captivity narratives in a transatlantic and interimperial context frame three case studies of the representation of captivity in the writing of American-born authors. Chapter 1 focuses on the relationship between Iberian accounts of captivity in the Mediterranean and in the Americas beginning in the sixteenth century. Instead of setting up a European paradigm against which colonial texts will be judged, the chapter emphasizes the mutual nature of the exchange by showing how fictional and historical accounts of captivity among Muslims—in such texts as Miguel de Cervantes Saavedra's *Los trabajos de Persiles y Sigismunda: Historia setentrional* (1617) and João Carvalho Mascarenhas's *Memoravel relaçam da perda da nao "Conceicam"* [sic] *que os turcos queymarão à vista da barra de Lisboa* (1627)—exhibit strategies developed in sixteenth-century New World accounts like Álvar Núñez Cabeza de Vaca's *Relación y comentarios* (1542, 1555). The transatlantic itinerary traced in the chapter shows how writing captivity on both sides of the Atlantic engages the problematization of the categories of truth and fiction that critics have argued to be central

30. Juan Bautista Túpac Amaru, *Memorias del hermano de Túpac Amaru, escritas en Buenos Aires* (Buenos Aires, 1976), 57, 62. Juan Bautista did not enjoy the "happy captivity" of Hassan al-Wazzan nor encounter the favorable reception enjoyed by the *Description of Africa* in sixteenth-century Europe; his memoir was only discovered in an Argentinian archive in the early twentieth century and was first published in Lima in 1941 as *Cuarenta años de cautiverio (memorias del Inka Juan Bautista Túpac Amaru)*. On the existence of medicinal gardens among the Nahua in Mesoamerica, which predate those of Europe, see Doris Heyden, "Jardines botánicos prehispánicos," *Arqueología mexicana,* X (2002), 18–23, esp. 23. Parrish describes the valorization of Africans and Amerindians as "primitive" yet credible sources of natural, botanic, and medical knowledge in the colonial British Atlantic world—and colonial whites' self-representation as necessary arbiters in the transmission of "potentially toxic" native and African knowledge to Europe—in *American Curiosity,* 215–306, esp. 217, 247.

to the rise of the novel. The simultaneous appeal to the captivity narrative's status as credible and pleasurable is an example of cultural exchange between the New World and the Old rather than of unidirectional influence from the center to the margins of empire. As narratives of intercultural contact, the tales of captivity produced at and for the center of empire are just as marked by cultural (as well as material) commerce with America as New World narratives are marked by their commerce with Old World literary forms and texts.

Chapter 2 is dedicated to el Inca Garcilaso de la Vega's history of Hernando de Soto's 1539 expedition to southeastern North America. Although he began to write it decades earlier based on oral information from a survivor of the expedition, *La Florida del Inca* was published in Lisbon in 1605, almost a half century after the mestizo author's relocation to Spain from his native Peru. Garcilaso weaves several tales of captivity into the narrative of Soto's disastrous expedition, which resulted in the death of its leader, the abandonment of the enterprise, and the dispersal of its participants. One of the best known of these stories is that of Juan Ortiz, a Spaniard who was looking for signs of the lost Pánfilo de Narváez expedition in Florida when he was captured in 1528. A comparison of Garcilaso's version of the tale to those of other chroniclers highlights his presentation of Ortiz as a valuable and valorized mediator and interpreter. *La Florida* also refers to captives and exiles who, unlike Ortiz, privilege their own or the "other's" cultural identity to the detriment of coexistence. Garcilaso's negative portrayal of these figures and explicit identification with Juan Ortiz underscore his self-definition as a mestizo author working to mediate and legitimize a space between two cultures. Written about and from places that Garcilaso did not consider home, *La Florida del Inca* provides an opportunity to explore the mestizo writer's conflictive process of identification and self-authorization, a dissonance that is less conspicuous in Garcilaso's later work devoted to his native land of Peru, *Comentarios reales de los Incas* (1609).

Chapter 3 centers on *Cautiverio feliz y razón individual de las guerras dilatadas del reino de Chile* by the Chilean creole soldier Francisco Núñez de Pineda y Bascuñán. Like *La Florida,* the work describes both the failure of violent attempts at Spanish conquest and a happy captivity among Amerindians. Completed by 1673, Pineda's manuscript remained unpublished until the nineteenth century, although it appears to have circulated widely during the colonial period. The double title is not misleading: what Pineda offers is a generic hybrid alternating between the autobiographical account of his six-month captivity among Araucanian Indians in 1629 and a wealth of political and moral "digressions," mainly concerning the past, present, and future of the Spanish presence in Chile. The latter issues occupy the bulk of the more than three-hundred-page manuscript. Both memoir and tract, Pineda's twofold creation converges in one principal purpose: to squarely place the blame for the prolongation of the wars in Chile (i.e., the inefficacy of the conquest) on Spanish misrule, in particular the ineptitude, malice, and greed of Spanish administrators. Pineda uses his knowledge and experience both as a captive and as a creole, or "native son," of Chile to explain and critique the failure of Spanish imperialism in his homeland. While *Cautiverio feliz* is unique among my texts and colonial letters as a firsthand autobiographical account of captivity, Pineda's work is no less shaped by concerns of authority, knowledge, and cultural identity than the literary rewritings of conquest in *La Florida del Inca* and the text I turn to next, *Caramuru.*

If captives serve as a supporting cast of characters in Garcilaso's version of the Soto expedition, and in *Cautiverio feliz* the autobiographical voice of the captive takes center stage, José de Santa Rita Durão elevates the captive figure to the role of epic hero in *Caramuru: Poema épico do descobrimento da Bahia* (1781), which I address in Chapter 4. Durão's version of the legend of the sixteenth-century castaway Diogo Álvares "Caramuru" and his indigenous wife, Paraguaçu, presents both the most transculturated captive of any of the texts under study and the most successful portrait of Iberian colonialism in the Americas. *Caramuru* thus carries to an extreme the tendency of other authors to present the captive's transculturation, not as a threat, but as an aid to imperial expansion. At the same time, the extent of the captive's transformation and the agency of his indigenous consort reveal the tensions within the colonial project and its representation and problematize the notion of a uniform and monolithic imperial system of differentiation and categorization.

The final chapter turns from the function of captivity in texts of the Spanish and Portuguese Empires to the role of Spanish and Portuguese captives—as well as English captives of the Spaniards and Portuguese—in English writing about the Americas. Here we also find captives and captured texts valued for their ability to purvey knowledge that fosters the work of empire building, offsetting the taint of cultural difference that might have rendered them suspect to both their own and their captors' societies. The chapter first examines how the English anthologizers Richard Hakluyt and Samuel Purchas incorporate Iberian sources—frequently texts captured by pirates—into their travel collections, *Principal Navigations of the English Nation* (1589, 1598–1600) and *Hakluytus Posthumus; or, Purchas His Pilgrimes* (1625).

The dependence on "captive" Iberian sources of knowledge in these anthologies as well as in Sir Walter Ralegh's *Discoverie of the Large, Rich, and Bewtiful Empyre of Guiana* (1596) complicates the authors' frequent anti-Spanish, anti-Catholic rhetoric, which has sometimes been interpreted as a sign of implacable nationalist opposition. The accounts of English captives of Amerindians, Spaniards, and Portuguese further demonstrate the crossing of national and religious borders in the production of firsthand knowledge about the New World, and English captives-cum-authors like Francis Sparrey, Peter Carder, and Anthony Knivet reveal flexible identities and narrative strategies that are similar to those of their Iberian counterparts. The chapter concludes with a consideration of England's and Anglo-America's most famous captive, John Smith, who explicitly argues for the authority granted by New World experience even as he freely incorporates the experiences of others into his historiographic and autobiographical works. John Smith's dependence on Iberian sources—perhaps even for his tale of rescue by Pocahontas—points up the circulation of Iberian texts in England and illustrates how a common European project of knowledge production and religious dissemination in the New World at times transcends national and even religious divisions.

As all of the texts examined in this book demonstrate, the site of captivity reveals the constructed nature of borders and binarisms. This book's attention to written works usually ascribed to distinct national and linguistic traditions—and especially to the texts and individuals that circulated between empires and across the Atlantic—also seeks to reveal the artificial nature of some of the borders that currently delimit scholarly fields. As captives show us, linguistic, geographic, and cultural borders are not impassable, and crossing boundaries can allow a mutually enriching dialogue across cultures—without crossing out difference.

chapter one : THE "TRUE HISTORY" OF CAPTIVITY NARRATIVES IN THE IBERIAN EMPIRES

In 1586, an English sailor named Peter Carder regaled Elizabeth I with the story of his "strange adventures, and long living among cruell Savages" in Brazil. A participant on Sir Francis Drake's 1577 expedition, Carder was the only survivor of his pinnace when it was separated from the rest of the ships and wrecked on the southwest coast of Brazil in 1578. After several months of "being well entertained" by Amerindians he calls "Tuppan Basse" (Tupinambá), Carder procured leave to seek an English or French ship on the coast in order to return to his homeland. Instead, he ended up in the hands of the Portuguese, one of whom helped him to avoid imprisonment by the Portuguese authorities. Carder eventually boarded a ship of English and Portuguese merchants bound for England, although he was "re-captured" by two "English Ships of warre" on the way home. When Charles Howard, lord high admiral of England, learned of his story, he brought Carder to Queen Elizabeth in the palace of Whitehall, "where it pleased her to talke with me a long houres space of my travailes and wonderfull escape . . . and afterward bestowed 22. angels on me, willing my Lord to have consideration of me." In 1625, the Anglican cleric Samuel Purchas published a version of Carder's account in his voluminous collection of travel narratives, *Hakluytus Posthumus; or, Purchas His Pilgrimes,* where he describes Carder's tale as "unmatchable by any English for the rare adventures, disadventures, and manifold succession of miseries in those wilde Countries, and with those wilder Countrimen of Brasilia." Both Carder and Purchas apparently viewed an emphasis on suffering and travail as more useful in promoting the narrative than acknowledging the favorable treatment and considerable freedom that the captive had enjoyed among the Tupinambá as well as the Portuguese.[1]

1. Samuel Purchas, *Hakluytus Posthumus; or, Purchas His Pilgrimes Contayning*

Carder was not the first to narrate his Brazilian captivity to Europeans. The German Hans Staden, who was held for nine months by the Tupinambá some thirty years earlier, promoted his narrative in much the same way in *Warhafftig Historia unnd Beschreibung einer Landtschafft der wilden, nacketen, grimmigen Menschfresser leuthen, in der Newenwelt America gelegen* (1557). The book enjoyed substantial and sustained commercial success, with multiple editions in German and translations into Dutch, Flemish, and Latin in the sixteenth and seventeenth centuries. Whereas Purchas's version of Carder's account emphasizes the delightful appeal of its strangeness, Staden's epilogue stresses his account's veracity, even though "the contents of my book will seem strange to many." "This cannot be helped," he concedes; "nevertheless I was not the first, nor shall I be the last, to undertake voyages and see strange lands and peoples. Those who have had similar experiences will not laugh at my relation, but will take it to heart." Staden suggests the vital and ongoing contribution of travelers and, particularly, captives like himself to the new geographic, ethnographic, and natural-historical knowledge that sometimes provoked European incredulity. But his admonition indicates that he expected some readers to be merely amused by his account of misadventures among cannibals.[2]

In his introduction, the book's editor—Thomas Dryander, a professor of medicine in Marburg—even more explicitly links the captive's knowledge to scientific discoveries. Dryander offers the various standard defenses of

---

a History of the World in Sea Voyages and Lande Travells by Englishmen and Others, 20 vols. (Glasgow, 1905–1907 [orig. publ. London, 1625]), XVI, 145–146, 150. An "angel" was a common gold coin equal to ten shillings (one half pound). I discuss Carder in more detail in Chapter 5.

2. I cite from the English translation, Hans Staden, *The True History of His Captivity,* ed. and trans. Malcolm Letts, Broadway Travellers (London, 1928), 169. For an inventory of Staden's German editions and subsequent translations, see Rubens Borba de Moraes, *Bibliographia brasiliana . . . ,* 2 vols. (Amsterdam, 1958), II, 280–286. Samuel Purchas translated Staden's work but declined to include it in *Hakluytus Posthumus* because, he claims, he had already glutted readers with "like Savage arguments," such as Carder's captivity narrative; see Purchas, *Hakluytus Posthumus,* XVII, 56. On travel narrators' and novelists' similar responses to critiques of untruthfulness, see Percy G. Adams, *Travel Literature and the Evolution of the Novel* (Lexington, Ky., 1983), 80–102; on the transition from "strange but true" to "strange, therefore true" in seventeenth-century claims to historicity, particularly in the travel narrative, see Michael McKeon, *The Origins of the English Novel, 1600–1740* (Baltimore, 1987), 46–47, 54–55, 111.

Staden's truthfulness (the virtue and honesty of Staden's father, the simplicity of his language, the existence of other eyewitnesses who could challenge his account) while acknowledging the common view that all travelers are liars because their accounts of exotic and distant lands are unverifiable. To rebut this assumption, the editor enumerates astronomical and cosmographical examples of presumed impossibilities that have been proved to be true through experience and investigation. Dryander here antedates Francis Bacon's proposals to reform natural philosophy through empirical observation by nearly a half century, himself drawing on more than a half century of Iberian experiential knowledge. The predictability of eclipses, the existence of the antipodes, and the habitability of the Torrid Zone are among the strange phenomena thought to be impossible by the "common people" but now undoubted by those "skilled in science." Professor Dryander acknowledges that it is the "many voyages of the Spaniards and Portuguese" that have established the certainty of the latter two facts.[3]

Dryander affirms that Staden decided to publish his account only for the purpose of glorifying God and demonstrating his mercy, echoing Staden's claim about his motivations in his epilogue. Nevertheless, terrestrial concerns clearly balance spiritual ones in the descriptive, ethnographic book 2, "A True and Brief Account of All That I Learnt concerning the Trade and Manners of the Tuppin Inbas, Whose Captive I Was." And Dryander asserts that he dedicated the work to Prince Philip, landgrave of Hesse, because the prince is a "great lover of such things, and of all that appertains to astronomy and cosmography." Yet as a former captive of the Catholic emperor Charles V after the defeat of the Protestant Shmalkaldic League in Germany (1546–1552), Philip was surely just as intrigued by Staden's narrative of captivity

3. See Thomas Dryander's introduction in Staden, *True History,* 21–29 (quotations on 23, 24, 26). On early modern techniques for establishing the veracity of testimony (of travelers and others), see McKeon, *Origins of the English Novel,* 108–109, and Steven Shapin, *A Social History of Truth: Civility and Science in Seventeenth-Century England* (Chicago, 1994), 212–227. Sixteenth-century Iberian writers frequently used navigational and autobiographical experience to critique classical views about the inhabitability of the Torrid Zone and the nonexistence of the antipodes; see, for example, José de Acosta, *Historia natural y moral de las Indias,* ed. Edmundo O'Gorman (Mexico City, 1940 [orig. publ. Seville, 1590]), 31–42, and Inca Garcilaso de la Vega, *Comentarios reales de los Incas,* ed. Aurelio Miró Quesada ([Caracas], 1976 [orig. publ. Lisbon, 1609]), I, 9–12. See also Antonio Barrera-Osorio, *Experiencing Nature: The Spanish American Empire and the Early Scientific Revolution* (Austin, Tex., 2006), 102–103.

and redemption, about which he "interrogated . . . and examined" Staden in the presence of Dryander and others. Perhaps Philip enjoyed hearing another former captive speak "a long houres space of [his] travailes and wonderfull escape," as much as his coreligionist Queen Elizabeth did while listening to Peter Carder's tale. Both narratives' simultaneous claims to "strangeness" and "truth" continue to enthrall audiences today, for Carder's and Staden's accounts have been retold in numerous printed and film versions that insist on both dimensions.[4]

The successful dissemination and favorable reception of Carder's and Staden's narratives undoubtedly owe in part to Europeans' familiarity with accounts of captivity in North Africa and Turkey. The second edition of Staden's *Warhafftig Historia*—published in Frankfurt in 1557—replaces the original woodcuts depicting Staden among the Tupinambá with illustrations made by Jörg Breu for a 1515 German edition of Ludovico de Varthema's narrative of travels in Africa and Asia, which had been reprinted in Frankfurt as recently as 1548. In 1554, the Frankfurt publisher of Staden's account had used the same images to illustrate an edition of Hans Schiltberger's *Reisebuch,* which describes the author's travels as a captive in the Ottoman

4. Staden, *True History,* 28, 169. Purchas claimed that Staden's work "[contains] little light for the Countrie, and the People" and found it excessively focused on "his owne Tragedies"; see Purchas, *Hakluytus Posthumus,* XVII, 56. In contrast, a modern anthropologist has asserted that Staden casts a "brilliant shaft of light" on Tupi cannibalism (Neil L. Whitehead, "Hans Staden and the Cultural Politics of Cannibalism," *Hispanic American Historical Review,* LXXX [2000], 721–751, esp. 751). For a response to Whitehead that emphasizes Staden's textual sources and literary self-consciousness, see Michaela Schmölz-Häberlein and Mark Häberlein, "Hans Staden, Neil L. Whitehead, and the Cultural Politics of Scholarly Publishing," *Hispanic American Historical Review,* LXXXI (2001), 745–751. Modern anthologies containing Peter Carder's account include Edward E. Leslie, *Desperate Journeys, Abandoned Souls: True Stories of Castaways and Other Survivors* (Boston, 1988); Charles Neider, ed., *Great Shipwrecks and Castaways: Firsthand Accounts of Disasters at Sea* (New York, 1952). Leslie introduces his material by stressing both its truth and its "diverting" qualities (*Desperate Journeys,* xviii). Staden's account has inspired two Brazilian films, Nelson Pereira dos Santos's *Como era gostoso o meu francês* (1971) and Luiz Alberto Pereira's *Hans Staden* (1999), and his captivity has been fictionalized in diverse novels dealing with colonial Brazil, from Arthur Lobo d'Avila's *Os Caramurús: Romance histórico da descoberta e independência do Brazil* (Lisbon, 1900) to Assis Brasil's *Paraguaçu e Caramuru: Paixão e morte da nação tupinambá* (Rio de Janeiro, 1995).

Empire between 1396 and 1427. The oriental imagery of the woodcuts in Staden's Frankfurt edition suggests the weight of Europe's prior contact with Islam on the representation of the New World, and the deployment of Breu's illustrations in both captivity narratives suggests the interchangeability of Muslim and Tupinambá captors in the European imagination. However, some of Breu's woodcuts portray individuals wearing the characteristic feathered skirts and headdresses of the Tupinambá, which surely derive from images of Brazilian Indians like the broadside accompanying a 1505 Augsburg edition of Amerigo Vespucci's *Mundus novus* (Plates 2 and 3). The Frankfurt edition of *Warhafftig Historia* thus includes images that some readers, at least, would associate with the Tupinambá captors described by Staden. Although bibliographers and critics are technically right to affirm that the derivative illustrations of the Frankfurt edition have "no connection" with Staden's text, the woodcuts indicate the global circulation and multidirectional influence of representations of exotic "others," particularly through narratives of captivity.[5]

5. See Ludovico de Varthema, *Die ritterliche unnd lobwirdige Reyss des . . . Ritter, unnd Landfahrer, Herrn Ludovico Vartomans, von Bolonia, sagend von den Landen Egypto, Syria, von beiden Arabia, Persia, India, und Ethiopia* (Frankfurt, 1548 [orig. publ. Augsburg, 1515]); Johannes Schiltberger, *Ein wunderbarliche unnd kürtzweilige History, wie Schildtberger, einer auss der Stadt Munchen in Beyern, von den Turcken gefangen, in die Heydenschafft gefuret und wider heimkommen ist, sehr lustig zu lesen* ([Frankfurt, 1554]); and Hans Staden, *Warhafftig Historia unnd Beschreibung einer Landtschafft der wilden, nacketen, grimmigen Menschfretter leuthen . . .* (Frankfurt, 1557). The latter two were published by Weygandt Han. Four editions of Staden's *Warhafftig Historia* were published in 1557, two in Marburg and two in Frankfurt (the second Frankfurt imprint may be a reissue). The Frankfurt edition is generally believed to have been produced after one or both of the imprints from Marburg; see Joseph Sabin, *Bibliotheca Americana: A Dictionary of Books Relating to America, from Its Discovery to the Present Time* (Amsterdam, 1962), XXIII, 115. Sabin refers to the woodcuts' derivation from Varthema's 1548 edition and asserts their lack of connection to Staden's text. See also Borba de Moraes, *Bibliographia brasiliana,* II, 280. Annerose Menninger points out the possible influence of Varthema's and Schiltberger's best-selling travel narratives on Staden's account but does not discuss the common use of Jörg Breu's illustrations; see Menninger, "Hans Stadens *Warhaftige Historia:* Zur Genese eines Bestsellers der Reiseliteratur," *Geschichte in Wissenschaft und Unterricht,* XLVII (1996), 509–525, esp. 516–517. On Breu's illustrations in Varthema's 1515 Augsburg edition, see Stephanie Leitch, "'Better Than the Prodigies': The Prints of Hans Burgkmair, Jörg Breu, and the Marvels of

PLATE 2. *Woodcut by Jörg Breu in Hans Staden,* Warhafftig Historia *(Frankfurt, 1557), derived from Ludovico Varthema,* Die ritterlich un[d] lobwirdig Rayss *(Augsburg, 1515). Photo courtesy of Edward E. Ayer Collection, The Newberry Library, Chicago*

PLATE 3. *Woodcut of South American Indians in Amerigo Vespucci,* Dise Figur anzaigt uns das Volck und Insel die gefunden ist durch den christenlichen Künig zü Portigal . . . *(Augsburg, 1505–1506). Spencer Collection, The New York Public Library, Astor, Lenox and Tilden Foundations*

This chapter is dedicated to exploring the connections between accounts of Old and New World captivity, connections that are figuratively and literally illustrated in the woodcuts of the Frankfurt edition of Staden's *Warhafftig Historia.* The use of images created for a popular Italian story of a journey through the Middle East and India to illustrate German accounts of captivity in both Brazil and Turkey shows how travel narratives (and their illustrations) traversed linguistic, national, and imperial borders as fluidly as the voyagers themselves. But early modern Iberia is a particularly rich site for observing the circulation of representations of captivity, given Spain and Portugal's proximity and vulnerability to a powerful Islamic empire at the same time that they were pursuing their own overseas exploration and conquest. Indeed, stories of Moorish and Turkish captivity appear in a variety of genres in sixteenth- and seventeenth-century Iberia, and these models were adopted and adapted for representing captured conquistadors—whether because of shipwreck or warfare—in the New World. However, the relationship of influence does not proceed only in this direction. Accounts of captivity among Muslims were also affected by the discovery of a "new world" of non-Christian peoples, information about whom was disseminated in Europe through the reports of explorers and conquistadors as well as captives like Peter Carder and Hans Staden. The New World impact on Old World texts can be traced in terms of specific images and references, as a closer look at the image on the title page of Staden's second edition will reveal. But the remainder of this chapter focuses less on an influx of new information than on what might be called formal or rhetorical impact: the way captivity

the New World" (Ph.D. diss., University of Chicago, 2005), 162–207. Leitch points out Breu's possible sources for Tupinambá iconography, including the Augsburg Vespucci broadsheet of 1505, and describes his use of the feather costume to depict certain castes in India as well as the inhabitants of Sumatra and Java (180–181, 199–202). On Varthema's immensely popular account of travels in Egypt, Syria, Arabia, Persia, India, Pegu, Sumatra, Java, and the Moluccas, see Joan-Pau Rubiés, *Travel and Ethnology in the Renaissance: South India through European Eyes, 1250–1625* (Cambridge, 2000), 125–163. Varthema generally traveled in disguise as a renegade Mamluk, but he was discovered as a Christian and imprisoned in Aden (Yemen). Following the conventional captivity plot, he claims to have been freed through the intervention of the sultan's wife, who fell in love with him; see George Percy Badger, ed., *The Travels of Ludovico di Varthema in Egypt, Syria, Arabia Deserta and Arabia Felix, in Persia, India, and Ethiopia, A.D. 1503 to 1508,* trans. John Winter Jones (London, 1863), 65–73.

narratives are told and sold to their audience, the objectives and potentially productive results of their telling.[6]

Among the texts examined in this chapter, only that of Hans Staden explicitly invokes the title of "true history," a notoriously ambiguous and widely used label that was applied to both novelistic and historiographic texts in the early modern period. But the similar claims of both historicity and strangeness, instrumentality and delight, in the remaining narratives demonstrate the same instabilities and anxieties regarding truthful representation that have been associated with the explosion of "true histories" in the sixteenth and seventeenth centuries and with the "rise of the novel" in the eighteenth. This chapter explores the profitable use of the rhetoric of veracity as well as the marvelous in narratives of the Iberian Atlantic world. To do so, it traces a route that criss-crosses not only oceans but genres, languages, and topographies, from Álvar Núñez Cabeza de Vaca's account of shipwreck and captivity in North America to tales of Algerian captivity in Cervantes's novels and a Portuguese pamphlet by João Carvalho Mascarenhas, to the story of a Spanish castaway in the Caribbean whose peregrinations mirror those of its author, el Inca Garcilaso de la Vega. Like Hans Staden and Peter Carder—who remind us that transnational and transconfessional crossings inevitably intersected transatlantic ones, as well—all of these narrators assert

6. J. H. Elliott's famous dictum about the "uncertain" or "blunted" impact of the New World on European consciousness in *The Old World and the New, 1492–1650* (Cambridge, 1970) has been challenged by those who have investigated published works about and references to the Americas in European literature; see Elliott's comments on this work and his slightly revised perspective in "Final Reflections: The Old World and the New Revisited," in Karen Ordahl Kupperman, ed., *America in European Consciousness, 1493–1750* (Chapel Hill, N.C., 1995), 391–408, esp. 394–395. Héctor Brioso Santos reviews the scholarship on the presence of the New World in Spanish literature in *América en la prosa literaria española de los siglos XVI y XVII* (Huelva, Spain, 1999), 16–22. For an approach to this issue focused specifically on the work of Cervantes, see Diana de Armas Wilson, *Cervantes, the Novel, and the New World* (Oxford, 2000). In *Turks, Moors, and Englishmen in the Age of Discovery* (New York, 1999), Nabil Matar analyzes the influence of images of American Indians on representations of Muslims in Britain, but he states that the reverse superimposition occurred in the Spanish case, given Spain's prior extensive contact with Islam (98). On the popularity of the theme of captivity among Muslims in Spanish Golden Age literature, see, for example, George Camamis, *Estudios sobre el cautiverio en el Siglo de Oro* (Madrid, 1977); Miguel Ángel Teijeiro Fuentes, *Moros y turcos en la narrativa áurea (El tema del cautiverio)* (Cáceres, Spain, 1987).

their unique abilities to transmit an accurate account of distant lands and exotic peoples and to captivate their audience with tales of misadventures that rival anything found in romance fiction. As we will see in Cabeza de Vaca and Mascarenhas as well as in the works by American-born authors discussed in subsequent chapters, the twofold appeal of authenticity and the extraordinary is all the more urgent and effective for former captives seeking to participate in Iberia's imperial projects. More broadly, the dual strategy points to the New World contribution to the epistemological and generic transformations associated with early modern Europe: the valorization of firsthand experience in the production of knowledge and the reconceptualization of verisimilitude and the marvelous in intellectual debates, which reflects a "major cultural transition in attitudes toward how to tell the truth in narrative," as Michael McKeon puts it in his account of the origins of the English novel. Perhaps a "true history" of such phenomena as the rise of the novel and the scientific revolution could shed the Eurocentric and Anglocentric valence of these terms by taking into account the true histories of Iberian shipwreck and captivity.[7]

THE NEW WORLD OF ALGERIAN CAPTIVITY

The circuitous provenance of the Tupinambá iconography in the Frankfurt edition of Hans Staden's *Warhafftig Historia* suggests a far from simple relationship of influence between European images of exotic "others" in the Middle East, Asia, and the Americas, and the different title pages of the Frankfurt and the Marburg editions confirm the complexity of the exchange. In the Marburg title page illustration, a naked savage reclines in a hammock while munching on a human foot while other limbs roast over a fire nearby. The Frankfurt edition title page evokes (and indeed originally referred to)

7. McKeon, *Origins of the English Novel,* 20. McKeon identifies this "major cultural transition" and the resulting instability in generic categories with the period from 1600 to 1740, but such a transition was well under way in the Iberian context in the sixteenth century. See Mary M. Gaylord, "The True History of Early Modern Writing in Spanish: Some American Reflections," *Modern Language Quarterly,* LVII (1996), 213–225, which analyzes the impact of the discovery of the New World on the proliferation of true histories in sixteenth-century Spanish writing. Gaylord points out that the wide use of the label of "true history" points to "an underlying cultural anxiety about the very nature of historical truth and the capacity of written language to know it and to transmit it" (218).

a geographically and culturally distinct scene: a fully dressed executioner dismembers a human body before a brick oven, with an assistant by his side and aged, Tupinambá-looking figures (naked with staffs and feather headdresses) looking on in the background (Plate 4). In its original context, the illustration depicted the euthanasia and ritual cannibalism of old and infirm members of the community in Java, as described by Varthema. However, Breu might have borrowed some elements of the composition from an illustration of Tupi cannibalism in a Strasbourg edition of Vespucci's letter to Pier Soderini, *Disz Büchlin saget . . .* (1509) (Plate 5). On the title page of Staden's *Warhafftig Historia,* the same image suggests the threat of cannibalism to Hans Staden himself, if we may identify the melancholic naked, bearded figure seated on the right with the naked, bearded captive that appears throughout the Marburg woodcuts. Both title pages emphasize a distinctive and potentially marketable feature of Staden's narrative of captivity, the fact that he was a captive to cannibals—the "man-munching people" identified in the title.[8]

An influential early-seventeenth-century description of Algiers—the *Topographia e historia general de Argel* (1612), published under the name of Diego de Haedo—also invokes cannibalism in a way that confirms not only the proximity and interchangeability of occidental and oriental captors in the European imagination but also the potential impact of the former on the latter. In a dialogue describing the cruel treatment of Christian captives by Moors and Turks in Algiers, one interlocutor asks himself, "Siendo todos estos bárbaros, moros y turcos, tan hambrientos de la sangre cristiana, [que] se regalen tanto con los tormentos y dolores de los pobres cristianos cautivos, cómo no han dado en lo que hacían los indios occidentales en los tiempos pasados y hoy día hacen los calibas, que comen a los que cautivan en la guerra?" [Since these Moorish and Turkish barbarians are so thirsty for Christian blood, and enjoy so much the torments and pain of the poor Christian captives, how is it that they have not discovered what the Occidental Indians did in times past and what the cannibals now do, who eat those whom they capture in war?] The speaker is the Portuguese doctor Antonio de Sosa, the probable author of the *Topographia* and a companion of Cervantes as a captive in Algiers. Sosa here uses New World captors as a

8. For the description of the cannibalism of the elderly and infirm in Java, see Badger, ed., *Travels of Varthema,* trans. Jones, 255–256. Leitch compares Breu's illustration with that of the Strasbourg Vespucci in "'Better than the Prodigies,'" 201–202.

Warhafftig Historia
vnnd beschreibung einer Landtschafft
der Wilden/Nacketen/Grimmigen Menschfres-
ser Leuthen/ in der Newen welt America gelegen / vor vnd
nach Christi geburt im Land zu Hessen vnbekant/biß auff dise ij. nechst ver-
gangene jar / Da sie Hans Staden von Homberg auß Hessen
durch sein eygne erfarung erkant/vnd jetzund
durch den truck an tag
gibt.

Dedicirt dem Durchleuchtigen Hochgebornen Herrn/
H. Philipsen Landtgraff zu Hessen / Graff zu Catzen-
elnbogen/ Dietz / Ziegenhain vnd Nidda/ seinem G. H.

Mit einer vorrede D. Joh. Dryandri / genant Eychman/
Ordinarij Professoris Medici zu Marpurgk.

Inhalt des Büchlins volget nach den Vorreden.

PLATE 4. *Title page of Hans Staden,* Warhafftig Historia *(Frankfurt, 1557), with woodcut by Jörg Breu, derived from Ludovico Varthema,* Die ritterlich un[d] lobwirdig Rayss *(Augsburg, 1515). Photo courtesy of Edward E. Ayer Collection, The Newberry Library, Chicago*

Von der neüwē Welt

vmb welches willē wir dannzemal nit wenig belustiget gewesen. Von welcher leüt sitten (da wir sie haben gesehen/ hond wir die seitmal die bequemlicheit sich begibt/ auch vnderweil herein wöllen ziehen.

Von irē leben vnd sitten

PLATE 5. *Woodcut of South American Indians in Amerigo Vespucci,* Disz Büchlin saget wie die zwe durchlühtigste Herre her Fernandus . . . *(Strasbourg, 1509). Photo courtesy of Edward E. Ayer Collection, The Newberry Library, Chicago*

point of comparison for those of the Old in order to communicate to readers the full extent of Moorish barbarity.[9]

The learned Dr. Sosa might have read about Tupi cannibalism in a text like Staden's. But during his own captivity in Algiers, he could quite possibly have learned of it from Brazilian Indians themselves, for he includes "indios de las Indias de Portugal, del Brasil y de la Nueva España" [Indians from the Indies of Portugal, of Brazil, and of New Spain] in the long list of renegades in Algiers, which represents virtually every nationality in Christendom. Like the illustrations in the Frankfurt edition of Staden, the *Topographia's* catalog of renegades suggests the interconnected nature of the East and West Indies as well as the Mediterranean world for sixteenth- and seventeenth-century Europeans. These connections were also made metaphorically, for according to the *Topographia,* the redemption of Christian captives produced such a wealth of human commerce that the Turks, who controlled Algiers since 1518, spoke of the city "como nosotros acá de las Indias de Castilla y Portugal" [as we do here of the Indies of Castile and Portugal].[10]

9. Diego de Haedo, *Topografía e historia general de Argel* (Madrid, 1929 [orig. publ. Valladolid, 1612]), II, 125–126. Antonio de Sosa appears in the text as an interlocutor in the three dialogues that constitute the second and third volumes of the modern edition. Haedo claims in the dedication to have polished and edited the text "composed" by his uncle, the archbishop of Palermo of the same name. However, Camamis persuasively argues that Sosa—whom we know through the testimony he provided about Cervantes's captivity upon his release—was the real author of the *Topographia;* see Camamis, *Estudios sobre el cautiverio,* 124–150, and Miguel de Cervantes Saavedra, *Información de Miguel de Cervantes de lo que ha servido á S. M. y lo que ha hecho estando captivo en Argel . . . ,* ed. Pedro Torres Lanzas (Madrid, 1981), 155–166. Although it rests on internal textual evidence, the attribution has been widely accepted; see Emilio Sola, "Antonio de Sosa: Un clásico inédito amigo de Cervantes (historia y literatura)," in *Actas del primer coloquio internacional de la Asociación de Cervantistas* (Alcalá de Henares, Spain, 1990), I, 409–412, and María Antonia Garcés, *Cervantes in Algiers: A Captive's Tale* (Nashville, Tenn., 2002), 32–34, 67–80. As I discuss later in this chapter, although Haedo might have suppressed the Portuguese authorship of the *Topographia,* the favor was returned by the Portuguese author of the *Memoravel relaçam da perda da nao Conceiçam* (Lisbon, 1627), which clearly plagiarizes from the *Topographia.*

10. Haedo, *Topografía,* I, 51–53, II, 88. For similar connections (geographic and metaphorical) between Algiers and the Indies, see Francis Knight, *A Relation of Seaven Yeares Slaverie under the Turkes of Argeire, Suffered by an English Captive Merchant . . .* (London, 1640), 32, 55; Gabriel Gómez de Losada, *Escuela de trabajos,*

The *Topographia* attests—and surely, after its publication, contributed—to Iberian fears of being taken captive by Moorish and Turkish corsairs in the sixteenth century: the text estimates the number of Christian captives in Algiers in the 1570s at no fewer than twenty-five thousand. Indeed, the *Topographia*'s depiction of the brutal treatment of Christian captives in Algiers well illustrates the cultural work of captivity narratives in early modern Iberia: to reinforce a Catholic identity while demonizing a powerful religious enemy and imperial rival. Other contemporary treatises, like Jerónimo Gracián's *Tratado de la redempción de captivos: En que se cuentan las grandes miserias, que padecen los Christianos, que están en poder de infieles, y quan santa obra sea la de su Rescate* (1609), were published specifically to promote the raising of alms for the ransom of captives by religious orders. According to Ellen Friedman, such accounts supported official government policy by reinforcing the public's perception of the horrors of North African captivity. In the same year as Gracián's publication, even the Moors who had converted to Christianity, the Moriscos, were expelled from Spain, in part because of fears about their potential collaboration with the Ottoman Empire.[11]

---

en quatro libros dividida: Primero del cautiverio mas cruel, y tirano: Segundo noticias, y govierno de Argel: Tercero, necessidad y conveniencia de la redempcion de cautivos christianos: Quarto, el mejor cautivo rescatado (Madrid, 1670), xlii–xliii, 223. In his discussion of what he calls the "Renaissance Triangle," Matar offers numerous examples of the multidirectional circulation of people between England, the Mediterranean, and the New World; he suggests that Amerindians were taken to North Africa and sold as slaves by Spaniards and New Englanders. See *Turks,* 83–107, esp. 100.

11. On the number of Christian captives in Algiers, see Haedo, *Topografía,* I, 47. Knight puts the number at 60,000 in 1640; see *A Relation of Seaven Yeares,* 51. On Redemptionist activity, see Ellen G. Friedman, *Spanish Captives in North Africa in the Early Modern Age* (Madison, Wis., 1983), 105–164; Mercedes García-Arenal and Miguel Ángel de Bunes, *Los españoles y el norte de África: Siglos XV–XVIII* (Madrid, 1992), who estimate the number of captives ransomed by the religious orders at 15,500 between 1575 and 1764 (see 284–285). Friedman argues that, because of the profitability of redemption, the treatment of captives by Moors and Turks did not exceed the standards of the epoch, despite the sensationalist depiction of torture in texts seeking to raise money for ransom; see her discussion of the Crown's support of Redemptionist activity in *Spanish Captives,* 128. On Jerónimo Gracián's *Tratado de la redempción de captivos* (Brussels, 1609) and other historical and theatrical works seeking to raise alms for ransom, see Enrique Fernández, "*Los tratos de Argel:* Obra testimonial, denuncia política y literatura terapéutica," *Cervantes: Bulletin of the Cervantes Society of America,* XX, no. 1 (Spring 2000), 7–26. Both Gracián's *Tratado*

Yet the more radical difference of the New World and its inhabitants could also be used to vilify an already-known religious and political enemy. Sosa describes his captivity in Algiers as

> aquel nuevo mundo tan diferente y extraño, que imaginó Demócrito, y que Anaxarco o su discípulo persuadió al ambicioso Alexandro; do tanto que entra en [él] captivo, nada halla de lo que había en el otro de do viene. Porque acá halla otro Dios, otra ley, otros templos, otros sacerdotes, otras cerimonias, otras costumbres, otro hablar, otro escribir al revés, otro comer en el suelo, otro sentarse en cuquillas, otro talle, otro vestido y otro trato y aun otro vivir, en todo muy diferentes. Acá no hay justicia, sino fuerza; no dar, sino robar; no templanza alguna, sino todo crápula y lujuria; no fortaleza, sino temeridad; no verdad, sino mentira; no amistad, sino cada uno para sí; no lealtad, sino engañarse unos a otros.

> that new world so different and strange, which Democritus imagined, and of which Anaxarchus or his disciple persuaded the ambitious Alexander; where as soon as the captive enters, he does not find anything like the other world from which he came. Because here he finds another God, another law, other temples, other priests, other ceremonies, other customs, another language, another writing backwards, another eating on the ground, another sitting on one's heels, another figure, another manner of dress, another usage and even another way of life, in everything very different. Here there is no justice, only force; no giving, only stealing; no temperance at all, but only drunkenness and lust; no strength, only recklessness; no truth, only lies; no friendship, but rather everyone for themselves; no loyalty, only deceiving one another.

Sosa generalizes the binary opposition between human captives and bestial captors, "nosotros" [us] and "los otros" [others], to their respective cultures, with the former always occupying the positive pole and the latter, the negative. Despite the classical source for the comparison that opens the passage, the consciousness of another New World surely inflects the narrator's con-

---

and another work discussed by Fernández, Antonio de Olave's *El glorioso martyrio del padre fray Andrés de Espoleto* ([Medina del Campo, 1543]), are bound with works reporting on and exhorting the propagation of Christianity in the New World, confirming the compatibility for readers of the North African and American arenas of religious confrontation and expansion.

struction of Algerian otherness, just as the reference to Brazilian cannibals allows him to dramatize the barbarism of Turkish captors.[12]

For Sosa, the loss of liberty in a site of such radical difference and strangeness inevitably transforms a Christian captive, even if he does not turn renegade:

> Un infelice cautivo queda desta suerte con el cautiverio tan manco, tan falto de una tan grande, tan notable parte de su proprio ser y valor, y siendo semejante y tan emparejado con un bruto y vil animal, y finalmente, tan despojado de sí mismo, ¿qué valor puede ser el suyo? ¿O en qué cuenta se ha de tener, sobreviniéndole una tan extraña mudanza y transmutación tan nueva y tan desigual?

> An unhappy captive thus becomes through his captivity so maimed, so missing in such a great and notable part of his being and value, and being similar and so equal to a brute and vile animal, and finally, so deprived

12. Haedo, *Topografía,* II, 25. The reference is apparently to the Greek atomist philosophers Democritus's and Anaxarchus's theories of infinite worlds, which, according to Plutarch, provoked the following response from Alexander: "Alexander wept when he heard Anaxarchus discourse about an infinite number of worlds, and when his friends inquired what ailed him, 'Is it not worthy of tears,' he said, 'that, when the number of worlds is infinite, we have not yet become lords of a single one?'" See Plutarchus, *Moralia,* ed. and trans. W. C. Helmbold (Cambridge, Mass., 1939), VI, 178–179. Nevertheless, "nuevo mundo" would surely have had other, more contemporary associations for readers. The passage recalls another Democritus, that of Juan Ginés de Sepúlveda's *Democrates alter* (also known as *Democrates secundus;* it was completed in 1545 but remained unpublished until 1892). In Sepúlveda's dialogue, which prompted his famous debates with Bartolomé de Las Casas in the 1550s, "Democrates" justifies the Spanish conquest of the New World by affirming the inhumanity of Amerindians, who, after Spanish domination and evangelization, "tanto se diferencian de su primitiva condición como los civilizados de los bárbaros . . . casi cuanto los hombres de las bestias" [are as different from their primitive condition as the civilized from the barbarous, almost as much as men from beasts]; see Sepúlveda, *Demócrates segundo,* in Ángel Losada, ed. and trans., *Obras completas* (Salamanca, 1997), III, 68. The construction of Amerindians as inferior beings is explicit throughout the text, and as Anthony Pagden explains, it resembles and parallels his "detailed vilification" of Turks elsewhere; see Pagden, *Lords of All the World: Ideologies of Empire in Spain, Britain, and France, c. 1500–1800* (New Haven, Conn., 1995), 100.

> of himself, what can his value be? Or how is he to understand himself, having been overcome by such a strange alteration and transmutation, so new and so unstable?

Sosa's interlocutor in the dialogue responds that the only appropriate name for such a being is "monstruo, porque, en efecto, quien es tan al contrario y al revés de los otros hombres, no conviene que se llame hombre" [monster, because indeed, it is not appropriate for someone who is so opposite and contrary to other men to be called a man]. The representation of the captive as animal or monster complicates the binary opposition between civilized Christians and inhuman Muslims that the *Topographia* elsewhere constructs. However, attributing the dehumanization to captivity in Algiers maintains the hierarchy between Christian civilization and Islamic barbarism. In marked contrast to the *Topographia,* Álvar Núñez Cabeza de Vaca readily acknowledges the physical and psychic difference that captivity in a new world entails yet characterizes the transformation as a source of knowledge and empowerment.[13]

FROM CAPTIVE TO CAPTAIN OR SHIPWRECK TO AUTHORSHIP: ÁLVAR NÚÑEZ CABEZA DE VACA

Castaways, not *Captives,* is the title of the modern English translation of Álvar Núñez Cabeza de Vaca's *Relación* (1542 and 1555), an account of his travels and travails in North America that is more commonly known as *Naufragios.* Cabeza de Vaca was one of four survivors (together with Andrés Dorantes, Alonso del Castillo Maldonado, and Dorantes's African slave, Estevanico) of the original six hundred who embarked on Pánfilo de Narváez's expedition to conquer and colonize Florida in 1527. Cabeza de Vaca himself invokes the trope of captivity to describe his misadventures, even though he acknowledges being held a slave during only part of the eight years that he wandered from the Gulf Coast of Florida to the western coast of Mexico. Most of the narrative is dedicated to his experiences as an independent trader and then as a respected healer among several indigenous groups. Yet when Cabeza de Vaca and his companions finally detect signs of Spaniards, they immediately praise God "por querernos sacar de tan triste y miserable captiverio" [for being pleased to rescue us from so sad and miserable a captivity]. Although his narrative focuses on hardship and suffering, Cabeza de Vaca

13. Haedo, *Topografía,* II, 17–18.

presents his captivity as an ultimately enabling rather than debilitating experience. Writing his narrative transforms the "sad and miserable captivity" into a productive service that embraces the dual purpose of providing useful and accurate information as well as edifying entertainment.[14]

What are the "undeniable traces of Christians" that signal Cabeza de Vaca's approximation to his culture of origin? The most notable signs of "home" and "civilization" are, paradoxically, misery and absence: "lugares despoblados y quemados," "la gente tan flaca y enferma, huída y escondida toda" ["(places) deserted and burned," "the people so thin and ill, all of them fled and hidden"]. Later, he and his companions learn directly of the Spanish presence that such desolation indicates: "Contáronnos cómo otras veces habían entrado los cristianos por la tierra, y habían destruido y quemado los pueblos, y llevado la mitad de los hombres y todas las mujeres y muchachos, y que los que de sus manos se habían podido escapar andaban huyendo" ["They . . . told us how on many occasions the Christians had entered the land and destroyed and burned the villages and carried off half the men and all the women and children, and that those who had managed to escape from their hands were wandering and in flight"]. Cabeza de Vaca's efforts to distinguish himself from the Spanish perpetrators of such wanton cruelty become apparent in his first encounter with the Christians whose "undeniable traces" he has observed. The Christians unsuccessfully insist to the incredulous Amerindians that Cabeza de Vaca, Dorantes, and Castillo are Spaniards like them:

14. Álvar Núñez Cabeza de Vaca, *Naufragios y comentarios,* ed. Roberto Ferrando (Madrid, 1984), 129; Cabeza de Vaca, *Castaways: The Narrative of Alvar Núñez Cabeza de Vaca,* ed. Enrique Pupo-Walker and trans. Frances M. López-Morillas (Berkeley, Calif., 1993), 110. For a similar comparison of his journey to a "captivity," see *Naufragios y comentarios,* 97; *Castaways,* 71. I cite from a modern edition and translation of Cabeza de Vaca's *La relación y comentarios del governador Álvar Núñez Cabeça de Vaca, de lo acaescido en las dos jornadas que hizo a las Indias . . .* (Valladolid, 1555); earlier, Cabeza de Vaca had published the portion of the text dedicated to his North American travels in *La relacion que dio Alvar Nuñez Cabeça de Vaca de lo acaescido enlas Indias enla armada donde iva por governador Pa[n]philo de Narbaez . . .* (Zamora, 1542). Rolena Adorno and Patrick Charles Pautz offer a transcription and translation of the 1542 text in *Álvar Núñez Cabeza de Vaca: His Account, His Life, and the Expedition of Pánfilo de Narváez,* 3 vols. (Lincoln, Nebr., 1999), I, 14–283. They also review the textual history of the *Relación* and other narratives of the Narváez expedition in III, 3–118, and they explain the adoption of the title "Naufragios" in III, 42, 90–91.

> Los indios tenían en muy poco o en nada de lo que les decían; antes, unos con otros entre sí platicaban, diciendo que los cristianos mentían, porque nosotros veníamos de donde salía el sol, y ellos donde se pone; y que nosotros sanábamos los enfermos, y ellos mataban los que estaban sanos; y que nosotros veníamos desnudos y descalzos, y ellos vestidos y en caballos y con lanzas; y que nosotros no teníamos cobdicia de ninguna cosa, antes todo cuanto nos daban tornábamos luego a dar, y con nada nos quedábamos, y los otros no tenían otro fin sino robar todo cuanto hallaban, y nunca daban nada a nadie; y de esta manera relataban todas nuestras cosas y las encarescían, por el contrario, de los otros.

> The Indians paid little or no heed to what they were told; rather, they talked with one another saying that the Christians were lying, for we came from where the sun rises and they from where it sets; and that we cured the sick and they killed the healthy; and that we had come naked and barefoot and they were well dressed and on horses and with lances; and that we did not covet anything, rather we returned everything that they gave us and were left with nothing, and the only aim of the others was to steal everything they found, and they never gave anything to anyone; and so they told all our deeds and praised them, in contrast to the others.

Through his *Relación,* Cabeza de Vaca himself takes over the task of telling "all our deeds and [praising] them, in contrast to the others." Unlike the *Topographia,* here it is the Spaniards who are the uncivilized "others," culminating the gradual shift evident throughout the account in the referents of "nosotros" [us] and "ellos" [them], or "los otros" [the others]. In this passage, the pronoun expressing the identity of the writing subject resists the categorization of "us" and "them" as Christian and pagan, Spaniard and Amerindian, civilized and savage.[15]

15. Cabeza de Vaca, *Naufragios y comentarios,* ed. Ferrando, 127, 129, 131–132; Cabeza de Vaca, *Castaways,* 107–108, 110, 113–114. The latter passage has garnered much attention from critics as evidence of Cabeza de Vaca's transformed identity; see, for example, Tzvetan Todorov, *The Conquest of America: The Question of the Other,* trans. Richard Howard (New York, 1984), 199; and Manuel Broncano, "De cautivos y cautiverios," in María José Álvarez, Manuel Broncano, and José Luis Chamoso, eds., *La frontera: Mito y realidad del Nuevo Mundo* (León, Spain, 1994), 167–181, 174. But as Todorov points out, Cabeza de Vaca never "forget[s] his goal, which is to escape and rejoin his own people," and the "very fact of writing a narrative of his life clearly indicates his solidarity with European culture"; see *Conquest,* 198–199.

We have no way of knowing, of course, whether the pronoun confusion of the previous passage is a relic of the real confusion that Cabeza de Vaca felt upon returning to Spanish society. What we do know is that such confusions occur alongside conventional arguments for colonization and evangelization and that Cabeza de Vaca's account in fact earned him a role in these imperial enterprises. After presenting his *Relación* to Charles V, he was appointed governor of the struggling colony in the Río de la Plata region of South America. His controversial expedition there, which ended with his being taken captive by his own compatriots and returned to Spain in chains, is narrated in the *Comentarios* that were published together with a revised edition of the *Relación* in 1555. If we attend to Cabeza de Vaca's stated goals in the prologues to both the 1542 and the 1555 publications, the unstable and shifting sense of "nosotros" and "los otros" appears to be intentional.[16]

As the title of *Relación* indicates, Cabeza de Vaca's work originates as a legal document, a *relación de servicios* [relation of services] rendered to an authority from whom the writing subject hopes to earn recompense or reward. Cabeza de Vaca's prologue to the 1542 edition, dedicated to Charles V, reveals his attempt to present his account of captivity as a form of service to the Crown, in the hopes of facilitating his transition from captive to captain:

> No me quedó lugar para hazer más servicio deste, que es traer a Vuestra Magestad relación de lo que en nueve años por muchas y muy estrañas tierras que anduve perdido y en cueros, pudiesse saber y ver, ansí en el sitio de las tierras y provincias y distancias dellas, como en los mantenimientos y animales que en ellas se crían, y las diversas costumbres de muchas y muy bárbaras naçiones con quien conversé y viví, y todas las otras particularidades que pude alcançar y conoscer que dello en alguna

16. On Cabeza de Vaca's advocacy of "peaceful conquest," which became official imperial policy with the New Laws of 1542, see Rolena Adorno, "Peaceful Conquest and the Law in the *Relación* (Account) of Álvar Núñez Cabeza de Vaca," in Francisco Javier Cevallos-Candau et al., eds., *Coded Encounters: Writing, Gender, and Ethnicity in Colonial Latin America* (Amherst, Mass., 1994), 75–86; José Rabasa, *Writing Violence on the Northern Frontier: The Historiography of Sixteenth-Century New Mexico and Florida and the Legacy of Conquest* (Durham, N.C., 2000), 31–83; and Ralph Bauer, *The Cultural Geography of Colonial American Literatures: Empire, Travel, Modernity* (Cambridge, 2003), 30–76. On Cabeza de Vaca's pursuit of a royal commission and his governorship in Río de la Plata, see Adorno and Pautz, *Álvar Núñez Cabeza de Vaca,* I, 378–395.

manera Vuestra Magestad será servido. . . . Lo qual yo escreví con tanta çertinidad que aunque en ella se lean algunas cosas muy nuevas y para algunos muy diffíciles de creer, pueden sin dubda creellas, . . . y bastará para esto averlo yo offrescido a Vuestra Magestad por tal.

No opportunity was afforded me to perform more service than this, which is to bring Your Majesty an account of what I learned and saw in ten years during which I wandered lost and naked through many and very strange lands, as well as the location of the lands and provinces and their distances, their supplies of food and the animals that live there, and the diverse customs of many and very barbarous nations with whom I spoke and lived, and all the other details that I could learn and know that may in some wise be of service to Your Majesty. . . . I wrote it with great certainty that, though many new things are to be read in it, and things very difficult for some to believe, they may believe them without any doubt; . . . and suffice it to say that I have offered the account to Your Majesty as truth.

Like Hans Staden, Cabeza de Vaca invokes the "strange but true" claim so common among early modern travel writers, for clearly the veracity of his writing must be guaranteed for it to be of service to the Crown. He also stresses that the value of his writing-as-service is linked to the knowledge that only a captive or someone immersed in a foreign culture could provide: not just geographic information but cultural and linguistic knowledge that will be useful for future conquests.[17]

Cabeza de Vaca's appointment as governor of Río de la Plata proves his success in this respect and illustrates—to an even greater degree than Peter

17. Cabeza de Vaca, *Relación,* in Adorno and Pautz, *Álvar Núñez Cabeza de Vaca,* I, 14–283, esp. 18–20; Cabeza de Vaca, *Castaways,* 4. On the role of legal documents like the *relación* (report or deposition) in the centralized, bureaucratic state of the sixteenth-century Spanish Empire and their relationship to fictional and historiographic narrative, see Roberto González Echevarría, "The Law of the Letter: Garcilaso's *Comentarios,*" in González Echevarría, *Myth and Archive: A Theory of Latin American Narrative* (Durham, N.C., 1998), 43–92. On Cabeza de Vaca's transformation of writing into a form of service equivalent to conquest, see Beatriz Pastor Bodmer, *Discursos narrativos de la conquista: Mitificación y emergencia* (Hanover, N.H., 1988), 210–211; Lucía Invernizzi S.C., "*Naufragios* e *Infortunios:* Discurso que transforma fracasos en triunfos," *Dispositio/n,* XI (1986), 99–111; and Sylvia Molloy, "*Naufragios,* de Alvar Núñez Cabeza de Vaca: Una retórica de la crónica colonial," *Nueva revista de filología hispánica,* XXXV (1987), 425–449.

Carder—the potentially profitable results of narrating a tale of misadventure in a foreign land. Cabeza de Vaca is clearly conscious of the power of rhetoric to create or enhance his self-image, and he even slightly edits the 1555 version to increase his own protagonism in several events. *Comentarios,* the account of his expedition to Río de la Plata—written by his secretary, Pero Hernández, but clearly under his direction—attempts to confirm the value of the knowledge and experience he boasts of in the prologue to the *Relación.* The governor is repeatedly shown to be a successful mediator with hostile tribes, presumably because of his linguistic abilities and familiarity with indigenous customs. At the same time, he prohibits the men in his company from contact with the natives owing to the men's lack of experience, which he fears will only provoke conflict. In contrast, Cabeza de Vaca appears in the *Comentarios* peacefully negotiating with Amerindians, and the text repeatedly highlights his role as a successful mediator.[18]

The *Comentarios* offer a persuasive case for the captain's virtue and heroic behavior, again in contrast to "other" Spaniards (his insubordinate and corrupt compatriots). Indeed, Cabeza de Vaca was eventually successful at exonerating himself of the charges against his governorship. However, the prologue suggests that Cabeza de Vaca ultimately rested his fame and authority on writing rather than actions—and on writing of captivity and misfortune rather than heroic deeds. He presents the 1555 text as a form of service to Prince Charles, the grandson of the emperor to whom he had dedicated the earlier work. Cabeza de Vaca promises to "[abrir] los ojos" [open the eyes] of the young prince with respect to the Crown's faraway domains and subjects awaiting evangelization. His text can thus serve, alongside the Infante's knowledgeable tutors who are praised in the proem, to instruct and cultivate the future monarch himself. Cabeza de Vaca's heightened self-aggrandizement in the 1555 publication is tied to increasing confidence in the power of his writing to gratify and enlighten readers of the highest rank.

18. On the differences between the 1542 and 1555 editions, see Adorno and Pautz, *Álvar Núñez Cabeza de Vaca,* III, 86–97. On the order not to communicate or trade with natives because of their "falta de experiencia" [lack of experience], see Cabeza de Vaca, *Naufragios y comentarios,* ed. Ferrando, 164; for examples of Cabeza de Vaca's mediation, see 156, 176–178, 195–196. The insistence on Cabeza de Vaca's benevolence and successful negotiation in these passages surely responded to accusations of his violence and injustice toward Amerindians as *adelantado.* On the controversy over his governorship, see Adorno and Pautz, *Álvar Núñez Cabeza de Vaca,* III, 102–114.

By extension, of course, the *Relación y comentarios* is assured to be edifying entertainment for all its readers. At this point in his career, authorship was surely of greater interest to Cabeza de Vaca than boarding another ship to perform heroic deeds in a distant land.[19]

The prologue also explains why he chose to publish a slightly edited version of the earlier account alongside the present narrative:

> [Los *Comentarios*] van juntos con mis primeros sucesos, porque la variedad de las cosas que en la una parte y en la otra se tractan y la de mis acontescimientos detenga a Vuestra Alteza con algún gusto en esta lección. Que cierto no hay cosa que más deleite a los lectores que las variedades de las cosas y tiempos y las vueltas de la fortuna, las cuales, aunque al tiempo que se experimentan no son gustosas, cuando las traemos a la memoria y leemos son agradables.
>
> [These *Commentaries*] appear together with my first adventures, so that the variety of the things that are represented in one part and the other and the variety of my experiences may detain Your Highness with some pleasure in the reading. Because it is certain that there is nothing that delights readers more than the varieties of things and times and reversals of fortune, which, although they are not pleasant at the time we experience them, are agreeable when we remember and read them.

Such praise of literary diversity and readerly enjoyment, which could be taken from the pages of Renaissance theorists like Torquato Tasso or Alonso López Pinciano in their revisions of Aristotelian poetics, might seem incompatible with Cabeza de Vaca's insistence on accuracy and truth. However, by framing his dual account of misfortunes in North and South America as a work of edifying and delightful literature as well as a text of historical accuracy, Cabeza de Vaca seeks to author-ize himself in both senses: as an

19. Cabeza de Vaca, *Naufragios y comentarios,* ed. Ferrando, 148–150. On Cabeza de Vaca's exoneration, see Adorno and Pautz, *Álvar Núñez Cabeza de Vaca,* I, 401. Adorno and Pautz also point out that the existence of chapter divisions in the 1555 edition reflect a new conception of the work, now destined for a broader audience: "Unlike the 1542 publication, which had been directed to the emperor and aimed at a mostly professional, Indies-oriented audience accustomed to reading long, unbroken reports, the new edition and its companion *Comentarios,* and most especially its proem, were geared to engage a wider range of readers" (III, 89).

author able to captivate his readers and as an authoritative source on American geography and ethnography.[20]

Cabeza de Vaca's success in these capacities is evident not only in the commission and pardon that he received from the Crown but also in the wider reception of his work that we can glimpse in an early-seventeenth-century peninsular novel, Félix Lope de Vega Carpio's *El peregrino en su patria* (1604). Here the inveterate pilgrim abroad returns to authorize "The Pilgrim at Home," as the novel's title might be translated. The first Golden Age Byzantine novel—an Iberian genre of prose fiction that emulated ancient Greek novels like Heliodorus's *Historia aethiopica,* rediscovered in 1531 and translated into Spanish in 1554—*El peregrino en su patria* incorporates the usual variety of episodes that alternately separate and unite the lover-

20. Cabeza de Vaca, *Naufragios y comentarios,* ed. Ferrando, 147. On the principle of variety in Renaissance literary criticism, see Alban K. Forcione's discussion of Torquato Tasso in Forcione, *Cervantes, Aristotle, and the "Persiles"* (Princeton, N.J., 1970), 27–30. On the delight provoked by multiplicity and variety, see Tasso, "Discourses on the Heroic Poem" (1594), in Allan H. Gilbert, ed. and trans., *Literary Criticism: Plato to Dryden* (New York, 1940), 466–503, esp. 499, and Alonso López Pinciano, *Philosophia antigua poética,* ed. Alfredo Carballo Picazo (Madrid, 1953 [orig. publ. Madrid, 1596]), II, 53. Many narrators of shipwreck and captivity tales invoke the topos of the pleasure of recalling and retelling past misfortunes. The anonymous author of *Viaje de Turquía* (completed in 1557–1558 but first published in Madrid, 1905), writes, "Como los marineros, después de los tempestuosos trabajos, razonan de buena gana entre sí de los peligros pasados . . . ansí a mí me ayudará a tornar a la memoria la cautividad peor que la de Babilonia, la servidumbre llena de crueldad y tormento, las duras prisiones y peligrosos casos de mi huida" [Just as sailors gladly reflect on past dangers after the hardships of a storm, . . . so it will help me to remember a captivity worse than that of Babylon, a slavery full of cruelty and torture, the difficult prisons and the dangerous circumstances of my escape]; see *Viaje de Turquía (La odisea de Pedro de Urdemalas),* ed. Fernando García Salinero (Madrid, 1985), 11. See also the prologue to Afonso Luís's *Naufrágio que passou Jorge d'Albuquerque Coelho, capitão, e governador de Paranambuco* (Lisbon, 1601), "Assim como a memoria dos dias alegres, e felices, conforme a openião de alguns Philosophos, causa tristeza, e dor em outros estados diferentes, assim a memoria dos males, e dos trabalhos, fora delles, causa deleitação, e contentamento" ["Just as the recollection of happy and prosperous days, according to what some philosophers tell us, causes sadness and grief when we find ourselves in very different circumstances, so, on the other hand, does the recollection of past toils and tribulations give us happiness and contentment when we are no longer enduring them"]. I cite from a modern edition of the 1601 pamphlet (which is the second edition; there are no extant copies of the

protagonists, including shipwrecks, captivities, and, of course, pilgrimages. Unlike most Byzantine novels, however, Lope's sets these misadventures on Spanish soil rather than in exotic locales. Through the restricted spatial and temporal limits (the events are nearly contemporaneous with the novel's writing), Lope seeks to augment the narrative's plausibility for his readers. He thus disregards Tasso's recommendation to situate events in distant lands (including the "countries recently discovered") in order to increase verisimilitude. For this reason, he must resort to other means to establish the narrative's authenticity.[21]

One of the ways in which he accomplishes this in one seemingly fantastic episode is by citing the narrative of another *peregrino* [pilgrim], who, in fact, wandered quite far from his *patria:* Cabeza de Vaca's *Relación.* We read that

---

first), Afonso Luiz Piloto and Bento Teyxeyra, *Naufragio e prosopopea* (Recife, 1969), and Afonso Luís, "Shipwreck Suffered by Jorge D'Albuquerque Coelho, Captain and Governor of Pernambuco," in C. R. Boxer, ed. and trans., *Further Selections from the Tragic History of the Sea, 1559–1565 . . .* , Works Issued by the Hakluyt Society, 2d Ser., no. 132 (Cambridge, 1968), 109–157, esp. 112.

21. Tasso, "Discourses," in Gilbert, ed. and trans., *Literary Criticism,* 465–503, esp. 488. Nevertheless, Lope approvingly refers to Tasso in a passage that reveals his preoccupation with verisimilitude: "Las [cosas] que no tienen apariencia de verdad no mueven, porque, como dice en su *Poética* Torcato Taso, donde falta la fe, falta el afecto o el gusto de lo que se lee. . . . El ir suspenso el que escucha, temeroso, atrevido, triste, alegre, con esperanza o desconfiado, a la verdad de la escritura se debe; o a lo menos, que no constando que lo sea, parezca verisímil" [Things that do not have an appearance of truth are not moving, because, as Torquato Tasso says in his *Poetics,* where faith is lacking, the effect or pleasure in what is being read is also missing. The listener's suspense, fear, boldness, sadness, joy, hopefulness, or doubt, are all owed to the truth of the writing; or at least, if not its truth, its verisimilar appearance]; see Félix Lope de Vega Carpio, *El peregrino en su patria,* ed. Juan Bautista Avalle-Arce (Madrid, 1973), 334–335. On Lope's use of narratorial interventions to assure the reader of the account's veracity, see Javier González Rovira, *La novela bizantina de la Edad de Oro* (Madrid, 1996), 217. The genre known in Spanish as the *novela bizantina* is equivalent to what is usually called "(Greek) romance" in English. On the differences between Greek and chivalric romance and the popularity of Heliodorus in early modern Spain, see Diana de Armas Wilson, *Allegories of Love: Cervantes's "Persiles and Sigismunda"* (Princeton, N.J., 1991), 111–123. Margaret Anne Doody challenges the commonplace distinction between ("idealizing") romance and ("realistic") novel and argues for the novelistic status of ancient Greek prose fiction like the *Aethiopica;* see Doody, *The True Story of the Novel* (New Brunswick, N.J., 1996), xvii.

the protagonist's prison companion, Everardo, was able to miraculously heal him,

> con medicamentos y palabras, que siendo soldado había aprendido, cosa de cuya verdad ni disputo ni dudo, porque si las hierbas y las piedras tienen virtud, ¿por qué ha de faltar a las palabras santas? Pues Fernán Nuñéz *[sic],* perdido entre los indios, afirma haber sacado a uno de ellos un pedernal de una flecha, que había dos años que al lado del corazón tenía cubierto de carne y aun haber resucitado un muerto; que habiéndolo escrito un capitán cristiano de tanta opinión y nobleza debe creerse, porque a Dios todo es posible.

> with medicine and words, which as a soldier he had learned, a thing whose truth I neither dispute nor doubt; because if stones and herbs have this ability, why not holy words? For Fernán Núñez *[sic],* lost among the Indians, claims to have extracted from one of them the flint of an arrow, which for two years was near his heart and covered by flesh, and even to have resuscitated a dead man, and having been written by a Christian captain of such high opinion and nobility, it should be believed, because for God, nothing is impossible.

Despite Lope's confusion regarding Álvar Núñez Cabeza de Vaca's first name, the episodes referred to are clearly those recounted in chapters 22 and 24 of the *Relación* (although the resuscitation of the dead man was not witnessed by Cabeza de Vaca but reported to him by others). Ironically enough, the distant "New World" that Lope deliberately excludes in order to increase verisimilitude is here invoked to confirm the narrative's veracity. More precisely, Lope draws on the writings of a "Christian captain" whose authority is guaranteed by the account of his experience "lost among the Indians" and whose "high opinion" is surely derived more from his rhetorical skills than from his exploits as a captain. If Cabeza de Vaca's road from captive to captain entails a detour through authorship, the path of influence from Heliodorus's *Aethiopica* to Lope's *El peregrino en su patria* appears to make a brief detour through the New World via Cabeza de Vaca's true history of captivity and misfortune.[22]

22. Lope de Vega, *Peregrino en su patria,* ed. Avalle-Arce, 95. On Cabeza de Vaca's 1555 publication as an "act of public advocacy designed to confirm the restoration of

In a letter of 1590 to the Council of the Indies, Miguel de Cervantes Saavedra presented, like Cabeza de Vaca, his experience as a captive as a type of service to the Crown, in the hopes of gaining a post in the Indies. Although he did not enjoy the same success as Cabeza de Vaca in this bid, Cervantes clearly shared his awareness of the literary appeal of a narrative of capture and escape from a foreign land. In one of the best-known interpolated tales of the first part of *Don Quijote* (1605), Ruy Pérez de Viedma, the "captive captain," introduces his oral account of captivity by calling attention to its marvelous as well as its truthful aspect: "Y así, estén vuestras mercedes atentos, y oirán un discurso verdadero a quien podría ser que no llegasen los mentirosos que con curioso y pensado artificio suelen componerse" ["Accordingly, should your graces be pleased to listen to me, you will hear a true tale that may well be superior to those lying narratives framed by strange and labored tricks and artifices"]. Even without the captain's reference in his tale to "un soldado español llamado tal de Saavedra" ["a Spanish soldier named Saavedra"], the reality of Miguel de Cervantes's captivity in Algiers from 1575 to 1580 would probably still inspire some readers to seek out the portions of true discourse in a tale evidently composed with its own share of "strange and labored artifices." For example, George Camamis credits Cervantes with inaugurating, with Antonio de Sosa, the treatment of captivity as a contemporary historical phenomenon in Golden Age literature, which he attributes to these men's personal experience as fellow captives. But Cervantes shows Pérez de Viedma's listeners at the inn to be just as captivated by the fabulous nature of the tale as by the narrator's claims to veracity. As don Fernando declares:

> Por cierto, señor capitán, el modo con que habéis contado este estraño suceso ha sido tal, que iguala a la novedad y estrañeza del mesmo caso. Todo es peregrino, y raro, y lleno de accidentes que maravillan y suspenden a quien los oye; y es de tal manera el gusto que hemos recebido en escuchalle, que aunque nos hallara el día de mañana entretenidos en el mesmo cuento, holgáramos que de nuevo se comenzara.

---

the *adelantado*'s good name and assure his place in history," see Adorno and Pautz, *Álvar Núñez Cabeza de Vaca,* III, 92.

The way you've told this extraordinary story, my dear sir, beautifully matches its unusual strangeness. Every bit of it is interesting, and distinctly uncommon, and full of episodes that astonish and captivate anyone hearing it, and we've listened to you with such delight that, even should you begin it all over again, and tomorrow would find us occupied with exactly the same tale, we would be equally delighted.

The captive captain has elicited just the pleasurable response sought by Álvar Núñez Cabeza de Vaca from the princely reader of his *Relación y comentarios*.[23]

With its depiction of captivity in exotic locales, Cervantes's posthumously published *Los trabajos de Persiles y Sigismunda: Historia setentrional* (1617) represents the other pole of Camamis's bipartite analysis: Byzantine captivity, which constitutes the "literary," or "idealized," counterpart of Moorish or Turkish captivity accounts based on "historical reality." In this model, captivity among pirates or other "barbarians" serves as a test of the protagonists' faithfulness to their respective lovers rather than as proof of a Christian captive's faith in the hands of infidels. In the prologue to his *Novelas ejemplares*

23. Cervantes, *Información,* ed. Lanzas, 12; Miguel de Cervantes Saavedra, *El ingenioso hidalgo don Quijote de la Mancha,* ed. Luis Andrés Murillo (Madrid, 1978 [orig. publ. Madrid, 1605]), I, 472, 486, 514; Cervantes, *The History of That Ingenious Gentleman Don Quijote de la Mancha,* trans. Burton Raffel (New York, 1995), 256, 264, 291; Camamis, *Estudios sobre el cautiverio,* 235–236. The bibliography on Cervantes's captivity and his literary treatment of the topic is immense; see, for example, Juan Bautista Avalle-Arce, "La captura de Cervantes," *Boletín de la Real Academia Española,* XLVIII (1968), 237–280; Michael McGaha, "Hacia la verdadera historia del cautivo Miguel de Cervantes," *Revista canadiense de estudios hispánicos,* XX (1996), 540–546; Diane E. Sieber, "Mapping Identity in the Captive's Tale: Cervantes and Ethnographic Narrative," *Cervantes: Bulletin of the Cervantes Society of America,* XVIII, no. 1 (Spring 1998), 115–133; Garcés, *Cervantes in Algiers.* A book particularly concerned with distinguishing historical references and verisimilar elements from literary motifs is Ottmar Hegyi, *Cervantes and the Turks: Historical Reality versus Literary Fiction in "La Gran Sultana" and "El amante liberal"* (Newark, N.J., 1992). For a review of biographical studies of Cervantes's captivity, see Alberto Sánchez, "Revisión del cautiverio cervantino en Argel," *Cervantes: Bulletin of the Cervantes Society of America,* XVII, no. 1 (Spring 1997), 7–24. Like Camamis, Rovira associates the increased popularity of captivity as a literary motif in the sixteenth and seventeenth centuries with its accurate reflection of historical reality; see *La novela bizantina,* 140.

(1613), Cervantes himself affirms that the *Persiles* "se atreve a competir con Heliodoro" [dares to compete with Heliodorus], whose *Historia aethiopica* Camamis identifies as the prototypical novel of captivity. As we will see, Cervantes incorporates all of these sources and sites of captivity into the *Persiles,* together with the New World setting excluded from Camamis's binary division.[24]

Alongside the episodes of the lovers' separation through captivity on remote islands and piratical ships, at one point the protagonists encounter, much like don Quijote, a narrator of a true history of Algerian captivity. In book 3, chapter 10, Auristela, Periando, and their companions come upon a large crowd gathered around two young men dressed as recently ransomed captives, who enthrall their audience with a horrifying tale that is visually accompanied by heavy chains and a painted canvas. Among the audience are the town's two mayors, one of whom is an ex-captive himself and thus able to expose the falsehood of the young men's story. However, the ridiculous detail of his questions—"¿cuántas puertas tiene Argel, y cuántas fuentes y cuántos pozos de agua dulce?" ["how many entrances are there to Algiers and how many freshwater fountains and wells?"]—divulges a distinct dose of Cervantine irony. As Alban Forcione has argued, the interrogation and the captive's response, "La pregunta es boba" ["That's a dumb question"], humorously dramatize contemporary literary debates, deflating the pretensions of neo-Aristotelian critics' recommendations for achieving verisimilitude. Both Torquato Tasso and Jacopo Mazzoni advocate locating events far enough from the realm of readers' direct knowledge so that the facts cannot be disputed. However ironic Cervantes's commentary on neo-Aristotelian criticism, the situation also demonstrates the proximity of Algerian captivity for a Spanish public. The mayor invokes the authority of firsthand experience, as well as his legal authority, to punish the young men for attempting to solicit money through their false tale, threatening them with a flogging and a sentence to the galleys.[25]

24. Camamis, *Estudios sobre el cautiverio,* 141, 234; Miguel de Cervantes Saavedra, *Novelas ejemplares,* ed. Harry Sieber (Madrid, 1995 [orig. publ., Madrid, 1613]), I, 53. Rovira, *La novela bizantina,* 140–143, also discusses captivity as a theme inherited from the novels of classical antiquity and follows Camamis's distinction between "historical" and "literary" narratives, the latter including the Byzantine novel, books of chivalry, and novellas.

25. Miguel de Cervantes Saavedra, *Los trabajos de Persiles y Sigismunda,* ed. Juan Baustista Avalle-Arce (Madrid, 1969 [orig. publ. Madrid, 1617]), 343, 346–347;

However, one of the young men—the "mozo hablador" [talkative youth]—manages to talk the mayor out of such rigorous punishment, declaring, "No hemos robado tanto que podemos dar a censo, ni fundar ningún mayorazgo; apenas granjeamos el mísero sustento con *nuestra industria, que no deja de ser trabajosa,* como lo es la de los oficiales y jornaleros" ["We haven't stolen so much, not enough to start an estate or set one up for our heirs. We scarcely make enough to earn a miserable living by *our wits, which takes as much work* as the jobs of tradesmen or day-laborers"]. The counterfeit captives (actually students from Salamanca) claim that they are not seeking to decieve their listeners but merely to earn a living on their way to Italy or Flanders in order to serve in the royal army, or, as they put it, "a romper, a destrozar, a herir y a matar los enemigos de la santa fe católica que topáramos" ["to break, smash, maim, and kill all the enemies of the holy Catholic faith we might run into"]. In other words, their goal is similar to Álvar Núñez Cabeza de Vaca's: to go from captives to captains in the service of imperial and religious expansion and to use their narrative of captivity quite literally to get them there. The "talkative youth" then attempts to convince the mayor that not only is their fiction-weaving "industria" [industry, ingenuity] as laborious as other occupations but that it can also be a service to the king: "Dejen a los míseros que van su camino derecho a servir a su Majestad con la fuerza de sus brazos y con *la agudeza de sus ingenios"* ["Leave the poor people alone who are going straight to serve His Majesty with the strength of their arms and *the keenness of their minds"].* The counterfeit captives illuminate the strategic ingenuity of Cabeza de Vaca's own literary labors to fashion himself as a resilient servant of the Crown.[26]

The loquacious student's speech, though perhaps no less fictitious than the account of captivity, yields rather profitable results for the narrator and his companion. "Por Dios," one of the mayors confesses, "que este mancebo

---

Cervantes, *The Trials of Persiles and Sigismunda: A Northern Story,* trans. Celia Richmond Weller and Clark A. Colahan (Berkeley, Calif., 1989), 247–249. On Cervantes's commentary on the debates about verisimilitude in this episode, see Forcione, *Cervantes, Aristotle, and the "Persiles,"* 170–186. On the recommendation to write about distant realms, see Jacopo Mazzoni, "On the Defense of the Comedy (Selections)" (1587), in Gilbert, ed. and trans., *Literary Criticism,* 358–403, esp. 389 ("the poet is able to feign a complete story dealing with a king, if only he feigns it of a country strange and remote" [389]); and see Tasso, "Discourses," ibid., 488.

26. Cervantes, *Los trabajos de Persiles y Sigismunda,* ed. Avalle-Arce, 348–349 (emphasis added); Cervantes, *Trials of Persiles and Sigismunda,* trans. Weller and Colahan, 249–250.

ha hablado bien, aunque ha hablado mucho, y que no solamente no tengo de consentir que los azoten, sino que los tengo de llevar a mi casa y ayudarles para su camino" ["Goodness, . . . this young man has spoken well, even though he's said too much, and not only will I not allow their lashing but I'm going to take them to my house and give them some help for their trip"]. Even the ex-captive mayor's reaction has changed, and his inclination to punish the false captives has been transformed into a desire not only to provide them with lodging but also to help them spin a better tale: "No quiero que vayan a vuestra casa, sino a la mía, donde les quiero dar una lición de las cosas de Argel, tal que de aquí adelante ninguno les coja en mal latín, en cuanto a su fingida historia" ["I don't want them to go to your house, but to mine, where I'll give them a lesson on things about Algiers, so that from now on no one will catch them making mistakes in their Latin, I mean, in their made-up story"]. The success of the student's discourse is thus unrelated to the authenticity of his narrative.[27]

Of course, verisimilitude is likely to increase this success, which is what the mayor's intervention is meant to accomplish. Indeed, the next day, upon leaving town, the protagonists again encounter the false captives, who affirm that "iban *industriados* del alcalde, de modo que de allí adelante no los podían coger en mentira acerca de las cosas de Argel" ["they were moving on, having been so well coached by the mayor that from then on no one would be able to catch them in any lies about anything having to do with Algiers"]. The counterfeit captives' tale now echoes the aesthetic principles articulated by the narrator at the beginning of the chapter: "[A la fábula] conviene guisar sus acciones con tanta puntualidad y gusto, y con tanta verisimilitud, que a despecho y pesar de la mentira, que hace disonancia en el entendimiento, forme una verdadera armonía" ["[Fiction] must be prepared with such accurate details and good taste, and with such an appearance of fact, so that notwithstanding and despite its untruth, which unavoidably generates some dissonance in the mind, its structure may be truly harmonious"]. Like the captive captain's ambiguous invocation of "lying narratives framed by strange and labored tricks and artifices," which his "true discourse" actually exceeds in curiosity, the narrator of the *Persiles* both opposes *fábula* [fiction] to *historia* [history] and asserts the desirability of the former's imitation of the latter. Or is it the reverse? The narrator also states, "No todas las cosas que suceden son buenas para ser contadas" ["Not everything that happens

27. Cervantes, *Los trabajos de Persiles y Sigismunda,* ed. Avalle-Arce, 349–350; Cervantes, *Trials of Persiles and Sigismunda,* trans. Weller and Colahan, 251.

makes good telling"], suggesting that the fabulous should be among the criteria for any narrative act—for *historia* in both of the senses used in this passage (story and history).[28]

The dual claims of sixteenth- and seventeenth-century prose writers to pleasurable novelty as well as to historical truth or verisimilitude have long been associated with neo-Aristotelian theoretical discussions in European intellectual circles. If Cabeza de Vaca's work was not an authoritative source for Cervantes's Byzantine novel as it was for Lope's, his prologues point to the way in which texts representing the New World inflected these debates. As Mary Gaylord points out, "It was not only the humanist, academic rediscovery of Aristotle's *Poetics* that made verisimilitude and the marvelous the burning questions of the day. Rather, the lived experience of astonishingly new worlds, and the urgent need of Spaniards in Europe and America to write about them, put the earnest historian and the literary liar in the same boat." Both types of writers, Gaylord explains, "had to deal in and with things 'not here': fiction, with scenes and characters that weren't here by definition . . . ; contemporary history, with radically new scenes 'not here,' because dramatically increased physical distance precluded the widespread sharing of experience." We have already seen Hans Staden's and Cabeza de Vaca's concern that the "new things" described in their accounts be accepted "without any doubt." These issues, as we will see in future chapters, are further complicated when the "not here"—the New World—is the "here" of the writer, when the "radically new scenes" remote from European readers are

28. Cervantes, *Los trabajos de Persiles y Sigismunda,* ed. Avalle-Arce, 343, 350 (emphasis added); Cervantes, *Trials of Persiles and Sigismunda,* trans. Weller and Colahan, 246, 252. On the ambiguous implications of the full passage containing these remarks, including the double meanings of *fábula* [fable or plot] and *historia* [history or story] exploited by Cervantes, see Forcione, *Cervantes, Aristotle, and the "Persiles,"* 178–186, esp. 180–181. On Cervantes's sources for literary theory and his comments on verisimilitude in the *Persiles* and other works, see E. C. Riley, *Cervantes's Theory of the Novel* (Oxford, 1962), 1–13, 179–199. Barbara Fuchs emphasizes how the performative dimensions of this episode subvert Spanish imperial ideology: "The performance of the false captives—presumably improved by the mayor's teachings—undoes the authenticity of a resistant Spanish identity by suggesting that it can be successfully pirated. . . . Even when exposed as frauds, the captives' tales retain their appeal, an appeal that has somehow become separated from the ideological reaffirmation they ostensibly provided." See Fuchs, *Mimesis and Empire: The New World, Islam, and European Identities* (Cambridge, 2001), 162.

the familiar territory of American-born authors (and the captives they write about).[29]

Cervantes's contemporary Sebastián de Covarrubias discusses the distinction between *fábula* and *historia* in a way that points directly to the New World influence on the epistemological instabilities exposed by Cervantes and Cabeza de Vaca. In his *Tesoro de la lengua castellana o española* (1611), Covarrubias unequivocally defines *fábula* in a way that recalls the captive captain's "lying narratives": "una narración artificiosa, inventada para deleitar y entretener, de cosas que ni son verdad ni tienen sombra della" [an artful narration, invented to delight and entertain, of things that are neither true nor have a shadow of truth]. However, a new realm of historical writing soon begins to cast its shadow over the boundaries between truth and fiction, verisimilitude and the marvelous:

> Los que habéis leído las Corónicas de las Indias, cosa que passó ayer, tan cierta y tan sabida, mirad quántas cosas hay en su descubrimiento y en su conquista, que exceden a quanto han imaginado las plumas de los vanos mentirosos que han escrito libros de cavallerías, pues éstas vendrá tiempo que las llamen fábulas y aun las tengan por tales los que fueren poco aficionados a la nación Española y para evitar este peligro, se había de haber defendido que ninguno las escribiera poéticamente en verso, sino conservarlas en la pureza de la verdad con que están escritas, por hombres tan graves y tan dignos de fe, sin atavío, afeite, ni adorno ninguno.

> Those of you who have read the Chronicles of the Indies, a thing that happened yesterday, so well known and certain, look at how many things there are in the discovery and conquest that exceed what has been imagined by the vain liars who have written books of chivalry. For there will come a time when these chronicles are called fables, and they are even held to be so by those that have little fondness for the Spanish nation, and to avoid this danger, no one should have been permitted to write chronicles

29. Gaylord, "The True History," *Modern Language Quarterly*, LVII (1996), 219, 220. Lennard J. Davis refers to the "undifferentiated matrix" of "news/novels discourse" from which the genre of the novel emerged in Davis, *Factual Fictions: The Origins of the English Novel* (New York, 1983), 42–70. See also William Nelson, *Fact or Fiction: The Dilemma of the Renaissance Storyteller* (Cambridge, Mass., 1973). Both critics rely on exclusively European texts and phenomena (for example, the printing press) to explain these features of early modern discourse.

poetically in verse, but rather they should be preserved in the purity of the truth with which they are written, by men so grave and so trustworthy, without any adornment or embellishment.

Covarrubias's concern for distinguishing the history of the conquest from the vain fables of the books of chivalry, which the former actually surpass in curiosity, articulates the challenge posed by the New World and its chroniclers not only to the categories of truth and fiction but also to the good faith of the (Christian) historian and the very defense of the Spanish nation (and its empire).[30]

Covarrubias's definition clearly links the issues of historiographic authority and textual authenticity to cultural anxiety about defending the borders of imperial sovereignty as well as of national and religious identity. As we will see in Chapter 5, Covarrubias perhaps need not have been so concerned about the incredulity of a hostile European readership, for Iberian accounts of the New World served as both models of inspiration and sources of information even for "those that have little fondness for the Spanish nation." The well-known royal edicts from the 1530s and 1540s prohibiting the importation of fictional works into the Spanish colonies derived from concerns about another group of readers who might have had trouble distinguishing "truth" from "fables": Amerindians. The 1543 edict signed by Prince Philip (later Philip II) states that

> llevarse a las dichas Indias libros de romance y materias profanas y fábulas, ansí como son libros de Amadís y otros desta calidad de mentirosas historias se siguen muchos inconvenientes, porque los indios que supieren leer, dándose a ellos, dexarán los libros de sana y buena dotrina y leyendo los de mentirosas historias, deprenderán en ellos malos costumbres y vicios; y demás desto, de que sepan que aquellos libros de historias vanas han sido compuestos sin haber pasado ansí, podría ser que perdiesen la abtoridad y crédito de nuestra Sagrada Scriptura y otros libros de dotores santos, creyendo, como gente no arraigada en la fe, que todos nuestros libros eran de una abtoridad y manera.

> much harm results from taking to the Indies books in the vernacular of profane and imaginative character such as those about Amadis and

30. Sebastián de Covarrubias Orozco, *Tesoro de la lengua castellana o española,* ed. Martín de Riquer (Barcelona, 1943 [orig. publ. Madrid, 1611]), 579–580.

others of this type of lying histories, because the Indians able to read turn to them, forsaking works of sound and proper doctrine; from these false tales they learn evil practices and vices. Moreover, since they do not know those frivolous books were written about what did not happen, it is possible that the authenticity and authority of our Holy Scriptures and the writings of learned saints may suffer because, since they [the Indians] are not firmly grounded in the faith, they may regard all books of equal truth and authority.

Barbara Fuchs has argued that European critical debates about truth and romance, as exemplified in Tasso's theoretical and literary work, share the anxieties of these edicts and thus "project the American experience of reading, with its vagaries of authorized and unauthorized textual interpretation, onto the European literary landscape." As Covarrubias's anxious remarks make clear, however, the threat comes not only from native or foreign readers but also from the writers of New World narratives themselves, like Cabeza de Vaca or Alonso de Ercilla (whose epic *La Araucana* [1569] is surely the chronicle written "poetically in verse" to which he refers).[31]

Despite such preoccupations, both Cabeza de Vaca and Cervantes's talkative youth reveal the success with which captivating "true histories" could legitimize loyal subjects ready to serve the imperial state. Cabeza de Vaca's text explicitly appropriates the legal genre of the relación de servicios, and Cervantes presented his own captivity as a form of service in an *Información,* a legal document through which returning captives from North Africa corroborated their preservation of Christian faith and loyalty to the Spanish Crown. As Roberto González Echevarría argues in "The Law of the Letter," sixteenth-century novelists and New World chroniclers alike appropriated the notorial rhetoric employed in such documents in the effort to legitimize "the voice which narrates the story."[32]

31. See Irving Leonard, *Books of the Brave: Being an Account of Books and of Men in the Spanish Conquest and Settlement of the Sixteenth-Century New World* (Berkeley, Calif., 1992 [orig. publ. Cambridge, Mass., 1949]), 81–84. The 1543 edict is transcribed in José Toribio Medina, *Biblioteca Hispano-Americana, 1493–1810,* 7 vols. (Santiago de Chile, 1898–1907), VI, xxvi–xxvii; I cite from Leonard's translation in *Books of the Brave,* 82. See also Fuchs, *Mimesis and Empire,* 24.

32. González Echevarría, "Law of the Letter," in González Echevarría, *Myth and Archive,* 70. Garcés explains how returning captives commonly presented texts like Cervantes's *Información:* "When a Spanish captive in Algiers or any other Muslim

The episode of the counterfeit captives, in fact, dramatizes the use of legal documents as a source of authorization as humorously as it does contemporary debates about verisimilitude. After the students' departure, the mayors approach the pilgrim protagonists and ask for their true history, presumably also a narrative in either pictorial or oral form: "¿Vosotros, señores peregrinos, traéis algún lienzo que enseñarnos? ¿Traéis otra historia que hacernos creer por verdadera, aunque la haya compuesto la misma mentira?" ["Do you, too, my good pilgrims, have some canvas with you to show us? Did you also bring with you some story you'll want us to believe is true, even though it might have been made up by Falsehood itself?"]. In response, one of the pilgrims takes out the "patentes, licencias y despachos que llevaban para seguir su viaje" ["letters of authorization, permission, and safe-conduct for their journey"] and tells (off) the authority: "Por estos papeles podrá ver vuesa merced quién somos y adónde vamos, los cuales no era menester presentallos, porque ni pedimos limosna, ni tenemos necesidad de pedilla" ["These papers will show Your Grace who we are and where we're going even though we weren't obliged to present them since we're neither begging nor do we have any need to"]. Such legal and written authorization of identity is certainly not as captivating as the students' performance. The pilgrims' papers—an account of pilgrimage, if you will, rather than captivity—are initially less successful than the false captives', since neither mayor is able to read. The documents end up in the hands of the *escribano* [town clerk], and perhaps because his own livelihood depends on producing such papers, the legalistic display of identity finally earns the favorable reaction already awarded to the students' tale, for he offers them shelter for the night in his home.[33]

In these scenes, Cervantes presents two distinct narrative approaches to the production of identity, which are conflated in the "peregrino, y raro" [strange and rare] but true discourse of both of the captive captains we have met thus far: Ruy Pérez de Viedma and Álvar Núñez Cabeza de Vaca. On

---

city was ransomed, he would write an *Información* on his life and habits during his captivity not only on his personal services, but also as a proper justification vis-à-vis the civil authorities and the Inquisition of having sustained his Catholic faith and not having renounced it among the infidels"; see *Cervantes in Algiers,* 99. For a reading of the "Captive's Tale" in *Don Quijote* as a relación de servicios, see Sieber, "Mapping Identity," *Cervantes: Bulletin of the Cervantes Society of America,* XVIII, no. 1 (Spring 1998), 130.

33. Cervantes, *Los trabajos de Persiles y Sigismunda,* ed. Avalle-Arce, 350; Cervantes, *Trials of Persiles and Sigismunda,* trans. Weller and Colahan, 251.

one hand, the pilgrims offer a supposedly truthful and unmediated (artless) rendition of identity as an authorized account of their place of origin, route, and destination. On the other hand, the students present an artful performance of an assumed identity through a narrative of feigned travel, which nevertheless conforms to the laws of verisimilitude. However, both narrative modes respond to similar motivations and achieve nearly identical effects. *Don Quijote*'s ex-captive, as well as *Persiles*'s various travelers, all manage to attract an audience as well as earn a place to stay, a home away from home, by displaying their itinerant identities and narrating their journeys, whether true or false.

Los trabajos de Persiles y Sigismunda opens with an actual rather than feigned scene of captivity, this one with New World intimations. The hero, Periandro, is held hostage on a remote "Isla Bárbara" [Barbaric Isle], ostensibly located somewhere in the North Sea, by "barbarians" who intend to cannibalize the foreigner's heart. If Periandro's captors are as savage and cruel as the Turks in the *Topographia* and the false captives' tale, the threat of ritual cannibalism recalls European apprehensions about the Occident rather than the Orient. Some critics have indicated classical sources for the Isla Bárbara episodes, but Diana de Armas Wilson points out their unmistakable New World hallmarks: the cannibals "trade in gold and pearls, fight with bows and arrows, communicate by signs or through a kidnapped female interpreter, and sail about in rafts constructed with *bejucos*—a specifically Caribbean *(taíno)* signifier." Other scholars have similarly attempted to identify Cervantes's sources for these details in New World chronicles like el Inca Garcilaso de la Vega's *Comentarios reales de los Incas.* Whether or not Cervantes found inspiration in a specific text for the "Barbaric Isle" episodes, the experience of a Spanish castaway on another part of the island suggests the potential (re)productive effects of shipwreck and captivity in a New World setting. In this sense, the novel participates in what George Mariscal calls "a vast cultural project struggling to make sense of previously unimagined worlds and peoples," like the works of Cabeza de Vaca or Garcilaso.[34]

34. De Armas Wilson, *Cervantes, the Novel, and the New World,* 71; George Mariscal, "*Persiles* and the Remaking of Spanish Culture," *Cervantes: Bulletin of the Cervantes Society of America,* X, no. 1 (Spring 1990), 93–102, esp. 102. On Cervantes's possible sources in New World historiography, see Rodolfo Schevill and Adolfo Bonilla y San Martín, introduction, in Miguel de Cervantes Saavedra, *Persiles y Sigismunda* (Madrid, 1914), I, v–xlvi, esp. xxvi–xxix; Stelio Cro, "Cervantes, el *Persiles* y la historiografía indiana," *Anales de literatura hispanoamericana,* IV (1975),

In chapters 5 and 6 of book 1, Antonio, known as the "bárbaro español" [Spanish barbarian], recounts his tale of shipwreck and survival on the Barbaric Isle to the protagonists after their escape from the cannibals. His tale appears to be the inverse of a narrative of subjection, for he describes his arrival and first contact with the native Ricla in terms that attempt to preserve (and assert the superiority of) his identity as a male Spaniard. Antonio relates how, after being shipwrecked on an apparently abandoned shore, he spies a "barbarian girl," whom he startles with his alien presence and proceeds to "captivate," both physically and emotionally:

> Pasmóse viéndome . . . y cogiéndola entre mis brazos sin decirla palabra, ni ella a mí tampoco, me entré por la cueva adelante, y la traje a este mismo lugar donde agora estamos. Púsela en el suelo, beséle las manos, halaguéle el rostro con las mías, e hice todas las señales y demostraciones que pude para mostrarme blando y amoroso con ella. Ella, pasado aquel primer espanto . . . se reía y me abrazaba, y sacando del seno una manera de pan hecho a su modo, que no era de trigo, me lo puso en la boca, y en su lengua me habló, y a lo que después acá he sabido, en lo que decía me rogaba que comiese. Yo lo hice ansí porque lo había bien menester.

> She was stunned to see me . . . ; clasping her in my arms without saying a word to her, nor she to me, I went straight into the cave and brought her to this same spot where we are right now. I placed her on the ground, kissed her hands, caressed her face, and made every sort of gesture and sign I could to show her I was gentle and loving. Once she got over her first fright . . . she would laugh and embrace me, and then taking from her clothes a special kind of bread not made of wheat, she put it in my

---

5–25; and de Armas Wilson, *Cervantes, the Novel, and the New World.* Schevill and Bonilla and de Armas Wilson point to el Inca Garcilaso de la Vega's *Comentarios reales* as a possible source for the Barbaric Isle's ritual cannibalism; see Schevill and Bonilla, introduction, in Cervantes, *Persiles y Sigismunda,* I, xxviii; de Armas Wilson, *Allegories of Love,* 114. Riley, on the other hand, points out the resemblance of the opening chapters to the story of Iphigenia, which was used by Aristotle and his sixteenth-century followers to illustrate the value of peripety and anagnorisis to achieve the effect of the marvelous without arousing doubt; see *Cervantes's Theory of the Novel,* 184. López Pinciano—Cervantes's probable source for Aristotelian theory—summarizes the Iphigenia tale in *Philosophia antigua poética,* ed. Carballo Picazo, II, 18–19.

mouth and spoke to me in her language, asking me, I later learned, to eat it. I ate because I really needed to.

The self-aggrandizing details in Antonio's tale—the young native woman's captivation at the sight of the Spaniard, the repetition of the male "I" as the subject of actions and the female as their recipient or object—do not disguise the fact that the male Spaniard is still dependent upon the indigenous woman for survival.[35]

Such an idealized depiction of the indigenous woman as docile and welcoming calls to mind the gentle and peace-loving natives that occasionally appear in Columbus's letters and journal, an image later consolidated in Bartolomé de Las Casas's defense of Amerindians and in the discourse surrounding the "noble savage." As in the texts of Columbus and Las Casas, as well, the emphasis on the tractability of the native "other" conveys the ease with which their conversion and civilization may take place, as Ricla herself affirms when she takes over Antonio's account of their encounter: "Yo, simple y compasiva, le entregué un alma rústica, y él—merced a los cielos—me la ha vuelto discreta y cristiana" ["I, simple and compassionate, turned my rustic soul over to him, and he, with Heaven's grace, has returned it to me wise and Christian"]. Her other "entregas" [surrenders] to the would-be colonizer are even more typical of the commerce sought by Europeans in the New World: "Entreguéle el cuerpo . . . y deste entrego *[sic]* resultó haberle dado dos hijos. . . . En veces le truje alguna cantidad de oro, de lo que abunda esta isla, y algunas perlas que yo tengo guardadas, esperando el día, que ha de ser tan dichoso, que nos saque desta prisión y nos lleve adonde con libertad y certeza y sin escrúpulo seamos unos de los del rebaño de Cristo" ["I surrendered my body to him . . . and this surrender resulted in the two children. . . . At various times I've brought him pieces of gold that abound on this island, and some pearls that I've stored away waiting for the day, bound to be a happy one, that will take us out of this prison and to a place where, freely and surely and with nothing to worry us, we'll be among the flock of Christ"]. Ricla's assimilation to her Spanish lover's religion and culture is

35. Cervantes, *Los trabajos de Persiles y Sigismunda,* ed. Avalle-Arce, 80; Cervantes, *Trials of Persiles and Sigismunda,* trans. Weller and Colahan, 39. On the echoes of an idealized New World encounter between a male Spaniard and a female Amerindian in this episode, see Cro, "Cervantes," *Anales de literatura hispanoamericana,* IV (1975), 5–25.

so complete that she even adopts his perspective of her homeland as a site of captivity from which she yearns to escape.[36]

Nevertheless, Ricla's role is not entirely passive. It is her conclusion to the "variable historia" [eventful story] that earns the admiration of their listeners; she also teaches Antonio her language, thus assuring that he does not leave the Barbaric Isle unaffected by his experience. Indeed, Antonio's nickname, "el español bárbaro" [the Spanish barbarian], indicates the extent of his transformation. He even appears with his family dressed in animal skins—his mixed-blood son wielding a bow and arrow—upon their arrival in Lisbon. Their strange appearance incites such wonder and admiration that they are urged to exchange their "barbarian" clothes for pilgrims' attire, in order to attract less attention. The public's excitement at such a novel spectacle recalls the reception of Amerindians in Portugal and elsewhere in Europe, such as that of a Brazilian Indian sent by Pedro Álvares Cabral to Lisbon, as described by the Jesuit Simão de Vasconcelos in his *Chrônica da Companhia de Jesu do estado do Brasil* (1663): "Foi recibido em Portugal com alegria do Rei, e do Reino. Não se fartavam os grandes, e pequenos de ver, e ouvir a fala, gesto, e meneios daquele novo indivíduo da geração humana" [He was received in Portugal with the delight of the king and of the realm. Neither old nor young tired of seeing and hearing the speech, gesture, and manners of that new individual of the human race]. Even more than the transculturated Spaniard, Ricla and her mestizo children, Constanza and Antonio, call to mind the "new individuals" encountered through Iberia's expansion in the New World.[37]

Significantly, it is the bicultural figure of Antonio's son who offers the legalistic display of identity—the "letters of authorization"—following the episode of the wayward students. His use of notorial documents reflects, on a miniature scale, the "allegory of legitimation" that González Echevarría has identified in both the picaresque novel and New World chronicles like el Inca Garcilaso's *Comentarios reales*. Yet notorial discourse and the rheto-

36. Cervantes, *Los trabajos de Persiles y Sigismunda,* ed. Avalle-Arce, 82–83; Cervantes, *Trials of Persiles and Sigismunda,* trans. Weller and Colahan, 41.

37. Cervantes, *Los trabajos de Persiles y Sigismunda,* ed. Avalle-Arce, 279; Cervantes, *Trials of Persiles and Sigismunda,* trans. Weller and Colahan, 196; Simão de Vasconcelos, *Crônica da Companhia de Jesus,* 3d ed. (Petrópolis, Brazil, 1977 [orig. publ. Lisbon, 1663]), 55–56. Mariscal highlights how Antonio the younger and his sister Constanza represent the "bicultural consequences of the encounter between Spain and its Others"; see *"Persiles," Cervantes,* X, no. 1 (Spring 1990), 97.

ric of true history are not enough for these peregrine characters to narrate their travels and travails in foreign lands. Previously, upon their arrival in Lisbon, the pilgrims had employed the same technique as the false captives and ordered a large canvas to be painted of their story. It is Antonio the younger, again, who describes the pictures—including both his parents' and Periandro's "captivities" on the Barbaric Isle—to those who insist on hearing their account. After meeting the counterfeit captives, we know what a dramatic and effective performance such a narrative can make. Cervantes once again confounds the true history of the pilgrims—of his novel as a whole—with the "strange artifice" of the students.[38]

Cervantes's simultaneous appeal to verisimilitude and the marvelous, truth and artifice, and instruction and entertainment in his narrations of captivity comes as no surprise: this ambiguity has been described as a defining feature of his theory of the novel and sometimes of the novelistic genre as such. As we have seen in Cabeza de Vaca's *Relación y comentarios,* however, authors of "true histories" of shipwreck and captivity were using similar techniques to frame accounts of New World novelties in the sixteenth century. In the seventeenth century, as well, some ostensibly historical works not only embrace the dual rhetorical strategies exploited by Cabeza de Vaca's and Cervantes's narrators but also highlight the transformative effects of the New World on European bodies as well as texts.[39]

38. González Echevarría, "Law of the Letter," in González Echevarría, *Myth and Archive,* 70–71; Cervantes, *Los trabajos de Persiles y Sigismunda,* ed. Avalle-Arce, 281; Cervantes, *Trials of Persiles and Sigismunda,* trans. Weller and Colahan, 197. Elizabeth Bearden reads the painted canvases in the *Persiles* as a hybrid cultural product inspired by Mexican pictographic codices, which served an authenticating, juridical function in the colonial context. She argues that Antonio the younger's role as the *lienzo*'s mestizo interpreter affords him "a narratival agency that gives the barbarian a voice while it readjusts the European idea of the art of memory to an indigenous model"; see Bearden, "Painting Counterfeit Canvases: American Memory *Lienzos* and European Imaginings of the Barbarian in Cervantes's *Los trabajos de Persiles y Sigismunda,*" *PMLA,* CXXI (2006), 735–752, esp. 741, 749.

39. On Cervantes's treatment of the novelistic functions of pleasure and profit and of the categories of history, fiction, verisimilitude, and the marvelous, see Riley, *Cervantes's Theory of the Novel,* 81–88, 163–199. Davis defines the novel by its "constitutive ambivalence toward fact and fiction," although his Anglocentric narrative of the emergence of the novel denies the novelistic status of anything preceding the eighteenth century, even *Don Quijote;* see *Factual Fictions,* 212.

NOVEL TOPOGRAPHIES, IBERIAN RELATIONS: JOÃO CARVALHO MASCARENHAS'S *Memoravel relaçam*

Although Portuguese captives were abundant in North Africa, particularly after King Sebastian's defeat at Alcácer-Quibir in 1578, accounts of captivity do not appear to have enjoyed quite the same literary vogue that they experienced in Spain. Narratives of shipwreck, on the other hand, clearly fascinated a wide Portuguese readership. Numerous *relações de naufrágio* [shipwreck accounts] were published in the latter half of the sixteenth and the first half of the seventeenth centuries in pamphlet form, sometimes in multiple editions. Bernardo Gomes de Brito consolidated their popularity in the eighteenth century with his publication of twelve such accounts in the *História trágico-marítima* (1735–1736), as did various counterfeit editions of seventeenth-century pamphlets printed around the same time. Shipwreck tales have sometimes shared the fortune of captivity narratives among modern critics who argue for their disruptive potential in imperial discourse, narrating as they do the failure of exploration and conquest. However, like Cabeza de Vaca, early modern writers, editors, and censors had no trouble reconciling shipwreck accounts with imperial goals, often citing their useful information about the lands reached or about the actions that affected the number of lives lost throughout the ordeal. That a certain segment of readership prized the narratives for their instructional value is evident in the frequency with which castaways themselves refer to previous shipwrecks in an attempt to guide their actions: one narrative even relates how a copy of an earlier shipwreck account "was found among the castaways and passed eagerly from hand to hand."[40]

40. Charles R. Boxer, "An Introduction to the *História Trágico-Marítima,*" in *Miscelânea de estudos em honra do Prof. Hernâni Cidade* (Lisbon, 1957), 48–99, esp. 93. Boxer's essay summarizes the publication history of each of the shipwreck pamphlets, beginning with the twelve gathered in Bernardo Gomes de Brito, *História trágico-maritíma* (Lisbon, 1735–1736); see also Boxer, "An Introduction to the *História Trágico-Marítima:* Some Corrections and Clarifications," *Quaderni portoghesi,* V (1979), 99–112. For an approach to shipwreck narratives that emphasizes their "counterideological impulse," see Josiah Blackmore's *Manifest Perdition: Shipwreck Narrative and the Disruption of Empire* (Minneapolis, Minn., 2002), 41. However, Blackmore also acknowledges the narratives' didacticism and affirmation of imperial ideology, particularly in Brito's eighteenth-century collection (41–45, 108–119). Although the theme of captivity in sixteenth- and seventeenth-century Portuguese literature has been less widely studied than in the Spanish context, examples

One account that did not make it into Brito's now canonical volumes, although it has appeared in other collections of Portuguese shipwreck narratives, is João Carvalho Mascarenhas's *Memoravel relaçam da perda da nao Conceiçam,* first published in Lisbon in 1627. The work's abbreviated title and pamphlet form have long allowed it to be read within the genre of Portuguese shipwreck narratives. The account relates no shipwreck, however, and might more properly be designated a narrative of captivity. The first part, *Relação da perda da nau Conceição,* narrates the ship's attack and destruction by seventeen Turkish vessels within sight of Lisbon and the transport of the captured Portuguese to Algiers, where they are sold into slavery. The second section, *Nova descrição da cidade de Argel,* offers a description of Algiers that, as we will see, is anything but new. The final part, *Dos sucessos que tiveram os cativos,* includes thirteen chapters relating the martyrdom, conversion, and escape of various Christian captives in Algiers and the Mediterranean. Mascarenhas, a well-traveled soldier of whom we know little other than from the narrative, states in the preface that his motivation for writing stems from

> ver que, sendo a cidade de Argel perseguição contínua da cristandade, . . . e donde há, somente dêste nosso reino, mais cativos que de outro algum, e que, havendo nêle tantos soldados, tantos letrados, tantas pessoas graves e doutas, não houvesse quem escrevesse dela algum tratado moderno em nossa língua, ocupando por ventura a sutileza de seus engenhos em livros de menos importância.

> seeing that, even though the City of Algiers is the constant persecution of Christianity, . . . and even though there are, only from this kingdom, more captives than from any other, and that among them there are so many soldiers, so many men of letters, so many serious and learned per-

abound in a variety of genres: Luis de Camões refers to the North African captivity of Prince Fernando in canto 4 of *Os Lusíadas* (Lisbon, 1572); one of the survivors of the Portuguese defeat at Alcácer-Quibir, Diogo Bernardes, included a series of poems on his captivity in his *Várias rimas ao Bom Jesus* . . . (Lisbon, [1594]); Fernão Mendes Pinto's autobiographical *Peregrinação* (Lisbon, 1614) narrates the author's adventures—including thirteen captivities—in the East Indies; and Gaspar Pires de Rebelo's novel *Infortúnios trágicos da constante Florinda* (part 1, 1625; part 2, 1633) incorporates a tale of Turkish captivity among the many "tragic misfortunes" of its lover-protagonists. See Rebelo, *Infortúnios trágicos da constante Florinda* (Lisbon, 1707), 279–281.

sons, there is none who has written about it in a modern treatise in our language, perhaps because they are occupying the subtlety of their wits in books of less importance.

Despite acknowledging earlier that captives are "matéria de pouca estima" [material of low esteem], Mascarenhas promotes his own work by underscoring the lack of and urgent need for texts in Portuguese about Algerian captivity. However, he need not have looked farther than his Iberian neighbors—who at the time shared a sovereign—to find other works on which to mold his account.[41]

Mascarenhas found such a source in what may be the work of another Portuguese author, if Camamis, Emilio Sola, and María Antonia Garcés are right about the attribution of the *Topographia e historia general de Argel* to Antonio de Sosa. Mascarenhas's debt to the *Topographia* is most immediately obvious in the section called *Nova descrição da cidade de Argel.* This section appears to have been lifted from the first part of Sosa's work, the *Topographia o descripción de Argel y sus habitadores y costumbres.* Mascarenhas offers a nearly word-for-word translation of the *Topographia* at times,

41. João Carvalho Mascarenhas, *Memorável relação da perda da nau Conceição,* in Damião Peres, ed., *Viagens e naufrágios célebres dos séculos XVI, XVII e XVIII,* I (Oporto, 1937), 21–142, esp. 25, 27–28. The first edition, *Memoravel relaçam da perda da nao "Conceicam"* [sic] *que os Turcos queimarão à vista da barra de Lisboa, varios successos das pessoas que nella cativarañ . . . ,* was printed in Lisbon in 1627. An eighteenth-century counterfeit edition slightly alters the title's wording and gives the author's name as João Tavares Mascarenhas; see Boxer, "Introduction to the *História Trágico-Marítima,"* in *Miscelânea de estudos,* 77–80. The English ex-captive Francis Knight made a similar claim of being the first to write about Algiers in Knight, *A Relation of Seaven Yeares Slaverie* (1640), which, like Mascarenhas's (and Staden's) account, is divided into "A True and Strange Relation" of captivity and a "Second Booke" dedicated to the "discription of Argeire." In the prologue, Knight asserts that "none, to my knowledge, hath ever devulged in Print, the estate and condition of Captives in that place of *Argeire.*" However, readers in England did have access to Spanish descriptions of Algiers and its Christian captives in the English translations of the first part of *Don Quijote* (Miguel de Cervantes Saavedra, *The History of the Valorous and Wittie Knight-Errant, Don-Quixote of the Mancha* [trans. Thomas Shelton] (London, 1612) and Gonzalo de Céspedes y Meneses's *Poema trágico del español Gerardo y desengaño del amor lascivo,* published as *Gerardo the Unfortunate Spaniard; or, A Patterne for Lascivious Lovers . . . ,* trans. L[eonard] D[igges] (London, 1622).

and although the organization and distribution of the chapters differ, the basic information found in nearly all of the *Relaçam's* thirteen chapters can be traced to different passages in the *Topographia,* which is a good deal longer (forty-one chapters). The similarities between the descriptions of Algiers generally correspond to facts that both authors might have acquired through other sources or through their own observation; they are, after all, describing the same city in which they were held captive. Yet the frequency of these coincidences and the similar turns of phrases used to present them suggest that Mascarenhas had access to the *Topographia* when writing his account.[42]

However, Mascarenhas would not have been the first to mine the *Topographia's* pages. Camamis shows how writers as diverse as Lope de Vega and the ex-captive Diego Galán model their descriptions of Algiers on passages from the *Topographia.* Camamis dedicates the most attention to Gonzalo de Céspedes y Meneses's "immense debt" to Sosa in his Byzantine novel, *Poema trágico del español Gerardo y desengaño del amor lascivo* (1615): not only the description of Algiers but various anecdotes in the *Poema trágico* are borrowed from Sosa's text. Céspedes y Meneses, in fact, may offer a clue to Mascarenhas's knowledge of the *Topographia.* The Spanish author

42. Compare, for example, the following passages: "Aunque en toda la muralla cuanta es en torno hay muchas torres y torreones o caballeros, pero como todos sean a la antigua, y muy flacos, solamente de siete se puede hacer caso" [Although along the whole wall there are many turrets and large fortified towers or cavaliers, but since they are all old and very weak, only seven are worth noting] and "Em tôda a muralha há muitas tôrres, ameias e seteiras e cavaleiros, mas sòmente de sete se pode fazer menção porque são terraplenados e com alguma artelharia mas tudo fraco e muito antigo" [Along the whole wall there are many towers, battlements, embrasures and cavaliers, but only seven are worth mentioning because they are embanked and have some artillery, but they are all weak and very old]; see Haedo, *Topografía,* I, 34, and Mascarenhas, *Memorável relação,* in Peres, ed., *Viagens e naufrágios célebres,* I, 79. The description of the organization of the divan *(duana* or *aduana)*—the general council of the janissary militia that governed Algiers—coincides even to the point of the salaries earned by each post; see Haedo, *Topografía,* I, 63–67, and Mascarenhas, *Memorável relação,* in Peres, ed., *Viagens e naufrágios célebres,* I, 91–92. Paul Teyssier's French translation acknowledges but does not explore the intertextual relationship, affirming only that, because of the similarities in the descriptions of Algiers, Mascarenhas surely knew the *Topographia;* see Mascarenhas, *Esclave à Alger: Récit de captivité de João Mascarenhas (1621–1626),* ed. and trans. Paul Teyssier (Paris, 1993), 10.

was exiled in Lisbon in the 1620s, and in 1625 the Portuguese printer António Álvares published the third edition of *Poema trágico.* Only two years later, António Álvares published Mascarenhas's *Memoravel relaçam,* which borrows from some of the same passages in the *Topographia* as Céspedes y Meneses's novel.[43]

Camamis finds Céspedes y Meneses's most egregious copying of the *Topographia* in the interpolated tale of the captivity and martyrdom of Fernando Palomeque. The story is based on the tale of Juan Cañete and other episodes included in the *Topographia*'s second dialogue, *Diálogo de los mártires,* which presents cases of Christian captives who are horrifically put to death but who retain their faith until the end. Mascarenhas might have found the same inspiration for the third section of his relation, *Dos sucessos que tiveram os cativos.* The initial chapters of this section follow quite closely the structure of the *Diálogo de los mártires,* with three successive cases of virtuous captive martyrdoms presented chronologically. The section proceeds with even more intriguing episodes: repentant renegades, picaresque adventurers, escape attempts, cross-cultural love affairs, revenge plots, and the miraculous reunion of a captive Sicilian woman with her exiled galley-slave son, "ficando ambos em uma hora livres, por tam diferente caminho e tam nunca imaginado meio" [both being freed at the same time through such a different path and such unimaginable means]. The literary resonance of these episodes, so common to the Byzantine novel and other contemporary fictional genres, suggests that the proximity between Céspedes y Meneses's novel and Mascarenhas's *relação* is not only by way of their common source, a historical treatise. Both also resort to the "strange and labored artifice" of the Byzantine—and the Cervantine—novel.[44]

43. On Galán's, Lope's, and Céspedes's borrowings from the *Topographia,* see Camamis, *Estudios sobre el cautiverio,* 151–170, 214–215. The Portuguese writer Francisco Manuel de Mello mentions sharing information with Céspedes for the writing of his *Historia de Felipe IV,* also published in Lisbon in 1631, and he praises Céspedes's fondness for the Portuguese as "justo agradecimento á boa hospedagem que achou em Lisboa, donde muitos annos viveo, depois de perseguido e desterrado da patria" [proper gratitude for the good hospitality that he found in Lisbon, where he lived for many years, after being persecuted and exiled from his homeland]; see Francisco Manuel de Mello, *Epanaphoras de varia historia portugueza . . .* (Lisbon, 1660), 123.

44. Mascarenhas, *Memorável relação,* in Peres, ed., *Viagens e naufrágios célebres,* I, 137. On Céspedes's plagiarism of the *Topographia* in the tale of Fernando Palomeque, see Camamis, *Estudios sobre el cautiverio,* 163–170. Another case of cross-linguistic

Mascarenhas's prologues recognize the confluence, particularly evident in the third section, of the goals of instruction, service, and entertainment through a truthful as well as delightful narration. Like Hans Staden, Mascarenhas dedicates his work to a patron familiar with captivity, the prior of Óbidos dom Pedro de Menezes, whose father and grandfather had died as hostages in North Africa. Recognizing that anyone can fall captive—including members of the royal family and nobility, as Portugal had dramatically experienced in the battle of Alcácer-Quibir—Mascarenhas asserts the exemplary, didactic nature of his work ("o que tem notícia de coisas semelhantes já sabe como se há-de haver nelas" [those who have news of similar things will already know how they are to behave when it happens to them]). He also frames the account, much like Cabeza de Vaca, as a sort of relación de servicios:

> Ponho debaixo do amparo e favor de V. M. esta minha relação, porque nela apresento também a V. M. meus trabalhos, pois todos os que conto passaram por mim e em todos os sucessos que relato me achei, tirando outros muitos que tive na Índia, de que não trato; e todos em serviço de sua Majestade, que por esta razão ficam sendo de mais qualidade e merecimento.

> I place this my relation under your protection and favor, because in it I also present to you my travails, since all of the ones that I recount happened to me and I was present in all of the events that I relate, as well as many others that I had in India, which I do not address; and everything in the service of His Majesty, and for this reason they are of higher quality and worthy of recognition.

---

plagiarism suggests Céspedes's role in disseminating the *Topographia* in Portugal. Céspedes's story of Fernando Palomeque inspired an anonymous eighteenth-century Portuguese pamphlet, once again incorrectly labeled "new": *Nova relaçaõ, e verdadeira noticia exposta ao publico, do grande cazo, que succedeo a hum cavalheiro italiano, e a outro valerozo espanhol, chamado Pedro Pisarro na cidade de Argel* (Lisbon, 1763). The pamphlet adheres to the structure of Céspedes's version, with a recent captive finding a martryr's bloodstains during a walk through Algiers and begging his companions to tell him the story. The interpolated account of Pedro Pisarro follows Céspedes's Palomeque tale, including the different passages lifted from the *Topographia,* nearly word for word. The pamphlet concludes in a second part, *Relação dos rigorosos martirios, que padeceo . . . Pedro Pisarro na cidade de Argel* (Lisbon, 1763).

In the prologue, Mascarenhas similarly insists on the account's status as true history in light of his eyewitness testimony as well as the plainness of his rhetoric: "Meu intento foi contar verdades (que em tudo o que escrevo como testemunha de vista poderei jurar), pelo que me pareceu não ser necessário adôrno de palavras, nem linguagem floreada, que esta muitas vezes serve mais de escurecer e confundir a história, que de a declarar e dar gôsto a quem a lê" [My intention was to tell the truth (for I can swear to everything that I write as an eyewitness), for which adornment or flowery language did not seem necessary, for these many times serve more to obscure and confuse the history than to declare it and give pleasure to the reader]. The pleasure extends to the author, as well, for Mascarenhas concludes the prologue by invoking the pleasure derived from retelling past misfortune, as had Cabeza de Vaca in his dedication to the 1555 *Relación y comentarios.*[45]

Mascarenhas also coincides with Cabeza de Vaca's affirmation of the reliable, firsthand nature of his testimony about foreign lands despite the novelty of its content. When telling of some Christian captives' plot to escape, Mascarenhas reiterates, "Trato de mim nesta história, porque, como testemunha de vista, a contarei mais ao certo e mais particularmente" [I speak of myself in this history, because, as an eyewitness, I will tell it more veraciously and with more detail]. And Mascarenhas's claim to eyewitness authority is, at one point, explicitly based on his travels in the New World (and beyond) rather than his travails in Algiers. This "digression"—an autobiographical intrusion into the otherwise detached perspective of the description of Algiers—represents Mascarenhas's most significant deviation from his Iberian source text and puts him into contact with other topographies as well as narrative models.[46]

Mascarenhas's chapter dedicated to the "orchards and farms" surround-

45. Mascarenhas, *Memorável relação,* in Peres, ed., *Viagens e naufrágios célebres,* I, 25–27, 137. "Pôsto que o contentamento de contar trabalhos passados me pode ficar por prémio, o ser bem aceita o terei por tam grande, quanto é o gusto com que a ofereço" [Although the contentment of telling past labors suffices as my reward, a good reception will be as great a prize to me as the pleasure with which I offer it] (28). A modern reader, Charles Boxer, praises both the truthful and delightful dimensions of the Mascarenhas text, calling it "more convincing and enthralling than Cervantes' treatment of [the theme of captivity] in *El trato de Argel, los baños de Argel* and chapters xxxix and xl of *Don Quijote de la Mancha";* see Boxer, "Introduction to the *História Trágico-Marítima,*" in *Miscelânea de estudos,* 92.

46. Mascarenhas, *Memorável relação,* in Peres, ed., *Viagens e naufrágios célebres,* I, 114.

ing Algiers initially seems to follow the *Topographia*'s chapter on the same topic. Both depict an Edenic setting, from Haedo's "infinitos jardines, huertas, viñas . . . todo regado con infinitas fuentes de aguas claras" [infinite gardens, orchards, and vineyards . . . all watered by infinite fountains of clear water] to Mascarenhas's "jardins, quintas, hortas e pomares, que são os melhores e mais viçosos, frescos, e abundantes de frutas e de fontes e ribeiras de água, que eu vi" [flower and vegetable gardens, farms, and orchards, which are the best and most vibrant, fresh, and abundant of fruit and fountains and brooks that I have ever seen]. Yet whereas Haedo calls on classical and familiar references to construct the locus amoenus ("realmente no se pueden imaginar más temperos de Tesalia ni huertos alcinocos que los jardines de Argel" [truly one cannot imagine more fruitful soil of Thessaly nor gardens of *alcino* [a plant native to Spain] than the gardens of Algiers]), Mascarenhas offers the evidence of his extensive travels. Because of its length, I quote only the first and last geographical references of this startling declaration:

> De maneira que eu, tendo visto alguma parte do mundo, até esta idade de trinta e oito anos de que sou—como foi: no Brasil, indo por terra, do Rio Grande até a Paraíba e Pernambuco, e daí à Baía, estando em todos os lugares, aldeias, engenhos, que há em tôda esta costa, de uma parte até a outra . . . ; vi todo o condado de Catalunha, o reino de Aragão e de Castela e êste de Portugal,—até agora não vi terra mais fresca de jardins, mais abundante de frutas, mais barata de mantimentos, mais copiosa de fontes, nem de clima mais temperado . . . do que é a cidade de Argel, que permita o Ceu seja ainda desta corôa.
>
> So that I, having seen some part of the world up until the age of thirty-eight that I am now—such as Brazil, going by land, from the Great River until Paraíba and Pernambuco, and from there to Bahia, visiting all the hamlets, villages, and plantations that there are along the coast, from one part to the other . . . ; I saw all of the County of Catalonia, the Kingdom of Aragon, of Castile, and this one of Portugal—but until now I have never seen a land with fresher gardens, more abundant in fruit, cheaper in supplies, more copious in fountains, nor one with a more temperate climate . . . than this city of Algiers, which may God yet allow to belong to this Crown.

Between Brazil and Iberia, the New and Old World, appears a geographic compendium that displays the global reach of Portuguese navigation, even after the fifteenth- and sixteenth-century heyday (Mozambique, Mombaza, Mourima, the Red Sea, India, Diu, Ormuz, Caldea, Persia, Arabia Felix, Arabia Deserta, Bizerta, Tunis, the Azores, Sardenia, Corsica, Menorca, Mallorca, Nice, Florence, Pisa, Genoa, etc.). The insistent first-person verbs ("vi"; "passei"; "estive"; "fui"; "vim"; "sem haver nêle pequeno lugar que não visse" [I saw; I passed; I was in; I went; I came; without there being any small place I didn't see]), followed by an appeal to conquest (at a time in which Portugal had all but abandoned its imperial enterprises in North Africa), suggest a rhetoric of exploration inherited from chronicles of discovery. Mascarenhas here reflects what Anthony Pagden calls the "autoptic imagination" of sixteenth-century accounts of the New World, the appeal to the unique authority of the eyewitness as opposed to the authoritative canon of the ancient philosophers, the Bible, and the church fathers. Yet the broad geographical extent of Mascarenhas's travels reminds us that the "New World" of European exploration and expansion was not limited to the Western Hemisphere.[47]

Along with other areas of Portuguese exploration, conquest, and trade, the New World thus makes its way into the "New Description" of Algiers as a source of the author's claim to credibility. The New World had already insinuated itself through the reference to "brazis, de nova Espanha, e do Prestes João" [Brazilians, from New Spain, and from Prester John], which concludes Mascarenhas's list of the provenance of "Christian" captives and renegades in Algiers, a list surely modeled on the one found in the *Topographia*. However, unlike the author of the *Topographia,* Mascarenhas claims personal acquaintance with not only Algiers but also the New World and

47. Ibid., 84–86; Haedo, *Topografía,* I, 200. On the "autoptic imagination," see Anthony Pagden, *European Encounters with the New World: From Renaissance to Romanticism* (New Haven, Conn., 1993), 51–56; see also Walter D. Mignolo, "El metatexto historiográfico y la historiografía indiana," *MLN,* XCVI (1981), 358–402, esp. 386–390. In a response to Elliott's notion of the "blunted impact" of the New World on Old World consciousness, Joan-Pau Rubiés argues that Europeans would not have "regarded the American discoveries as something essentially separate from the new accounts of Africa and Asia brought about by the Portuguese and those who followed them, or from any other accounts of exotic peoples in the Levant, Russia or Central Asia." In this sense, Rubiés points out, we should be "adding up all these accounts into our estimate of the extent to which Europeans wrote about, published about, and read about exotic lands and peoples throughout the Renaissance"; see Rubiés, "Travel Writing and Humanistic Culture: A Blunted Impact?" *Journal of Early Modern History,* X (2006), 5–6, 131–168.

beyond and uses this experience to support the authenticity of his portrait of the city. The reference to exploits in more distant and exotic lands marks the *Memoravel relaçam's* difference from its textual source and exposes its resemblance to the "true histories" of Peter Carder, Hans Staden, Cabeza de Vaca, and still another castaway, Pedro Serrano.[48]

A CAPTIVATING TALE OF SHIPWRECK: EL INCA GARCILASO DE LA VEGA'S PEDRO SERRANO

Like Mascarenhas's interpolated autobiographical itinerary in the description of Algiers, the tale of Pedro Serrano, narrated in chapter 8 of Garcilaso's *Comentarios reales,* is something of a digression in a work otherwise dedicated to the preconquest history of Garcilaso's Peruvian homeland. Although announced earlier, it appears in a chapter dedicated to "La descripción del Perú," where Garcilaso explains, "Antes que pasemos adelante, digamos aquí el suceso de Pedro Serrano que atrás propusimos, porque no esté lejos de su lugar y también porque este capítulo no sea tan corto" [Before we proceed, let us tell here the story of Pedro Serrano that I proposed earlier, so that it won't be far from its place and also so that this chapter won't be so short].[49]

Despite the apparently offhand nature of its interpolation, the Pedro Serrano tale has long captured the attention of readers and critics. Enrique Pupo-Walker highlights its literary qualities and the echoes of "shipwreck and rescue novellas" found in the episode. Other scholars have asserted a reverse direction of influence, noting, not Garcilaso's inspiration in fictional European works like the Byzantine novel, but rather his influence on them, like Cervantes's *Persiles y Sigismunda* and Daniel Defoe's *Robinson Crusoe.* Such speculations about direct sources and influences are probably unverifiable, but they can remind us of the transnational as well as transatlantic context of two "key figures in the rise of their respective national novels," as Diana de Armas Wilson argues. A modern English readership, on the other hand, would be more likely to associate the Pedro Serrano tale with Peter Carder's account, for two modern collections of "true histories" of shipwreck open their volumes with the stories of these two castaways in the New World.[50]

48. Mascarenhas, *Memorável relação,* in Peres, ed., *Viagens e naufrágios célebres,* I, 72. Haedo's comparable list of renegades is found in *Topografía,* I, 53.

49. Garcilaso, *Comentarios reales,* ed. Quesada, I, 23.

50. Enrique Pupo-Walker, *La vocación literaria del pensamiento histórico en*

In any case, the plot will surely sound familiar to readers of *Robinson Crusoe.* Pedro Serrano is the sole survivor of a shipwreck on a deserted Caribbean island, where he uses his "industria" [industry, ingenuity] to gather food, water, and fuel, make a fire, and build shelter. It is three years before Serrano encounters another human being: not a native like Crusoe's Friday, but another Christian castaway like himself. Serrano's appearance has changed so much at this point that his compatriot fails to recognize him, in a scene reminiscent of the return of Cabeza de Vaca and other captives: "Cuando se vieron ambos, no se puede certificar cuál quedó más asombrado de cuál. Serrano imaginó que era el demonio que venía en figura de hombre para tentarle en alguna desesperación. El huésped entendió que Serrano era el demonio en su propia figura, según lo vio cubierto de cabellos, barbas y pelaje" [When they saw each other, it is hard to say who was the more surprised of whom. Serrano imagined that it was the devil coming in the shape of a man to tempt him to some desperate act. The guest understood that Serrano was the devil himself, seeing him covered with hair, beard, and hide]. Garcilaso describes how, owing to inclement weather, Serrano has grown such excessive hair on his body that he has the appearance of a wild boar. Like many scenes of the captive's return, it is speech that assures both parties of each other's Spanish and Christian identity. Serrano begs God to deliver him from the devil, whereas the castaway recites the Credo to back up his affirmation that "soy cristiano como vos" [I am a Christian like you].[51]

América: Desarrollo de la prosa de ficción, siglos XVI, XVII, XVIII, y XIX (Madrid, 1982), 56; de Armas Wilson, *Cervantes, the Novel, and the New World,* 48. In their edition of the *Persiles,* Schevill and Bonilla mention the "strange adventure" of Pedro Serrano as a possible source of inspiration for Antonio's shipwreck tale, as well as for Defoe's *Robinson Crusoe;* see introduction, in Cervantes, *Persiles y Sigismunda,* xxvii–xxviii. John D. Leckie was apparently the first to argue for the relationship between Pedro Serrano and *Robinson Crusoe* in "A Spanish Robinson Crusoe," *Chamber's Journal,* XI (1908), 510–512. See also David Fausett, *The Strange Suprizing Sources of Robinson Crusoe* (Amsterdam, 1994), who points out other possible connections to Garcilaso's *Comentarios reales* (I, 4, 36–38). The shipwreck collections featuring both Carder and Serrano are Neider, ed., *Great Shipwrecks and Castaways,* and Leslie, *Desperate Journeys;* the titles of both volumes emphasize the historicity that scholarship on Serrano's tale has tended to underplay.

51. Garcilaso, *Comentarios reales,* ed. Quesada, I, 21, 25. For an English translation, see Garcilaso, *First Part of the Royal Commentaries of the Yncas,* ed. and trans. Clements R. Markham (London, 1869). I offer revised versions of Markham's

After four years of some quarrels but mainly cooperation—Serrano apparently has no need to assert his absolute mastery over the island, like Crusoe—the castaways are rescued by a passing ship, again while saying the Credo and crying out in the name of our Lord, "que de otra manera sin duda huyeran los marineros, porque *no tenían figura de hombres humanos*" [for otherwise the mariners would certainly have fled from them, for *they did not have the appearance of human men*]. The insistence implicit here on judging a person's humanity and identity through words and actions rather than appearances, however strange and inhuman they may seem, is relevant to Garcilaso's project in two senses. On one hand, the emphasis on common identity despite external differences supports his praise of his Inca ancestors' civilization as a precursor and transition to Christianity, parallel to that of the Greeks and Romans. On the other hand, the episode strengthens his own claims to an authentic Christian and Spanish identity, surely a concern to a mestizo like himself in a society increasingly intolerant of "New Christians."[52]

In fact, Pedro Serrano's barbarous appearance—the external evidence of his misfortunes—plays an important role in his future fortunes. His "inhuman figure" turns the recitation of his tale, which begins on board the ship, into a visual performance: he and his companion "admiraron a cuan-

---

translations because of the translator's tendency to trim and alter references to Pedro Serrano's abundant body hair.

52. Garcilaso, *Comentarios reales,* ed. Quesada, I, 26 (emphasis added). On Garcilaso's presentation of the Incas as precursors to Christianity and comparable to the ancient civilizations of Persia, Egypt, Greece, and Rome, see ibid., I, 36–38; Garcilaso, *Historia general del Perú* (Lima, 1959 [orig. publ. Córdoba, 1617]), I, 9–10. Fuchs argues, in contrast to other critics who have speculated about Garcilaso's sympathies for the Moriscos who rebelled in the Alpujarras uprising (1568–1571), that "Garcilaso probably perceived no connection between himself and the Moriscos, and the fact that *others* might make such a connection made it even more imperative that he distance himself from them"; see *Mimesis and Empire,* 73. In the dedication to Philip II of Garcilaso's translation of León Hebreo's *Dialoghi d'amore,* entitled *La traduzion del indio de los tres dialogos de amor de Leon Hebreo, hecha de italiano en español por Garcilasso Inga de la Vega* (Madrid, 1590), Garcilaso boasts of his participation in the suppression of the Alpujarras rebellion; there is a facsimile of this edition in León Hebreo, *Diálogos de amor,* ed. Miguel de Burgos Núñez, trans. Garcilaso (Seville, 1989). Garcilaso also reproduced the dedication in his prologue to the *Historia general del Perú,* I, 12–15.

tos los vieron y oyeron sus trabajos pasados" [caused wonder to everyone who saw them and heard their past travails]. And Serrano puts his visible transformation to profitable use in Europe. There, Serrano's wondrous appearance and strange tale become something of a relación de servicios:

> Pedro Serrano llegó acá y pasó a Alemania, donde el Emperador estaba entonces: llevó su pelaje como lo traía, para que fuese prueba de su naufragio y de lo que en él había pasado. Por todos los pueblos que pasaba a la ida (si quisiera mostrarse) ganara muchos dineros. Algunos señores y caballeros principales, que gustaron de ver su figura, le dieron ayudas de costa para el camino, y la Majestad Imperial, habiéndolo visto y oído, le hizo merced de cuatro mil pesos de renta.

> Pedro Serrano arrived here and went on to Germany, where the emperor then was; he wore his hide as it was, so that it would be proof of his shipwreck and what he had experienced. In every village through which he passed along the way (if he chose to show himself) he made much money. Some lords and principal knights, who liked to see his figure, paid the cost of his journey, and His Imperial Majesty, having seen and heard him, was pleased to grant him an income of 4,000 pesos.

The castaway's "industry"—like that of Cervantes's false captives—is here evident in his itinerant performance, which earns him concrete rewards, if not a governorship like Cabeza de Vaca's. Garcilaso highlights Serrano's participation in his self-fashioning as an ex-castaway, denoting his choice not to shave, to "show himself," and to leave his hair waist length even after seeing the emperor. Serrano's hirsute body is the visible proof of his shipwreck account, offered to his audience for direct contemplation. His savage appearance is also a visual counterpart to Antonio de Sosa's description of the captive's transformation in the *Topographia* ("such a strange alteration and transmutation," so "new and so unstable" that he should not be "called a man"). Yet whereas Sosa questions the captive's humanity because of his loss of liberty, Serrano's "inhuman figure" is no evidence of a loss of human qualities. His barbarous aspect denotes, not a "wild man," but a true history of adventure, misfortune, and royal service, and Garcilaso is careful to highlight its reception as such. Serrano's physical transformation not only authenticates his account but also is a source of astonishment that reaps him material benefits. His "inhuman figure" permits his favorable recognition as an imperial subject by the emperor himself.[53]

Serrano follows Cabeza de Vaca's trajectory by choosing to return to the land of his original tribulations, although he dies before he can enjoy his new fortunes there. Both of these castaways' true histories illustrate a strategy employed by other American-born writers, as we will see in subsequent chapters: the transformation of difference from a negative attribute into a positive and productive one. El Inca Garcilaso himself takes up this ambivalent strategy: in the prologue to his *Historia general del Perú,* Garcilaso describes his encounter with an eminent Spanish schoolmaster who criticized him for daring, as "un antártico, nacido en el Nuevo Mundo" [an Antarctic Indian, born in the New World], to translate a renowned humanist work, León Hebreo's *Dialoghi d'amore,* from Italian into Spanish. Garcilaso counters the negative appraisal of his New World origins by praising his compatriots' nobility in arms, agriculture, and liberal and mechanical arts. He concludes with an anecdote about the reception of Peruvian textiles in Spain. Among the excellent "domestic arts" of his homeland, he refers to the

> traje de vestidos, cortados al talle, de que pudo ser muestra admirable y gustosa una librea natural peruana que dió que ver y admirar en esta ciudad de Córdoba, en un torneo celebrado en la fiesta de la beatificación del bienaventurado San Ignacio . . . cuya traza y forma al natural yo di al Padre Francisco de Castro, y, si la pasión no me ciega, fue la cuadrilla más lucida y celebrada, y que llevaba los ojos de todos por su novedad y curiosidad.

> costumes, made to fit, of which an admirable and pleasing example is the native Peruvian livery, which was much seen and admired in this city of Cordoba in a tournament held during the celebration of the beatification of the blessed Saint Ignatius . . . , whose design and form I gave, without

53. Garcilaso, *Comentarios reales,* ed. Quesada, I, 26; Haedo, *Topografía,* II, 17–18. Serrano's use of his hirsute appearance to authenticate his account avoids the contradiction that Stephen Greenblatt identifies in travel narrators' reliance on eyewitness testimony: "The problem with eyewitness accounts is that they implicitly call attention to the reader's lack of that very assurance—direct sight—that is their own source of authority"; see Greenblatt, *Marvelous Possessions: The Wonder of the New World* (Chicago, 1991), 34.

art or affectation, to Father Francisco de Castro. And if prejudice does not blind me, the team wearing it was the most magnificent and celebrated, and captured the attention of all through its novelty and curiosity.

Garcilaso surely hoped that his own text would attain a similar reception as "fruta nueva del Perú" [new fruit of Peru], as Philip II apparently referred to Garcilaso's translation of León Hebreo.[54]

Like Pedro Serrano with his hairy body, the Spaniards in Peruvian attire are the most "magnificent and celebrated" of the festival because of the "novelty and curiosity" of their appearance. In contrast to early modern curiosity cabinets, which would render New World artifacts "the ultimate context-less objects," the text articulates the productive and performative functions of Peruvian works in a new context. The transculturated aspect of the Spaniards does not diminish the religiosity of the festival but rather enhances it by capturing the attention of a wide audience. The praise of the Peruvian costumes sustains a form of self-aggrandizement, as well, since Garcilaso is the "author" of the "admirable and pleasing" design. Again, we find a confluence of appeals to truth and artifice: Garcilaso's claim to represent Inca costumes "without art or affectation" contrasts with the evident artifice of Spaniards dressed as Incas. Garcilaso is as aware as Pedro Serrano of the selling points of New World figures as well as narratives, for he introduces the Serrano tale as "un caso historial de grande admiración" [a historical case of great admiration]. The story's historicity is confirmed by Garcilaso's claim to have heard it from someone who knew Pedro Serrano. Yet both the story and the livery are also characterized by *admiración,* in both senses of the word in Spanish: admiration and astonishment.[55]

54. Garcilaso, *Historia general del Perú,* I, 9, 16–17.

55. On curiosity cabinets, see Pagden, *European Encounters with the New World,* 33; Garcilaso, *Historia general del Perú,* I, 21, 26. The tale of Pedro Serrano does appear to be loosely based on a historical case: the shipwreck and survival of one "Maestre Joan" on the same Serrana island that Garcilaso identifies as the place of Serrano's shipwreck (and to which, Garcilaso argues, Pedro Serrano gave his name). Maestre Joan's account has been published as "Relación y derrotero del viaje que hizo el Maestre Joan en el golfo de Méjico a varias islas y especialmente a la de la Serrana," in Luis Torres de Mendoza, ed., *Colección de documentos inéditos, relativos al descubrimiento, conquista y organización de las antiguas posesiones españolas de América y Oceanía, sacados de los Archivos del Reino, y muy especialmente del de Indias,* X (Madrid, 1868), 57–65. Robert F. Marx published a translation of this ac-

Garcilaso's anecdote about the Peruvian costumes can serve as an emblem for the transatlantic itinerary traced in this chapter. The Incan livery is not merely set off as a wondrous example of an exotic New World but participates in and has an effect on the Spanish, Christian festival. Similarly, texts about New World captivity were not simply presented and received (or ignored) in Iberia as a distinct genre about a distant land, incommensurable with literary depictions of captivity in the Byzantine novel or testimonials of Moorish and Turkish captivity. Rather, New World accounts participated in and helped to shape peninsular discourses about captivity, inflecting the descriptions of captives and captors, the strategies of authorization, and the claims about the utility (reader's instruction or entertainment, author's benefit) of Old World captivity narratives, whether fictional or historical. A recognition of mutual transatlantic influence need not overlook or underestimate the prior existence of an Iberian discourse on captivity owing to centuries of contact and conflict with Muslims. However, a true history of the captivity narrative in early modern Iberia should take into account authors and texts from the New World as well as the Mediterranean.

Furthermore, a true history of the generic and epistemological transformations of early modern Europe should also take into account the role played by true histories of shipwreck and captivity. These narratives both reflect and exploit the "questions of truth" that so preoccupied writers of the age and that are often linked to the rise of the novel. Several of the castaways discussed in this chapter—Peter Carder, the *Persiles*'s Antonio *el bárbaro,* and Pedro Serrano—have been cited as possible sources of inspiration for Defoe's *Robinson Crusoe,* often considered by Anglophone critics to be the first modern novel. But the connection between novelistic genres and true histories of shipwreck and captivity should perhaps be sought less through

---

count, which he wrongly attributes to Pedro Serrano, in "Pedro Serrano: The First Robinson Crusoe," *Oceans,* VII, no. 5 (September-October, 1974), 50–55. The Pedro Serrano tale and Maestre Joan's relación coincide in little more than a few details. Predictably, Maestre Joan affirms the utility of his account based on the navigational information he has provided to the "piloto mayor de su Magestad" [chief pilot of His Majesty] and to the chartmaker Francisco Gutiérrez. He also creates narrative interest through the more fantastic claim to have seen the devil on the island ("de una forma peor de la que con que le pintan" [in a worse form than he is painted]), which perhaps inspired Garcilaso's rendition of the two castaways' first encounter; see "Relación y derrotero," 62–64. I thank Domingo Ledezma for bringing Maestre Joan's account to my attention.

specific sources and influences than through their common appropriation of diverse rhetorical strategies.[56]

Early modern narrators of captivity may base their authority in part on eyewitness testimony, but they openly acknowledge the way artifice mediates in the construction of a delightful yet edifying tale. Mediation also plays a thematic role in the works that I examine in the following chapters: ex-captives are portrayed, like Cabeza de Vaca, as skillful mediators and interpreters, thanks to their unique familiarity with European and Amerindian cultures. If Pedro Serrano's body allows him to perform a transculturated identity, these texts also perform the intermediary character of the captives they describe, drawing from as well as helping to transform multiple traditions and genres.

56. De Armas Wilson's *Cervantes, the Novel, and the New World* critiques nationalist approaches to the "rise of the novel" and emphasizes the importance of the imperial and transnational context to such "foundational" novelists as Cervantes and Defoe (45–48, 76–77). The linkage of truth claims and entertainment in both captivity narratives and novels merits further investigation. On the connections between novelistic rhetoric and travel narratives more broadly, see Adams, *Travel Literature.* Nancy Armstrong and Leonard Tennenhouse specifically explore the role of Anglo-American captivity narratives in the origins of the English novel through their production of an authorial consciousness in Armstrong and Tennenhouse, *The Imaginary Puritan: Literature, Intellectual Labor, and the Origins of Personal Life* (Berkeley, Calif., 1992), 196–216. However, the critics pay little heed to the flourishing of both novels and captivity narratives in the Iberian context, which are, as we have seen, much more than "curiosities" (203). Although focused, like Armstrong and Tennenhouse, on the origins of the English novel, McKeon's chapter on Cervantes does recognize the "enormous influx of colonial wealth to the Iberian peninsula" as a distinctive feature of early modern Spain and one of the contextual differences that helps to explain Cervantes's novelistic achievement a full century before the rise of the English novel; see *Origins of the English Novel,* 293–294. This book extends the consideration of "colonial influx" to the New World texts and subjects that also affected epistemological and social categories in early modern Europe.

chapter TWO : CAPTIVITY, EXILE, AND INTERPRETATION IN EL INCA GARCILASO DE LA VEGA'S *La Florida del Inca*

TRANSATLANTIC (DOUBLE) CROSSINGS

The end of *La Florida del Inca* (1605) is difficult to reconcile with its mestizo author's reputation for the reconciliation of contraries. El Inca Garcilaso de la Vega (1539–1616) concludes his account of Hernando de Soto's expedition to Florida (1539–1543) with a tale of Floridians in Spain, whose displacement reflects the author's own distance from his Peruvian homeland since his early twenties. This chapter traces *La Florida*'s multiple crossings—of territories and oceans, cultures and languages—in order to explore the relationship between Garcilaso's strategies of self-authorization and his reworking of the motifs of captivity and exile. For Garcilaso, transplanted individuals like captives and exiles are essential to transmitting accurate and useful knowledge across cultural borders, yet *La Florida*'s final episode offers a negative example of such a mediating role. It becomes a narrative of a double crossing: a transatlantic round-trip and a duplicitous revenge.[1]

Ostensibly, Garcilaso's purpose in the last chapter is to memorialize the religious men who have sacrificed their lives in the evangelization of Florida, as he has already done for their military counterparts. But when he describes a group of eight Jesuit missionaries accompanied on their journey to Florida by an indigenous "señor de vasallos" [lord of vassals], Garcilaso's narrative urge takes over: "De cómo vino a España será bien que demos cuenta" ["It will be well for me to give here the following account of how this Indian came to Spain"]. According to Garcilaso, this cacique, whom he later refers to as "don Luis," was one of seven Amerindians brought to Spain by Pedro

1. See Aurelio Miró Quesada Sosa, *El Inca Garcilaso* (Madrid, 1948), 241–243, for an example of the traditional reading of Garcilaso as "an example of harmony and synthesis," a mestizo humanist whose mission it was to "integrate opposites."

Menéndez de Áviles after his second expedition to Florida. Despite their apparent willingness to leave their homeland—Garcilaso claims that they came "de buena amistad" [in good friendship]—the Floridians resist assimilating to Spanish culture. Although they are eventually baptized, they maintain their dress and language. Their contact with Garcilaso's "author"—Gonzalo Silvestre, a participant on the Soto expedition—reveals the extent of their antipathy toward Spaniards. When he asks them for news of Florida, they contemptuously respond, "¿Dejando vosotros esas provincias tan mal paradas como las dejasteis queréis que os demos nuevas de ellas? . . . De mejor gana le diéramos sendos flechazos que las nuevas que nos pide" ["Having left those provinces as desolate as you did, do you want us to give you news of them? . . . We would more willingly give him arrow blows than the information he requests of us"]. Indeed, given the devastating effects of the Soto expedition on the indigenous societies of southeastern North America, such a scornful refusal to provide information is hardly surprising. Silvestre seems undecided about whether to praise, blame, or fear their display of audacity by shooting great arrows into the air: "Contándome esto mi autor me decía que se espantaba de que no se las hubiesen tirado a él, según son locos y atrevidos aquellos indios, principalmente en cosa de armas y valentía" ["In telling me of this incident, my author admitted that he feared they might shoot at him, since Indians are foolish and rash, especially in matters that concern arms and valor"]. As in Garcilaso's ambiguous portrait of indigenous hostility toward Spaniards throughout *La Florida,* the Amerindians' threat might be interpreted as either insolent barbarism or laudable bravery.[2]

2. Inca Garcilaso de la Vega, *La Florida del Inca,* ed. Sylvia Lynn Hilton (Madrid, 1986 [orig. publ. Lisbon, 1605]), 584–585; English translations are from [Garcilaso], *The Florida of the Inca,* ed. and trans. John Grier Varner and Jeannette Johnson Varner (Austin, Tex., 1951), 640–641. Throughout this chapter, page numbers will follow the quotations from these texts in parentheses. Translations of brief passages from *La Florida* that are presented without quotation marks are my own. I will refer to what Spaniards called "La Florida" as "Florida" in this chapter in order to avoid confusion with the title of Garcilaso's work. The official account of Pedro Menéndez de Áviles's 1565 expedition explains that the Floridians in Spain were in fact taken as hostages to ensure the safety of the Spaniards left in Florida; see Gonzalo Solís de Merás, *Pedro Menéndez de Avilés, Adelantado Governor and Captain General of Florida: Memorial,* trans. Jeannette Thurber Connor (Deland, Fla., 1923), 236. Summarizing archaeological research about the impact of Spanish contact on native societies of this region, Jerald T. Milanich describes widespread depopulation and culture change as a result of both disease and military action; see Milanich, ed., *The*

Six of the Floridians die shortly after baptism, whereas the last—don Luis—requests permission to return to his homeland, promising to disseminate the Catholic faith "como buen cristiano" [like a good Christian]. Don Luis's own conversion, however, has been far from complete. Once the Spanish missionaries are on his own turf, he abandons them in an isolated place while he presumably goes to prepare his compatriots to receive the faith. After two weeks, the missionaries tire of waiting for him to return and send a few brothers to seek him out. When he sees them, the cacique belies his pretense of serving as an intermediary. Instead, he fulfills the threat made to Gonzalo Silvestre: "Como traidor apóstata, sin hablarles palabra, los mató con gran rabia y crueldad" (585) ["As a traitor apostate and without uttering a word, [he] slew them both with great rage and cruelty" (642)]. After killing all of the missionaries, the Amerindians seize and mock their Bibles, Breviaries, and bibelots, the very symbols of their faith. However, such anti-Christian behavior does not go unpunished, for three of the Amerindians reportedly fall dead when they remove a cross from the missionaries' belongings.[3]

Hernando de Soto Expedition (New York, 1991), xviii. Marvin T. Smith also reviews the evidence for the demographic collapse of indigenous populations after the sixteenth century in Smith, "Indian Responses to European Contact: The Coosa Example," in Jerald T. Milanich and Susan Milbrath, eds., *First Encounters: Spanish Explorations in the Caribbean and the United States, 1492–1570* (Gainesville, Fla., 1989), 135–149.

3. The following information about don Luis can be gathered from documents in the Archivo General de Indias, studied and summarized by Paul E. Hoffman in *A New Andalucia and a Way to the Orient: The American Southeast during the Sixteenth Century* (Baton Rouge, 1990), 183–187, 244–245. An indigenous nobleman named Paquiquineo was taken by Antonio Velázquez on a voyage to the Florida coast in 1561; he was given his Christian name in honor of the viceroy of New Spain, don Luis de Velasco. After an audience with Philip II, don Luis was sent with Dominican friars to return to Florida by way of New Spain, but in Mexico City he fell ill, was baptized, and remained to receive religious instruction. Four years before the Jesuit mission recounted by Garcilaso, don Luis accompanied two Dominicans on a reconnaissance voyage in which he failed to find his homeland. In *The Spanish Jesuit Mission in Virginia, 1570–1572* (Chapel Hill, N.C., 1953), Clifford M. Lewis and Albert J. Loomie provide transcriptions and translations of the various Spanish accounts of the 1570 mission, including Garcilaso's avowed source, Pedro de Rivadeneyra's *Vida del P[adre] Francisco de Borja* (Madrid, 1592); see 15–18 on the discrepancies in these sources with respect to don Luis's place of origin and activities before 1570. An ambiguous reference in Ralph Hamor's *True Discourse of the Present Estate of Virginia* (London, 1615) has led some scholars to identify don Luis as the father or the brother

Garcilaso's version of this oft-told story of indigenous treachery and Jesuit martyrdom illustrates the conflictive nature of his sympathies and identifications, as the son of an Inca noblewoman and a Spanish conquistador retelling the history of a failed Spanish conquest. Garcilaso follows his Jesuit source for the episode, Pedro de Ribadeneyra, in recounting the divine retribution accorded to the impious Amerindians. However, he also concludes that the Jesuits' spilled blood cries, not for "venganza como la de Abel, sino misericordia como la de Cristo Nuestro Señor, para que aquellos gentiles vengan en conocimiento de su eterna magestad, debajo de la obediencia de nuestra madre la Santa Iglesia Romana" (586) ["vengeance like that of Abel, but for mercy like that of Christ Our Lord, so that these pagans may come into the knowledge of His Eternal Majesty under the obedience of Our Mother the Holy Roman Church" (643)]. Like the Spanish accounts, Garcilaso condemns don Luis's treason and apostasy and calls for future evangelization. Yet his inclusion of a firsthand encounter with don Luis in Spain establishes the Floridian's justifiable resentment toward Spaniards for devastating his homeland. The passage shows just how difficult it is to declare where Garcilaso's loyalties lie or to resolve his incompatible allegiances in a neat synthesis of harmonious mestizo identity. Such a synthesis would require concealing the violence incited by cultural imposition that is all too palpable in this passage.[4]

The narrative of Hernando de Soto's exploration of Florida thus begins and ends with the violence and loss connected to geographical displacement and cultural conflict. Garcilaso opens *La Florida del Inca* by indulging in a retrospective digression about Captain Soto's previous participation in the conquest of Peru, where, because of political strife and tyranny, "se perdió aquel imperio" (72) ["the kingdom of the Incas was lost" (4)]. The violent conclusion of Soto's subsequent expedition is thus prefigured in its opening

---

of Powhatan, who famously held John Smith captive in 1607; Hamor explains that the Chickahominies' hatred of the Spaniards and willingness to fight with the English against them is because *"Powhatan's* father was driven by them from the *west-Indies* into those parts" (13). Helen C. Rountree rebuts these connections through chronological evidence in Rountree, *Pocahontas, Powhatan, Opechancanough: Three Indian Lives Changed by Jamestown* (Charlottesville, N.C., 2005), 26–28. However, the episode points up the English belatedness to the colonial scene and the fact that their relations with the Amerindians were always mediated by prior indigenous contact with the Spaniards; I take up this issue more fully in Chapter 5.

4. On the divine retribution, see the excerpt from Rivadeneyra's *Vida del P[adre] Francisco de Borja,* in Lewis and Loomie, *Spanish Jesuit Mission,* 144.

lines, and the recursive motif is, not conquest, but loss. The mourning of imperial loss, introduced with respect to Garcilaso's Inca heritage, eventually characterizes the failure to establish a Spanish settlement in Florida as well.

Like the recursive structure of the captivity narrative, the circle traced by *La Florida* would seem to promote synthesis, but confusion and discord prevail. After all, integration would curtail the need for bicultural interpreters like Garcilaso. In contrast to the Floridians' refusal to communicate, Garcilaso highlights his willingness to narrate ("it will be well for me to give here the following account"), which replicates that of his Spanish source ("in telling me of this incident, my author . . ."). Indeed, Garcilaso describes his "principal intento" (545) in writing the account as providing information to promote the conquest and evangelization of Florida, particularly in light of the threat of French Protestant colonization. Garcilaso himself fostered this intention by giving copies of his work to Franciscan missionaries on their way to the region, apparently assuming that the final scene of slaughtered clerics would not be enough to dissuade them from their mission. In his later work *Historia general del Perú* (1617), Garcilaso writes how a Peruvian-born clergyman had requested copies of *La Florida* from him in 1612, in order for the missionaries to "saber y tener noticia de las provincias y costumbres de aquella gentilidad" [know and have information about the provinces and customs of those heathen peoples].[5]

If Garcilaso's act of mediation serves an imperial desire for knowledge about its non-European subjects, his account also documents the refusal to render information, as well as other instances of intercultural violence and miscommunication. Garcilaso's ambivalent position is neither that of the imperial authority who demands news about the New World nor of the resistant subaltern who repudiates the demand. *La Florida del Inca* both draws on and takes the place of the conquistadors' eyewitness accounts of the region, like that requested from Menéndez de Áviles after Philip II had seen the Floridians that the captain brought back with him. Garcilaso's locus of enunciation lies between that of the Florida Indians in Spain, representatives of the Crown's new subjects, and that of Menéndez as royal subject ordered, and authorized, to write about Florida by the Crown. Or rather, Garcilaso embraces and redefines both positions, presenting the American origins that he shares with the Floridian captives as authorization for his writing. In so

5. Inca Garcilaso de la Vega, *Historia general del Perú* (Lima, 1959 [orig. publ. Córdoba, 1617]), II, 783.

doing, he goes beyond simply providing news of Florida to serve the cause of imperial and religious expansion. He also accounts for the imperial violence that has left the province in "desolation," provoking, in turn, the "rage and cruelty" of the Floridians toward the Spanish missionaries. Nevertheless, Garcilaso concludes this episode—and the volume—by calling for Christian mercy rather than justifying revenge. As José Rabasa points out, Garcilaso here essays a discourse on tolerance, one that would extend to and authorize "his own Indianness," as he so often identifies himself. Garcilaso's use of the final episode to underscore a lesson of mercy implicitly condemns both Spaniards and Amerindians for violence toward strangers in foreign lands.[6]

Rabasa reads Garcilaso's self-identification as an "Indian writer" as a strategy that moves beyond a simple inversion of values that would reinforce the binary opposition between colonizer and colonized. Such an analysis aligns Rabasa with other modern scholars who have similarly avoided the critical trap of identifying Garcilaso as either an acculturated Spaniard or an immutable Amerindian. José Antonio Mazzotti argues that Garcilaso's "internal complexity," evident in his discordant versions of Cuzco's indigenous past in the *Comentarios reales de los Incas* (1609), bears witness to "the emergence of a new voice: the dominated yet privileged colonial subject." Mazzotti's *Coros mestizos del Inca Garcilaso* addresses this subject by delineating the stylistic and thematic features of his work that would be legible to an Andean rather than a European audience. The present chapter will also describe Garcilaso's articulation and legitimation of this new voice, not through his representation of his own Inca heritage, but through his manipulation of a topic familiar to Iberian readers: captivity.[7]

6. Solís de Merás, *Memorial,* trans. Connor, 243. See José Rabasa, *Writing Violence on the Northern Frontier: The Historiography of Sixteenth-Century New Mexico and Florida and the Legacy of Conquest* (Durham, N.C., 2000), 223.

7. See Rabasa, *Writing Violence,* 207; José Antonio Mazzotti, "The Lightning Bolt Yields to the Rainbow: Indigenous History and Colonial Semiosis in the *Royal Commentaries* of el Inca Garcilaso de la Vega," *Modern Language Quarterly,* LVII (1996), 197–211, esp. 211; Mazzotti, *Coros mestizos del Inca Garcilaso: Resonancias andinas* (Lima, 1996). In *El Inca Garcilaso y el humanismo renacentista* (Buenos Aires, 1949), Luis A. Arocena attacks the analysis of Garcilaso's essential "Indianness" in Luis Valcárcel's *Garcilaso el Inca: Visto desde el ángulo indio* (Lima, 1939), but Arocena errs in the opposite direction by only focusing on Garcilaso's Renaissance humanist influences. For other studies that, like Rabasa and Mazzotti, emphasize complexity and contradiction rather than focus on one side or the other of Garcilaso's mestizo identity or asserting a harmonious synthesis between the two, see

Garcilaso's versions of the captivity narrative focus on the transformative power of captivity and the empowerment of the transformed captive. Bilingual and bicultural knowledge, as well as more obvious indicators such as dress and physical appearance, evince the captive's transformation. Instead of using captivity either to underscore or erase cultural difference, Garcilaso highlights the captive's potential role as a mediator or interpreter who, like himself, is familiar with both of the cultures in contact. Garcilaso paints a favorable portrait of captives who embrace this role and thus foster mutual knowledge and respect between different groups and condemns those who favor a single cultural identity to the detriment of coexistence. The positive presentation of the captive-intermediary does not invert or subvert the dynamics of colonial power but rather authorizes the position of interpreter.

Margarita Zamora has examined Garcilaso's self-construed role as interpreter in the *Comentarios reales de los Incas* within the context of Renaissance humanist philology. The Renaissance understanding of hermeneutics as "an act of mediation which is faithful to the essence or 'idea' of the original," and the concomitant respect for the art of translation, provide a framework for assessing Garcilaso's literary and historiographic projects, from his version of León Hebreo's *Dialoghi d'amore* to his interpretation of Inca history for European readers in the *Comentarios reales.* Language and mediation are also central features in Garcilaso's adaptation of Iberian models for representing captivity. In *La Florida,* captivity often occasions linguistic confusion, but it also generates interpreters who can clarify misunderstandings and thus contribute to the work of conquest. Garcilaso shows how linguistic tumult, concurrent with the act of conquest, can produce interpreters at the same time that it creates a need for them. The existence of linguistic difference and confusion precludes the cultural universality with which Garcilaso is often associated, but it allows him to affirm the importance of mediators who are able to cross linguistic and cultural, as well as geographic, boundaries.[8]

Antonio Cornejo Polar, "El discurso de la armonía imposible (El Inca Garcilaso de la Vega: Discurso y recepción social)," *Revista de crítica literaria latinoamericana,* XIX (1993), 73–80; Sara Castro-Klaren, "Writing Subalterity: Guaman Poma and Garcilaso Inca," *Dispositio/n,* XIX (1994), 229–244; and Doris Sommer, "At Home Abroad: El Inca Shuttles with Hebreo," in Susan Suleiman, ed., *Exile and Creativity: Signposts, Travelers, Outsiders, Backward Glances* (Durham, N.C., 1998), 109–142.

8. Margarita Zamora, *Language, Authority, and Indigenous History in the* "Comentarios reales de los Incas" (Cambridge, 1988), 8. Susana Jákfalvi-Leiva ar-

Like the "Captive's Tale" in *Don Quijote,* whose first part was published the same year as *La Florida del Inca,* Garcilaso's work stages a scene of its own reception in the final chapters. The viceroy and residents of Mexico City call upon the surviving members of the expedition, who have finally arrived at the viceregal capital, to relate their exploits. Garcilaso here takes advantage of the opportunity not only to remind his readers of important episodes in the book but also to mold their reactions through the example of the listeners, whose response is made clear through a series of verbs: "Admiráronse . . . Maravilláronse . . . Espantáronse . . . Gustaron . . . Estimaron en mucho . . . Abominaron . . ." (573–574) ["They were amazed . . . They marvelled at . . . They were astonished . . . They were pleased . . . They were profoundly impressed . . . They abhorred" (627–628)]. Like Álvar Núñez Cabeza de Vaca, Hans Staden, and so many other narrators of captivity, Garcilaso knew that tales of adventure among exotic peoples in foreign lands were capable of inspiring dramatic emotional responses and thus would be a selling point of his text. However, in keeping with Renaissance history's principal didactic intention—not only to inform readers but to inspire them to action—the ultimate and ideal response to Garcilaso's history of Florida is also laid out before the readers: "Finalmente holgaba mucho de oír el visorrey la grandeza de aquel reino . . . para las cuales cosas crecía el deseo del visorrey de hacer la conquista" (575) ["And finally it made [the viceroy] very happy to hear of the [greatness] of that kingdom. . . . And because of these things, his desire to make the conquest increased" (629)]. Garcilaso's explicit intent to encourage conquest and conversion finds ready ears in the viceroy, the first to hear an account of the Soto expedition.[9]

The first episode to provoke the admiration of the Mexican audience—

gues that, rather than a secondary or preliminary literary activity for Garcilaso, the activity of translation informs all of his work; see Jákfalvi-Leiva, *Traducción, escritura, y violencia colonizadora: Un estudio de la obra del Inca Garcilaso* (Syracuse, N.Y., 1984), 15.

9. On Renaissance historiography's use of language to move the will of the reader and impel him/her to action, see Zamora, *Language, Authority, and Indigenous History,* 12–14; William J. Kennedy, *Rhetorical Norms in Renaissance Literature* (New Haven, Conn., 1978), 1–8, and 189–191. Hugo Rodríguez-Vecchini reads this scene as an example of Garcilaso's many self-reflexive assertions of his account's verisimilitude; see his *"Don Quijote* y *La Florida del Inca," Revista iberoamericana,* XLVIII (1982), 587–620, esp. 616.

again, like that of Ruy Pérez de Viedma's listeners in the *Quijote*—is a tale of captivity. Juan Ortiz, a native of Seville, was captured by Floridians in 1528 while looking for Pánfilo de Narváez's expedition (which resulted in another narrative of captivity that would serve as a source for Garcilaso, Cabeza de Vaca's *Relación*). Ortiz remained in captivity until the arrival of Soto in 1539. The survivors describe the captive as being cruelly tortured by his first master, Hirrihigua, but then enjoying the kindness and generosity of the cacique Mucozo. The appearance of the Ortiz captivity tale at the beginning of the conquistadors' narration—when, in fact, it had occurred some eleven years before their arrival—reveals the significance of this account within Garcilaso's own narrative and thus merits closer investigation. The tale of Juan Ortiz, as we will see, gains paradigmatic importance in *La Florida del Inca* because it is an example of the very process that the tale relates: the emergence of a hybrid result of intercultural relations.

In a narrative that often recounts multiple episodes in a single chapter, Garcilaso devotes a substantial amount of text—the first eight chapters of book 2, part 1—to the story of Juan Ortiz's captivity and release. Garcilaso treats the episode with significant depth and length in comparison to the other known accounts of the Soto expedition. Juan Ortiz, in fact, appears in all of these narratives as well as in a letter written by Soto to Cuban officials describing the expedition's initial activities. All of these accounts underline his role as interpreter and guide once he is recovered by the Spaniards, attesting to his undisputed importance to the expedition. The brief relation by the royal factor Luis Hernández de Biedma begins with the Spaniards learning of Ortiz's survival through Amerindian informants. The version based on the diary of Rodrigo Ranjel, Soto's private secretary, mentions the expedition's encounter with Juan Ortiz but includes nothing about his previous captivity. The Fidalgo d'Elvas's (Gentleman of Elvas) *Relaçam verdadeira dos trabalhos que o governador dom Fernando de Souto e certos fidalgos portugueses passarom no descobrimento da provincia da Frolida* [sic] (1557) also mentions Ortiz early in the text (chapter 8), and it comes closest to resembling Garcilaso's version in the retrospective narration of Ortiz's captivity. However, the incident spans only a few pages and remains unconnected to the rest of the narrative; its significance lies in the invocation, rather than the manipulation, of a literary commonplace.[10]

10. An English translation of Hernando de Soto's "Letter at Tampa Bay to the Justice and Board of Magistrates in Santiago de Cuba" is included in Edward Gaylord Bourne, ed., *Narratives of the Career of Hernando de Soto in the Conquest of*

Garcilaso differs from these authors not only in his expansive treatment of the episode but in its framing. The first chapter of book 2, part 1, narrates Soto's entry into Florida and arrival at the town governed by Hirrihigua, a cacique whose fear and loathing of Spaniards leads him to abandon his home when he learns of their coming. He continues to refuse the governor's attempts to establish peace and repudiates all Spanish gifts, messages, and promises. Garcilaso is initially reticent to divulge the reasons for this hostility, which are related to a betrayal and offense that he suffered at the hands of the previous leader of a Spanish expedition: "El indio se había reducido a su amistad, y, durante ella, no se sabe por qué causa, enojado Pánfilo de Narváez, le había hecho ciertos agravios que por ser odiosos no se cuentan" (115) ["[Pánfilo de Narváez] had converted the Indian to friendship; then, for some unknown reason, he had committed certain abuses against the cacique which are of too odious a nature to be told here" (60–61)].

Florida . . ., trans. Buckingham Smith (New York, 1904), II, 159–165. Luis Hernández de Biedma's "Relacion del suceso de la jornada que hizo Hernando de Soto," presented to the Council of the Indies in 1544, was published in Buckingham Smith, ed., *Colección de varios documentos para la historia de la Florida y tierras adyacentes* (London, 1857), I, 47–64; Smith's translation, entitled "Relation of the Conquest of Florida," is in Bourne, ed., *Narratives of the Career,* II, 3–40. Rodrigo Ranjel's account is known to us only through the version that Gonzalo Fernández de Oviedo y Valdés included in book 17, chaps. 22–28, of his *Historia general y natural de las Indias,* which was first published in its entirety in 1851; Oviedo's text is based on Ranjel's diary and oral information provided to him by Ranjel sometime before 1546. See Oviedo, *Historia general y natural de las Indias,* ed. Juan Pérez de Tudela Bueso (Madrid, 1959 [orig. publ. 1535]), II, 153–181. Bourne first translated the account into English in "A Narrative of de Soto's Expedition Based on the Diary of Rodrigo Ranjel," in Bourne, ed., *Narratives of the Career,* II, 43–150. The Fidalgo d'Elvas's *Relaçam verdadeira dos trabalhos que o governador dom Fernando de Souto e certos fidalgos portugueses passarom no descobrimento da provincia da Frolida* [sic] was published in Évora in 1557. The author is anonymous, but according to the publisher's prologue, he was one of the several known Portuguese participants in the expedition. It was first translated into English by Richard Hakluyt in *Virginia Richly Valued, by the Description of the Maine Land of Florida Her Next Neighbor* (London, 1609); I will cite from Buckingham Smith's translation, *True Relation of the Vicissitudes That Attended the Governor Don Hernando de Soto and Some Nobles of Portugal in the Discovery of the Province of Florida,* in Bourne, ed., *Narratives of the Career,* I, 1–223. Finally, the "Cañete fragment"—the extant portion of a précis of a narrative written by Fray Sebastián de Cañete, which also mentions a captive Spaniard—was discovered in the late twentieth century in the Archivo

We will later learn that these "agravios" are grave indeed—throwing his mother to the dogs to be eaten and cutting off the cacique's nose—but Garcilaso judiciously saves this information for a point in the narrative when it can justify Hirrihigua's own cruelty. Despite his initial silence regarding this offense, Garcilaso reveals a need to explain Hirrihigua's refusal of contact with Spaniards:

> Y para que se vea mejor la rabia que este indio contra los castellanos tenía, será bien decir aquí algunas crueldades y martirios que hizo en cuatro españoles que pudo haber de los de Pánfilo de Narváez, que, aunque nos alarguemos algún tanto, no saldremos del propósito, antes aprovechará mucho para nuestra historia. (115)

> In order to present a better picture of the rage Hirrihigua felt for the Castilians, it will be well to show here the cruelties and martyrdoms he himself had inflicted upon four of Pámphilo de Narváez' men whom he succeeded in capturing. To a certain extent we may be digressing; yet we will not be leaving the main purpose of the story, and the digression will contribute much to the value of our history. (61)

Garcilaso carefully converts a reason to be silent ("too odious . . . to be told here") into the reason to narrate ("in order to present a better picture"). At the same time, he transforms an apparent digression—textual wanderings

---

General de Indias. A transcription can be found in Eugene Lyon, "The Précis of the *Relación* of Fray Sebastián de Cañete and Other Soto Narratives," in Raquel Chang-Rodríguez, ed., *Beyond Books and Borders: Garcilaso de la Vega and "La Florida del Inca"* (Lewisburg, Pa., 2006), 91–96; earlier, he published an English translation in Milanich, ed., *Hernando de Soto Expedition,* 453–454. I mainly cite from Bourne's *Narratives of the Career of Hernando de Soto,* which includes the translations of Elvas and Biedma first published by Buckingham Smith in 1866 under the same title, along with Bourne's own translation of Oviedo/Ranjel. Milanich reprints excerpts from both volumes in *Hernando de Soto Expedition* and another two-volume set in English—Lawrence A. Clayton, Vernon James Knight, Jr., and Edward C. Moore, eds., *The De Soto Chronicles: The Expedition of Hernando de Soto to North America in 1539–1543* (Tuscaloosa, Ala., 1993)—includes new translations of Biedma and Ranjel, as well as other accounts and documents related to the expedition. For more information on all these sources and the relations between them, see the essays included in Patricia Galloway, ed., *The Hernando de Soto Expedition: History, Historiography, and "Discovery" in the Southeast* (Lincoln, Nebr., 1997).

that reflect those of his characters—into a direct contribution to his "main purpose." The objective of the tale is to locate the origin of discord between Spaniards and Amerindians in Spanish treachery while making native hostility the ostensible focus of the narrative. Thus, whereas the other narratives focus on the result of the captivity—the discovery of Ortiz and his subsequent service as an interpreter—Garcilaso's point of departure is its cause, "the rage Hirrihigua felt for the Castilians." Just as in his account of don Luis, Garcilaso presents Hirrihigua's rage as motivated by previous Spanish misdeeds in the region.

To illustrate Hirrihigua's fury, then, Garcilaso initiates a flashback to the capture of four Spanish soldiers, three of whom are immediately tortured and killed. The young Juan Ortiz is spared only because of the merciful intervention of the cacique's wife and daughters. These women continue to defend and comfort him during the trying months of his captivity until Hirrihigua's thirst for revenge becomes implacable, even after Ortiz earns the respect of others by slaying a lion in the night while guarding a child's dead body. The eldest daughter, however, saves the Spaniard by sending him to a neighboring leader, Mucozo, who hopes to marry the girl and thus is likely to comply with her request.

Thus far, many elements of the Juan Ortiz captivity tale would resonate with peninsular readers. Hirrihigua's mistreatment of Ortiz recalls the depictions of cruel captivity among Moors and Turks, such as the captive martyrdoms described in the "Diálogo de los mártires" in the *Topographia e historia general de Argel.* The intervention of the captor's wife and daughters to save and eventually free Ortiz recalls a well-known motif in medieval and Renaissance literatures: that of the "enamored Muslim princess" who converts to Christianity and flees with her father's captive. The *Relaçam* also invokes the motif by showing Juan Ortiz to escape with the aid of his captor's daughter. Unlike *La Florida,* however, the Fidalgo d'Elvas's version does not include an amorous relationship between the cacique's daughter and Mucozo, perhaps allowing readers to identify her more with the model of the captor's daughter enamored of the Christian captive. The woman's liaison with Mucozo in *La Florida* permits Garcilaso to spotlight the nobility of the indigenous leader, since he must sacrifice marrying his beloved because of his defense of Juan Ortiz.[11]

11. Diego de Haedo, "Diálogo de los mártires," in Haedo, *Topografía e historia general de Argel* (Madrid, 1929 [orig. publ. Valladolid, 1612]), III, 1–192. Garcilaso invokes the term "martirio" [martyrdom] to describe the deaths of the other three

The second stage of Ortiz's captivity, among Mucozo's people, invokes a very different model of captive-captor relations, but one that can also be found in peninsular literature. Mucozo's treatment of Juan Ortiz recalls the chivalric interaction between the Christian captain Narváez and his noble Moorish captive Abindarráez in the anonymous novella *El Abencerraje* (1561) and the many ballads relating their legendary encounter during the Reconquest. However, Garcilaso inverts the relationship, making the Christian the grateful captive rather than the benevolent captor. Garcilaso relates how Ortiz arrives safely and is warmly received by Mucozo, who sympathizes with the Spaniard's sufferings and promises to treat him differently: "Le oyó con lástima de saber los males y tormentos que había pasado, que bien se mostraban en las señales de su cuerpo. . . . Respondióle que fuese bien venido y se esforzase a perder el temor de la vida pasada, que en su compañía y casa la tendría bien diferente y contraria" (123) ["(Mucozo) listened with compassion to his account of the sufferings and torments he had experienced, evidences of which were clearly revealed by the scars on his body. . . . More-

---

captives, and Ortiz uses it to inform the cacique Mucozo about his treatment by Hirrihigua; see *La Florida,* ed. Hilton, 115, 122; [Garcilaso], *The Florida,* 61, 71. On the daughter's interventions to spare Juan Ortiz, see Fidalgo d'Elvas, *Relaçam verdadeira,* xxiv–xxv; Bourne, ed., *Narratives of the Career,* trans. Smith, I, 28–30. Despite Garcilaso's well-known disavowal of chivalric fiction in book 2, part 1, chap. 27, Garcilaso includes a scene familiar to readers of *Amadís* and *El caballero Cifar:* that of the child's corpse carried off by a lion that the hero extraordinarily slays; see Amalia Iniesta Cámara, "Novelas de caballerías, bizantina e italiana en *La Florida del Inca,*" *Anales de literatura hispanoamericana,* II (1982), 39–50, esp. 42. On the echoes of European fiction in *La Florida*—especially the novela bizantina, discussed in Chapter 1, above—see also Aurelio Miró Quesada Sosa, "Creación y elaboración de *La Florida del Inca,*" *Cuadernos americanos,* III, no. 18 (November–December 1989), 152–171; and Lee Dowling, "*La Florida del Inca:* Garcilaso's Literary Sources," in Galloway, ed., *Soto Expedition,* 98–154. On the motif of the "enamored captor's daughter," see Mohja Kahf, *Western Representations of the Muslim Woman: From Termagant to Odalisque* (Austin, Tex., 1999), 33–38; and Harriet Goldberg, "Captivity as a Central Node in Hispanic Popular Legends: There's Something about a Prisoner," in Delia V. Galván, Anita K. Stoll, and Philippa Brown Yin, eds., *Studies in Honor of Donald W. Bleznick* (Newark, N.J., 1995), 49–58. Other New World instances can be found in many of the texts addressed in this book, from the Barbaric Isle's Ricla in the *Persiles* to Brazil's Paraguaçu and Virginia's Pocahontas.

over, he assured him of his welcome and urged him to make an effort to forget the fear of his former existence; for, he said, in his house and company he would find life very different from what he had known previously" (72)]. Ortiz's captivity tale already provokes the ideal response in its first listener, an indigenous cacique.[12]

If Ortiz's ordeal as Hirrihigua's captive has left its mark on his body, the subsequent eight years of "happy captivity" with Mucozo also leave an indelible imprint on both the Spaniard and his captor. Mucozo defies not only the demands of his family but his own interests by refusing to surrender the captive to Hirrihigua: "Tuvo por mejor perder (como lo perdió) el casamiento que aficionadamente deseaba hacer con la hija de Hirrihigua y el parentesco y amistad del cuñado que volver el esclavo a quien lo pedía para matarlo" (124) ["Rather than return the slave to be slaughtered by his former master, he chose to abandon all possibility of a marriage with Hirrihigua's daughter, whom he ardently desired and subsequently lost, and at the same time to forfeit his friendship and kinship with Urribarracuxi" (73)]. In this sense, Mucozo's characterization exceeds that of the gallant Moor in *El Abencerraje,* for Abindarráez's strength, virtue, and nobility are undermined by his emotional captivity to his beloved, Jarifa. Mucozo's parallel in the happy captivity of *El Abencerraje* is, not the Moorish captive, but the Christian captain, who also chooses to uphold his honor and virtue at the expense of being with the woman he loves. One version of *El Abencerraje*

12. On the various sixteenth-century editions of the anonymous narrative known as *Abencerraje* (1561, 1562, 1565), see Francisco López Estrada, "Introducción," in López Estrada, ed., *El Abencerraje (novela y romancero)* (Madrid, 1993), 13–126, esp. 13–19; he discusses the subsequent literary appropriations of the tale (19–23) and the relationship between the novels and *romances* (ballads) inspired by the legend (67–79). López Estrada also reviews the literary antecedents of what many readers take to be the tale's dominant theme, "the lesson of generosity," and compares the work to contemporary Italian *novellas* that, similar to *La Florida,* praise the behavior of benevolent Muslim captors toward their Christian captives (28–43). For an example of a reading focused on religious tolerance, see Claudio Guillén, "Individuo y ejemplaridad en el *'Abencerraje,'*" in Guillén, *El primer Siglo de Oro: Estudios sobre géneros y modelos* (Barcelona, 1988), 109–153, which explores how the idealized relationship between Narváez and Abindarráez contradicts historical reality as well as official discourse on Muslims in Spain. Israel Burshatin, in contrast, characterizes *El Abencerraje* as a "self-flattering depiction of Christian control over the Moor and his world"; see Burshatin, "Power, Discourse, and Metaphor in the *Abencerraje,*" *MLN,* XCIX (1984), 195–213, esp. 197.

includes the tale of Narváez's previous abandonment of an adulterous relationship when he learns that his beloved's husband has spoken well of him; as Laura Bass has analyzed, Narváez restores patriarchal order by subordinating heterosexual desire to homosocial bonds. Mucozo, however, subordinates not only heterosexual desire but also homosocial bonds with his own kin—his brother-in-law Urribarracuxi, who acts as a proxy for Hirrihigua in the effort to recover Ortiz—to his love for the Christian captive, whom he treats "como a propio hermano muy querido" (123) ["as a very much beloved brother" (72)]. For Garcilaso, Mucozo's exemplarity resides in his recognition of a male foreigner as worthy of emotional investment.[13]

Garcilaso not only praises Mucozo's conduct with respect to his captive but also contrasts it with the treatment of captives and hostages among Europeans. Without inverting the identification of Europe with civilization and America with barbarism, Garcilaso's incisive comparison unsettles and complicates such categories as he refers to the cacique who,

> aunque bárbaro, lo hizo con este cristiano muy de otra manera que los famosísimos varones del triunvirato que, en Laino, lugar cerca de Bolonia, hicieron aquella nunca jamás bastantemente abominada proscripción y concierto de dar y trocar los parientes, amigos y valedores por los enemigos y adversarios. Y lo hizo mucho mejor que otros príncipes cristianos que después acá han hecho otras tan abominables y más que aquélla. . . . Los cuales . . . sólo por vengarse de sus enojos, entregaron los que no les habían ofendido por haber los ofensores, dando inocentes por culpados,

13. In "Homosocial Bonds and Desire in the *Abencerraje," Revista canadiense de estudios hispánicos,* XXIV (2000), 453–471, Laura R. Bass draws on Eve Kosofsky Sedgwick's analysis of the management of homosocial desire through heterosexual love triangles in nineteenth-century English novels (*Between Men: English Literature and Male Homosocial Desire* [New York, 1985]). Mary M. Gaylord calls Abindarráez a "prisoner of Love," and "if the Moor is doubly a captive—captive both of a Christian knight and of his own Moorishness—, [Narváez] is doubly a victor"; see Gaylord, "Spain's Renaissance Conquests and the Retroping of Identity," *Journal of Hispanic Philology,* XVI (1991–1992), 125–136, esp. 132. The old man in *El Abencerraje* who recounts Narváez's abandonment of the adulterous relationship concludes, "El caballero a mi parescer usó de gran virtud y valentía, pues venció su misma voluntad" [It seems to me that the gentleman was very virtuous and brave, for he defeated his own will]; see López Estrada, ed., *El Abencerraje,* 158. Although the circumstances are different, Garcilaso implies that a similar appraisal could be made of Mucozo's behavior.

> como lo testifican las historias antiguas y modernas, las cuales dejaremos por no ofender oídos poderosos y lastimar los piadosos. (124)

> although a barbarian, behaved toward this Christian in a manner far different from that of the famous Triumvirate of Laino (a place near Bologna), which made a never sufficiently abominated proscription and agreement to exchange relatives, friends, and protectors for enemies and adversaries. And, too, his behavior was much more admirable than that of other Christian princes who since then have made bargains equally odious, if not more so. . . . These Christians, solely to avenge their anger, exchanged people who had not offended them for those who had, thus giving up the innocent for the guilty. To this fact, both ancient and modern histories testify, but we shall abandon this subject lest we offend powerful ears and grieve the pious. (73–74)

Garcilaso may have avoided offending "powerful ears" by suppressing specific details about "these Christians," but he has said enough to point out the relativism of the charge of barbarism—as well as to demonstrate his familiarity with classical and contemporary European practices and representations of captivity ("ancient and modern histories"), within and against which he composes his tale of Juan Ortiz.

Garcilaso's praise of Mucozo's superiority to Christians is only lightly veiled by his didactic discourse: "Basta representar la magnanimidad de un infiel para que los príncipes fieles se esfuercen a le imitar y sobrepujar, si pudieren, no en la infidelidad, como lo hacen algunos indignos de tal nombre, sino en la virtud y grandezas semejantes" (124–125) ["It suffices to represent the magnanimity of an infidel so that princes of the Faith may make efforts to imitate and if possible surpass him—not in infidelity, as some do who are undeserving of the title of Christian, but in virtue and similar excellences" (74)]. God and human nature "muchas veces en desiertos tan incultos y estériles producen semejantes ánimos para mayor confusión y vergüenza de los que nacen y se crían en tierras fértiles y abundantes de toda buena doctrina, ciencias y religión cristiana" (125) ["many times produce such souls in sterile and uncultivated deserts to the greater confusion and shame of people who are born and reared in lands that are fertile and abundant in all good doctrines and sciences, as well as the Christian religion" (74)]. If Garcilaso's metaphors belie an unwavering Eurocentric perspective on the relationship between civilization and Christianity, the explanation for this counterexample points to an important authorial strategy. Garcilaso's claim to narrative and historiographic authority is dependent upon the confusion of categories such as these, which would otherwise exclude an American-born mestizo writer from intellectual production, as Garcilaso himself suggests through an incident recounted in the prologue to his *Historia general del Perú.* And as Garcilaso constantly points out, "confusion" is inextricably bound up with the process of conquest itself, as with any intercultural contact.[14]

Linguistic misunderstanding is perhaps the most common example of confusion cited by Garcilaso, whose task is to clarify what a monolingual or monocultural observer would be incapable of comprehending. Garcilaso often alludes to the danger of misinterpreting unfamiliar speech "conforme a su deseo" [according to one's desires], as in the famous passage about the name of Peru in *Comentarios reales* (originally intended, according to Garcilaso, for inclusion in *La Florida*). A similar example of linguistic confusion appears in the Ortiz narrative, when Garcilaso finally returns to Governor Soto, the hero of his story. He affirms that Soto decided to rescue Ortiz after hearing a garbled version of his captivity upon arriving in Hirrihigua's village. But Soto's response is actually a rather belated one. The real confusion arose previously, when an Amerindian captured by Juan de Añasco on an earlier expedition mentioned the name "Orotiz" to his Spanish captors:

> Y como a este mal hablar del indio se añadiese el peor entender de los buenos intérpretes que declaraban lo que él quería decir, y como todos los oyentes tuviesen por principal intento el ir a buscar oro, oyendo decir al indio Orotiz, sin buscar otras declaraciones, entendían que llanamente decía que en su tierra había mucho oro, y se holgaban y regocijaban sólo con oírlo nombrar, aunque en tan diferente significación y sentido. (125–126)

But the pronunciation of the name was defective, and the understanding of the good interpreters who were declaring what he desired to say was

14. As mentioned in Chapter 1, Garcilaso relates his encounter with a scholar who questioned his audacity to translate León Hebreo's *Dialoghi d'amore* into Spanish, being "un antártico, nacido en el Nuevo Mundo, allá debajo de nuestro hemisferio, y que en la leche mamó la lengua general de los indios del Perú" [an Antarctic Indian, born in the New World, there underneath our hemisphere, and who nursed in his mother's milk the general language of the Indians of Peru]; see Garcilaso, *Historia general del Perú,* I, 16.

even worse. Therefore, when those listening, whose principal aim was to go in search of gold, heard him say Orotiz, they asked for no further interpretation but understood him to declare flatly that in his land there was much *oro* or gold. Thus they cheered and made merry just with hearing the word named, although with such different meaning and sense. (74–75)

The confusion may be comical, but its implications—and consequences for Ortiz—are quite serious. Many chroniclers complain that the Spanish colonizers are more interested in finding gold than saving Amerindian souls, but Garcilaso shows the ill effects of their deliberate misinterpretations—reminiscent of those of Columbus—even on one of their own. Significantly, this scene is not corroborated by any of the other sources dedicated to the Soto expedition. Its similarity to other passages in Garcilaso's works, such as the "Perú" anecdote cited above, suggests a clever manipulation of Ortiz's name on Garcilaso's part. He demonstrates his ability to interpret not only indigenous languages more accurately but Spanish itself, all the while pointing out the conquistadors' misplaced ambitions.[15]

According to Garcilaso, Soto himself recognizes the importance of reliable interpretation to avoid such misunderstandings, and this is one of his reasons for trying to recover the Spanish captive: "Le pareció sería bien enviar por [Juan Ortiz], así por sacarlo de poder de indios como porque lo había menester para lengua e intérprete de quien se pudiese fiar" (126) ["The Governor concluded that it would be wise to send for him; first, to

15. On the confusion that generated the name of Perú, see Inca Garcilaso de la Vega, *Comentarios reales de los Incas,* ed. Aurelio Miró Quesada ([Caracas], 1976), I, 15; Garcilaso, *La Florida,* ed. Hilton, 562; [Garcilaso], *The Florida,* ed. and trans. Varner and Varner, 614. As Garcilaso explains in the *Comentarios reales,* "Perú"—which the Spaniards take to be the name of the land—conflates the proper name of the native they interrogate ("Berú") with his mention of a nearby body of water ("Pelú," or river). Columbus's misinterpretations of indigenous speech—particularly in the effort to confirm the existence of gold—are well known; see, for example, the entry for October 21 in the logbook of his first voyage (Cristóbal Colón, *Textos y documentos completos: Relaciones de viajes, cartas y memoriales,* ed. Consuelo Varela [Madrid, 1982], 41–42; Cecil Jane, trans., *The Journal of Christopher Columbus* [London, 1960], 39–41). Faulty indigenous interpretation is not exempt from Garcilaso's critique; in *Historia general del Perú,* Garcilaso holds the interpreter Felipillo's ignorance of Spanish responsible for the deaths of Atahuallpa and Huascar Inca, decisive moments in the fall of the Inca Empire (*Historia general,* I, 96).

remove him from the hands of the Indians, and then to provide the army with a much needed interpreter whom he could trust" (75)]. In his letter to officials in Cuba, Soto acknowledges his reliance on natives captured to serve as interpreters and guides ("old men of authority . . . who have information of the country farther on"), but he also questions their fidelity: "Of what these Indians say I believe nothing but what I see." Garcilaso shows that such suspicions might have sometimes been well founded, even if vengeful Spaniards acted improperly upon them. According to the Fidalgo d'Elvas, before departing Spain, Soto unsuccessfully attempted to recruit a mediator whose Spanish allegiance was more assured: Álvar Núñez Cabeza de Vaca. Juan Ortiz offers a similar profile, as a Spaniard with extensive experience as a captive.[16]

In Garcilaso's version, the cacique Mucozo also recognizes Juan Ortiz's value as a trustworthy intermediary. After informing Ortiz of the Spanish presence, Mucozo immediately sends him to the Spaniards and charges him with nothing less than a peace mission: "Iréis al general español y, de vuestra parte y mía, le suplicaréis que en remuneración de lo que a él y a toda su nación en vos he servido . . . , tenga por bien de no hacerme daño en esta poca tierra que tengo y se digne de recibirme en su amistad y servicio" (126–127) ["Go therefore to the Spanish general and request in my name as well as your own, that as a recompense for the favor I have rendered him and all of his nation through my kindness to you . . . , he not deem it expedient to do me harm in this little land of mine, and that he deign to receive me into his fellowship and service" (76)]. Ortiz offers the decorous answer of a knight

16. Soto, "Letter at Tampa Bay," in Bourne, ed., *Narratives of the Career,* trans. Smith, II, 161–162. On Soto's proposal to Cabeza de Vaca, see Fidalgo d'Elvas, *Relaçam verdadeira,* v–vi; Bourne, ed., *Narratives of the Career,* I, 6–7. As the Fidalgo d'Elvas points out, Cabeza de Vaca sought an appointment of higher status; he had gone to court seeking the *adelantamiento* of Florida for himself, only to find it had already been granted to Soto. Garcilaso condemns the Spaniards' execution of an indigenous guide who had intentionally led them astray in *La Florida,* ed. Hilton, 480–481; and *The Florida,* ed. and trans. Varner and Varner, 513–515. For a survey of some of the captured natives and European ex-captives who served as interpreters for the Portuguese, Spanish, French, and English in the New World, see Francis Xavier Luca, "Re-'interpreting' the Conquest: European and Amerindian Translators and Go-betweens in the Colonization of the Americas, 1492–1675" (Ph.D. diss., Florida International University, 2004), 41–184. Luca argues that European ex-captives could be as subject to suspicions about their loyalties as abducted Amerindians (180–184).

of chivalry, but one that is infused with the formulaic language of notorial rhetoric and the relación de servicios. He thanks Mucozo for his kindness, extols his virtue and courtesy, and assures him reciprocal treatment from the Spaniards once he has given "muy larga relación y cuenta al capitán español y a todos los suyos para que se lo agradeciesen y pagasen en lo que al presente en su nombre les pidiese y en lo por venir se ofreciese" (127) ["a liberal account of all such things to the Spanish Captain and his men that they too might in turn express their gratitude and make recompense with what he at present was going to ask of them in the Cacique's behalf and also with whatever might arise in the future" (76)]. Ortiz and Mucozo recognize that mediation is effected through narration, in which an insider's knowledge is transferred to a foreign public in order to promote intercultural understanding. Of course, it is Garcilaso who delivers this promised oral account of Ortiz's captivity in writing, thus deserving a similarly grateful response from his audience. Indeed, Garcilaso himself hopes for such a reaction to the "very long relation and account" of his own (and his father's) services to the Spanish Crown, which he brings before the Council of the Indies and, disappointed, later intersperses throughout his writings.[17]

17. In his unsuccessful bid to earn compensation for his father's services and his mother's patrimony, described in the *Historia general del Perú,* Garcilaso depicts his father's controversial behavior toward Gonzalo Pizarro as that of a captive obeying the code of chivalry. Garcilaso's father had given his horse to Pizarro following the latter's victory over the king's forces at Huarina, an act that would later inspire charges of treason in the work of some historians (Francisco López de Gómara, Agustín de Zárate, Diego Fernández). Garcilaso defends his father's action in terms of both his captive status and his friendship with Pizarro: "Fuese mi padre de tanto ánimo, esfuerzo y valentía, que se apease de su caballo y lo diese a su amigo. . . . No faltará quien diga que fue contra el servicio del Rey, a lo cual diré yo que un hecho tal, en cualquiera parte que se haga . . . merece honra y fama" [My father was of such courage, fortitude, and valor that he got down from his horse and gave it to his friend. . . . There will be those who say this was against the service of the king, to which I will respond that such a deed, wherever it is done, deserves honor and fame]; see *Historia general del Perú,* I, 388, II, 537, 571. Garcilaso lauds his father for doing as Juan Ortiz did: serving both opponents without betraying either. John Grier Varner argues that the captain's conduct at Huarina "was a simple gesture which found precedent in many accounts of medieval and Renaissance chivalry; but the circumstances under which it was rendered strengthened suspicion and subjected Garcilaso to malicious rumors which could never be completely allayed"; see Varner, *El Inca: The Life and Times of Garcilaso de la Vega* (Austin, Tex., 1968), 79. Garcilaso's representation of

As the stage shifts from the Amerindian village to the encounter between Amerindians and Spaniards, the parallels between Garcilaso and the ex-captive mount. Garcilaso constructs the episode in a way that credits the Floridians, and Juan Ortiz himself, with the initiative for the captive's return to Christian society. Whereas other accounts of the Soto expedition emphasize the Spanish "discovery" of Juan Ortiz, in Garcilaso's version the Spaniards are actually backtracking when Ortiz, sent by Mucozo in the company of fifty Amerindians, comes upon them. Garcilaso is careful to point out that Ortiz is not the same as when he left Spanish society: captivity has transformed him as well as his captor. Ortiz himself does not initially discern this change, indicated by his appearance, and he rejects his companions' advice to hide from the approaching Spaniards:

> confiado en que era español y que los suyos le habían de reconocer luego que le viesen, como si viniera vestido a la española o estuviera en alguna cosa diferenciado de los indios para ser conocido por español. El cual [Ortiz], como los demás, no llevaba sino unos pañetes por vestidura y un arco y flechas en las manos y un plumaje de media braza en alto sobre la cabeza por gala y ornamento. (128)

> being confident that, since he was a Spaniard, his countrymen would recognize him the moment they beheld him—as if he had been attired in Spanish clothes or something else that might differentiate him, instead of being equipped as he was like the natives with nothing but some loin cloths on his body, a bow and arrows in his hand, and for ornament, plumage half a fathom in height upon his head. (78)[18]

---

an act of suspected treason as praiseworthy service (within Spanish cultural norms) is parallel to his valorization of his own mestizo identity, a condition that also prompted suspicions of betrayal among both Amerindians and Spaniards. Garcilaso reinterprets his father's apparent vacillation as an intentional, mediating gesture of positive consequences, as he does with the native Andean "captives" who serve their Spanish masters by returning to the Amerindian camp during the day in order to bring food and supplies to the Spaniards at night; see *Historia general del Perú,* I, 197–198.

18. On the "discovery" of Juan Ortiz, see Soto, "Letter at Tampa Bay," in Bourne, *Narratives of the Career,* trans. Smith, II, 160–161: "At my arrival here I received news of there being a Christian in the possession of a Cacique, and I sent Baltazar de Gallegos . . . to endeavour to get him. He found the man a day's journey from this place,

The lack of recognition by an ex-captive's compatriots is common to tales of captivity in peninsular drama and fiction as well as colonial chronicles. In his *Historia verdadera de la conquista de Nueva España* (1632), Bernal Díaz del Castillo describes the Spanish reaction to the appearance of Jerónimo de Aguilar—the Spaniard rescued from captivity on the Yucatán Peninsula, who later served as Cortés's interpreter—in similar terms to that of *La Florida*. Here the soldier Andrés de Tapia brings Aguilar back to Cortés's camp, where rumor has already spread of the Spanish captive's return:

> Ciertos españoles preguntaban al Tapia qu[é] es del español, aunque iba allí junto con él, porque *le tenían por indio propio, porque de suyo era moreno e tresquilado a manera de indio esclavo,* e traía un remo al hombro e una cotara vieja calzada y la otra en la cinta, e una manta vieja muy ruin e un braguero peor. . . . Pues desque Cortés lo vio de aquella manera, también pic[ó] como los demás soldados y preguntó al Tapia que qué era del español.

> Several Spaniards asked Tápia where the Spaniard was? although he was walking by his side, for *they could not distinguish him from an Indian as he was naturally brown and he had his hair shorn like an Indian slave,* and

---

with eight or ten Indians, whom he brought into my power." Ranjel's account likewise attributes the first sighting of Ortiz and his native companions, and their subsequent pursuit, to the Spaniards; see Oviedo, *Historia general y natural,* ed. Tudela Bueso, II, 155; Bourne, ed., *Narratives of the Career,* II, 56. Garcilaso's depiction of Ortiz's physical appearance coincides with other accounts. Biedma writes that Ortiz "venía desnudo como ellos, con un arco y unas flechas en la mano, labrado el cuerpo como Indio: como los Christianos los toparon pensaron que eran indios que venían a espiar la gente" ["came naked like them, with a bow and some arrows in his hands, his body wrought over like theirs. They who discovered the natives thought they were come to spy out the condition of our people"]; see Smith, ed., *Colección de varios documentos,* I, 47; Bourne, ed., *Narratives of the Career,* II, 3–4. The Fidalgo d'Elvas describes the captive in similar terms, but like Biedma and Soto, he attributes more agency to the Spaniards in their recovery of Ortiz than Garcilaso does: "Saindo ao campo chão [Baltasar de Gallegos] vio dez ou onze índios, antre os quaes vinha um christão despido e como andava queimado do sol e trazia os braços lavrados a uso dos índios, e nenhuma cousa deferia delles" ["When Baltasar de Gallegos came into the open field, he discovered ten or eleven Indians, among whom was a Christian, naked and sun-burnt, his arms tattoed after their manner, and he in no respect differing from them"]; see Fidalgo d'Elvas, *Relaçam verdadeira,* xxiii; Bourne, ed., *Narratives of the Career,* I, 26.

> carried a paddle on his shoulder, [and] was shod with one old sandal and the other was tied to his belt, he had on a ragged old cloak, and a worse loin cloth. . . . When Cortés saw him in this state, he too was deceived like the other soldiers, and asked Tápia; "Where is the Spaniard?"

The Spaniard Gabriel Lobo Lasso de la Vega's version of these events, included in his epic poem *Mexicana* (1588, 1594), also indulges in a detailed description of Aguilar's exotic appearance. In this scene, the captive and three indigenous companions present themselves before a group of Spaniards:

> Ven que de la barquilla van saliendo
> cuatro robustos jóvenes membrudos,
> trenzados los cabellos y desnudos.
> En tierra saltan, de arcos ocupadas
> las manos y de agudos pasadores,
> de palo y pedernal anchas espadas,
> matizadas de varios mil colores:
> piernas, brazos y caras esmaltadas,
> de cárdeno color muchas labores,
> los bezos de la boca agujereados
> de sortijones de oro atravesados.
>
> They see emerge from the boat
> four strong, muscular youths,
> naked, with hair braided.
> They come ashore, their hands engaged
> with bows and sharp arrows,
> broad swords of wood and flint,
> of a thousand different tints;
> their legs, arms, and faces adorned
> with an elaborate purple hue,
> their perforated lips
> pierced with large rings of gold.[19]

19. Bernal Díaz del Castillo, *Historia verdadera de la conquista de la Nueva España,* ed. Miguel León-Portilla (Madrid, 1984 [orig. publ. 1632]), I, 135 (emphasis added); Díaz del Castillo, *The Discovery and Conquest of Mexico, 1517–1521,* ed. Genaro García, trans. A. P. Maudslay (New York, 1956), 45 (emphasis added); Gabriel Lobo

Such scenes of "anti-anagnorisis" can also be found in Spanish literature dealing with the captive's return from Turkish or Algerian captivity. In the "Captive's Tale" of *Don Quijote,* for example, Ruy Pérez de Viedma relates to his listeners at the inn how a young shepherd, the first person they encounter upon their arrival in Spain, fears a Moorish attack because of their appearance:

> Dimos voces, y él, alzando la cabeza, se puso ligeramente en pie, y a lo que después supimos, los primeros que a la vista se le ofrecieron fueron el renegado y Zoraida, y como él los vio en hábito de moros, pensó que todos los de la Berbería estaban sobre él; y metiéndose con estraña ligereza por el bosque adelante, comenzó a dar los mayores gritos del mundo, diciendo: "—Moros, moros hay en la tierra! ¡Moros, moros! ¡Arma, arma!" Con estas voces quedamos todos confusos, y no sabíamos qué hacernos.

> We called out and, raising his head, he jumped right up and, as we afterwards learned, the first thing he saw was our renegade and Zoraida and, since they were wearing Moorish clothing, was convinced that all of Barbary was after him and went running through the nearby wood, leaping like a rabbit and screaming, with the wildest yells ever heard,
>
> "Moors, the Moors have landed! Moors, Moors! To arms, to arms!"
>
> This frantic shouting completely confused us, and we didn't know what to do.

The ex-captive and his entourage are as bewildered as the shepherd until they recognize the source of his misunderstanding and have the renegade exchange his Turkish attire for that of a Christian captive.[20]

Their confusion and that of the unsuspecting shepherd are not nearly as severe as that of the Spaniards who encounter Aguilar in Lobo Lasso de la Vega's *Mexicana.* In this tale, the captive's voice—his ability to speak Spanish—make him all the more uncanny, foreign in appearance yet familiar in speech to the Spanish conquistadors (and the readers of the poem). The

---

Lasso de la Vega, *Mexicana (1594),* ed. José Amor y Vázquez (Madrid, 1970 [orig. publ. Madrid, 1588]), 28.

20. Miguel de Cervantes Saavedra, *Don Quijote de la Mancha,* ed. Luis Andrés Murillo (Madrid, 1978), I, 511; Cervantes, *The History of That Ingenious Gentleman Don Quijote de la Mancha,* trans. Burton Raffel (New York, 1995), 281.

poet registers their confusion when they hear Aguilar interrogate their own identity:

"¿Por ventura, señores, sois cristianos?"
  De tal pregunta todos admirados,
confusos y suspensos respondieron:
"Sí, somos," temerosos y turbados,
que por la estigia sombra la tuvieron.
Mirábanle y mirábanse alterados,
que cuando la española lengua oyeron,
por hombre tan remoto pronunciarse,
no pudieron dejar de no admirarse.

"By chance, sirs, are you Christians?"
  Everyone was confused, dazed,
and at such a question amazed,
and taking him for the Estygian ghost
they responded, "Yes, we are," in fright.
They gazed at each other and at him, altered:
for when they heard the Spanish language
pronounced by a man so strange,
they couldn't fail to be bewildered.

Here speech distinguishes the foreign from the familiar, however uncanny the juxtaposition between the two. Bernal Díaz's more or less historically based Aguilar is far less eloquent, but he does manage to mumble "Dios y Santa María y Sevilla" [God and St. Mary and Seville] so that the Spaniards are able to identify him through the holy trinity of religion, homeland, and native language.[21]

21. Lobo Lasso de la Vega, *Mexicana,* ed. Amor y Vázquez, 28. Mary Gaylord describes the unsettling implications of this scene, which she reads as emblematic of the "alteration" suffered by all those involved in the conquest of America: "The surprise of seeing and hearing a barbarian turns into the much more mysterious experience of seeing the barbarian while hearing the neighbor. . . . This is the disquieting experience that Freud, three centuries later, would characterize as *unheimlich,* in which something familiar becomes wrapped in mystery, while something strange simultaneously acquires a disturbing air of familiarity"; see Gaylord, "Jerónimo de Aguilar y la alteración de la lengua (la *Mexicana* de Gabriel Lobo Lasso de la Vega)," in

Unlike Aguilar in either of these versions, Juan Ortiz is curiously unable to utter a word in Spanish to make himself known. He cannot even pronounce the name of his place of origin: "Dio grandes voces diciendo 'Xivilla, Xivilla', por decir Sevilla, Sevilla" (129) ["He cried in a loud voice, 'Xivilla, Xivilla,' by which he intended to say, 'Sevilla, Sevilla'" (79)]. The captive no longer purely belongs to either his fatherland or his mother tongue. His loss of Spanish has perhaps more of a historical than a literary precedent, for it is corroborated by several of the accounts of the Soto expedition, where it is often the only thing mentioned about him. Biedma claims that the Spaniards nearly killed Ortiz "por que él sabía poco nuestra lengua que ya la tenía olvidada; acordose de llamar a Nuestra Señora, por donde fue conocido ser el Christiano" [because he knew little of our language which he had already forgotten; he remembered to call upon Our Lady, whereby he was recognized as a Christian]. Despite this providential inspiration, it still takes him several days to regain fluency in his native language, during which time he interjects four or five "Indian" words for each one spoken in Spanish. Hernando de Soto more optimistically writes of Ortiz's loss and recovery of Spanish: "We rejoiced no little over him, for he speaks the language; and although he had forgotten his own, it directly returned to him." The Cañete fragment—the truncated summary of a narrative of the Soto expedition written by a participant friar—briefly mentions Juan Ortiz and also confirms that he had forgotten his own language.[22]

In contrast, two other eyewitness sources—the Fidalgo d'Elvas's *Relaçam verdadeira* and Oviedo's rendition of Rodrigo Ranjel's diary—present an

José Antonio Mazzotti, ed., *Agencias criollas: La ambigüedad "colonial" en las letras hispanoamericanas* (Pittsburgh, 2000), 73–97, esp. 80, 84. For the final quotation, see Díaz del Castillo, *Historia verdadera,* ed. León-Portilla, I, 135.

22. Soto, "Letter at Tampa Bay," in Bourne, ed., *Narratives of the Career,* trans. Smith, II, 160–161. See Biedma's account in Smith, ed., *Colección de varios documentos,* I, 47, and Bourne, ed., *Narratives of the Career,* II, 4, although I have offered my own translation of this passage. For the Cañete fragment, see Lyon, "Précis," in Chang-Rodríguez, ed., *Beyond Books and Borders,* 91–96. Ortiz's loss of Spanish would hardly be surprising after a decade of not speaking it. Similar declarations by ex-captives of their loss of their native tongue can be found in Juan Falcón's *declaración* regarding his Araucanian captivity (1599–1614) and Isaac Jogues's account of his captivity among the Mohawks (1642–1643); see Horacio Zapater Equioz, "Testimonio de un cautivo: Araucanía, 1599–1614," *Historia,* XXIII (1988), 295–325, esp. 317; and Richard VanDerBeets, ed., *Held Captive by Indians: Selected Narratives, 1642–1836* (Knoxville, Tenn., 1973), 4.

Ortiz articulate in Spanish and able to confirm his identity through speech in the manner of Lobo Lasso's Aguilar. The Fidalgo d'Elvas writes, "O christão [v]indo um de cavallo com a lança sobre elle, começou a bradar christão sou señores nam me mateis, nem mateis estes indios, que elles me ham dado a vida" ["The Christian, seeing a horseman coming upon him with a lance, began to cry out, 'Do not kill me, cavalier; I am a Christian! Do not slay these people; they have given me my life!'"]. In Ranjel/Oviedo's text, Ortiz pleads only for his own life, stressing his identification with them in terms of religion and birthplace: "Señores, por amor de Dios y de Sancta María no me matéis: que yo soy cristiano, como vosotros, y soy natural de Sevilla y me llamo Joan Ortiz" ["Sirs, for the love of God and of Holy Mary, slay not me; I am a Christian like yourselves and was born in Seville, and my name is Johan Ortiz"]. The more elaborate exchanges in these versions follow literary models of the returning captive and make Garcilaso's account stand out by contrast.[23]

RECAPTURING LANGUAGE

Why, then, does Garcilaso depart from the model of foreign appearance/familiar speech upon the captive's return to "civilized" society? Ortiz does manage, of course, to prove his Christian identity in Garcilaso's account (Garcilaso here cites Juan Coles, a possibly apocryphal written source): "En este paso, añade Juan Coles, que, no acertando Juan Ortiz a hablar castellano, hizo con la mano y el arco la señal de la cruz para que el español viese que era cristiano" (129) ["In describing this incident, Juan Coles adds that, failing in his efforts to speak Castilian, Juan Ortiz made a sign of the cross with his hand and his bow so that his opponent might recognize him as a Christian" (79)]. Garcilaso pauses here to insert a rather lengthy autobiographical digression, which allows him not only to replace Coles's signature with his own but also to present the depiction of the captive as a self-portrait and Ortiz as his alter ego:

> Porque, con el poco o ningún uso que entre los indios había tenido de la lengua castellana, se le había olvidado hasta el pronunciar el nombre de la propia tierra, como yo podré decir también de mí mismo que por no haber tenido en España con quién hablar mi lengua natural y materna,

23. Fidalgo d'Elvas, *Relaçam verdadeira,* xxiii; Bourne, ed., *Narratives of the Career,* I, 27, II, 57; Oviedo, *Historia general y natural,* ed. Tudela Bueso, II, 155.

> que es la general que se habla en todo el Perú (aunque los incas tenían otro particular que hablaban entre sí unos con otros), se me ha olvidado de tal manera que, con saberla hablar tan bien y mejor y con más elegancia que los mismos indios que no son incas, porque soy hijo de palla y sobrino de incas, que son los que mejor y más apuradamente la hablan por haber sido lenguaje de la corte de sus príncipes y haber sido ellos los principales cortesanos, no acierto ahora a concertar seis o siete palabras en oración para dar a entender lo que quiero decir, y más, que muchos vocablos se me han ido de la memoria, que no sé cuáles son, para nombrar en indio tal o tal cosa. (129–130)

> Since there had been little or no opportunity for Juan Ortiz to speak Castilian among the Indians, he had forgotten even so much as how to pronounce the name of his native land. But I shall be able to say the same for myself, for having found no person in Spain with whom I may speak my mother tongue, which is the one generally used in Peru (although the Incas have a special language that they employ in speaking among themselves), I have so forgotten it that I cannot construe a sentence of as many as six or seven words which will convey my meaning, and I cannot remember many of the Indian terms necessary to name such and such an object. (79–80)

Garcilaso thus takes advantage of the narrative of a Spaniard among Amerindians to recount his own tale of exile from both fatherland and mother tongue. This corroborates his account for readers who, familiar with other descriptions of the return of captives, may not readily accept Ortiz's loss of his native language. "Esto he sacado por la experiencia del uso o descuido de las lenguas que las ajenas se aprenden con usarlas y las propias se olvidan no usándolas" (130) ["Thus I have found through experience that one learns the words of a strange language by using them, but that he likewise forgets those of his own language by failing to use them" (80)]. His recourse to autobiography allows him to assert his authority as an eyewitness. At the same time, the introduction of firsthand experience does not so much detract from Garcilaso's reshaping of the Ortiz tale into a delightful captivity narrative as add to its suspense: "Volviendo a Juan Ortiz, que lo dejamos en gran peligro de ser muerto por los que más deseaban verlo vivo" (130) ["But let us return to Juan Ortiz, whom we left in great danger of being destroyed by those who of all others desired to see him alive" (80)].

Like the captive, Garcilaso has been affected by the linguistic confusion that inevitably arises from intercultural contact. Prolonged absence from one's homeland—whether because of captivity or exile—means that the language in which one feels at home may have changed. Lee Dowling argues that Garcilaso offers a novel and personal guarantee of truth to his readers by affirming "his unique perception of events that derive[s] from his *own identity as a Mestizo.*" In fact, here Garcilaso uses not only his indigenous or mestizo origins but his distance from his native land and tongue to assure his narrative and historiographic authority. Garcilaso's bicultural and transatlantic experience both inflects and authorizes his representation of captivity.[24]

The identification of an American exile in Spain with a Spanish captive in the Americas relativizes the very categories of "home" and "abroad," "native" and "foreign." Furthermore, by identifying his situation with that of Juan Ortiz, Garcilaso subtly transplants the site of intercultural contact and conflict from the borders to the center of the Spanish Empire (as he does, as well, with the tale of Floridians in Spain at the end of the book). Spain had long since adopted a policy of excluding cultural and religious "others" from within its borders: Jews had been forced to leave Spain or convert to Christianity since 1492, and although the definitive expulsion of the Moriscos would not occur until 1609, Garcilaso himself had participated in the suppression of the Alpujarras uprising in 1570. Garcilaso reminds Spanish readers that bicultural subjects like him cannot be safely relegated beyond the boundaries of a monocultural empire but continue to exist in their midst. Yet Garcilaso does not unequivocally celebrate his "voyage in" from the colony to the metropolis, in Edward W. Said's terminology. Like the hostile Floridians who confront Gonzalo Silvestre, Garcilaso also recognizes the loss incurred by his passage to Spain.[25]

Garcilaso's stance toward his native language in this passage differs significantly from his usual claim to superior knowledge of Quechua, as exemplified in the "Advertencias acerca de la lengua general de los indios del Perú" preceding his later work, *Comentarios reales*. His position seems less

24. Dowling, *"La Florida del Inca,"* in Galloway, ed., *Soto Expedition,* 124.

25. On Garcilaso's participation in the suppression of the Alpujarras rebellion, see Chapter 1, note 52, above. Edward W. Said describes the "voyage in" of twentieth-century colonial intellectuals and authors as a "conscious effort to enter into the discourse of Europe and the West, to mix with it, transform it, to make it acknowledge marginalized or suppressed or forgotten histories"; see his *Culture and Imperialism* (New York, 1993), 216.

of a contradiction when he points out that the captive's or exile's native language, although capable of being lost, is not irrecoverable. "Es verdad que, si oyese hablar a un inca, lo entendería todo lo que dijese y, si oyese los vocablos olvidados, diría lo que significan" (129) ["It is true that I would understand all that were said should I hear an Inca speak, since I would remember the meaning of forgotten words" (80)]. If lack of use results in the loss of one's native tongue, then the opposite must also be true: recovery of a language is possible through its practice. In this sense, exile does not merely provoke loss since it can also prompt the need to recapture cultural and linguistic memory and thus inspire creativity. Certainly Garcilaso's desire to use and write about his native language and culture increased as time elapsed since his departure from Peru.[26]

Similarly, according to Garcilaso, Juan Ortiz's loss of fluency in Spanish is far from permanent. Even if he has difficulty speaking Spanish, he can understand it immediately. The very next day, he is able to relate a compelling account, presumably in Spanish, about his years of captivity and his knowledge of the land: "Amplió la relación que de su vida hemos dado y de nuevo relató otros muchos tormentos que había pasado, que causaron compasión a los oyentes" (132–133) ["[He] enlarged upon the story we have given of his life, telling of many more tortures he had endured, all of which

26. In the "Advertencias acerca de la lengua general de los indios del Perú," Garcilaso affirms his role as preserver of Quechua even in Spain, in marked contrast to his acknowledgment of linguistic loss in *La Florida:* "Yo harto hago en señalarles con el dedo desde España los principios de su lengua para que la sustenten en su pureza, que cierto es lástima que se pierda o corrompa, siendo una lengua tan galana" [I do enough in pointing out from Spain the principles of the language so that it can be maintained in its purity, for it surely would be a shame if it were lost or corrupted, being such an elegant language]; see *Comentarios reales,* ed. Quesada, I, 8. See Manuel Burga, "El Inca Garcilaso de la Vega: Exilio interior, ambigüedad y segunda utopía," in Burga, *Nacimiento de una utopía: Muerte y resurrección de los Incas* (Lima, 1988), 271–309, on Garcilaso's literary progression toward topics "closer to home": from a translation of a philosophical work from Italian into Spanish, to the history of an expedition to Florida based on information provided by others, to his final volumes dedicated to the history of his homeland both before and after the Spanish conquest, in which he offers his own experience and that of his family as testimony. Garcilaso's work elicits a similar question to the one posed by Suleiman in the introduction to her *Exile and Creativity: Signposts, Travelers, Outsiders, Backward Glances* (Durham, N.C., 1998), 1–6: "Is this distance (from one's native tongue) a falling away from some original wholeness and source of creativity, or is it on the contrary a spur to creativity?" (2)

moved his listeners to pity" (84)]. Ortiz is again successful at provoking the compassion of his listeners, this time his Spanish compatriots. Whereas Ortiz recovers his native language through listening and speaking in the presence of Spaniards, Garcilaso, who also would never return to his homeland, does so through reading and writing. He preserves and demonstrates his knowledge of the Inca language and culture not only through his own literary work but through correspondence with friends and family in Peru.

Although far from permanent, Ortiz's loss of his native language is still the element that most distinguishes Garcilaso's version of his tale from other captivity narratives, including other accounts of the Soto expedition. The mestizo author recognizes that languages and cultures cannot just be added together or superimposed without some surplus or loss, and he hardly propounds captivity or exile—involuntary absence from one's native culture and language and immersion into another—as a way to harmoniously synthesize differences or resolve intercultural tensions. Captives and exiles can assuage that tension by using their bicultural knowledge to mediate between disparate groups, but they cannot make it disappear. Rather than effacing conflict, their existence contributes to the confusion of categories, and categories cannot be violated without leaving behind some evidence of violence.[27]

MEDIATING EX-CAPTIVES

The Ortiz tale is an example of how Garcilaso, describing intercultural tension on American soil, transmits it to his European readers as well. The principal objective of framing the episode within European literary models of captivity may be to reduce the "otherness" of Amerindians for European readers. However, there is also a parallel defamiliarization of the captive figure and the trope of captivity itself. Whereas peninsular Byzantine novels such as Lope de Vega's *El peregrino en su patria* and Cervantes's *Persiles y*

27. For other critical readings emphasizing the tensions and conflicts, rather than harmonious synthesis, in Garcilaso's work, see note 7, above. Francisco A. Ortega also points out the nonproductive, noncommunicative dimensions of Garcilaso's writing in his trauma-centered reading of the *Comentarios reales* and *Historia general del Perú,* concluding that Garcilaso offers "a sober reminder of the profound complexities that exist at the heart of inter-cultural communication: accession to multiple worlds does not always mean finding a place of rest and comfort" (Ortega, "Trauma and Narrative in Early Modernity: Garcilaso's *Comentarios reales* [1609–1616]," *MLN,* LXVIII [2003], 393–426, esp. 421).

Sigismunda present captivity as a test of religious faith or amorous faithfulness, Garcilaso attributes no spiritual or moral significance to Juan Ortiz's captivity. If the nobility and virtue of anyone's character is proved, it is that of Mucozo. Juan Ortiz is neither more nor less Christian when he reenters Spanish society, and Garcilaso feels no need to present captivity as a means to induce Ortiz's penitence or purification, an allegorization common to captivity narratives from Heliodorus to Cabeza de Vaca to Mary Rowlandson. Ortiz's transformation is, not metaphorized or interiorized, but physically, culturally, and linguistically visible. Accordingly, Ortiz does not praise God for his return to Spanish society, and he only gradually readopts a Spanish style of dress.[28]

Ortiz's captivity, then, does not represent a trial to be passively endured in order to demonstrate the strength of his Spanish and Christian identity and prove his resistance to the captors' power. Ortiz's value to both groups lies in the extent of his transculturation—his bilingualism and familiarity with a foreign culture, without losing all ties to his own—rather than in his imperviousness to assimilation. Garcilaso eulogizes "the faithful interpreter" Juan Ortiz thus: "En todo aquel descubrimiento no había servido menos con sus fuerzas y esfuerzo que con su lengua, porque fue muy buen soldado y de mucho provecho, en todas ocasiones" (496) ["Throughout the entire exploration he had served no less with his forces and strength than with his tongue, for he was an excellent soldier and of much help on all occasions" (533)]. The strained rectification of Ortiz's portrait merely confirms that the previous narrative has emphasized the captive's role as a knowledgeable interpreter rather than as a soldier who depends on brute strength. In legitimizing the role of the captive interpreter, Garcilaso redefines the source of power as linguistic and cultural information rather than force. Captivity and exile can be an empowering, rather than a humbling, experience.[29]

28. Dowling argues that the reduction of Amerindian "otherness" is "Garcilaso's primary intention in *La Florida*"; see "*La Florida del Inca*," in Galloway, ed., *Soto Expedition*, 117. On the Christianization and allegorization of Spanish Byzantine novels like Lope de Vega's *Peregrino en su patria*, see Javier González Rovira, *La novela bizantina de la edad de oro* (Madrid, 1996), 158. On the spiritual interpretation of Puritan captivity narratives, see Richard Slotkin, *Regeneration through Violence: The Mythology of the American Frontier, 1600–1860* (Middletown, Conn., 1973), 94–145. On Juan Ortiz's gradual readoption of European clothing, see Garcilaso, *La Florida*, ed. Hilton, 131; [Garcilaso], *The Florida*, ed. and trans. Varner and Varner, 81.

29. The importance of Ortiz's service as an interpreter is confirmed by all of the accounts of the Soto expedition. Soto himself acknowledges Ortiz's value in his letter

Before comparing the Ortiz tale to other instances of captivity and exile, we must note the captive's role in the conclusion of the episode and in the rest of *La Florida.* Just as Garcilaso enlarges the frame of the Ortiz captivity tale by initiating it with Hirrihigua's violent response to Narváez's cruelty, he also stretches the lighthearted and egalitarian mood resulting from Mucozo's treatment of Ortiz through several chapters. Chapter 7 relates the warm welcome given to the ex-captive, followed by Soto's reception of Mucozo. Ortiz serves as an interpreter in the formal exchange of gratitude, deference, and promises of service between the Floridian and the Spanish leaders, which once again highlights their parity. Mucozo's conformity to Spanish ideals of nobility and generosity motivates the Spaniards to admire and reciprocate his virtuous behavior: "El adelantado Hernando de Soto y el teniente general Vasco Porcallo de Figueroa y otros caballeros particulares aficionados de la discreción y virtud del cacique Mucozo se movieron a corresponderle en lo que de su parte, en agradecimiento de tanta bondad, pudiesen premiar" (134) ["The Adelantado Hernando de Soto, the Lieutenant General Vasco Porcallo de Figueroa, and other individual cavaliers and admirers of the eloquence and virtue of the chieftain were moved by their appreciation of such goodness to make a suitable return with whatever each on his part was able to award" (85)].

---

to officials in Cuba: "This interpreter puts a new life into us, in affording the means of our understanding these people, for without him I know not what would become of us"; see Bourne, ed., *Narratives of the Career,* trans. Smith, II, 162. Ortiz reappears as an interpreter and close adviser to Soto most frequently in the accounts of Garcilaso and the Fidalgo d'Elvas (not surprisingly, since these are the longest narratives). His death is duly noted as a great loss by many of these sources, the Fidalgo d'Elvas's being perhaps the most eloquent on the difficulty of proceeding without Ortiz: "Foi tão grande inconviniente para o prepósito de descobrir ou querer sair da terra falecer Joam Ortiz que pera saber dos índios o que elle em quatro palavras declarava, com o moço havia mistér todo o dia: e as mais das vezes entendia ao revés o que se perguntava: por donde muitas vezes acontecia o caminho que um dia andavam e as vezes dous e tres tornarem atrás e andarem por esses matos perdidos de uma parte pera outra" ["The death was so great a hindrance to our going, whether on discovery or out of the country, that to learn of the Indians what would have been rendered in four words, it became necessary now to have the whole day; and oftener than otherwise the very opposite was understood of what was asked; so that many times it happened the road that we travelled one day, or sometimes two or three days, would have to be returned over, wandering up and down, lost in thickets"]; see Fidalgo d'Elvas, *Relaçam verdadeira,* cxx; Bourne, ed., *Narratives of the Career,* I, 147.

The motif of reciprocity, so dear to the *El Abencerraje* paradigm of genteel captivity, comes into play here and in several other passages involving Ortiz and Mucozo. The next chapter uses a comical scenario to reinvoke the Floridians' legitimate fears of unmediated hostility by Spaniards: Mucozo's mother comes to the camp, "muy ansiosa y fatigada de que su hijo estuviese en poder de los castellanos" (134) ["very uneasy and troubled that her son should be in the power of the Castilians" (86)] and worried that Soto will do to her son what Pánfilo de Narváez did to Hirrihigua. Governor Soto assures her that, because of Mucozo's benevolence toward Juan Ortiz, neither she nor her son deserve any mistreatment. The mother also recommends reciprocal treatment but understands it differently: "A la partida dijo a Juan Ortiz que librase a su hijo de aquel capitán y de sus soldados como su hijo lo había librado a él de Hirrihigua y de sus vasallos" (135) ["On parting [she] told Juan Ortiz that he should liberate Mucozo from that captain and his soldiers just as Mucozo had liberated him from Hirrihigua and his vassals" (87)]. The mother's anxiety is highly amusing to the Spaniards and her son, but her mention of past violence casts a shadow on the festivities—if not for the participants, then for the readers who know the fate of Hirrihigua's mother and so many other Amerindians at the hands of Soto and his men. In the end, mutual respect and reciprocal kindness are merely a glimpse of what could have been.

As if to negate the specter of violence, Garcilaso returns in the following chapter to two more tales of happy captivity and mutual benevolence, neither of which is mentioned in other sources. The first, that of Pedro Grajales, is a miniature reproduction of Juan Ortiz's captivity with Mucozo, but his captor, unexpectedly, is none other than Hirrihigua. The Amerindians capture Grajales in a surprise attack without bloodshed, then regale him with food and assurances that they will not mistreat him as they had Juan Ortiz. The Spaniards soon recover him and themselves capture several Floridian women and children, but even in this short time Grajales has become nearly unrecognizable as a Spaniard: "Apenas le conocieron los castellanos, porque, aunque el tiempo de su prisión había sido breve, ya los indios le habían desnudado y puéstole no más de con unos pañetes, como ellos traen" (138) ["The Spaniards for their part hardly recognized their comrade since in the brief time he had been captured, the Indians removed his clothes and dressed him in some loin cloths such as they themselves wear" (91)]. Once again, the ex-captive is able to mediate between previously hostile Spaniards and Amerindians by telling of his captors' goodwill. In order to reciprocate

Hirrihigua's benevolence, Soto releases the women and children he had captured;

> y les dijo que les agradecía mucho el buen tratamiento que a aquel español habían hecho y las buenas palabras que le habían dicho, en recompensa de lo cual les daba libertad para que se fuesen a sus casas y les encargaba que de allí en adelante no huyesen de los castellanos ni les hubiesen temor, sino que tratasen y contratasen con ellos *como si todos fueran de una misma nación,* que él no había ido allí a maltratar naturales de la tierra, sino a tenerlos por amigos y hermanos. (139, emphasis added)

> then he expressed his gratitude for the good treatment and the gracious words they had extended his countryman; and in recompense for their kindness, he gave them permission to go to their homes. He charged them, however, that from that time forward not to flee or fear the Castilians, but to deal and traffic with them *as if all were of the same nation;* for, he said, he had not come to their land to mistreat the natives but to make friends and brothers of them. (91–92, emphasis added)

Soto here voices Garcilaso's dream of pacific integration between Amerindians and Spaniards who treat and respect one another as equals—friends, brothers, compatriots. When Soto reencounters Mucozo a few chapters later, Garcilaso again indulges in a moving declaration of mutual affection and respect between the two leaders, in a dialogue reminiscent of the exchange of courtly missives between Abindarráez, Narváez, and the king of Granada at the end of *El Abencerraje.*[30]

In the second, brief mention of captivity in this chapter, Garcilaso shows how the Floridians are capable of treating their prisoners so fairly that they hardly seem like captives at all. Two Spaniards, the mariner Hernando Vintimilla and the page Diego Muñoz, are quickly able to return to Spanish society, despite—and perhaps because of—their acceptance into Amerindian society: "No los mataron ni les dieron la mala vida que habían dado a Juan Ortiz, antes los dejaron andar *libremente como a cualquier indio de ellos,* de tal manera que pudieron después estos dos cristianos, con buena maña que para ello tuvieron, escaparse de poder de los indios" (139, emphasis added) ["They did not kill these men or even maltreat them as they had done Juan

30. López Estrada, ed., *El Abencerraje,* 147.

Ortiz. On the contrary, they permitted them to go about *as freely as any one of themselves,* and in consequence both cunningly contrived to escape" (92, emphasis added)]. The cycle of captivity tales concludes by pointing out that it is possible to mollify even the fiercest of enemies, like Hirrihigua, through kind words and good works: "De manera que, con las buenas palabras que el gobernador envió a decir al cacique Hirrihigua y con las buenas obras que a sus vasallos hizo, le forzó que mitigase y apagase el fuego de la saña y rabia que contra los castellanos en su corazón tenía" (139) ["Thus it was that by sending friendly messages to Hirrihigua and by doing good deeds for his vassals, the Governor eventually forced that Cacique to mitigate and extinguish the fire of rage which he carried in his heart for the Castilians" (92)]. Even if Governor Soto is credited with cooling Hirrihigua's rage, Garcilaso has structured the episodes in such a way that Spanish treachery is responsible for the cacique's initial hostility. Amerindian benevolence interrupts the subsequent chain of violent actions, beginning, in its stead, a series of friendly encounters.[31]

31. Garcilaso revisits the episode of Muñoz and Vintimilla later in the text and reiterates his conclusions about Spanish culpability. He affirms that they were captured "más por culpa de los mismos españoles presos que por gana que los indios hubiesen tenido de hacerles mal" (251) ["more through their own fault than through any desire on the part of the natives to do them harm" (229)]. In the case of Diego Muñoz, Garcilaso blames the refusal of his adult companions to share the fish that they had caught using the Floridians' equipment. Their openly hostile attitude stands in blatant contrast to the Amerindians' gentle words and generosity: "Con buenas palabras, de ellas en español y de ellas en indio, [los indios] les dijeron: 'Amigos, amigos, gocemos todos del pescado.' Pedro López, que era hombre soberbio y rústico, les dijo: 'Andad para perros, que no hay para qué tener amistad con perros.' Diciendo esto, echó mano a su espada e hirió a un indio que se le había llegado cerca" (251) ["Twenty men addressed the Christians kindly, some speaking in Spanish and some in their own tongue. 'Friends, friends,' they said, 'let us all enjoy the fish.' Pedro López, who was a crude and arrogant individual, replied: 'Dog! We don't have to traffic with dogs.' With that he grasped his sword and wounded an Indian who had come near" (229–230)]. In response to such aggression, the Floridians kill López, gravely wound another Spaniard, and take the young Muñoz captive. Hernando Vintimilla, on the other hand, is captured because of his own verbal insolence toward natives who similarly request to share in the shellfish he has collected. Interestingly, the violence that Garcilaso emphasizes in each of these incidents is of a linguistic nature, a recurrent motif in *Comentarios reales* and *Historia general del Perú,* although usually presented through misinterpretation rather than verbal abuse.

Garcilaso thus favorably presents captivities in which fair treatment results in an amicable and respectful relationship between Spaniards and Amerindians. He is less approving of those who abandon their culture of origin to fully integrate into another society. Tales of Floridian equivalents to North American "White Indians" or Mediterranean renegades appear in the second half of *La Florida.* When Coza, another noble and well-spoken cacique, receives the Spanish expedition, his people regale the Spaniards to such an extant that "ningún encarecimiento basta a decir el amor y cuidado y diligencia con que les servían" (344) ["no exaggeration is sufficient to describe the affection, care and diligence with which these Indians ministered unto them" (344)]. Coza pleads with the Spaniards to stay and settle, asserting the superiority of his province, but Soto insists on continuing on to the coast. Such is the governor's "fin principal" ["principal purpose"]: "ir a este puerto para empezar a hacer su población" (346) ["to reach this port and begin a settlement" (346)].[32]

Although Garcilaso, as we will see, disapproves of Soto's decision to move on, he also disparagingly remarks on one participant's choice to stay. Garcilaso underscores this deserter's low status as well as the uncertainty of his religion and place of origin: "En el pueblo de Coza quedó huido un cristiano, si lo era, llamado Falco Herrado. No era español ni se sabía de cuál provincia fuese natural, hombre muy plebeyo, y así no se echó menos hasta que el ejército llegó a Talise" (346) ["One of the Christians (if he was a Christian), named Falco Herrado, deserted the army in the town of Coza. The native land of this man was not known, but he was not a Spaniard; and since he was a very plebeian person, he was not missed until the army arrived at Talise" (346–347)]. Herrado's name corroborates his lack of Spanish and Christian identity, suggesting as it does the facial branding of Moorish captives to indicate their slave status ("herrado") or his wayward, erroneous choice of residence ("errado"). Herrado's repudiation of Soto's attempt to recover him recalls the initial hostility of Hirrihigua and Fernando Vintimilla: "Muy desvergonzadamente envió a decir con los indios que fueron con los recaudos del gobernador que por no ver ante sus ojos cada día a su capitán . . .

32. Hernando de Soto's contract with Charles V clearly states that his commission is to colonize two hundred leagues of Florida; see Smith, ed., *Colección de varios documentos,* 141; Milanich, ed., *Soto Expedition,* 284–285. As we will see, Garcilaso emphasizes these obligations to criticize the expedition's failure to settle in Florida.

quería quedarse con los indios" (346) ["He very shamelessly sent Indians with messages to inform the Governor that rather than see before him each day the captain . . . he preferred to remain among the Indians" (347)]. As with Hirrihigua, however, Garcilaso also includes an explanation for this rejection, for Herrado claims that it is because of prior mistreatment by the captain, "que le había reñido y maltratado de palabra" (346) ["who had reprimanded and verbally insulted him" (347)]. And like Juan Ortiz, Herrado can expect very different treatment from Coza, who sends word to Soto that he will honor Herrado "exceedingly" rather than force him to return. What might have been an unhappy captivity among Spaniards becomes a pleasant one among Floridians.[33]

In the same village as Herrado, another non-Christian captive of Spaniards also stays behind, perhaps less voluntarily: "Quedó un negro enfermo que no podía caminar, llamado Robles, el cual era muy buen cristiano y buen esclavo. Quedó encomendado al cacique y él tomó a su cargo el regalarle y curarle con mucho amor y voluntad" (347) ["A sick Negro named Robles, who was a very fine Christian and a good slave, was left in this same town of Coza because he was unable to walk. He was entrusted to the Cacique, who undertook personally and with much love and willingness to restore him to health" (347)]. Both Herrado's and Robles's desertion of the expedition affords Garcilaso an opportunity to spotlight indigenous hospitality toward foreigners, whether Christian Spaniards or not. But Garcilaso also shows a way in which these individuals, despite their abandonment of Spanish society, can still serve an intermediary role. Garcilaso concludes the chapter by explaining his inclusion of these rather tangential episodes: "Hicimos caudal de estas menudencias para dar cuenta de ellas para que, cuando Dios Nuestro Señor sea servido que aquella tierra se conquiste y gane, se advierta a ver si quedó algún rastro o memoria de los que así se quedaron entre los naturales de este gran reino" (347) ["Now all these trifles we have considered worth-

33. The 1734 *Diccionario de autoridades* offers as one of the definitions of "herrar" "poner en la cara a los esclavos una nota o señal para que sean conocidos por tales, y cogidos en caso de hacer fuga. En España se hace con los Moros, y se les pone en la frente o en las mexillas una S y un clavo" [to put on the face of slaves a mark or sign so that they will be recognized as such, and caught in case of escape. In Spain it is done to the Moors, and they put on their forehead or on their cheeks an S and a nail] (S + *clavo,* nail = *esclavo,* slave); see *Diccionario de la lengua castellana, en que se explica el verdadero sentido de las voces, su naturaleza y calidad, con las phrases o modos de hablar, los proverbios o refranes, y otras cosas convenientes al uso de la lengua,* IV (Madrid, 1734), 147.

while to give in minute detail so that when Our Lord God may be served by the land's being conquered and won, someone may be reminded to ascertain if there is any trace or memory of those who stayed among the natives of that great kingdom" (347)]. Garcilaso suggests how deserters might one day contribute to Spanish colonization, even if only as a shared cross-cultural memory.

A similar potential role is ascribed to Diego de Guzmán, who later abandons the expedition. Unlike Herrado, Guzmán is identified as a noble and wealthy Sevillian who possesses a serious moral defect: gambling. He forfeits everything—horse, weapons, even clothing—in his "pasión y ceguera" ["passion and blindness"] for his vice, but the one stake he cannot bear to lose is his Amerindian lover. Instead of surrendering her, he escapes with the cacique's daughter and goes to live among her people. Garcilaso speculates that Guzmán's "passion," this time inspired by carnal desire, has once again blinded him: "Se supo que la india era hija del curaca y señor de aquella provincia Naguatex, moza de diez y ocho años y hermosa en extremo, las cuales cosas pudieron haberle cegado para que inconsideradamente negase a los suyos y se fuese a los extraños" (451) ["It was learned that the girl was a daughter of the Curaca and lord of the province of Naguatex, was extremely beautiful and was only eighteen years of age. These were circumstances which could have so blinded this man as to make him inconsiderately desert his own people and join the company of strangers" (477–478)]. Garcilaso's condemnation of Guzmán's actions confirms that he does not associate his own displacement from Peru with the Spaniard's self-exile, as he does with Juan Ortiz's experience.[34]

The Floridians now play mediator in a hostile dialogue between the renegade Guzmán and the Spaniards who hope to convince him to return. Garcilaso shows how the Spaniards blame the wrong party by threatening the Amerindians that, if he does not come back, they will all be killed. If a gentle-

34. José Juan Arrom reads this episode autobiographically, as a love story that exemplifies the synthesis of Garcilaso's mixed parentage and loyalties; see Arrom, "El Inca Garcilaso de la Vega o la crónica como investigación filosófica y comentario social," in Arrom, *Imaginación del Nuevo Mundo: Diez estudios sobre los inicios de la narrativa hispanoamericana* (Mexico, 1991), 137–160, esp. 149. However, the episode's focus is on the interaction of groups (the Spaniards' and Floridians' negotiations over Guzmán) rather than individual lovers. Garcilaso does not attempt to justify Guzmán's actions in the way that Bernal Díaz del Castillo does for Gonzalo Guerrero, the captive who chooses to stay in his adopted homeland because of his wife and children; see Díaz del Castillo, *Historia verdadera,* I, 130.

man like Guzmán does not return to "civilization," they can only assume that the natives have murdered him. The Amerindians suggest a way of verifying his identity and proving his existence, telling Soto, "Mande escribirle una carta y pídale que se venga o responda a ella, para que por su letra, pues nosotros no sabemos escribir, se vea cómo es vivo" (453) ["Have a letter written to him in which you request that he come in person or answer your communication, for by his handwriting, since we ourselves cannot write, it may be seen that he still lives" (479)]. The Floridians (or rather, Garcilaso) recognize reading and writing as the distinctive marks of European civilization, capable of not only identifying a person's provenance but asserting authority and substantiating the truth of the spoken word.

The Amerindian who takes the letter to Guzmán returns after three days "con la misma carta que había llevado, y en ella trajo el nombre de Diego de Guzmán escrito con carbón, que lo escribió para que viesen que era vivo, y no respondió otra palabra" (453) ["with the identical letter he had carried. Upon this letter, however, the Spaniard had scrawled his name in charcoal as evidence that he still lived. But that Christian answered not another word" (480)], a telling sign of his repudiation of Spanish society. Nevertheless, as an *hidalgo* of sound origin, Guzmán is even more deserving of redemption than Falco Herrado:

> Si quedando con la reputación y crédito con que entre los indios de Naguatex quedó, les hubiese después acá predicado la Fe Católica como debía a cristiano y a caballero, pudiéramos no solamente disculpar su mal hecho, empero loarlo grandemente, porque podíamos creer que hubiese hecho mucho fruto con su doctrina, según el crédito que generalmente los indios dan a los que con ellos lo tienen. (454)
>
> If continuing with the reputation and confidence with which he remained among the Indians of Naguatex, he afterward preached to them of the Catholic Faith, as ought a Christian and a cavalier, I not only could excuse his miserable behavior but could praise it highly; for according to the credence that the Indians generally give to those who hold with that faith, I could believe that he might have borne much fruit with this doctrine. (481)

If he were to use his position to propagate Christianity, Guzmán's abandonment of the expedition would not only be excused but lauded. He would be, like Garcilaso, a mediator working to make his own culture more familiar and more acceptable to others. Guzmán's and Herrado's rejection of European society and their resulting absence from the written record would consign their deeds to oblivion if Garcilaso's own narrative did not compensate for this lack. The parallel between Guzmán's evangelizing work in Florida and Garcilaso's labor of writing in Spain underscores the extent to which Garcilaso's praise of mediation contributes to imperial and religious expansion, not its subversion.[35]

EXILES FROM PARADISE

As *La Florida* progresses, we begin to see the connection between the loss of history and memory—which Garcilaso, after all, is attempting to remedy by writing this account of Soto's expedition—and the loss that results from the expedition itself. Garcilaso's employment of such terms as "fruto" ["fruit"] and "pérdida" ["loss"], evident in the passage cited above, turns increasingly insistent as the failure of the Soto expedition becomes more apparent. Garcilaso begins to foreshadow the conclusion at the end of book 3, just over halfway through *La Florida*. Here, he points out the futility of the Spaniards' expectations through an anecdote about an expeditioner named Juan Vego. Vego's horse is greatly coveted by his companions, who

> le ofrecieron muchas veces siete y ocho mil pesos por él para la primera fundición que hubiese, porque las esperanzas que nuestros castellanos a los principios y medios de su descubrimiento se prometían fueron tan ricas y magníficas como esto. Mas Juan Vego nunca quiso venderlo, y acertó en ello, porque no hubo fundición, sino muerte y pérdida de todos ellos, como la historia lo dirá. (399)

35. Garcilaso's treatment of tales of desertion differs significantly from the rather matter-of-fact narration of them that is found in the *Relaçam*. There, Guzmán's case is not presented as a coherent narrative at all: alluded to in chapter 31, only in chapter 35 do we encounter the anticlimactic account of Guzmán's fate: "Em Chaguete os índios por mandado do Cacique vieram de paz e disseram que o christão que alli ficara nam queria vir. O governador lhe escreveo e mandou tinta e papel pera que respondesse" (cxlix) ["To Chaguete, by command of the Cacique, the Indians came in peace, and said, that the Christian who had remained there would not come. The Governor wrote to him, sending ink and paper, that he might answer" (185)]. Although here the initiative to write is Soto's own—not the Amerindians' suggestion as in Garcilaso—Guzmán's response is similarly presented as a signature only, and Soto promptly gives up seeking his return.

> offered many times to give him seven and eight thousand pesos for it when they should receive their first division of spoils, for the prospects which our Castilians promised themselves in the initial and middle stages of the exploration were as rich and magnificent as this. But Juan Vego would never sell his horse, and he showed good judgment in not doing so, for there was to be no melting of metals, and instead only the death and loss of everyone, as our history will reveal. (410–411)

"Sad and lamentable" is how Garcilaso describes the day that the Spaniards finally decide to abandon the expedition, having lost their leader and nearly half the participants and having failed to find any mineral wealth or to fulfill any of the expeditions' goals as stated in the charter. Garcilaso complains that the Spaniards "desampararon y dejaron perdido el fruto de tantos trabajos como en aquella tierra habían pasado y el premio y galardón de tan grandes hazañas como habían hecho" (526) ["were abandoning the fruit of the numerous hardships they had experienced in that land, and were forfeiting the guerdon and reward for the magnificent and heroic deed they had accomplished" (570)]. The concluding pages reinvoke the motifs of fruit and loss, as Garcilaso offers the following explanation for the ultimate failure of the conquistadors' heroic deeds that he has extolled throughout the narrative: "Todo lo cual se consumió y perdió sin fruto alguno por dos causas: la primera, por la discordia que entre ellos nació, por lo cual no poblaron al principio, y la segunda, por la temprana muerte del gobernador" (579) ["All these things were consumed and lost fruitlessly for two reasons: first because of the dissension that sprang up among these Spaniards and prevented their settling in the beginning, and then because of the early death of the Governor" (634)].

Garcilaso's contemporaries concurred that the Soto expedition was a failure. Oviedo reproaches the Spaniards and Soto, in particular, even more severely than Garcilaso does. Oviedo's perspective is palpable in the questions that a "historian"—presumably Oviedo himself—poses to a participant on the expedition. Why did the governor and his army take so many slaves and beautiful young women from each province? Why did they detain caciques and principal men after these had given the Spaniards all they had? Why did they never stop to rest anywhere? In sum, "aquello ni era poblar ni conquistar, sino alterar e asolar la tierra e quitar a todos los naturales la libertad, e no convertir ni hacer a ningún indio cristiano ni amigo" ["such a course was, not settlement or conquest, but rather disturbing and ravaging the land and depriving the natives of their liberty without converting or making a single Indian either a Christian or a friend"]. The gentleman's lame responses provoke Oviedo's general condemnation of the expeditioners—"¡Oh gente perdida, oh diabólica cobdicia, oh mala conciencia!" ["Oh, wicked men! Oh, devilish greed! Oh, bad consciences!"]—but his critique quickly narrows to the flaws of their leader: "Oid, pues, letor, católico, y no lloréis menos los indios conquistados que a los cristianos conquistadores dellos, o matadores de sí y de esotros, y atended a los subcesos deste gobernador mal gobernado, instruido en la escuela de Pedrarias de Avila, en la disipación y asolación de los indios de Castilla del Oro" ["Give ear, then, Catholic reader, and do not lament the conquered Indians less than their Christian conquerors or slayers of themselves, as well as others, and follow the adventures of this governor, ill governed, taught in the school of Pedrarias de Avila, in the scattering and wasting of the Indians of Castilla del Oro"]. In contrast to Oviedo's pointed denunciations of Soto's abduction and enslavement of Amerindians, Garcilaso leaves the leader's reputation relatively unsullied by attributing the practice of captive-taking more generally to "los nuestros" (409) ["our men" (423)].[36]

Thus Garcilaso develops a different explanation for the failure of the expedition. Whereas Oviedo condemns Soto for insisting on continuing the expedition after men and resources are spent, Garcilaso praises Soto's resolve, which is challenged by attempts at mutiny and desertion. When he learns of rumors of another rebellion among his soldiers, Soto chastises them:

> ¿Qué es esto, soldados y capitanes? . . . ¿A qué deseáis volver a España? ¿Dejastes en ella algunos mayorazgos que ir a gozar? ¿A qué queréis ir a México? ¿A mostrar la vileza y poquedad de vuestros ánimos, que, pudiendo ser señores de un tan gran reino donde tantas y tan hermosas provincias habéis descubierto y hollado, hubiésedes tenido por mejor

36. See Oviedo, *Historia general y natural,* ed. Tudela Bueso, II, 172–173; Bourne, ed., *Narratives of the Career,* trans. Smith, II, 117–119. On Oviedo's vituperation of Soto throughout the narrative, see Martin Malcolm Elbl and Ivana Elbl, "The Gentleman of Elvas and His Publisher," in Galloway, ed., *Soto Expedition,* 45–97, esp. 57–61, 80–81, where they compare Oviedo / Ranjel to the Fidalgo d'Elvas extensively. In contrast to Oviedo, the Fidalgo d'Elvas rarely criticizes the actions of the governor and never appraises the expedition as a failure. Rabasa argues that Oviedo's "negative judgments of de Soto have more to do with a denunciation of de Soto's adventurism than with a 'humanization' of Oviedo's attitude toward Indians," pointing out that the writer elsewhere condones violence toward Amerindians in the service of colonization and evangelization; see *Writing Violence,* 190.

> (desamparándolas por vuestra pusilanimidad y cobardía) iros a posar a casa extraña y a comer a mesa ajena, pudiéndola tener propia para hospedar y hacer bien a otros muchos? ¿Qué honra os parece que os harán cuando tal hayan sabido? Habed vergüenza de vosotros mismos . . . y desengaños *[sic]*, que mientras yo viviese, nadie ha de salir de esta tierra, sino que la hemos de conquistar y poblar o morir todos en la demanda. (432–433)

> Soldiers and captains! What is this? . . . Why do you want to return to Spain? Did you leave family estates there to enjoy? Why do you want to go to Mexico? To disclose the baseness and littleness of your own souls? Possessed now of the power to become lords of such a great kingdom as this where you have discovered and trodden upon so many and such beautiful provinces, have you deemed it better (abandoning them through your pusillanimity and cowardice) to go and lodge in a strange house and eat at the table of another when you can have your own house and table with which to entertain many? What honor do you think they will pay you when they have learned as much? Be ashamed of yourselves. . . . And be undeceived, for as long as I live, no one is to leave this land before we have conquered and settled it or all died in the attempt. (451–452)

Soto does in fact "die in the attempt": Garcilaso narrates his death of fever, which occurred about two years after landing on the coast of Florida, and offers him an extensive eulogy. His wishes were indeed only respected as long as he lived, for as soon as he was dead, his men decided to forfeit the exploration and return to "civilization" in Mexico or Spain as soon as possible. Garcilaso does not refrain from condemning the decision, describing it as something that "después lloraron todos los días de su vida, como se suele llorar lo que sin prudencia ni consejo se determina y ejecuta" (476) ["they afterward lamented all the days of their lives, as those things customarily are lamented which are decided upon and executed without wisdom or counsel" (509)].[37]

37. After narrating Soto's death, Garcilaso eulogizes him—surely with some irony—as a "magnánimo y nunca vencido caballero, digno de grandes estados y señoríos e indigno de que su historia la escribiera un indio" (469) ["magnanimous and never conquered cavalier who was worthy of great titles and estates and undeserving that his history be written by an Indian" (499)]. Although he valorizes Álvar Núñez Cabeza de Vaca as a textual source, Garcilaso similarly chastises him for his

The discourse of loss and remorse continues until the arrival of the Spaniards in Mexico, where distance begins to transform their memories. The appalling condition of the Pánuco settlement at which the survivors arrive inspires unfavorable comparisons with the land they left behind: "notaron que todo cuanto en el pueblo habían visto no era más que un principio de poblar y cultivar miserablemente una tierra que con muchos quilates no era tan buena como la que ellos habían dejado y desamparado" (566) ["[they] realized that the whole of what they had seen in that town was no more than a start at settling and miserably cultivating a land which, with its many fine qualities, was inferior to the one they themselves had forsaken" (618)]. Garcilaso shows the Spaniards continuing to mourn "el bien que habían perdido" (567) ["the good they had lost" (619)] until they recall Soto's explicit warning (quoted above) and acknowledge its validity. What we witness, in fact, is the aggrandizement of lived experience through memory, a transformation that eventually leads to the telling of a fabulous tale to a Mexican audience. More disturbingly, the survivors' profound regret at leaving Florida leads them to violently turn on one another "con rabia y deseo de matarse" (567) ["with rabidness and a desire to kill" (620)]. Although released from their sufferings in Florida—which, as for Cabeza de Vaca, might have seemed like a captivity, an unwanted exile in a hostile foreign land—the survivors are captivated by their memories. Indeed, the overall movement that the Soto expedition inscribes is not that of "removal without return," which Ralph Bauer associates with narratives of conquest and the "centrifugal cultural

---

desire to return and not stay in the land where he had so much success: "Habiéndoles hecho Dios Nuestro Señor tanta merced que llegaron a hacer milagros en su nombre, con los cuales habían cobrado tanta reputación y crédito con los indios que les adoraban por dioses, no quisieron quedarse entre ellos, antes, en pudiendo, se salieron a toda prisa de aquella tierra y se vinieron a España a pretender nuevas gobernaciones, y, habiéndolas alcanzado, les sucedieron las cosas de manera que acabaron tristemente, como lo cuenta todo el mismo Alvar Núñez Cabeza de Vaca, el cual murió en Valladolid, habiendo venido preso del Río de la Plata, donde fue por gobernador" (77–78) ["Our Lord God was so merciful to the five who escaped that they succeeded in performing miracles in His name and thus gained such a reputation and esteem among the Indians that they were worshipped as deities. Nevertheless they did not want to remain in this land, and as soon as they were able to do so, [they] left very hastily and came to Spain to solicit new governorships. They succeeded in obtaining their desire, but many things occurred which were to bring them to a sad end, according to this same Alvar Núñez Cabeza de Vaca, who died in Valladolid after returning in chains from the Río de la Plata where he had gone as Governor" (12)].

dynamics initiated by European expansionism." Rather, the global structure of *La Florida* invokes the recursive movement of the captivity narrative: removal and return.[38]

As we know, however, captives do not return untransformed by their experience. Even if the Soto expedition survivors fail to recognize or appreciate their transformation, others do. The first sight of the survivors is described in a similar way to the return of captives. Even the Mexican natives' initial impression is that of amazement and nonrecognition: "El cacique se estuvo todo el día con los españoles . . . admirado de los ver tan negros, secos y rotos" (564) ["The Cacique remained through that day with the Spaniards . . . he was amazed at seeing them so lean, sunburned and broken" (616)]. Upon entry into the Spanish settlement at Pánuco, the expeditioners "no llevaban otros vestidos sino de gamuza y cueros de vaca, de pieles de osos y leones y de otras salvajinas, que más parecían fieras y brutos animales que hombres humanos" (565) ["were wearing no clothes save chamois and cowhide and the skins of bears, lions and other savage beasts. Indeed they appeared more like wild animals than human beings" (617)]. Like the fur-clad family of "Antonio el bárbaro" in *Persiles y Sigismunda,* or the *Comentarios reales'* furry castaway Pedro Serrano, the appearance of the survivors provokes as much amazement as their tale of misadventure and also confirms its truth. During their passage from Pánuco to Mexico, Amerindians and Spaniards alike come to marvel at the unusual crossbreeds: "Por los caminos salían a verlos así castellanos como indios en grandísimo concurso y se admiraban de ver españoles a pie, vestidos de pieles de animales y descalzos en piernas. . . . Espantábanse de verlos tan negros y desfigurados, y decían que bien mostraban en su aspecto los trabajos, hambre, miserias y persecuciones que habían padecido" (568) ["Along the roads a very great concourse of people, Castilians as well as Indians, thronged to see them; and the crowd were amazed to behold Spaniards afoot, bare-legged, and clothed in animal skins. . . . Moreover the onlookers were shocked at seeing our people so sunburned and haggard, and declared that they showed clearly in their appearance the labors, hunger, miseries and persecutions they had suffered" (621)].

The Fidalgo d'Elvas's *Relaçam* corroborates the transformed appearance of the survivors but insists on their being immediately provided with the appropriate Spanish attire in Pánuco and again in Mexico City; the concern

38. Ralph Bauer, "Imperial History, Captivity, and Creole Identity in Francisco Núñez de Pineda y Bascuñán's *Cautiverio feliz," Colonial Latin American Review,* VII (1998), 59–82, esp. 60–61.

for proper dress preoccupies both ordinary citizens and the viceroy alike. The gifts of Spanish clothing are presented as unusually significant acts of kindness: the inhabitants of Mexico City, for example, "com muita cortesia pedindo-lhe por mercê, cada um pera sua casa levava os com que se atrevia, e dava-lhe de vestir, cada um o milhor que podia: de maneira que o que menos vestido houve valia de xxx. cruzados acima" ["with great courtesy entreated for their companionship as favour, each one taking to his house as many as he dared, giving them for raiment all the best he could, the least well dressed wearing clothes worth thirty cruzados and upward"]. Garcilaso, by contrast, extols the survivors' own attire, however much it marks their transformation: "muy lindas y galanas pellejinas que, como hemos dicho, las había hermosísimas en la Florida" (566) ["very handsome and elegant furs (for as we have said the furs in Florida are magnificent)" (618–619)]. According to Garcilaso, the Mexico City elite more highly esteem the furs and skins disdained by the expeditioners than the pearls that they have brought from Florida:

> Mas cuando vieron las mantas de martas y de las otras pellejinas que los nuestros llevaron, las estimaron sobre todo, y . . . las hicieron lavar y limpiar porque eran en extremos buenas, y con ellas aforraban el mejor vestido que tenían y las sacaban a plaza por gala y presea muy rica. . . . Todo lo cual era para los nuestros causa de mayor desesperación, dolor y rabia, viendo que hombres tan principales y ricos hiciesen tanto caudal de lo que ellos habían menospreciado. (570–571)

> But when they beheld the robes of marten and other furs that our men were wearing, they prized them above everything else; and . . . they had them washed and cleaned, for they were extremely good. With them they lined their best clothing and then wore them in the plaza as a very rich adornment. . . . All of this was cause for great despair, pain and rage among our men—this realization that such rich and illustrious people placed so high a value upon what they themselves had scorned. (624)

The survivors' regret over abandoning Florida is exacerbated when others recognize, through their transformed appearance, the region's natural and cultural wealth.[39]

Indeed, Garcilaso's earlier discussion of Floridian dress suggests that the

39. Fidalgo d'Elvas, *Relaçam verdadeira,* clxxvi; Bourne, ed., *Narratives of the Career,* trans. Smith, I, 218.

furs are less a product of nature than an exquisite artifact: "En lugar de capa, traen mantas abrochadas . . . de martas finísimas que de suyo huelen a almizque. Hácenlas también de diversas pellejinas de animales . . . los cuales pellejos aderezan en todo extremo de perfección" (81) ["Instead of cloaks they have robes. . . . Some are made of very fine marten fur and smell of musk, whereas others are of . . . different small skins. . . . These skins they dress to the utmost perfection" (16)]. The furs function, not as a sign of savagery, but as one of a different civilization. The survivors' semblance to wild beasts surely stems less from their attire than from their contempt for signs of transculturation, as well as from their violent acknowledgment of loss, savagely manifested in "furor y saña," "rabia y deseo de matarse" (567) ["fury [and rage]," "rabidness and a desire to kill" (619–620)].[40]

THE FRUITS OF CAPTIVITY AND EXILE: WRITING AND MEDIATION

Like the tales of deserters Guzmán and Herrado, then, the expedition in general corresponds to Garcilaso's notion of an unproductive captivity: both the Spaniards' refusal to assimilate and Guzmán's and Herrado's abandonment of Spanish society fail to produce two different kinds of fruit. These scenarios neither create transculturated mediators, and thus the conditions for coexistence, nor do they allow for the exchange of knowledge and information, and thus the generation of accurate and authoritative historical records. Whereas Guzmán's story cannot be told because he gave up writing, according to Garcilaso the conquistadors' account can most truthfully be told only by a historian whose bicultural experience authorizes him to tell it. Although he may wish to present himself as Gonzalo Silvestre's passive amanuensis in order to privilege the participant's eyewitness authority, Garcilaso does not conceal his active, essential role in the production of the history: "No le ayudaban poco, para volver a la memoria los sucesos pasados, las muchas preguntas y repreguntas que yo sobre ellos y sobre las particularidades y

40. See also Garcilaso's admiring descriptions of the dress of indigenous nobles in *La Florida,* ed. Hilton, 343, 348; *The Florida,* ed. and trans. Varner and Varner, 343, 349. Garcilaso elsewhere condemns a similar rejection of Amerindian customs, when some sixty Spaniards die after refusing an indigenous cure for a mysterious illness; see *La Florida,* 407–408; *The Florida,* 422. On this scene, see Raquel Chang-Rodríguez, *Violencia y subversión en la prosa colonial hispanoamericana, siglos XVI y XVII* (Madrid, 1982), 39.

calidades de aquella tierra le hacía" (65) ["The many questions which I put to him repeatedly concerning the details and qualities of that land helped him no little to recall these facts to mind" (xxxix)].

The work of conquest can thus either bear fruit (texts, subjects) or induce loss (of memory, of identity), depending upon the type of intercultural relations that one pursues. For Garcilaso, the ideal relationship between Spaniards and Amerindians would include both mutual respect for cultural differences and indigenous submission to the authority of the Spanish Crown and Catholic Church. This relationship can be facilitated through the labor of interpreters and mediators. It comes as no surprise, then, that Garcilaso associates the work of conquest with the task of writing and that his self-aggrandizement extends to the equation of his own written work with Soto's "heroica empresa" (546) ["heroic undertaking" (594)]. Although he reports his desire to have participated in the expedition, he affirms that his service to the Crown lies in another "trabajo" [work/labor]: writing the history of Florida. For Garcilaso, the information that he provides in his narrative is as valuable as exploration, and writing involves as much mobility and sacrifice in the service of evangelization and imperial expansion: "Y esto baste para que se dé el crédito que se debe a quien . . . tomó el trabajo de escribir esta historia vagando de tierra en tierra con falta de salud y sobra de incomodidades, sólo por dar con ella relación de lo que hay descubierto, para que se aumente y extienda nuestra Santa Fe Católica y la corona de España" (580) ["But let it suffice that just the credit which is due be bestowed upon one who . . . has taken the trouble to write this history, wandering from land to land, sick and exceedingly weary, solely to report what has been discovered in that great kingdom in order that our Holy Catholic Faith and the Crown of Spain may be augmented and understood" (636)]. European-born historians and anthologizers of New World expeditions like Gonzalo Fernández de Oviedo and Richard Hakluyt also authorize their work by presenting it as the product of travel and travail, but Garcilaso relocates the site of suffering from the New World to Spain while also using his firsthand knowledge of indigenous culture to authenticate his account.[41]

41. On Oviedo's self-authorization through the trope of suffering, see Anthony Pagden, *European Encounters with the New World: From Renaissance to Romanticism* (New Haven, Conn., 1993), 66; on Hakluyt's, see Mary C. Fuller, *Voyages in Print: English Travel to America, 1576–1624* (Cambridge, 1995), 153–156. For an example of Richard Hakluyt's use of the rhetoric of travel and travail, see his *Principal Navigations, Voyages, Traffiques, and Discoveries of the English Nation Made by Sea*

In the end, Garcilaso rewrites the recursive movement of the captivity narrative by associating captivity with exile, with a displacement that entails the transformation of the subject and not merely the expectation of return to an original wholeness. Garcilaso transforms the captivity narrative by focusing on the transformation, linguistic and otherwise, of the captive/exile, which can be either productive and empowering (if the transculturated subject seeks to mediate between disparate cultures) or fruitless and disabling (if the subject refuses the role of intermediary). Like exile, however, even if an "unproductive captivity" results in loss, it also inspires the need to recover or re-create memory through interpretation and narration. Exile and captivity can thus create intercultural mediators as well as assure colonial society's need of them.

It is therefore curious to note Garcilaso's refusal to mediate for his Inca relatives in Peru, who had sent him a petition to present to the Council of the Indies requesting exemptions because of their royal lineage. Garcilaso excuses himself to his Inca relatives at the end of the *Historia general del Perú* for not completing this task, claiming, "No me ha sido más posible, por estar ocupado en escrivir esta historia, que espero no haber servido menos en ella a los españoles que ganaron aquel Imperio que a los Incas que lo poseyeron" [I have not been able to do it, because I have been occupied in writing this history, with which I hope to have not served less the Spaniards who won that empire than the Incas who possessed it]. Garcilaso might have understood writing the history of his dual ancestry to be a more productive service of mediation than recourse to the legal system, which in his case had proved to be ineffectual. Ironically, but appropriately for this conflictive mestizo writer, Garcilaso perhaps gained most attention on both sides of the Atlantic when his work was interpreted as advocating violence, to which the prohibition of his work at the time of the eighteenth-century Tupac Amaru rebellion can attest.[42]

Garcilaso himself surely did not naïvely assume the power of mediation to bring about the peaceful integration of opposites: the violent scene with which *La Florida* concludes reminds us that the ultimate consequence of the intercultural contact he describes is, not harmony, but discord. Whether or

or Over-land to the Remote and Farthest Distant Quarters of the Earth at Any Time within the Compasse of These 1600 Yeeres, 12 vols. (Glasgow, 1903–1905 [orig. publ. London, 1589]), I, xxxix–xl; I discuss this text in Chapter 5.

42. Garcilaso, *Historia general del Perú,* II, 857. On the Incas' petition and the prohibition of the *Comentarios reales,* see Varner, *El Inca,* 328, 356, 379–383.

not Garcilaso was fully aware of the implications of his attempt to confuse cultural categories and assert his conflictive identity, the insistent presence of confusion in his work suggests that the only way to promote coexistence is to acknowledge the violent sources of that confusion, not erase or ignore them. It is appropriate, then, to conclude by recalling the "unhappy captivities" that in fact outnumber the happy ones recounted in *La Florida*.[43]

According to Garcilaso, unhappy captivities—mainly of Amerindians among Spaniards—can be traced back to the earliest Spanish expeditions to Florida. Garcilaso affirms that the capture of slaves to work in the gold mines of Santo Domingo was the primary motive for the third expedition to Florida, led by Lucas Vázquez de Ayllón. Describing the 130 Floridians who board the Spanish ship under false pretenses and are taken into captivity, Garcilaso laments, "Se dejaron morir todos de tristeza y hambre, que no quisieron comer del coraje del engaño que debajo de amistad se les había hecho" (76) "[(They all) perished of sorrow and starvation, for being angry at the deception done them under the guise of friendship, they had refused to eat" (10)]. The caciques who later spurn Soto's offers of friendship recall such deceptions and cite the Spanish practice of taking captives as one of the most important reasons to wage war. Although the most vituperous condemnations of Spanish behavior occur in the speeches of caciques like Vitacucho, whom Garcilaso depicts as an unrepentant savage, some of the accusations resemble the author's own critiques of the expedition: "Para poblar y hacer asiento no se contentan de tierra alguna de cuantas ven y huellan, porque tienen por deleite andar vagamundos, manteniéndose del trabajo y sudor ajeno" (172) ["They are not content to colonize and establish a site on some of the land that they see and tread upon because they take great pleasure in being vagabonds and maintaining themselves by the labor and sweat of others" (134)]. In his account of the rebellion incited by Vita-

43. Cornejo Polar accurately describes Garcilaso's discourse as one of "impossible harmony," in which the mestizo author oscillates between declaring the essential unity of Inca and Spanish cultures and worldviews and insinuating their incommensurable distinctiveness; see Polar, "El discurso de la armonía imposible," *Revista de crítica literaria latinoamericana,* XIX (1993), 73–80. Elsewhere, Polar points out how the violent conclusion of *Historia general del Perú* accords with this "impossible harmony": "It is no accident, then, that the Garcilaso's work intentionally concludes not with an image of synthesis and plenitude, but with its inverse, the execution of the 'good prince' Túpac Amaru I." See his *Escribir en el aire: Ensayo sobre la heterogeneidad socio-cultural en las literaturas andinas* (Lima, 1994), 97.

cucho—in which slaves turn on their masters with burning wood, pots of boiling food, crockery, chairs, and tables—Garcilaso describes the natives' actions as "no menos crueles y espantables que dignos de risa" (198) ["no less cruel and frightful than they were ludicrous" (165)]. Yet the captives' valiant desperation and their extermination by armed Spaniards represent a striking indictment of Spanish enslavement of Amerindians, however much Garcilaso lays the blame for the tragic outcome on Vitacucho. After reading of the innumerable captives taken by Spaniards throughout the expedition, the fears of Mucozo's mother are no more "digno de risa" ["laughable"] than the captives' unsuccessful uprising.[44]

Indeed, no Floridian experiences the happy captivity among Spaniards that Juan Ortiz enjoyed with Mucozo. Captivity is almost unremittingly violent when the tables are turned, although Garcilaso does not follow Bartolomé de Las Casas's depiction of passive and meek Amerindian captives. Captives also rebel against their Spanish captors, whether as a group or individually, and their families and compatriots work to negotiate their return. And the murder of captive mediators can be devastating to the Spaniards, as well. In terms just as strong as his censure of don Luis (the cacique who kills the Jesuit missionaries), Garcilaso condemns the Spanish revenge on a captive guide who leads the expedition astray but ultimately confesses to the deception. Instead of accepting his repentance, the Spaniards allow him to be torn apart and eaten by their dogs, which leaves them with no guide at all: "Esta fue la venganza que nuestros castellanos tomaron del pobre indio que les había descaminado, como si ella fuera de alguna satisfacción para el trabajo pasado o remedio para el mal presente, y después de haberla hecho, vieron que no quedaban vengados, sino peor librados que antes estaban, porque totalmente les faltó quien los guiase . . . y así se hallaron del todo perdidos" (481) ["Such was the vengeance that our Castilians wrought upon the miserable Indian who had misled them, as if it were of some satisfaction

44. See also Quigualtanqui's challenge to the Spaniards (466, 496) and the promise of liberation to two female slaves made by Quigualtanqui and his allies' messengers: "Tened paciencia, hermanas, y alegraos con las nuevas que os damos, que muy presto os sacaremos del cautiverio en que estos ladrones vagamundos os tienen" (512) ["Be patient, sisters, and rejoice in the news that we bring you, for very soon we are going to release you from the captivity in which you are held by these wandering thieves" (553)]. However, the women immediately inform their masters of the natives' "treachery"; once again, the captives' mediation serves the Spanish imperial cause.

to them for their past hardship or some remedy for their present ill. And after having done so, they found that they still were still unavenged and in fact more entangled than they had been before, for now they were entirely without a guide. . . . Hence they were utterly lost" (515–516)].[45]

Although this episode demonstrates the indispensable knowledge of captive mediators, whatever their ethnic origin, Garcilaso's tale of another Amerindian captive highlights the advantage of variable and contradictory identifications. In book 4, chapter 15, Garcilaso relates how a boy taken from the fierce warrior tribe of Tula—the only one whom the Spaniards manage to retain in captivity—is ordered by his captors to participate in the children's mock battles, and he eagerly complies. Elected as captain of one group, he effectively frightens his adversaries until he is commanded to switch sides: "Luego mandaban los españoles que el muchacho tula se pasase a la parte vencida y pelease contra la vencedora. El lo hacía así, y con el mismo apellido los vencía, de manera que siempre salía victorioso" (443) ["Then the Spaniards commanded the boy to pass to the side of the conquered and fight against the conquerors. This he did, and again with the name of Tula was triumphant. Thus he always came out victorious" (466)]. The captive's flexibility reflects that of Garcilaso, who alternately positions himself on the side of the conquerors and the conquered, defending both groups' nobility, valor, and motivations. Garcilaso's strategy is equally victorious, successfully using the various positions from which he writes to authorize his history.

The Spanish cruelty toward Amerindian captives in *La Florida* contextualizes the concluding episode of the narrative, which in this light appears more an act of revenge than one of treachery. Don Luis might not have been forcibly removed from his homeland, but the episode reveals what the results

45. See Bartolomé de Las Casas, *Brevísima relación de la destruición de las Indias,* ed. André Saint-Lu (Madrid, 1996 [orig. publ. Seville, 1552]), 77; Las Casas, *A Short Account of the Destruction of the Indies,* ed. and trans. Nigel Griffin (London, 1992), 12–13, where Las Casas describes the Spanish enslavement of Amerindian captives as "la más dura, horrible y áspera servidumbre en que jamás hombres ni bestias pudieran ser puestas" ["the harshest and most iniquitous and brutal slavery that man has ever devised for his fellow-men, treating them, in fact, worse than animals"]. Las Casas similarly describes the "dreadful atrocities" perpetrated by the Soto expedition on "poor, harmless natives"; see *Brevísima relación,* 154; *Short Account,* 103. For examples of the agency of indigenous captives in recovering their freedom or that of their relatives, see Garcilaso, *La Florida,* ed. Hilton, 411–412, 443; [Garcilaso], *The Florida,* ed. and trans. Varner and Varner, 425–427, 465.

would be if one followed the path suggested by another Spanish ex-captive in Florida, Hernando de Escalante Fontaneda. Fontaneda was a near contemporary of Garcilaso, born in Cartagena de Indias, although he describes his parents as *encomenderos* who "sirvieron a su magestad en aquellas partes del Perú, y después en la ciudad de Cartagena" ["served His Majesty in those parts of Peru, and afterwards in the city of Carthagena"]. Like Garcilaso, he was on his way to be educated in Spain when he was shipwrecked on the coast of Florida in 1545. He was held captive there for seventeen years before he was rescued by Pedro Menéndez de Áviles, whom he served as an interpreter and guide, just as Juan Ortiz had done for Hernando de Soto. Fontaneda's experience appears to cross those of Garcilaso and Juan Ortiz, yet Fontaneda's proposed solution for the conquest and evangelization of Florida could not be further from Garcilaso's proposals in *La Florida del Inca*. Fontaneda concludes his memoir,

> Son grandes flecheros y traidores y tengo por muy cierto que jamás serán de paz ni menos cristianos. Yo lo firmaré de mi nombre por muy cosa cierta porque lo sé. Si no toman mi consejo será trabajo y peor que antes. Que los cojan a buena manera convidándoles la paz y metellos debajo de las cubiertas a maridos y mujeres, y repartillos por vasallos a las islas y aún en tierra firma por dineros, como algunos señores en España compran al Rey vasallos; y desta manera habría maña y amenguándolos.

> They are great bowmen, and very faithless. I hold it for certain they never will be at peace, and less will they become Christians. I will sign this assertion with my name as a very sure thing, for I know what I say. If my counsel be not heeded, there will be trouble, and matters be worse than they were beforetime. Let the Indians be taken in hand gently, inviting them to peace; then putting them under deck, husbands and wives together, sell them among the islands, and even upon Terra Firma for money, as some old nobles of Spain buy vassals of the king. In this way, there could be management of them, and their number become diminished.

Although some readers might have taken the concluding tale of don Luis in *La Florida* as evidence of the indigenous "faithlessness" described by Fontaneda, Garcilaso's use of the story, along with accounts of other captive Amerindians, reveals the limitations as well as the violence of a proposal like Fontaneda's. Despite or perhaps because of his own relocation to Spain, Garcilaso argues that the only productive means of evangelizing and colonizing Florida is through Spanish settlement, not the abduction and diaspora of Amerindians.[46]

Indigenous captives are more common in *La Florida del Inca* than in the books discussed in the following chapters, even if they all share a focus on the transformed and empowered captive-mediator. Garcilaso allows the unhappy captivities of Amerindians among Europeans to disrupt the portrait of either an idealized, peaceful reconciliation or a successful conquest. The captivity of Amerindians moves to the background in *Cautiverio feliz* and all but disappears from the narrative of victorious imperial expansion in *Caramuru*. The creole authors of both of these texts more closely resemble Fontaneda than Garcilaso, in their insistence on the instrumental knowledge gained through being captives, without a concomitant concern for the effects of being captors.

46. See Hernando de Escalante Fontaneda, *Memoir of D° d'Escalante Fontaneda respecting Florida,* trans. Buckingham Smith (1854) (Miami, 1944), 19, 21, 72, 74. This edition includes a transcription of the Spanish original (66–75), which I have modernized with respect to spelling, punctuation, and word division in my quotations. Escalante Fontaneda asserts, "No hay hombre que tanto sepa de aquella comarca como yo que lo sé que la presente escribo porque estuve cautivo entre ellos dende niño de trece años hasta que fui de treinta años" ["No one knows that country so well as I know it, who writes this; for I was a captive among its inhabitants, from a child the age of thirteen years until I was thirty years old"], and he complains that the services of knowledgeable interpreters like himself have not been adequately compensated (17, 70).

chapter three : THE CAPTIVE SUBJECT & THE CREOLE AUTHOR IN FRANCISCO NÚÑEZ DE PINEDA Y BASCUÑÁN'S *Cautiverio feliz y razón individual de las guerras dilatadas del reino de Chile*

CREOLE ALIENATION

Like Álvar Núñez Cabeza de Vaca, Miguel de Cervantes, el Inca Garcilaso de la Vega, and so many others who bore arms to serve their monarch, Francisco Núñez de Pineda y Bascuñán (1607–1680) spent much of his life petitioning authorities for compensation and rewards in light of his and his father's services to the Crown during the Araucanian wars in Chile. Although he was finally granted a privileged position as *corregidor* of the wealthy region of Moquegua at the ripe age of seventy-two, Pineda died before ever reaching it. As José Anadón writes in his biography of the Chilean soldier, "He died as a transient in distant lands." Pineda's adult career as a "transient" far from his homeland seeking financial assistance recalls Garcilaso's relocation to Spain. Yet whereas Garcilaso presents both exile and captivity as potentially productive experiences, for Pineda, being forced to leave his patria is a far worse fate than the captivity he endured as a young man among the Mapuche, or (as the Spaniards referred to them) Araucanian, Indians of southern Chile. As he laments in his *Cautiverio feliz y razón individual de las guerras dilatadas del reino de Chile:* "Al cabo de mis años y de más de treinta y cuatro de servicios personales, me obligó la necesidad a salir de mi patria, pidiendo limosna por ajenos distritos para sustentar a mis hijos y buscarles remedio" [At the end of my years, and after more than thirty-four years of personal service, necessity obliged me to leave my homeland, begging for alms in foreign regions in order to support and find help for my children].[1]

1. José Anadón, *Pineda y Bascuñán, defensor del araucano: Vida y escritos de un criollo chileno del siglo XVII* ([Santiago], 1977), 185 (Anadón includes a "Memorial de don Francisco de Pineda y Bascuñán al gobernador Francisco Laso de la Vega," dated May 23, 1639, as an appendix to the biography [223–225]); Francisco Núñez

In another passage, Pineda relates this displacement to that of an entire class of *beneméritos,* or creole descendants of conquistadors, whose positions and territories had been usurped by newly arrived Spaniards with enough wealth to purchase, rather than earn, them:

> Con que se quedan en la calle desnudos los pobres beneméritos, y sus hijos sin tener un pan que comer; con que unos huyendo y otros desterrados, salen a buscar remedio a tierras extrañas, dejando más de fuerza que de grado el amor de la patria y el deseo entrañable de asisitirla en sus mayores trabajos y defenderla en sus conflictos y penalidades. ¿Cómo puede de esta suerte conseguirse en Chille la paz que se desea? cómo no ha de ser la guerra inacabable? que este es el principal fundamento de esta historia, de adonde vamos sacando estas ajustadas consecuencias.

> And so the poor, well-deserving ones are naked on the street, and their children without bread to eat; and so some fleeing and others exiled, they go to seek relief in foreign lands, leaving more by force than willingly their love of patria and their deep desire to aid it in its greatest hardships and defend it in its conflicts and sufferings. How can the desired peace be attained in Chile in this way? How can the war not be unending? For this is the principle foundation of this history, from which I will be extracting these fitting consequences.

---

de Pineda y Bascuñán, *Cautiverio feliz y razón individual de las guerras dilatadas del reino de Chile,* [ed. Diego Barros Arana], Colección de historiadores de Chile, III (Santiago de Chile, 1863), 390. Throughout this chapter, I cite from this edition, which is still more widely available in U.S. libraries than the more recent critical edition, *Cautiverio feliz,* ed. Mario Ferreccio Podestá and Raïsa Kordić Riquelme ([Santiago de Chile], 2001). The only extant manuscript, in the Archivo Nacional de Santiago de Chile, bears the date 1673, which is visibly corrected from 1663; see Ferreccio Podestá and Kordić Riquelme on the textual history of the work, in prologue, ibid., I, 7–9. Nestor Meza Villalobos argues that Pineda's understanding of "patria" departs from earlier notions by widening from city to *reino* [kingdom]; see *La conciencia política chilena durante la monarquía* (Santiago de Chile, 1958), 106. Throughout the text, Pineda refers to his "patria chilena" [Chilean patria] and distinguishes "hijos de la patria" [children of the patria] from "forasteros" [foreigners], who come from the peninsula as well as other American colonies; see, for example, discurso 4, chap. 37, "En que se prueba que los forasteros y advenedizos son enemigos de la patria" [In Which It Is Shown That Foreigners and Newcomers Are Enemies of the Patria], in *Cautiverio feliz y razón individual,* [ed. Barros Arana], 421–427.

Here Pineda uses the adjectives *desnudo* [naked] and *desterrado* [exiled] to describe the predicament of creoles like himself in seventeenth-century colonial Chile. Significantly, he identifies these circumstances as a cause rather than a result of the "unending war." Such qualifications may seem more apropos of castaways or captives in the early years of conquest and exploration than of an experienced creole soldier in the late seventeenth century. Pineda does, in fact, occasionally use these terms to describe his condition during the seven months he spent among Araucanians, but they do not detract from his overall presentation of a happy captivity. Whereas in other captivity narratives nudity and displacement would signal the captive's sufferings in a foreign, barbaric culture, in *Cautiverio feliz* they describe the misfortune of an ex-captive who has been estranged by the corruption and disorder rampant in his presumably civilized homeland.[2]

Nevertheless, frustration with colonial Hispanic society does not lead Pineda to reject his Spanish identity: captivity, however happy, is still captivity. Instead of indicating a radical inversion of loyalties, the shifting implications of *desnudo* and *desterrado* in *Cautiverio feliz* reveal the instability of binary oppositions between Amerindian and Spaniard in the Chilean context. Although Araucanians successfully resisted Spanish domination until well into the nineteenth century, Chile was a frontier society of intermittent warfare more than an unrelenting battleground between Spaniards and Amerindians. Rather than a "defender of the Araucanian," as he is described in the title of a modern biography, Pineda is concerned with the defense of impoverished creoles like himself or like the retired soldier who "clamó al

2. Pineda y Bascuñán, *Cautiverio feliz y razón individual,* [ed. Barros Arana], 484. Álvar Núñez Cabeza de Vaca stresses his and the other shipwreck survivors' nudity as a sign of their absolute loss; see Cabeza de Vaca, *Naufragios y comentarios,* ed. Roberto Ferrando (Madrid, 1984), 72; Cabeza de Vaca, *Castaways,* ed. Enrique Pupo-Walker and trans. Frances M. López-Morillas (Berkeley, Calif., 1993), 41. On clothing as a symbol of power, authority, and civilization in Cabeza de Vaca's *Relación* and other colonial accounts, see Mariselle Meléndez, "La vestimenta como retórica del poder y símbolo de producción cultural en la América colonial: De Colón a *El lazarillo de ciegos caminantes,*" *Revista de estudios hispánicos,* XXIX (1995), 411–439, esp. 414. *Cautiverio feliz* destabilizes the usual association between clothing and civilized European identity and between nudity and indigenous barbarism that Meléndez identifies in colonial accounts: for example, Pineda notes the practical purposes of being forced to strip down as a captive, and the Araucanians show a great deal of interest in appropriating Spanish clothing for use in their own festivities; see Pineda y Bascuñán, *Cautiverio feliz y razón individual,* [ed. Barros Arana], 35, 103, 515.

cielo . . . porque tenía su sueldo quitado y se hallaba desnudo, sin tener con que cubrir sus carnes ni a sus hijos" [cried out to heaven in protest because his salary had been taken away, and he found himself naked, without anything to cover his flesh nor that of his children]. The soldier's story appears amid Pineda's complaint about the authorities' refusal to remedy his own financial losses following the 1655 Araucanian rebellion, incurred through aiding besieged Spaniards at the fort of Boroa. Pineda's reapplication of terms like *desnudo* and *desterrado* to a creole's plight in colonial society suggests the tenuous nature of boundaries and definitions, not a reversal of expected associations. Indeed, the categories of "conqueror" and "conquered" are hardly applicable to the volatile Chilean frontier, just as place of origin fails to distinguish the "civilized" from the "barbarians" for a generation of creoles growing up with a sincere attachment to their American homelands. Like the captivity tales of *La Florida, Cautiverio feliz* exposes these instabilities rather than presents an inverted relationship of power between Amerindian and Spaniard.[3]

Whereas el Inca Garcilaso discovers the resemblance between his position as a New World historian in Spain and that of a Spanish captive in Florida while transcribing a secondhand account, Francisco Núñez de Pineda y Bascuñán's own past comprises a tale of border crossing that allows him to interrogate categories and construct a mediating authorial identity. Pineda's autobiographical account of his seven-month captivity among the Mapuche in 1629 would resonate with his compatriots, for the persistence of hostilities between Spaniards and Araucanians made captivity as familiar a reality as it was in the Mediterranean. Yet Pineda recounts his captivity, not to render a

3. Pineda y Bascuñán, *Cautiverio feliz y razón individual,* [ed. Barros Arana], 244; Anadón, *Pineda y Bascuñán, defensor del araucano.* Anadón finds evidence of Stockholm syndrome—psychological identification with one's captor, named after a 1973 hostage situation—in the captivity narratives of Hans Staden and Mary Rowlandson as well as Pineda; see Anadón, *Historiografía literaria de América colonial* (Santiago de Chile, 1988), 145–171. Gilberto Triviños describes the efforts in recent Chilean historiography to debunk the epic-inspired myth of a permanent, uninterrupted war between Spaniards and Araucanians and to recognize instead the existence of "frontier contact" characterized by more than domination and resistance; see Triviños, *La polilla de la guerra en el reino de Chile* ([Santiago de Chile], 1994), 77. Similarly, Sergio Villalobos identifies three distinct periods in the Araucanian conflict, with the last and longest, 1662 to 1883, characterized by "frontier relations" rather than violent confrontation; see Villalobos, *La vida fronteriza en Chile* (Madrid, 1992), 226.

vivid picture of the bitter consequences of war, to incite or justify animosity; rather, he seeks to explain the reasons for the conflict's persistence and to suggest the means of its resolution to the successive Spanish sovereigns to whom he dedicated the work, Philip IV and Charles II. Pineda derives his authority to inform the king on these matters from firsthand experience and knowledge as a captive and a soldier as well as from the scholarly erudition that he displays as a writer. The captivity narrative is thus integrated in both intention and theme with the diverse historical, religious, moral, and political commentary that constitutes the bulk of the text.[4]

As many scholars have noted, Pineda's resuscitation of his experience as a captive some thirty-five years after the fact responds to the author's present, pressing needs and concerns. Don Antonio de Acuña y Cabrera, the corrupt and incompetent governor of Chile at the time, had recently scorned Pineda's informed advice regarding the possibility of an Araucanian uprising. The subsequent rebellion of 1655 represented a military disaster for the Spaniards and cost Pineda both his home and fortune. Pineda links his personal frustration with the disrespect and financial loss that he has incurred (despite loyal service to his patria) to that of other disenfranchised creoles. Like Garcilaso, Pineda criticizes many of the Spanish policies and practices of imperial expansion and proposes an alternative model, which he argues would not only be more just toward himself and his fellow creoles but would benefit all parties involved by bringing the war to a close. Garcilaso and Pineda also coincide in their need to establish credibility as American-born writers within a Spanish tradition, and they do so in part by identifying themselves with the captives whose stories they relate. Pineda's critique, of course, is tied to the affirmation of his own qualities and contributions to the colonial system as a creole, an American of Spanish descent, rather than

4. Originally dedicated to Philip IV when a draft of the text was completed in 1663, the title page was visibly altered to consign the name of Charles II in 1673; see Ferreccio Podestá and Kordić Riquelme, prologue, in Pineda y Bascuñán, *Cautiverio feliz,* ed. Ferreccio Podestá and Kordić Riquelme, I, 7–10, esp. 7. Stuart B. Schwartz and Frank Salomon assert that, owing to prolonged warfare in Chile and later in the La Plata River basin, the Araucanian frontier is the only area in South America where Spanish captives came to constitute "an institutionalized category with a distinctive role"; see Schwartz and Salomon, "New Peoples and New Kinds of People: Adaptation, Readjustment, and Ethnogenesis in South American Indigenous Societies (Colonial Era)," in Salomon and Schwartz, eds., *The Cambridge History of the Native Peoples of the Americas,* III, *South America,* part 2 (Cambridge, 1999), 443–501, esp. 473.

as a mestizo who can claim a double heritage as his own. Pineda's roots in American soil rather than bloodlines mean that physical location and intellectual adeptness are more important than linguistic or racial difference in his construction of creole identity.[5]

As noted earlier, Garcilaso's praise of mediation—whether through captive interpreters or monotheistic Inca rulers—is undermined by his recognition of the violence of cultural imposition and the irreconcilability of differences. Pineda, on the other hand, starts by acknowledging certain borders delimiting Amerindian and Spanish culture, such as religious faith. He associates the violence of Chilean society not with the presence but with the lack of such exemplary Christians as he portrays himself to be during his captivity. Cultural differences would thus appear to be reconcilable through the universal practice of Christianity. However, Pineda's interest in redrawing boundaries to accommodate the figure of the creole forces him to rely on inversions and ambiguities that, as in the case of the terms *desnudo* and *desterrado,* collapse oppositions and lose their ability to designate cultural difference. Pineda's willingness to participate in and adopt certain Araucanian customs further destabilizes cultural borders and suggests that his success as a mediator and ultimately his authority depend on a limited degree of transculturation. Although both authors conceive of their work as a service to the imperial enterprise, they also reject conventional categories in their construction of a paradigm that befits a newly developing, albeit unpredictable and contradictory, sense of belonging.

5. Sergio Correa Bello, *El "Cautiverio feliz" en la vida política chilena del siglo XVII* (Santiago de Chile, 1965), and Ralph Bauer, *The Cultural Geography of Colonial American Literatures: Empire, Travel, Modernity* (Cambridge, 2003), 118–156, also analyze Pineda's work within the political and social context of the 1655 rebellion and its aftermath. Pineda complains of the financial damages he incurred during the siege of the fort of Boroa, where he was commander and owned property; not only had he not been present at the time of the siege because of a misguided order of the governor, but his resources had been depleted by the beleaguered Spaniards at the fort. Pineda complains that his request for reimbursement, although eventually granted, had been held up for more than a year, to his great inconvenience; see Pineda y Bascuñán, *Cautiverio feliz y razón individual,* [ed. Barros Arana], 241–243. On Acuña y Cabrera's weak regime (1650–1656), which encouraged slave raiding among Indians for his own family's profit—a practice that provoked the rebellion of 1655—see Eugene H. Korth, *Spanish Policy in Colonial Chile: The Struggle for Social Justice, 1535–1700* (Stanford, Calif., 1968), 177–187; Francisco A. Encina, *Historia de Chile* (Santiago de Chile, 1944), III, 235–259.

Pineda's ambivalent approach, like that of Garcilaso, has often been subjected to readings that focus on identifying his ultimate loyalties or his "hidden purpose." Yet Pineda's motives actually encompass the defense both of Araucanian virtue and of Spanish and Christian rule, since the affirmation of his authority in colonial society as well as literary history relies on providing a positive but accurate portrait of both groups with which he can claim intimate knowledge. Pineda's presentation of Spaniards and Amerindians is thus tempered by a familiarity that recognizes weaknesses as well as strengths and lays the blame for the "prolonged wars of Chile" on both groups as necessary. Pineda aspires to use this information to mediate and thus bring about an end to the hostilities. Nevertheless, for him, the end of the wars implies Araucanian acceptance of Spanish rule and Christianity. In his portrayal of the success of his mediation, the inevitably violent results of such an acceptance are less evident than they are in Garcilaso, although they are still present.[6]

6. On a "hidden purpose" in Pineda's work, see Yuzhuo Qiu, "El propósito enmascarado: Piñeda y Bascuñan y el *Cautiverio feliz,*" *Mester,* XXIII (1994), 101–111, esp. 108. For other readings that emphasize Pineda's use of the captivity narrative to underscore his knowledge, authority, and identity as a creole, see Raquel Chang-Rodríguez, *Violencia y subversión en la prosa colonial hispanoamericana, siglos XVI y XVII* (Madrid, 1982), 63–83; Carmen de Mora Valcárcel, *Escritura e identidad criollas: Modalidades discursivas en la prosa hispanoamericana del siglo XVII* (Amsterdam, 2001), 183–321; Bauer, *Cultural Geography of Colonial American Literatures,* 118–156, which is an elaboration of two earlier articles: "Creole Identities in Colonial Space: The Narratives of Mary White Rowlandson and Francisco Núñez de Pineda y Bascuñán," *American Literature,* LXIX (1997), 665–695; "Imperial History, Captivity, and Creole Identity in Francisco Núñez de Pineda y Bascuñán's *Cautiverio feliz,*" *Colonial Latin American Review,* VII (1998), 59–82. In *La polilla de la guerra en el reino de Chile,* 83–140, Triviños offers an overview and analysis of several tales of captives that appear in colonial documents and historical works, and in "'No os olvidéis de nosotros': Martirio y fineza en el *Cautiverio feliz,*" *Acta literaria,* XXV (2000), 81–100, Triviños identifies two types of captivity narratives in colonial Chile: "narratives of the (literal or symbolic) crucifixion of captives" and "narratives of 'barbarian kindness,'" 81–82. In the latter category, he includes Pineda's *Cautiverio feliz* and Diego de Rosales's *Historia general del reino de Chile,* which adheres to the former text quite closely in the account of Pineda's captivity given in book 7, chap. 11; see Rosales, *Historia general del reino de Chile, Flandes indiano,* ed. Mario Góngora, 2d ed. (Santiago de Chile, 1989 [orig. publ. Valparaíso, 1877–1878]), II, 1038–1042.

As a book-length autobiographical captivity narrative, *Cautiverio feliz* is unique in Chilean literary history, but many poetic and historiographic texts interpolate episodes of captivity—Spaniards among Araucanians as well as vice versa—in their narratives. Seventeenth-century Chilean readers would be familiar with representations of captivity according to the two models—abject and idealized—that we have encountered in peninsular literature and historiography. As in Spanish texts concerning the Muslim/Turkish conflict, ostensibly true accounts of unhappy captivities occasionally served, in Chile, to vilify the Spaniards' cultural and religious "others" and to corroborate the superiority of Christian culture and values. Alonso de Ovalle (1601–1651), a Jesuit historian and contemporary of Pineda, dedicates several chapters of his *Historica relacion del reyno de Chile* (1646) to the deplorable experiences of captives, many of whom had spent more than forty years in "cruel and miserable captivity" before returning to Spanish society upon the signing of a peace treaty in 1641. He paints a particularly vivid portrait of the plight of female captives, whose "miserias, y desdichas . . . [eran] tan desmedidas, y improporcionadas a los mesmos hombres, quanto más a la delicadeza de las mujeres, que no se podían oir sin lágrimas" [miseries and misfortunes . . . were so excessive and disproportionate even for men, and much more so for delicate women, that they could not be heard without tears]. Besides the excessive labor that they are forced to perform, one of the greatest cruelties that the Araucanians inflict on their female captives, according to Ovalle, is to dress them "como Indias" [like Indian women]. In fact, some captives even hide from their would-be redeemers because "es tal la verguença, y confusión, que tienen, particularmente las mujeres cautivas, de verse en tan vil traje delante de los Españoles" [the shame and confusion, particularly among the women captives, at being seen in such vile dress before Spaniards is so great]. That altered appearance could disguise a captive's Christian identity was as alarming in seventeenth-century Chile as it had been elsewhere in the Iberian empires. If the attire and appearance of Juan Ortiz and Jerónimo de Aguilar made them unrecognizable to their compatriots, for Ovalle, clothes have the power to unmake the Spanish woman.[7]

7. Alonso de Ovalle, *Historica relacion del reyno de Chile* (Rome, 1646), 259, 260, 263. The titles of the chapters dedicated to captives (book 6, chaps. 16–17) well indicate Ovalle's perspective on captivity among Araucanians: "Lo que han padecido los españoles en el duro cautiverio, que han tenido en poder de los indios más de quarenta

Yet women's bodies are even more revealing of the moral dangers of captivity, since others refuse to return "sólo de verguença, por no parecer delante de los suyos, y padecer la confussión, de que las vean cargadas de hijos de los Indios" [only out of shame, so that they won't have to appear before their relatives and suffer the confusion of being seen bearing the children of Indians]. In his *Memorias de los sucesos de la guerra de Chile,* the ex-soldier Gerónimo de Quiroga (1628–1704) similarly affirms the resistance of some Spanish women to return from captivity, but he attributes it to their moral and cultural degradation rather than shame or modesty. Describing the numerous Spanish women captured from La Imperial in 1599, Quiroga writes that the captors

> en un punto gozaron a todas las mujeres y en breve tiempo todas fueron como ellos, porque el trato familiariza las costumbres y dispone de manera las voluntades, que habiendo de conformarse con su suerte, infelices, sin mucha repugnancia les pareció lo feo, hermoso, y lo asqueroso aliviado. Yo conocí muchas señoras de éstas, mucho peores que los indios, tan desesperadas cuando al cabo de treinta o cuarenta años las sacaron del barbarismo, que bramaban por volverse a él.

> immediately possessed all the women and in a brief time the women were all like them, because contact makes customs familiar and shapes the will in such a way that, resigning themselves to their misfortune and without much repugnance, what was ugly seemed to them beautiful, and what was disgusting became a relief. I met many of these women, who were

---

años" [What the Spaniards Have Suffered in Their Cruel Captivity in the Power of Indians for More than Forty Years]) and "Dase fin a esta material y pondérase el más inconsolable trabajo, que han padecido los Españoles en este su cautiverio" [In Which This Material Is Concluded and the Inconsolable Hardship That These Spaniards Have Suffered in Their Captivity Is Considered]; see Ovalle, *Historica relacion,* 259–264. However, Ovalle lets slip some visual evidence that challenges his potrait of brutal captivity, especially for women. He personally witnesses the attempted ransom of one ex-captive who "venía tan fresca, y gorda, como si viniera, no de un cautiverio, tan pessado sino de un lugar de dilicias, y regalos" [came so fresh and fat that it seemed as if she came not from a difficult captivity but from a place of delight and pleasure]. Rather than question assumptions about Amerindian cruelty and barbarism, as Pineda does in *Cautiverio feliz,* Ovalle praises her appearance as proof of "el valor, con que estas cautivas han llevado su trabajo" [the courage with which these captive women have endured their hardship] (260).

much worse than the Indians, and so desperate that, when at the end of thirty or forty years they took them out of that barbarism, they howled to go back to it.

According to Quiroga, the barbarism of indigenous captors is so great that it inevitably spreads to Spanish captives and their mestizo descendants, whom he describes as "los más inicuos bárbaros que hay en estas Provincias" [the most iniquitous barbarians that there are in these provinces].[8]

In *Purén indómito,* an epic poem dating from the beginning of the seventeenth century, Diego Arias de Saavedra portrays Araucanian inhumanity in the cruel treatment, torture, and sacrifice of captives. The indigenous characters are consistently presented as "bárbaros gentiles, / idólatras, sin fe y sin razón" [barbarous gentiles, idolaters without faith or reason] and the way that female captives are forced to dress provokes an anxiety similar to that of Ovalle and Quiroga. The "bárbaro traje" [barbarous costume] is

tan mal hecho
que no señala talle ni cintura,
forma, garbo, faición, espalda o pecho;
y, demás de ser mala su hechura
áspero, deshonesto, corto, estrecho,

8. Ovalle, *Historica relacion,* 263; Jerónimo de Quiroga, *Memorias de los sucesos de la guerra de Chile* (1690), ed. Sergio Fernández Larraín ([Santiago de Chile, 1979]), 283–284. A similar portrait of the sufferings of captive women appears in Alonso González de Nájera's *Desengaño y reparo de la guerra del reino de Chile,* finished in 1614. Like Ovalle, González de Nájera notes that some captive women choose not to return because of their pregnancy, and, with respect to those who were ransomed, he amply describes the "hábito o por mejor decir desnudez con que venían" [dress, or, to put it better, nudity in which they came]; see González de Nájera, *Desengaño y reparo de la guerra del reino de Chile, donde se manifiestan las principales ventajas que en ella tienen los indios á nuestros españoles, y los engaños que de nuestra parte han sido causa de la dilación de su conquista, con un medio que promete brevedad para acabarla,* ed. José Toribio Medina, Colección de historiadores de Chile, XLVIII (Santiago de Chile, 1889), 68. Although González de Nájera's unmitigated view of indigenous barbarism is apparent elsewhere in his account, his identification of the Araucanians who most mistreat their captives as the ones who have had most contact with Spaniards (like *La Florida del Inca*'s Hirrihigua) unwittingly corroborates Pineda's assertion that Spanish, rather than Araucanian, violence and cruelty is responsible for the conflict; see *Desengaño y reparo de la guerra del reino de Chile,* 69.

tanto que se descubren las costillas
y llega, cuando mucho, a las rodillas.

formed so poorly
that it shows neither figure nor waist,
form, grace, features, back nor breast,
and besides being made so imperfectly,
it is so rough, immodest, short, and tight
that the ribs can be seen,
and at the very most it covers the knees.

For Arias de Saavedra, the "barbarous costume" disguises the Spanish woman's elegant figure with scanty and coarse attire, paradoxically revealing both too much and too little. Like the fur-clad survivors of the Soto expedition or Pedro Serrano's own furry body, the woman's transformed appearance is an external manifestation of transplanted experience, but here it only signifies suffering and the loss of a civilized identity. Pineda does not diverge from this model to the same extent as Garcilaso, who shows Spaniards extolling and adopting "barbarous" attire at the end of *La Florida del Inca* and bestowing rewards for its display in the Serrano tale of *Comentarios reales*. However, as we have seen, Pineda does challenge categorical assumptions by metaphorically relocating the lack of clothing to the Spanish side of the Chilean frontier.[9]

9. Diego Arias de Saavedra, *Purén indómito,* ed. Mario Ferreccio Podestá (Concepción, Chile, 1984 [orig. publ. Leipzig, 1862]), 640. In the first published edition, Diego Barros Arana attributed the work to Fernando Álvares de Toledo, author of another epic known as *Araucana II;* see Ferreccio Podestá, prologue, in Saavedra, *Purén indómito,* 11–87, esp. 34–49. The more recent attribution to Diego Arias de Saavedra is based on internal and external evidence. Among the hardships suffered by Chilean soldiers that Pineda laments is the lack of proper dress. Because of the greed of Spanish officials, the soldiers who are sent to Chile "salen de tal suerte de las embarcaciones, que parecen más indios que soldados, sin camisas ni espadas" [disembark from the ships in such a way that they seem more like Indians than soldiers, with neither shirts nor swords]. Later, Pineda criticizes the superiors who mock the very situation they have produced: "Hay algunos superiores . . . a los que se precian de libertados, descorteses y desmedidos en el lenguaje, llamando a sus soldados de indios vestidos" [There are some superiors who boast of being bold, rude, and insolent in their speech, calling their soldiers clothed Indians]; see *Cautiverio feliz y razón individual,* [ed. Barros Arana], 365–366. In *Guerra de Chile, causas de su duracion,*

Accounts of captivity in Chilean historiography and literature do not exclusively dwell on the female experience, although these examples demonstrate how the trials of the "weaker sex" might have been particularly persuasive of Amerindian barbarism. Nevertheless, other works of Chilean literature emulate the idealized presentation of Araucanians in Alonso de Ercilla y Zúñiga's *La Araucana* (1569) and take up another Spanish model of captivity, that of *El Abencerraje* (1561), by painting an exemplary portrait of intercultural relations. In *Restauración de La Imperial y conversión de almas infieles,* written around 1693, the Mercederian creole friar Juan de Barrenechea y Albis entertains the possibility of happy captivity, but only for Araucanians among Spaniards, not vice versa. Barrenechea y Albis sets his legendary account of an indigenous youth who ultimately adopts the culture of his Spanish captors during the same period as Pineda's captivity, 1628–1629. Although these years mark the end of the Jesuit-driven policy of "defensive warfare" (1612–1626) and the return to more aggressive slave raiding, Barrenechea points to benevolence and fair treatment as an alternative model of intercultural relations that could avoid armed hostility. However, his depiction of the captive-captor relationship implies the same stereotypes of Amerindian barbarism that inform the colonialist discourse of imperial historiography.[10]

---

medios para su fin, exemplificado en el govierno de don Francisco Lasso de la Vega (Madrid, 1647), Santiago de Tesillo also claims that the disheveled Chilean soldiers "no parecían Españoles" [did not seem like Spaniards] but attributes it to their own gambling rather than the corruption of Crown-appointed officials (40–41).

10. Juan de Barrenechea y Albis's "Restauración de La Imperial y conversión de almas infieles," whose manuscript is held at the Archivo Nacional de Santiago de Chile, remains unpublished except for the highly abridged version in José Anadón's *La novela colonial de Barrenechea y Albis (siglo XVII): Aventuras y galanteos de Carilab y Rocamila* (Santiago de Chile, 1983). A slightly different version of the tale appears in the *Coronicón sacro-imperial de Chile* by Francisco Xavier Ramírez, finished in 1805 but first published in 1994; see Ramírez, *Coronicón sacro-imperial de Chile,* ed. Jaime Valenzuela Márquez (Santiago de Chile, 1994), 195–202. Ramírez's source may be Barrenechea y Albis, for he was in possession of the earlier author's manuscript, but the variations in Ramírez's version and his reference to other sources suggest that the tale may have a legendary or historical basis; see Anadón, *La novela colonial de Barrenechea y Albis,* 54. For Barrenechea y Albis's biography and a summary of the plot of "Restauración de La Imperial y conversión de almas infieles," see José Toribio Medina, *Historia de la literatura colonial de Chile,* 3 vols. (Santiago de Chile, 1878), II, 336–349; a summary in English is in Thomas J. Tomanek, "Barrene-

In a structure that recalls that of *Cautiverio feliz, Restauración de La Imperial* interweaves the ill-starred adventures of the noble young lovers Carilab and Rocamila throughout its 630 pages. Among his other trials and tribulations, Carilab is twice held captive by Spanish forces and unjustly sentenced to death. Each time, he is spared through the intervention of a father of the Order of Mercy—the same order as that of the author—which, of course, had long been dedicated to the redemption of Christian captives among Muslims. Carilab's heroic comportment and chivalric devotion to Rocamila, the mestiza daughter of an Araucanian father and a captive Spanish mother, earn him the sympathy of Captain don Lorenzo Suárez de Figueroa, who agrees to release him in exchange for several Spanish prisoners held by another Araucanian chieftain. Carilab fulfills his word by returning with the captives before celebrating his marriage to Rocamila. He also converts to Christianity (again owing to the intervention of the author's alter ego, the Mercederian father) and promises never again to take up arms against the Spaniards. Although the account is cut short, later references in the text imply that the denouement involves Rocamila's conversion, the couple's baptism, and their decision to live out the rest of their lives in Christian society.[11]

Critics have long recognized the correspondences between Barrenechea y Albis's and Pineda y Bascuñán's accounts; one calls *Restauración de La Imperial* "the other side of the coin" with respect to *Cautiverio feliz,* for narrating essentially the same tale while inverting the roles of Spaniard and Araucanian in the captive-captor relationship. In both cases, the captives

---

chea's *Restauración de La Imperial y Conversión de Almas Infieles:* The First Novel Written in Spanish America," *Revue des langues vivantes,* XL (1974), 257–268.

11. On Barrenechea's work raising alms for the ransom of captives, see Toribio Medina, *Historia de la literatura colonial de Chile,* II, 336. Until the nineteenth century, the Mercederians actively raised money in the New World for the ransom of captives in North Africa; see Andrés Millé, *La Orden de la Merced en la conquista del Perú, Chile y el Tucumán y su convento del antiguo Buenos Aires, 1218–1804* (Buenos Aires, 1958), which cites a 1746 declaration issued by the Order of Mercy affirming its support for the ransom of captives among Araucanians, "con tal que esto no perjudique la limosna para redimir de entre los moros" [as long as it does not jeopardize the alms for redeeming those among the Moors] (234). On the ransom of captives in Argentina with funds originally destined for redemption in North Africa, see Susan Migden Socolow, "Spanish Captives in Indian Societies: Cultural Contact along the Argentine Frontier, 1600–1835," *Hispanic American Historical Review,* LXXII (1992), 73–99, esp. 80.

are sufficiently persuaded of their captors' generosity to defend their former enemies. More specifically, Barrenechea's portrait of reciprocal respect and generosity between captive and captor explicitly evokes the structure of *El Abencerraje* by presenting the Spaniards in the role of benevolent captors, whereas the pagan captive's virtues are limited to valor, vigor, and amorous devotion. However, *Restauración de La Imperial* does not reflect the tolerance of religious and cultural difference that *El Abencerraje* appears to underscore, for intercultural contact merely convinces the indigenous captive of the superiority of his captors' culture and religion, which is enough to lead him to abandon his own and adopt a Christian, civilized way of life.[12]

Pineda's captivity does not lead to a similar adoption of and by the "other" culture but instead ends with the captive's redemption and return home. As we will see, the creole captive can and does absorb qualities that he observes in his captors and adopt or participate in their cultural practices. However, he does not sever ties to his native culture or religion. Rather, Pineda suggests that the captive's ability to move peacefully and mediate between different groups is the result of knowledge gained through firsthand experience on both sides of the border. Despite the inversion of roles between Christian and Amerindian, then, Barrenechea's representation of captivity shares a similar purpose with that of Pineda. Both portray the creole in the role of knowledgeable mediator, familiar enough with both cultures to be able to bring an end to captivity and conflict, and they do so in a way that reflects the author's own marginal position with respect to his European sources and audience. In Barrenechea's text, the creole mediator appears in the figure of the Mercederian friar, whose intervention resolves Carilab's captivity and leads to the "conversion of infidel souls," which we know from the title to be the author's goal. *Cautiverio feliz,* on the other hand, presents a greater departure from the aforementioned literary models by turning the focus from the opposition between cultures (as in abject captivity) or the erasure of cultural difference (via an idealized captivity) to the transformative effect of cross-cultural experience on the captive. Although assumptions of cultural

12. On *Restauración de La Imperial* as the "other side of the coin" of *Cautiverio feliz,* see Domingo Amunátegui Solar, "Bosquejo histórico de la literatura chilena," *Revista chilena de historia y geografía,* IX (1914), 5–39, esp. 17. On the the traces of *El Abencerraje,* as well as Heliodorus's *Aethiopica* and Ercilla's *La Araucana* in the tale of Carilab and Rocamila, see Anadón, *Historiografía literaria de América colonial,* 205–228.

superiority and inferiority still dominate, they are not immutably linked to the binary categories of Spaniard and Amerindian but rather participate in the complex construction of creole identity as the in- (and go-)between.

ESSENTIAL DIGRESSIONS

Pineda interpolated his tale of captivity throughout the more than three hundred folios of his manuscript and never envisioned it as separable from or superior to the extensive citations and commentary in which it is embedded. Indeed, an exclusive focus on the narrative—a perspective that has resulted in several modern truncated editions—goes against the repeated affirmations of the author that it is "al intento de este libro las digresiones que haga, y no la historia que suscinta escribo" [to the purpose of this book the digressions that I make, and not the story that I succinctly write]. Both the captivity narrative and the political, historical, and moralizing "digressions" serve the common purpose of explaining the reasons for the continuation of the Chilean wars, alluded to in the second part of the work's bipartite title, *Razón individual de las guerras dilatadas del reino de Chile.*[13]

13. In 1878, José Toribio Medina lamented Pineda's "overbearing erudition" and proclaimed the work's universal literary status if Pineda had limited himself to recounting his adventures among the Araucanians, and in 1914, Domingo Amunátegui Solar recommended the publication of an abridged edition to foreground the work's novelistic dimension. See Toribio Medina, *Historia de la literatura colonial de Chile,* II, 334; and Amunátegui Solar, "Bosquejo histórico de la literatura chilena," *Revista chilena de historia y geografía,* IX (1914), 5–39, esp. 14. Several abridged editions that privilege the narrative of captivity have, in fact, been published: Alejandro Vicuña's biographical *Bascuñán, el cautivo* (Santiago de Chile, 1948); Francisco Núñez de Pineda y Bascuñán, *El cautiverio feliz,* ed. Ángel Custodio González ([Santiago de Chile], 1948); and Pineda, *Cautiverio feliz y razón individual de las guerras dilatadas del reino de Chile,* ed. Álvaro Jara and Alejandro Lipschutz (Santiago de Chile, 1973). Pineda himself recognized the prohibitive length of the work and offered his own abridged version in a *Suma y epílogo de lo más esencial que contiene el libro intitulado Cautiverio feliz, y guerras dilatadas del reino de Chile,* which reduces but in no way excludes all of the scholarly citations and commentary related to the state of affairs in Chile. The *Suma y epílogo* originally preceded the manuscript of *Cautiverio feliz* held at the Archivo Nacional in Santiago, Chile, but a more complete copy was found at the Bodleian Library at Oxford; see Pineda, *Suma y epílogo de lo más esencial que contiene el libro intitulado Cautiverio feliz, y guerras dilatadas del reino de Chile,* ed. Robert A. McNeil (Santiago de Chile, 1984). It is also included in *Cautiverio feliz,* ed. Ferreccio

Pineda's wanderings from the central story line could also be seen as metaphorically integrated with the subject matter reflected in the first part of his title, *Cautiverio feliz*. In a contemporary Spanish treatise on Christian captives in Algiers, Gabriel Gómez de Losada's *Escuela de trabajos* (1670)—whose full title evokes a captivity that is anything but happy—the author excuses the rambling quality of his work on precisely these grounds:

> Es condición humana desear variedad en las cosas. . . . Si a este libro le sucediere lo mesmo que a los Cautivos, merecerá mayores aplausos, por salir tan parecido a su assumpto, muchos destos encaminaban sus viajes a las Indias, y a otras partes del mundo, y sin tener la intención, fueron a parar a Argel; vamos muchas vezes en las jornadas que hazemos a parar al fin que no nos proponíamos al principio, ya sea acaso o a elección.

> It is a human condition to seek variety in things. . . . If what happens to the captives also happens to this book, the similarity to the subject matter will make it more worthy of applause; for many of these captives were on their way to the Indies, or other parts of the world, and unintentionally ended up in Algiers; on journeys we often end up somewhere that we did not plan at the beginning, whether by accident or by choice.

Gómez de Losada's acknowledgment of the parallel between textual and navigational detours calls attention to the fragility of Spanish imperial aspirations, the real and perhaps unexpected connection for many would-be conquistadors between New World exploits and captivity in Algiers, the "Indies of the Turks." Pineda's intentional digressions from the autobiographical captivity narrative more pointedly demonstrate the failure of these aspirations in Chile, but they also connect the New and Old World in a different sense. The frequent citation of biblical and classical sources renders his captivity among Araucanians more familiar to potential Euro-

---

Podestá and Kordić Riquelme, I, 73–232. Correa Bello describes the 1948 editions as "mutilated," justifiably taking issue with their failure to appreciate the relationship between the captivity narrative and Pineda's critique of contemporary Chile in the "digressions"; see *El "Cautiverio feliz" en la vida política chilena del siglo XVII*, 31–32. Other critics who assert the integration of narrative and "digressions" include Raquel Chang-Rodríguez, "El propósito del 'Cautiverio feliz' y la crítica," *Cuadernos hispanoamericanos*, CCXCVII (1975), 657–663; Mora, *Escritura e identidad criollas*, 183–321; Bauer, *Cultural Geography of Colonial American Literatures*, 118–156.

pean readers. Perhaps more important, the digressions demonstrate the American-born author's familiarity with an authoritative European tradition of knowledge.[14]

Following the author's claims that the "digresiones largas . . . son y han de ser el blanco principal de mi desvelo" [long digressions . . . are and should be the principal object of my concern], scholars have increasingly turned from the narrative of captivity to the political and juridical discourse of Pineda's text. An exclusive focus on these aspects, however, can lead to another reading of *Cautiverio feliz* as an inversion of expectations, as when Diego Barros Arana writes: "One is almost tempted to believe that those digressions constitute its true foundation, and that the narrative of his captivity is only an accessory. In this way, Bascuñán deprived his work of the greater part of its worth." As Ralph Bauer has described, the captivity narrative is far from "only an accessory" to Pineda's account. Bauer argues that, in contrast to the usual subordination of eyewitness accounts to the discourse of the imperial historian, in *Cautiverio feliz,* "eyewitness testimony contains historiographic discourse, not vice versa."[15]

14. Pineda y Bascuñán, *Cautiverio feliz y razón individual,* [ed. Barros Arana], 132. For Renaissance commentators' praise of digressions and variety as contributing to the delight of prose and poetic fiction, see Allan H. Gilbert, ed., *Literary Criticism: Plato to Dryden* (New York, 1940), 264, 271–272, 498–501. On the popularity of digressions and interpolated tales in Baroque literature, see Emilio Orozco Díaz, *Introducción al barroco,* ed. José Lara Garrido ([Granada], 1988), I, 113–149.

15. Pineda y Bascuñán, *Cautiverio feliz y razón individual,* [ed. Barros Arana], 297; Barros Arana, introduction, ibid., iii–vii, esp. vi. Bauer explains the distinction between Pineda's account and "imperial historiography": "Pineda's 'true history' is structured into five historical 'discursos' (each of which is itself divided into twenty-six 'capítulos'); but none of the different 'discursos' (nor the 'capítulos') are topically distinct from the others in content. Instead, the content of his 'true history' is entirely structured by the narrative of his experiences in captivity, into which are inserted his lengthy historiographic 'digresiones'"; see *Cultural Geography of Colonial American Literatures,* 142–143. For readings focused on Pineda's juridical and political discourse, see Correa Bello, *El "Cautiverio feliz" en la vida política chilena del siglo XVII;* Dennis Pollard, "The King's Justice in Pineda y Bascuñán's *Cautiverio feliz," Dispositio/n,* XI (1986), 113–135; Lucía Invernizzi S.C., "Recursos de la argumentación judicial-deliberativa en el *Cautiverio feliz* de Pineda y Bascuñán," *Revista chilena de literatura,* XLIII (1993), 5–30; Fresia Castillo Sánchez, "El discurso en *El cautiverio feliz (1673),*" in Juan Villegas Morales, ed., *Actas Irvine-92* (Irvine, Calif., 1994), V, *Lecturas y relecturas de textos españoles, latinoamericanos y U.S. latinos,* 227–234.

Pineda's captivity represents not only the basis for his own claims to experiential authority but also a source of other firsthand accounts:

> El principal blanco a que se han encaminado estos verdaderos discursos . . . ha sido el significar las causas y fundamentos que hallo para la dilacion de esta guerra de Chille; y para que se conozca con evidencia que lo que digo y escribo en este volúmen, es por ciertas relaciones adquiridas de los propios antiguos naturales, he fundádolos en historia de mi captiverio dichoso y feliz . . . ; a cuya causa me parece que de los entendidos y cuerdos no serán adicionadas las digresiones largas que se ofrecen para la materia propuesta.
>
> The principal goal to which these true discourses are directed . . . is to point out the causes and reasons for the prolongation of this war in Chile. And in order for it to be known with evidence that what I write and say in this volume has been acquired from certain relations obtained from the ancient natives themselves, I have grounded them in the history of my happy and fortunate captivity . . . ; for which reason it appears to me that, to the informed and wise, the long digressions that I offer for the proposed material will not seem excessive.

The captivity narrative both authorizes and is authorized by the historical, political, and moral digressions of his work. The eyewitness relations of Amerindians—which graphically describe Spanish treachery, injustice, and cruelty—support Pineda's arguments concerning the prolongation of the wars. At the same time, the extensive biblical and classical allusions render his transcription of indigenous oral accounts more trustworthy. Discursive heterogeneity is just as pertinent to the construction of creole authority as the ambivalent portrait of Amerindians and Spaniards. The creole writer displays the range of his discursive abilities just as the captive demonstrates his capacity to negotiate in a variety of cultural settings. If captivity amid another culture, like the creole patria itself, is a site of distance and difference with respect to the metropolis, *Cautiverio feliz* insists on showing that these qualities need not be associated with a lack of knowledge or power. For Pineda, distance and difference can actually be indicators of creole superiority (moral, spiritual, intellectual) to Spaniards in the Chilean context.[16]

16. Pineda y Bascuñán, *Cautiverio feliz y razón individual,* [ed. Barros Arana], 246. As Bauer points out, Pineda accepts the distinction promulgated by imperial

CROSSING BOUNDARIES: INVERSIONS AND (CON)FUSIONS

Pineda's construction of creole identity and authority generally follows two equally important steps. The first and most immediately apparent is what I have referred to as "inversion," in which boundaries are destabilized by showing that qualities associated with one category may be just as, or more, applicable to its opposite. Many of these revolve around the inverse relationship between captivity and misfortune: the poverty and injustice suffered by Chilean soldiers under Spanish administration contrasts with the abundance of food and drink as well as the fair treatment that Pineda receives during his happy captivity. Yet these ironic reversals are not ends in themselves. Pineda does not advocate an abandonment of Spanish civilization to join the natural paradise and social utopia of "noble savages." Rather, these inversions challenge perceived boundaries so that they can be redrawn, not discarded. Both steps—the crossing of boundaries and the affirmation of new ones—are integral to defining a creole identity distinct from peninsular Spaniards yet loyal to the Spanish Crown.[17]

Pineda characterizes his text by insisting, like Garcilaso, that he is uniquely capable of revealing the truth that has been obscured by Spanish writings about the colonies in general and Chile in particular: "El principal blanco a que se encaminan mis discursos, no es otro que hacer las verdades patentes" [The principal aim to which my discourses are directed is none other than

---

historians between "two kinds of Spaniards"—Chilean-born creoles and peninsular Spaniards—but inverts the moral hierarchy usually drawn between the two: "The Creoles, such as his father, appear as morally superior while the 'habitadores,' or Peninsular Spaniards who now govern Chile, imitate the 'primeros conquistadores' ('first conquerors'), whose corruption and vice were notorious"; see *Cultural Geography of Colonial American Literatures,* 132.

17. For a description of the misfortunes of Chilean soldiers, particularly their lack of food, clothing, and financial compensation, as well as the abuse heaped upon them by corrupt officials, see Pineda y Bascuñán, *Cautiverio feliz y razón individual,* [ed. Barros Arana], 376–383. Here Pineda asks, "Bien ponderadas todas estas desdichas, penalidades y trabajos que por mayor he referido, ¿habrá quien pueda decir, que haya ejército alguno de S. M. más oprimido, más trabajado, ni más mal socorrido que el de Chille, y con esto más humilde, más leal, ni más sufrido?" [After pondering all these misfortunes, sufferings, and hardships that I have summarized here, is there anyone who can say that Your Majesty has an army more oppressed, more weary, and more needy of assistance than that of Chile, and despite all this is the most humble, the most loyal, and the longest suffering?]

making the truth clear]. Pineda describes how he is compelled to offer his account after learning of "algunos escritos y obras de historia que han salido a luz y están para salir, de algunos acaecimientos de esta guerra de Chile, tan ajenos de la verdad como llevados de la adulación los más, y otros del propio interés" [some writings and historical works that have come out or are about to come out, concerning some events of this war in Chile, which are as far from the truth as most of them are carried away by adulation, and others by self-interest]. Although no less motivated by self-interest, Pineda makes the case for the authenticity of his account by contrasting it with such "escritos ociosos, fantásticos, quiméricos y fabulosos" [idle, fantastic, chimerical, and fabulous writings]. His warning about these works' potentially hazardous impact on the very foundations of Christian society echoes and expands that of Sebastián de Covarrubias in his definition of *fábula:* "Podemos decir que si tales escritores fabulosos, contemplativos y interesados dan sus obras a la estampa, es cierto que vacilará la fee por falta de la verdad, la justicia perecerá porque las leyes tendrán diferentes sentidos y el Evangelio en sus plumas muy gran riesgo de entenderse" [We can say that, if such fabulous, indulgent, and self-interested writers print their works, it is certain that faith will vacillate for the lack of truth, and justice will perish because the laws will have different meanings, and in their writings, the gospel will run a great risk of not being understood].[18]

Laden with the pessimism and disillusionment typical of his Baroque age, Pineda's text actually shows these consequences to have already taken effect. The author frequently invokes the image of an "upside-down world" as a reflection of the current state of the New World and Chile in particular, calling the latter a "cáos de confusión" [chaos of confusion] and affirming that "en Chille o en las Indias corren al revés todas las cosas, sin acertar a encaminarlas al verdadero camino de la razón y justicia" [in Chile or the Indies everything runs in reverse, without managing to be directed onto the truth path of reason and justice]. After referring to Augustine's claim that, with Christ's birth, the "true light" of justice would diminish the darkness in the world, Pineda writes, "Esto es cierto y se verifica en la Europa y en Castilla; y en la América Austral de nuestro reino muy al revés y al contrario se experimenta el caso; con que podemos decir que en este chileno hemisferio corren

18. Pineda y Bascuñán, *Cautiverio feliz y razón individual,* [ed. Barros Arana], 2–3, 5. See the definition of *fábula* in Sebastián de Covarrubias Orozco, *Tesoro de la lengua castellana o española,* ed. Martín de Riquer (Barcelona, 1943 [orig. publ. Madrid, 1611]), 579–580.

todas las cosas al trocado" [This is true and can been seen in Europe and Castile, but in our kingdom of southern America we experience very much the reverse and contrary; so that we can say that in this Chilean hemisphere everything runs backward]. Pineda dedicates several chapters to explaining the role of writing in the perpetuation of this chaos. At one point, he specifically blames the *letrados* for the fact that, in Chile, "ande todo de arriba abajo, porque están sin sentido nuestras leyes, pues los mesmos jurisperitos confiesan, que la ley no tiene más entendimiento que el que ellos quieren darle" [everything is upside down because our laws have no meaning, for the jurists confess that the law has no more understanding than that which they wish to give it]. Literary and judicial culture in Chile has a profoundly detrimental, even "barbaric," effect on society: "Serán sus letras, su ciencia y sabiduría, de nuestros reinos y provincias enemigos feroces y ponzoñosas fieras (como lo han sido), ántes que muralla, abrigo ni defensa: con que la paz que se busca y se solicita, es imposible se consiga" [Their letters, science, and knowledge will be ferocious enemies and poisonous beasts (as they have been) to our kingdom and provinces rather than a wall, shelter, or defense: and so it is impossible to attain the sought-after peace]. In contrast, Pineda presents his text as indeed fulfilling the role of "wall, shelter, and defense" of his patria. Writing is not inherently destructive or purposeless but can be a form of service to one's country and contribute to the cause of peace—and it is all the more culpable when it fails to do so.[19]

Thus whereas Garcilaso claims that "confusion" is the inevitable result of cross-cultural and cross-linguistic translation during colonization, Pineda identifies it as the product of a self-serving colonial bureaucracy that esteems

19. Pineda y Bascuñán, *Cautiverio feliz y razón individual,* [ed. Barros Arana], 356–357, 373, 384, 408, 411. Pineda affirms that his intention is not to censure learning and writing: "¿Quién podrá dudar de cuánta importancia sea la ciencia y sabiduría, principalmente en los que gobiernan y están puestos en altas dignidades, para que sus reinos, provincias y ciudades estén bien regidas, prudentemente gobernadas, y bastantemente defendidas? Mejores son las letras y la ciencia que las fuerzas (dice la sabiduría), y mejor que el fuerte, el varón prudente" [Who can doubt the importance of science and knowledge, principally in those who govern and enjoy high ranks, so that their kingdoms, provinces, and cities are well ruled, prudently governed, and sufficiently defended? Letters and science are better than force (wisdom tells us), and the prudent man is better than the strong one] (406). Much like Garcilaso or Cabeza de Vaca, Pineda asserts that the service performed in writing his account is even more valuable than that which he rendered as a soldier or captive.

obscurity and deception. His text is both a response to and a participation in the proliferation of legal writing that Ángel Rama and Roberto González Echevarría have described as integral to the Spanish colonization of the New World. Pineda extensively cites a university professor, Antonio Maldonado, on the multiplication of laws and their interpreters:

> ¿Qué diré de la multitud de sus profesores y su ciencia? muchos cursantes en las universidades, muchos graduados, muchos pasantes, muchos abogados, muchos jueces: grande es la multitud de tantos muchos. ¿Cuántos habrán leído enteramente el derecho? Pocos. ¿Cuántos le han entendido? Iba a decir ninguno: dígame alguno, si ya ha leído textos y glosas, ¿cómo le ha ido con la obscuridad del texto solo? cómo con la confusión, variedad, yerros, irresolución y infinidad de las glosas? . . . No, y en esto conforman todos con Aristóteles, que no se tiene la verdad en lo que de muchas maneras se entiende.
>
> What can I say about the multitude of professors and their learning? Lots of students in the universities, lots of graduates, lots of tutors, lots of lawyers, lots of judges: great is the multitude of so many "lots." How many of them have read the law in its entirety? Few. How many have understood it? I was going to say nobody: tell me, if someone has already read the texts and glosses, how has it gone with the obscurity of the text alone? How has it gone with the confusion, variety, errors, irresolution, and infinity of glosses? . . . No, and in this everyone agrees with Aristotle, that there is no truth in that which can be interpreted many ways.

The chaos promoted by Chilean society and its literary and judicial culture serve as both the inspiration and the obstacle to revealing the truth, for Pineda himself finds it necessary to "dilatar su descripción más de lo que quisiéramos, por ver si podemos salir al fin de estas confusas nieblas" [extend his description more than we would like, to see if we can finally leave this confusing fog]. Ironically enough, distancing oneself from chaos requires ever more wandering on the part of the author, both textually and physically.[20]

20. Pineda y Bascuñán, *Cautiverio feliz y razón individual,* [ed. Barros Arana], 373, 403. Roberto González Echevarría, in "The Law of the Letter: Garcilaso's *Comentarios,*" in González Echevarría, *Myth and Archive: A Theory of Latin American Narrative* (Durham, N.C., 1998), 43–92, follows Ángel Rama's formulation of "la

Deferment, as already suggested, is characteristic of Pineda's text—the long and rather tangential citation of Maldonado provides an example—and today's readers would be tempted to associate it with the work of "confusion," "variety," and "infinite commentary" that Pineda himself seems to deplore. However, our author differentiates his work from that of his contemporaries by declaring the central truth to which his text adheres: the "individual reason for the prolonged wars of Chile" of the work's title. According to Pineda, the explanation for the war's continuance is not subject to interpretation, at least by uninformed outsiders. The author presents himself as an imperial subject singularly able to disclose this truth to the king because of—and not in spite of—his distance from the center of the realm incurred by both his cross-cultural experience and his American origins.

Principally, Pineda's experience as a captive has revealed the false nature of Spanish stereotypes regarding Araucanians. He challenges, without inverting, assumptions about native difference through repeated affirmations that "la naturaleza de estos bárbaros infieles no es tan de bestia fiera como algunos la pintan, pues se sujetan mansos al halago y reconocen el bien agradecidos" [the nature of these barbarian infidels is not that of wild beasts as some paint it, for they subject themselves peacefully to flattery and they acknowledge kindness gratefully]. In contrast, the "evidente consecuencia" [evident consequence] that Pineda extracts from observing and interacting with Araucanians is that "somos y habemos sido mucho peores que idólatras gentiles" [we are and have been much worse than gentile idolaters]. His captors' final plea to him, in fact, involves the clarification of misconceptions among Spaniards about their character and cultural practices: "No os olvidéis de nosotros, significando a los españoles vuestros hermanos y compañeros, que no somos tan malos ni de inclinaciones tan perversas como nos hacen" [Don't forget about us, and tell your Spanish brothers and companions how we are not so bad nor of such perverse inclinations as they take us to be]. *Cautiverio feliz* may thus represent, as Gilberto Triviños argues, "the consummation of a desire": with the text, Pineda fulfills his captors' wish for him to remember and publicize his happy captivity among kind and civilized Araucanians. But the plea ascribed to the Araucanians also fulfills Pineda's own desire to present himself as a mediator valorized by both cultures.[21]

---

ciudad letrada" [the lettered city] in his discussion of the growth of state bureaucracy, the presence of the letrados, and the proliferation of legal documents in the Spanish colonies; see Rama, *La ciudad letrada* (Hanover, N.H., 1984).

21. Pineda y Bascuñán, *Cautiverio feliz y razón individual,* [ed. Barros Arana],

Nevertheless, Pineda's confidence in the ability to tell the truth alternates with an acknowledgment of the difficulties in recognizing it and of the fact that appearances can be even more deceptive when multiple cultures are involved. The captive is first portrayed as fearfully anticipating unrestrained violence on the part of his captors, which conforms to the cultural stereotypes that the author will eventually challenge. He dreads that his captors will recognize him as the son of Álvaro Núñez de Pineda, an experienced and well-known general in the Araucanian wars. The young captive first assumes so categorical an opposition between Spanish and Araucanian forces that rapprochement or reconciliation are unthinkable. "Considerándome preso y entre mis enemigos" [Considering myself a prisoner among my enemies], he writes, "se me vino a la memoria ser mayor el peligro y riesgo en que me hallaba, si me conociesen por hijo del maestro de campo general Álvaro Núñez de Pineda, . . . a cuya causa me pareció conveniente y necesario usar de cautelosas simulaciones, fingiéndome de otras tierras y lugares" [I realized the greater risk and danger in which I would find myself if they discovered that I was the son of the fieldmaster Álvaro Núñez de Pineda, . . . for which reason it seemed to me convenient and necessary to use careful simulations, pretending to be from other lands and places]. The captive seeks to redouble the distance between himself and his captors by feigning (in)difference, denying even the possibility of communication: "Aunque moderadamante lo común y ordinario de su lenguaje le entendía, más ignorante me hice en él de lo que la naturaleza me había comunicado" [Although I moderately understood the common and ordinary parts of their language, I made myself seem more ignorant of it than what nature had communicated to me].[22]

Whereas many captives struggle with initial ignorance of their captors' language, Pineda's already moderate proficiency indicates previous contact with the Araucanian tongue (even though he describes it as having been mysteriously "communicated by nature"). In fact, long-established interaction between the Araucanians and Spaniards makes the captivity scenario significantly different from those of the sixteenth century in this regard. Unfamiliarity and miscommunication are replaced by previous, although limited, intercultural knowledge espoused by figures that have crossed bor-

---

261, 303, 491; Triviños, "'No os olvidéis de nosotros,'" *Acta literaria,* XXV (2000), 98.

22. Pineda y Bascuñán, *Cautiverio feliz y razón individual,* [ed. Barros Arana], 22.

ders. One such figure is the Spanish-speaking Amerindian who has recently fled his Spanish master to join the Araucanian forces and who recognizes the young captive. Pineda transposes the misidentification-to-recognition scene, usually reserved for the captive's return, to the very beginning of the captivity tale. The captive's fear of reprisal appears to be justified as the Araucanian cries out, "Muera, muera luego este capitán sin remisión alguna, porque es hijo de Álvaro Maltincampo (que así llamaban a mi padre), que tiene nuestras tierras destruidas, y a nosotros aniquilados y abatidos" [Kill, kill now this captain without pardon, because he is the son of Álvaro Maltincampo (for that is how they called my father), who is the reason that our lands are destroyed and that we are annihilated and humiliated].[23]

Just when we seem to be back in the space of binary oppositions between "annihilators" and "annihilated," which can be inverted through revenge on the captured and vulnerable oppressor, Pineda shows the recognition to turn in his favor. Although he introduces what happens next as the merciful intervention of God, he also provides ample motivation for the actions of Lientur, a cacique who used to be friendly with Spaniards but had since been provoked to lead a rebellion against them. Lientur's formidable entrance, armed from head to toe and mounted on a fierce horse, first leads the captive to think that "venía a poner término a mis días" [he was coming to put an end to my days]. On the contrary, however, Lientur has come to defend his life: "Cuando aguardaba ver de la muerte el rostro formidable, me hallé con más seguras prendas de la vida" [When I expected to see the formidable face of death, I found myself with the surest signs of life]. The captive's perception of Araucanians is sharpened by his proximity to them as individuals, and he describes the sympathy apparent in the cacique's face, "en cuyas razones y apacible rostro . . . eché de ver la aflicción y pesar con que se hallaba por ha-

23. Ibid. Although Pineda refers to him despectively as an "indezuelo" [little Indian], he also justifies the man's abandonment and betrayal of his former masters: "Pocos días antes del subceso se había de nosotros ausentado y agregádose a los enemigos *por algunas vejaciones y tratamientos malos que había recebido (que lo cierto es que las más veces somos y habemos sido el origen de nuestras adversidades y desdichadas suertes)*" [A few days before the event, he had left us and and joined our enemies *because of some vexations and mistreatments that he had received (for it is certain that most often we are and have been the cause of our adversities and misfortunes)*] (emphasis added). Like Garcilaso's contextualization of Hirrihigua's hatred of Spaniards in *La Florida del Inca,* hostility is initially provoked by Spanish cruelty and injustice.

berme conocido en aquel estado" [in whose reasons and gentle countenance . . . I could see his affliction and grief at seeing me in that state].[24]

Thus although "Alvarito" (as his captors call him, after his father) thought that recognition of his true identity as Álvaro's son would bring about his death, Lientur's intervention causes it to have the reverse effect. First, the indigenous captain reidentifies Alvarito as "hijo del primer hombre que nuestra tierra ha respetado y conocido" [son of the first man who has respected and known our land] and therefore as one who can be associated with "el sosiego de nuestra patria" [the tranquility of our patria]. Lientur then uses his acquaintance with Alvarito's father to invoke the lesson of reciprocity in captivity that can also be found in *El Abencerraje, La Florida del Inca,* and *Restauración de La Imperial.* In a speech that adheres to a convention of Western historiography, Lientur declares,

> A mí consta del tiempo que asistí con él en sus fronteras, que después de pasada la refriega, a sangre fría a ningunos cautivos dio la muerte; antes sí les hizo siempre buen pasaje, solicitando a muchos el que volviesen gustosos a sus tierras, como hay algunos que gozan de ellas libres y asistentes en sus casas con descanso, entre sus hijas, mujeres y parientes, por su noble pecho y corazón piadoso. Y lo propio debes hacer generoso con este capitán tu prisionero, que lo que hoy miramos en su suerte podemos en nosotros ver mañana.

> It is clear to me, from the time I was with him on his frontier, that after the skirmish was over, he never killed any captives in cold blood. Rather, he always treated them well, allowing many to go happily back to their lands. There are many who enjoy their lands freely and in peace, accompanied in their homes by their daughters, wives, and relatives, because of his noble breast and compassionate heart. And the same generosity you should grant to this captain your prisoner, for what we see him suffering today could be our lot tomorrow.

24. Pineda y Bascuñán, *Cautiverio feliz y razón individual,* [ed. Barros Arana], 25. Santiago de Tesillo offers a very different picture of the cacique Lientur: "Lientur, y Patapiches, Capitanes de los rebeldes executaron sumas crueldades, y desacatos en las fronteras, quemando, y saqueando todas las estancias, cautivando mucho número de gente" [Lientur and Patapiches, captains of the rebels, performed supreme cruelties and impertinences on the borderlands, burning and sacking all the ranches and capturing a great number of people]; see *Guerra de Chile,* 8.

Lientur justifies his argument by describing his firsthand contact with Spaniards; like Pineda, Lientur makes his case and establishes his authority based on knowledge gained while inhabiting the border zone. Lientur convinces Maulicán, Alvarito's captor, to esteem and protect his captive: "Pues desde aquel punto y hora dio principio el señor de mi voluntad a tratarme con amor, con benevolencia y gran respeto" [For since that moment and hour the lord of my will began to treat me with love, benevolence, and great respect]. Alvarito is also induced to love his captor/benefactor, and the author is inspired to meditate on the value of "verdadera amistad" [true friendship] that he has unexpectedly discovered among his supposed enemies.[25]

TRUE FRIENDSHIP

The chapter dedicated to Lientur's speech is representative of Pineda's juxtaposition of narrative with "digression" in terms of citations and commentary on the writings of classical and religious scholars (Ovid, Cicero, Aquinas, and Theophilus, among others). These references support Pineda's affirmation of the superiority of the type of friendship that Lientur has demonstrated toward his father, even in his absence: "Enseñó también a los aduladores amigos este generoso capitán, a serlo como lo deben ser los que profesan una limpia y verdadera amistad, manifestándola en ausencia y con fervor, que entonces con ventajas sobresale y entre las más lúcidas amistades se descuella" [This generous captain also taught flattering friends how those who profess a pure and true friendship should act, manifesting their friendship in absence and with fervor, for then its advantages stand out, and it excels among the most illustrious friendships]. In contrast to the "aduladores amigos" [flattering friends] that Pineda everywhere associates with corrupt colonial administrators, he praises Lientur for his generous display

25. Pineda y Bascuñán, *Cautiverio feliz y razón individual,* [ed. Barros Arana], 25–27. On invented speeches in classical historiography, see R. G. Collingwood, *The Idea of History,* rev. ed. (Oxford, 1993 [orig. publ. Oxford, 1946]), 30–31. On el Inca Garcilaso's use of native speeches in *La Florida del Inca* to critique Spanish policies and practices, see Lee Dowling, *"La Florida del Inca:* Garcilaso's Literary Sources," in Patricia Galloway, ed., *The Hernando de Soto Expedition: History, Historiography, and "Discovery" in the Southeast* (Lincoln, Nebr., 1997), 98–154, esp. 111. See also Garcilaso's own response to potential objections about these speeches in his *La Florida del Inca,* ed. Sylvia L. Hilton (Madrid, 1986 [orig. publ. Lisbon, 1605]), 191–194.

of friendship "en ausencia sin embarazos de intereses ni afectación de lisonjas" [in absence and without the impediment of self-interest nor the affectation of flattery]. The key qualities that condition Lientur's friendship—truth and absence—are implicitly related throughout Pineda's account, for they also mark the value of the particular service that he is capable of rendering his distant interlocutor, the king. Absence—in terms of distance from the metropolis—is thus revalorized, in a move typical of creole writers. Pineda repeatedly decries "el poco premio que esperamos en regiones tan distantes y apartadas de la presencia de nuestro gran monarca, nuestro Rey y natural señor" [the little reward that we expect in regions so distant and remote from the presence of our great monarch, our king and natural lord]. Such remoteness enhances the worth of royal service: "Los trabajos, miserias y desdichas que [se] padecen en este afligido reino sin esperanzas de premio, son *más de estimar y agradecer que los méritos y servicios (por aventajados que sean) adquiridos y obrados en la presencia y a los ojos de nuestro Rey y natural señor*" [The hardships, miseries, and misfortunes that are suffered in this distressed kingdom without hope of reward are *more worthy of being esteemed and thanked than the merits and services (however superior they may be) acquired and performed in the presence and before the eyes of our king and natural lord*]. Again, Pineda's "trabajos" [hardships] apply equally to his experience as a captive in a distinct culture and as a creole soldier and writer in a land distant from the metropolis. Pineda concludes his discussion of Lientur's friendship with a reminder of his intention to explain why "la guerra de Chile es inacabable, más sangrienta y más dilatada: que es a lo que se encaminan mis discursos ciertos y verdaderos" [the war in Chile is unending, bloodier, and more prolonged, to which my certain and true discourses are dedicated]. The qualities of "true friendship" discovered in Lientur's speech are thereby reflected in his own "true discourse" and the political solutions that he proposes: namely, the greater involvement of creoles in colonial government.[26]

The subsequent chapter returns to the reasons behind Alvarito's capture,

26. Pineda y Bascuñán, *Cautiverio feliz y razón individual,* [ed. Barros Arana], 8, 10, 28 (emphasis added). The difference between "true" and "false" friendship, often drawing on classical typologies, was a popular topic in Renaissance moral philosophy as well as literature; see Ullrich Langer, *Perfect Friendship: Studies in Literature and Moral Philosophy from Boccaccio to Corneille* (Geneva, 1994). Pineda appropriates this tradition by using it to support his characterization of Amerindians and his implicit self-portrait as a creole author.

which also demonstrate the negative consequences of ignoring the good advice of a true friend. Pineda here links his writing not to the qualities of an indigenous leader but to those of his father, the fieldmaster Álvaro Núñez de Pineda. Our author argues that his capture could have been avoided had his father's advice been heeded by the governor of Chile at the time, Luis Fernández de Córdoba, whose government (1625–1629) sustained a series of disastrous military failures like those that would later plague Acuña y Cabrera. Pineda relates how the governor—in a scene that replicates his own interaction with Acuña y Cabrera on the eve of the 1655 rebellion—had failed to listen to Álvaro's sage counsel, which advised reinforcing his son's regiment immediately after an Araucanian attack: "Por la experiencia que tenía de tantos años, y el conocimiento de estos naturales rebeldes, estaba cierto sin poner alguna duda que el enemigo había de volver muy breve con una gruesa junta a molestar nuestras fronteras y a balaustrar con nuestro tercio" [From the experience of so many years, and the knowledge that he had of these rebellious natives, he was certain without any doubt that the enemy would return soon with a large assembly to vex our frontiers and to attack our infantry regiment]. Fernández de Córdoba apparently disparaged this advice with words that might have been ringing in Pineda's ears as he wrote his account: "Respondió el dicho gobernador, que era muy a lo viejo . . . porque otros consejos había más frescos y modernos" [The said governor responded that that was very passé . . . because there was other advice that was fresher and more modern].[27]

As Pineda frequently reminds the reader throughout the narration of the battle of Cangrejeras, which resulted in his capture, self-seeking officials who thus ignore the counsel of the aged and experienced should be held responsible for the suffering of their people. Thus the Spanish loss at Cangrejeras and Pineda's consequent capture are the product not only of Spanish cruelty toward Araucanians, which has incited the latter to seek revenge, but of the failure of the governor to follow the advice of a concerned and knowledgeable soldier. Pineda gives a biblical example of how "aunque nos adviertan lo que puede ser de nuestra conveniencia . . . no damos crédito jamás a lo que nos importa y es de nuestra mayor utilidad y provecho" [even when we are warned about that which may be advisable to us . . . we never give credit to that which matters to us and is to our greater utility and advantage]. Significantly, the example tells the story of the injustice suffered

27. Pineda y Bascuñán, *Cautiverio feliz y razón individual,* [ed. Barros Arana], 14.

by an Ammonite prince who had informed his Assyrian commander of the reasons behind Israel's release from captivity and was subsequently killed for his frankness. The digression, together with his reproach of the governor for disregarding his father's advice, reflects Pineda's concern for the current neglect among colonial officials of his own perspective, which is similarly informed by age and experience.[28]

Nevertheless, Pineda remains hopeful of the possibilities of the written word. He reproduces the governor's letter to his father informing him of his son's capture, followed by the missive that his father writes in response. Curiously, Álvaro Núñez de Pineda's letter laments the governor's failure to take his advice even more than his son's capture: "No he llegado a sentir tanto su pérdida, cuanto que en la ocasión que a V.S. dije y supliqué que reparase ese tercio para lo subcedido, me respondió que era muy a lo viejo" [I'm not as sorry about his loss as about the time I told and begged Your Lordship to repair that regiment in preparation for what has happened, and you answered that it was very passé]. Pineda again praises his father's forthrightness, now expressed in writing, and credits this letter with nothing less than his own rescue: "Esta resuelta carta fue el total instrumento de mi bien y origen principal de mi rescate; porque atendiendo el gobernador a la sobrada razón de mi padre . . . , tuvo por bien el callar y disimular esta carta. . . . Con que desde entonces puso mayor cuidado y solicitud en librarme de los trabajos y peligros de la vida en que me hallaba" [This resolute letter was the total instrument of my well-being and the principal origin of my ransom; because, when the governor attended to the abundant reasons of my father . . . , he found it wise to be quiet and pardon the letter. . . . And so he began to put more care and effort into liberating me from the hardships and life-threatening dangers that I faced]. If Pineda's explanation for his capture reflects the reasons for the prolongation of the Araucanian wars—namely, the moral failure, ignorance, and incompetence of those in power—then perhaps Pineda can imitate his father's example of effective writing by also remedying injustice and settling conflict through his truthful account, or at least convince the reader of his power to do so. How can captivities and wars be resolved? Fathers—for Pineda himself is one at the time of writing his account—know best. By linking their own generation to their fathers', creole writers like Pineda could simultaneously negate accusations of "creole degeneration" and affirm the value of their service that, like that of their fathers, encompasses both arms and letters. We have already seen Pineda's

28. Ibid., 20.

resentment toward the wave of letrados, lawyers and administrators proceeding from Spain who, as González Echevarría writes, "'reconquered' the new territories for the Crown" and "clipped the wings of the conquistador's aspirations." Because of the prolonged wars of Chile, creoles were particularly interested in affirming the importance of military service that continued the work of their fathers the conquistadors, since the creoles saw themselves as assuming more responsibility for defending the empire than the Spanish-born governors and administrators who would come and go as they desired or their fortune demanded. In this sense, Pineda compares his father, and by extension himself, to a biblical figure, an adviser to King David: "Estos son los ministros que deben estimar los superiores que gobiernan, y solicitar sus asistencias, para que *con resoluciones amorosas les digan las verdades . . . aunque sea a costa de sus propias conveniencias y autoridades*" [These are the ministers whom the governing superiors should esteem and whom they should ask for assistance, so that *with loving resolution they tell them the truth . . . even though it be at the cost of their own comfort and authority*]. Pineda's only hope for reward, respect, or power in colonial society rests on his ability to tell the truth seductively, but he recognizes that it is a decidedly risky endeavor.[29]

Pineda thus links danger to the act of telling the truth—"Decir verdades trae vinculadas en sí las heridas, la sangre y el abatimiento, y aun la muerte; pues no se puede ya vivir en estos tiempos sin la mentira y la adulación" [Telling the truth brings with it wounds, blood, defeat, and even death; for one cannot live in these times without lies and flattery]—which is more extreme than the peril that he has faced in battle or as a captive of Araucanians. As we have seen, the revelation of his true identity paradoxically brought about his salvation, at a moment when he most expected it to endanger his life. Here again, Pineda inverts expectations and displaces the site of anxiety and fear, as well as confusion and deceit, from captivity among "barbarians" to colonial "civilization." However, this is not to say that Pineda presents an absolutely idealized portrait of the captivity experience: to do so would undermine his claim to have served his king by surviving a trying ordeal. Alvarito's safety is not guaranteed by his master Maulicán's benevolence

29. Ibid., 30–31, 34 (emphasis added); González Echevarría, "Law of the Letter," in González Echevarría, *Myth and Archive,* 47. On the evolution of creole self-identification with the conquistadors, see Anthony Pagden, "Identity Formation in Spanish America," in Nicholas Canny and Anthony Pagden, eds., *Colonial Identity in the Atlantic World, 1500–1800* (Princeton, N.J., 1987), 51–93, esp. 58–65.

alone but must also be assured by the captive's own adeptness in hazardous situations.[30]

Thus if Lientur's intervention turns Maulicán from Alvarito's captor into his protector, the captive also participates in inverting the terms of their relationship. Early in their journey to Maulicán's homeland, Alvarito survives a dangerous crossing of a symbolic—and real—frontier, the Bío-Bío River, in which he not only refuses the opportunity to escape but also returns to save his master, who is thought to have drowned. Maulicán's response again reflects the ideal of courtly reciprocity, as we have seen in other invented speeches of indigenous leaders that are cast in European models:

> Cuando el [amo] mío me vio con su caballo de diestro, me empezó a abrazar y decir muy regocijado: capitán, ya yo juzgué que te habías vuelto a tu tierra; seas muy bien parecido, que me has vuelto el alma al cuerpo; . . . si hasta esta hora tenía voluntad y fervorosa resolución de rescatarte y mirar por tu vida, con esta acción que has hecho me has cautivado de tal suerte, que primero me has de ver morir a mí, que permitir que padezcas algún daño.

> When my master saw me with his bridled horse, he began to hug me and tell me joyfully: "Captain, I had already concluded that you had returned to your land; you have made a wonderful appearance, for you have returned my soul to its body; . . . if until now I have had the desire and fervent determination to ransom you and watch out for your life, with this action you have captivated me in such a way, that you will see me die before I permit that you suffer any harm.

The captive here enchants his captor with a demonstration of bravery, loyalty, and generosity, which makes him even more deserving of the favorable treatment that he has already begun to receive.[31]

Again, Pineda goes beyond the simple inversion of roles by describing his "captivation" of Maulicán according to a different model of captivity: one

30. Pineda y Bascuñán, *Cautiverio feliz y razón individual,* [ed. Barros Arana], 3.

31. Ibid., 38. Bauer astutely describes how the episode of the river crossing appropriates "the template of the European New World shipwreck narrative" and echoes "the many exotic accounts of hurricanes during the transatlantic crossing in the European New World shipwreck narratives"; see *Cultural Geography of Colonial American Literatures,* 151.

that consists of intercultural relations founded on mutual respect rather than force and violence. The reciprocal nature of this type of captivity is reflected in his own attitude toward his captor, as Pineda affirms in a ballad entitled "En agradecimiento a Maulicán mi amo, debido a sus agasajos y corteses acciones" [With Gratitude to My Master Maulicán, owing to His Kindnesses and Courteous Actions]:

Cautivo y preso me tienes
Por tu esfuerzo, no es dudable;
Mas con tu piadoso celo
Más veces me aprisionaste.
Mas podré decir, que he sido
Feliz cautivo en hallarme
Sujeto a tus nobles prendas
Que son de tu ser esmalte.

You hold me captive and prisoner
By your courage, there is no doubt;
But with your merciful devotion
You have captivated me more oft.
Yet I can say that I have been
A happy captive to find myself
Subject to your noble qualities
Which give luster to your character.

Alvarito's captivity with Maulicán is no longer based on his physical capture, for it has been superseded by an exemplary relationship that inspires mutual emotional or spiritual captivation.[32]

Such tales of reciprocity and noble comportment on both sides recall the *Abencerraje* model of idealized captivity that we also noted in Barrenechea y Albis's story of Carilab and Rocamila. *Cautiverio feliz* diverges from the latter by following the role reversal employed by Garcilaso in his presentation of Juan Ortiz's captor Mucozo: here again, the Amerindian is the benevolent captor, and the Spaniard, the faithful and appreciative captive. However, Pineda's captivity narrative does not entirely invert the tale of Barrenechea

32. Pineda y Bascuñán, *Cautiverio feliz y razón individual,* [ed. Barros Arana], 47.

y Albis: whereas the latter concludes with Carilab and Rocamila's conversion to the Christian faith and incorporation into Spanish society, Alvarito is not similarly enthralled by his captors' culture to the extent that he would abandon his own. Like Juan Ortiz, the creole captive maintains ties to his homeland, his native culture, and most of all his religion.

In fact, Pineda coincides with el Inca Garcilaso so far as to roundly condemn those Spaniards who, unlike him, completely rescind their Christian faith and "go native" by choosing to remain among Amerindians and assimilating to their way of life. During his stay with the cacique Tureopillan, Alvarito discovers that captive Spanish women have taught the cacique's mestizo children the rudiments of Christian prayer. Alvarito assumes the task of continuing their religious instruction at the behest of Tureopillan, and eventually he is responsible for catechizing and baptizing many indigenous children: significantly, he serves as an interpreter by teaching them to pray in their own language. When he asks an old man why they do not call on the few Spaniards already living among them for these tasks, the Araucanian responds, "Los españoles que habían quedado entre ellos, no eran captivos, sino era de los que por su gusto entre ellos estaban viviendo a su usanza, y no como cristianos, gozando del vicio y del ocio que los demás infieles, por cuya causa no querían ser baptizados por sus manos" [The Spaniards who had stayed among them were not captives but were those who wished to live there according to their customs and not like Christians, enjoying the vice and idleness of the other infidels, for which reason we don't want to be baptized by their hands]. Like Garcilaso, Pineda carefully distinguishes faithless renegades from Christian captives and only ascribes to the latter the ability to contribute to the cause of peace. According to Pineda, even the Araucanians condemn Spaniards who have thus abandoned their homeland and way of life: "Los miraban como a herejes (aunque eran sus compañeros)" [They saw them as heretics (even though they were their companions)]. For Pineda, peaceful intercultural relations are best promoted, not by assimilation, but by efforts to make the captive's culture understandable (and desirable) to the foreign society, as Alvarito does by translating Christian prayers.[33]

33. Ibid., 219.

In contrast to his censure of assimilated Spaniards among Amerindians, Pineda upholds the Araucanians as a model in light of their refusal to compromise their independence, homeland, or identity in captivity. As he points out, many even refuse to abandon their patria when captured,

> porque no hay nación en el mundo que tanto estime y ame el suelo donde nace, como esta de Chile, pues se ha visto en ocasiones llegar a cautivar algunos indios de los más ancianos y viejos, y por no salir de sus tierras, permitir los hiciesen pedazos antes que tener vida fuera de sus límites y contornos, y otros por sus mismas manos haberse dado la muerte.

> because there is no nation in the world that esteems and loves the soil on which it was born as much as this one of Chile, for it has been seen on occasions that, when some of the eldest Indians have been captured, in order not to leave their lands, they permit themselves to be hacked to pieces rather than live outside their surroundings and boundaries, and others have killed themselves with their own hands.

This characterization of Araucanian patriotism is exemplified in the captivity narrative by Maulicán's desire to return home, bringing his captive with him, which is realized at the end of the first of five *discursos* that comprise the text. Here, Pineda invokes the commonplace of the patria as "madrastra de sus hijos" [stepmother to its children], as well as an expression more familiar to modern ears: "No hay cosa más agradable ni más dulce que el propio suelo" [There's nothing more agreeable and sweet than one's homeland]; that is, there's no place like home. Maulicán's eagerness to go home, despite the excellent treatment that he and his party have enjoyed along the way, surely reflects Pineda's understanding of his own displacement. However happy his captivity, it does not lessen his desire to return home, even if that home is a far less pleasant "stepmother to its children."[34]

Pineda here follows his usual protocol by addressing the virtues of patriotism and homesickness first through the example of his indigenous captor

34. Ibid., 66–70. For a similar creole complaint about the patria as "mother of foreigners" (and by extension, stepmother of its children), see Pagden, "Identity Formation in Spanish America," in Canny and Pagden, eds., *Colonial Identity in the Atlantic World,* 59.

and then by incorporating biblical and scholarly digressions on the theme to support his arguments. The digressions, which mainly consist of commentary on certain biblical episodes, again link the captivity narrative to Pineda's critique of Chile's self-serving colonial regime. Referring to Saul's humble affirmations of his own inadequacy in response to the prophet Samuel's urgings to lead Israel as their king, Pineda laments:

> ¿Habrá alguno que diga con Saúl estas palabras? No por cierto, porque esto se acostumbraba cuando los oficios y dignidades buscaban a los más dignos sujetos, y no ellos a los oficios.
>
> ¡O! cómo debían los monarcas, príncipes y superiores imitar al supremo Rey de cielos y tierra, en buscar para los oficios preeminentes, no a los que los solicitan con dineros y favores, sino es a aquellos que los merecen por sus propios servicios, y por haber derramado su sangre en servicio de nuestro Rey y señor de su patria! que de esta suerte se consiguiera la paz y quietud que se desea.
>
> Would anyone repeat Saul's words? Certainly not, for that was customary when the offices and positions sought after the most worthy subjects and not the reverse.
>
> Oh! How the monarchs, princes, and superiors should have imitated the supreme king of heaven and earth in seeking to fill the preeminent offices, not with those who request it with money and favors, but with those who deserve it for their own services and for having spilled their blood in service of our king and lord of the patria! For by this means the sought-after peace and tranquillity could be attained.

Although Pineda affirms the relevance and centrality of this aside, he adds, "Esto baste por ahora, y volvamos a nuestro intento, que es decir, que aunque el extraño suelo mejor hospedaje hace al peregrino, no sé qué se tiene el amor de la patria o la propia habitación para el sosiego y descanso y para la quietud del ánimo" [That's enough for now, and let us return to our intention, which is to say that, although foreign lands offer better lodging to the pilgrim, I don't know what it is about the love of patria and home that calms and soothes the soul]. Just as the captive and his captors desire to return to their homelands, Pineda's excursus on the current political situation reverts to the commentary on patria and the narrative of captivity.[35]

35. Pineda y Bascuñán, *Cautiverio feliz y razón individual,* [ed. Barros Arana], 69.

Pineda's continuous play between digression and intent decenters his discourse just as his discussion of patriotism and foreignness challenges Eurocentric notions of the relationship between the center and margins of empire. According to Pineda, the margins can better serve the center if they are ruled not by Spanish "foreigners" but by those who, like Pineda, know the "marginal" space as their beloved patria. In another passage, he again cites a biblical figure, who declares that "ningún daño mayor . . . le puede venir a una república feliz, que lo que había de ser premio de sus hijos, se comunique por precio a los extraños" [no greater damage . . . can come to a happy republic than selling for a price to foreigners that which should be a reward for its children]. If the children of the patria are creole Chileans like Pineda, the peninsular Spaniards who usurp most positions in the colonial government are "foreigners" who only bring harm to the "happy republic." At other points, Pineda reiterates more explicitly this identification of peninsular Spaniards with foreigners: "Los que vienen a gobernarle forasteros, son siempre sus mayores enemigos, alborotando la guerra y destruyendo la paz" [Those that come to govern it as foreigners are always its greatest enemies, stirring up war and destroying the peace]. In contrast, he points out the benefits that creole rule in the colonies would hold for the empire as a whole:

> Considerando que en tantos siglos como ha que gobiernan a Chille forasteros (que es lo propio que enemigos, como queda probado) no ha tenido provecho ni utilidad de este reino, antes sí cada día recrecerse los gastos de su real patrimonio y dilatarse más la guerra; pudiera ser, como he dicho, que mudase rumbo, y trocando medicinas, fuese saludable ante todo para su patria algún natural y experimentado hijo de ella, que no sin misterio grande mandó Dios que no se pudiese nombrar rey o superior, sino fuese de entre los propios hermanos y compañeros.

> Considering that, in all the centuries that Chile has been governed by foreigners (who are the same as enemies, as has been proved), there has been no benefit or utility to this kingdom, but rather every day the expenses of the royal patrimony grow and the war is more protracted, it could be, as I have said, that if we change course and alter remedies, the most healthy thing for the patria would be some native or experienced child of it, for not without mystery did God command that a king or superior be named from among his own brothers and companions.

Pineda thus frames his argument in an economic and religious context that would surely appeal to his ideal reader, the king, while also insinuating a conception of Chile as a distinguishable entity within the empire—a patria, which implies certain rights as well as responsibilities of its citizens.[36]

The digressions make it clear that Pineda's acclaim of Araucanian patriotism is intended mainly to construct a new model of the creole patriot, which he himself exemplifies as a captive, soldier, and author of a text that explains the reasons for Chile's violent history and instability. The absorption of this feature of indigenous civilization to Pineda's self-portrait as a creole, a "native and experienced son of the patria," recalls his treatment of the cacique Lientur's true friendship. Both cases illustrate how creole writers identify distinctively American qualities in the interest of their own self-aggrandizement and revalorize their place of origin, despite its distance from the center of empire, by pointing out its ability to engender such superior characteristics among its nobler residents. At the same time, Pineda assures readers of his historiographic authority by invoking a tradition of European scholarship in the passages that extol Araucanians or the qualities they embody. Although creole writers frequently responded to theories of "creole degeneration" through the praise of American nature and cities as superior to their European counterparts, Pineda vindicates creole identity by lauding not just an American land but the points of contact with indigenous culture within that space.[37]

SITES OF CULTURAL IMMERSION

Contemporary readers of Pineda, however, would surely have questioned the nature and extent of his return to civilization and loyalty to his Hispanic patria after undergoing such a happy captivity beyond the Araucanian frontier. Although Pineda is eager to affirm the authority that his experience as a captive has granted him, he also seeks to assure his audience that he has not

36. Ibid., 118, 163, 422. For similar arguments for creole rule of the different "kingdoms" of the Spanish Empire, see Pagden, "Identity Formation in Spanish America," in Canny and Pagden, eds., *Colonial Identity in the Atlantic World,* 60–65.

37. On the creole exaltation of American space, see, for example, Bernard Lavallé, "Espacio y revindicación criolla," *Cuadernos hispanoamericanos,* CCCXCIX (1983), 20–39, rpt. in Lavallé, *Las promesas ambiguas: Ensayos sobre el criollismo colonial en los Andes* (Lima, 1993), 105–127.

been adversely affected by exposure to American "barbarism"—not only the natural environment, as seventeenth-century theories of climatic determination would assert, but cultural practices that he has observed and in which he might have participated. As Ralph Bauer indicates, part of Pineda's motivation for writing about his experience is to clarify exactly what he did and did not do as a captive, which corresponds to his overall aim to "hacer las verdades patentes" [make the truth clear]. Bauer argues that, similar to Mary White Rowlandson, the author of the first Anglo-American captivity narrative, *The Soveraignty and Goodness of God* (1682), Pineda defends the purity of his Spanish body and abiding adherence to Christian morality: "'True histories' about captives-completely-returned . . . construct colonial identities through a demonstration that American creoles did not 'go native' as a result of transculturation in the American environment, that creoles are, in fact, as 'Spanish' or 'English' as the Spaniards or English born in Europe." Indeed, as a sign of his maintenance of Spanish cultural and religious identity, Pineda insists that "todo el tiempo que asistí cautivo entre estos naturales, no falté a la obligación de cristiano" [the whole time that I was a captive among these natives, I never failed to fulfill my obligations as a Christian].[38]

As an example of Pineda's anxiety about cultural contamination, Bauer points to the author's response to a romantic theatrical representation of his captivity, which he describes as being performed in Lima shortly after his return. Pineda himself invokes the motif of the "enamored captor's daughter" in his account of how Maulicán's daughter secretly visits him and provides him with food while he is in hiding from enemy caciques. However, Pineda disputes the sexual relationship depicted in the *comedia* that was represented in Lima: "He significado este amoroso subceso con todas circunstancias, por haber sido los informes que hicieron en el Perú a quien hizo una comedia de las cosas de Chile, muy a la contra del hecho: porque representó estos amores muy a lo poético, estrechando los afectos a lo que las obras no se desmandaron" [I have described this amorous incident in detail because there were reports in Peru that made someone produce a comedy about Chile, totally against the facts: because it represented these loves very poetically, stretching the affection farther than the deeds went]. Although he claims here and elsewhere never to have gone astray in deed, Pineda does not shy from

38. Pineda y Bascuñán, *Cautiverio feliz y razón individual,* [ed. Barros Arana], 5, 251; Bauer, "Creole Identities in Colonial Space," *American Literature,* LXIX (1997), 678.

pointing out to his readers the temptation that beautiful indigenous women represent to him as a young captive. Whether his Araucanian companions offer him their daughters and sisters or the women themselves attempt to seduce him, sexual temptation appears to be the greatest danger that he faced while captive. On the occasion of one indigenous celebration, Pineda writes, "Jamás me vi más atribulado, ni más perseguido del demonio que en esta ocasión forzosa y inexcusable, porque [era] aplaudido de los caciques, y solicitado con amor y voluntad a sensuales apetitos" [I never found myself more afflicted and pursued by the devil than on this forced and inexcusable occasion, because it was applauded by the caciques and solicited with love and the pleasure of sensual appetite]. Shortly thereafter, a naked mestiza bathing in the river attracts his attention, and Pineda urges the reader to "[contemplar] un rato la tentación tan fuerte que en semejante lance el spíritu maligno me puso por delante" [contemplate for a while the powerful temptation that in such an episode the malignant spirit put before me].[39]

In an explanation of another such "amoroso subceso" [amorous incident], Pineda legitimates its inclusion by citing a classical authority—"como dijo Ovidio, que es conveniente y permitido en las historias trágicas entreverar algunos amorosos subcesos" [as Ovid said, it is convenient and permitted in tragic histories to interweave some amorous incidents]—and by expounding on the principle of literary variety in his poetic translation of the Ovid citation: "Que un jardín con varias flores / es a la vista agradable; / y así será más loable / lo vario en los escritores" [A garden with various flowers / is pleasing to the sight; / and so even more praiseworthy / is variety in those who write]. Pineda appeals to both the truthful and the pleasurable dimension of his narrative of captivity as much as sixteenth-century ex-captives like Álvar Núñez Cabeza de Vaca, and his incorporation of "amorous incidents," however tempered by disavowal, invites the romanticized interpretation of the Peruvian theatrical performance. A nineteenth-century copyist of *Cautiverio feliz,* in his prologue to a manuscript held at the Archivo Nacional in

39. Pineda y Bascuñán, *Cautiverio feliz y razón individual,* [ed. Barros Arana], 149–150, 289, 296. Triviños points out that, unlike other captives, Pineda does not seek to silence or hide his desire but rather converts it into material for his narrative; see "'No os olvidéis de nosotros,'" *Acta literaria,* XXV (2000), 81–100, esp. 84. Frequently cited in corroboration of the performance of the *comedia* in Lima is Guillermo Lohmann Villena's vague and cursory mention of it, which most likely is based on Pineda's text, since he offers no other source; see Villena, *El arte dramático en Lima durante el virreinato* (Madrid, 1945), 215.

Santiago, asserts the moral threat of the amorous incidents when he explains why he excluded them from his transcription:

> Esta obra parece una *novela* agraciada, y lastimosa, y por lo mismo conmueve a la curiosidad de su lectura: y assí me pareció cosa indecorosa propinar (ni aun con pretextos históricos) a los jóvenes de ambos sexos este veneno que trae la pésima recomendación de una verdadera comedia. Por cuyo motivo sin agraviar a las noticias historicas he bosquejado essos pasajes, sin darles el vivo de todos sus colores, con que aparecieron tan inmundos, como inhonestos.
>
> This work seems like a charming and lamentable *novel,* and for this reason it inspires the curiosity of the reader; thus it seemed improper to me (even with historic pretexts) to offer to the youth of both sexes this venom, which has the dreadful recommendation of a true comedy. For this reason, without affecting the historical information, I have outlined those passages without painting them in all their vivid colors, with which they appeared both indecent and immodest.

Like Pineda, the transcriber (identified by another hand on the manuscript as Father Buenaventura Aranguiz) bemoans that the captive's "true history" has been turned into a "true comedy." Yet the author himself has used these episodes to inculcate his work with the delightful effects of variety, and even the prudish Aranguiz confirms the captivating novelistic dimension of his narrative.[40]

40. Pineda y Bascuñán, *Cautiverio feliz y razón individual,* [ed. Barros Arana], 138; [Buenaventura Aranguiz, R.P.Fr.], "Prólogo del transcriptor," in Francisco Núñez de Pineda y Bascuñán, *Cautiverio feliz, y guerras dilatadas de Chylle,* Archivo Nacional, Santiago de Chile, MS Fondo Antiguo, XXXVIII, fol. 3–9, [5v] (emphasis added). The seventeenth-century Jesuit friar Diego de Rosales suggests the potential literary qualities of Chilean history in general in terms of the variety and pleasure recommended by Renaissance neo-Aristotelians. Rosales concludes his portrait of don Luis Fernández de Córdoba, the governor at the time of Pineda's captivity: "Y por ser tan leído y amigo de historias, deseó mucho ver escrita la historia general deste Reino, porque juzgó, que sería muy gustosa por haber sucedido tanta variedad de cosas y ser estos Indios tan valientes, y no haberlos podido sujetar el poder español ni los bríos y valentía de tan grandes y tan experimentados capitanes generales, como ha tenido este Reino" [Since he was so well read and so fond of histories, he very much desired

Although Pineda assures readers of his unwavering chastity, the sites of greatest temptation—bathing and festivities—reveal ways in which the creole captive traverses the very boundaries between Spanish and Amerindian culture that he seeks to maintain. Alvarito initially rejects participation in native practices such as daily baths and the celebrations that he usually describes as "borracheras" [drunken carousals]. Engagement in these activities would imply a cultural immersion (literal and figurative) that Pineda would not readily acknowledge. However, as his time in captivity progresses, Alvarito begins to join his captors in bathing and festive dancing. But in case readers were worried that Alvarito's transculturation was a unidirectional "Americanization," Pineda also shows ways in which he was able to affect members of the society in which he was held captive.

Daily bathing is the Araucanian custom that Pineda first and most willingly adopts. His claim of initial repugnance toward baths and his preoccupation with justifying his participation in them was surely conditioned by not only a Christian ideal of modesty but also the practice's association with Moorish culture. Indeed, bathing was one of the Islamic customs, like the use of the Arabic language, prohibited by the 1567 royal degree that provoked the Morisco uprising in Alpujarras. Pineda defends his change in attitude thus:

> Aunque a principios llegué a sentir el imitarles en aquella acción y costumbre, después me hice tanto al baño de por la mañana, que era el primero que acudía a él sin repugnancia, porque real y verdaderamente conocí y experimenté ser saludable medicina para la salud y para la conservación de la vida, pues en todo el discurso de mi vida me he hallado tan fuerte ni tan vigoroso como después que continué aquel ejercicio, y el haber vivido después acá con buena salud (a Dios las gracias principalmente) juzgo [haber sido] el haber quedado acostumbrado a refrescarme de mañana; que ya que no puedo ejecutar el baño (por no tener a mano cuando me levanto un cristalino arroyo a que arrojarme), me hago echar en la cabeza y en el celebro un cántaro de agua serenada de buen porte, después de haberme lavado los brazos y la cara.

---

to see written a general history of this realm, because he believed that it would be very pleasing, since such a variety of things have happened in it, and these Indians are so valiant that they have not been subjected by Spanish power nor by the vigor and valor of such great and experienced captains general as there have been in this kingdom]; see Rosales, *Historia general del reino de Chile,* II, 1043.

> Although at first I regretted imitating them in that action and custom, I later became so accustomed to bathing in the morning that I was always the first to do so, without repugnance, because I really and truly found and experienced it to be salutary medicine for health and the preservation of life; for in the whole course of my life I have never found myself to be so strong and vigorous as after continuing that practice, and I attribute living here later in good health (thanks principally be to God) to be a consequence of taking up the custom of the morning bath. And since I cannot implement the bath [as such] (since I do not have at hand a crystalline brook in which to throw myself when I rise in the morning), I have a pitcher of cool, clear water poured over my head, after washing my arms and face.

The elaborate justification that Pineda offers, based on the value of a daily bath for the preservation of good health, should not obscure the fact that he has wholeheartedly embraced participation in an activity that he initially found foreign and repugnant. Pineda's adaptation of the practice after he returns to Christian lands might resemble the Catholic form of baptism by pouring water over the head, but its Araucanian origins are crystal clear.[41]

Of course, the benefits and pleasures gained through this Araucanian custom do not match those that Pineda associates with the understanding of Christian doctrine, which he explains in the following pages to a curious *camarada* (his bed-partner and the son of another kind host, the cacique Luancura). This youth becomes Alvarito's first convert, who begs his Christian friend to baptize him and his family. The episode allows Pineda to demonstrate the ease with which Araucanians willingly befriend Christians and convert to their religion, if exposed to kind actions and good instruction rather than to the diabolical behavior that they have witnessed among most Spaniards. When Alvarito requests permission from Luancura to baptize his son, the cacique affirms that "recibiría grande júbilo y alegría en verlo

41. Pineda y Bascuñán, *Cautiverio feliz y razón individual,* [ed. Barros Arana], 156. The bracketed correction in this passage is based on the 2001 edition; see *Cautiverio feliz,* ed. Ferreccio Podestá and Kordić Riquelme, I, 452. On the 1567 prohibition of bathing in "artificial baths," both public and private, see Luis de Mármol Carvajal, *Historia del* [sic] *rebelión y castigo de los moriscos del reino de Granada* (Madrid, 1852 [orig. publ. Málaga, Spain, 1600]), 161; the Morisco response points out the lack of connection between public bathing and Islamic religious practices and that "por la mayor parte son los bañeros cristianos" [for the most part the bathers are Christians] (164).

hacer cristiano, porque él lo era antiguo y tuvo siempre buena voluntad a los españoles, aunque sus temeridades obligaron a aborrecer sus acciones" [he would receive great joy and happiness in seeing him made a Christian, because he had long been one and always had goodwill toward the Spaniards, although their recklessness had obliged him to hate their actions]. The Araucanians consistently note Alvarito's difference with respect to the wayward Christians that they have known or heard about through their ancestors. Thus even when Alvarito presses Luancura to admit that there must have been some good Christians among all the bad ones that he has described, the cacique responds, "Muy pocos y muy contados . . . los que lo parecían" [Very few and very numbered . . . are those who appeared to be so]. The captive's baptism of his indigenous captors reveals the influence that an exemplary Christian creole is capable of exerting over his pagan neighbors when they are treated with respect and kindness. The introduction of this particular custom among Araucanians mirrors—and perhaps mitigates for Pineda—his own transculturation, for he describes the baptism with the same action of pouring water from a pitcher that had earlier denoted his own adoption of the Araucanian practice of the morning bath.[42]

As evidence of Pineda's resistance to transculturation, Bauer cites the fact that "Pineda, who was forced to participate in sinful *fiestas* during his captivity, returns with revelations about the despicable Americanizations in colonial society," in which Spaniards engage in Mapuche dances and celebrations. However, Pineda is not intransigent in his condemnation of these festivities. Already in the first one in which he participates, related about midway through the first of the five discursos, an inclusive "we" appears, referring to both his Araucanian captors and himself. As the fiesta progresses, we can observe the vacillation between "nosotros" [us] and "los otros" [the others] that characterizes all of Pineda's captivity account. At the beginning, the first-person pronoun represents an uninformed outsider anxiously trying to fit into the spectacle he observes: "A imitación de los otros, fui haciendo lo que los demás hacían, que unos me brindaban a mí y yo brindaba a los otros" [In imitation of the others, I was doing what the rest were doing, and some drank a toast to me and I drank a toast to the others]. Soon, however, the first-person singular is replaced by the inclusive plural, which reveals the captive's sharing in his captors' pains as well as their pleasures: "Y de esta suerte comimos y bebimos muy a gusto, desquitando el ayuno que en el

42. Pineda y Bascuñán, *Cautiverio feliz y razón individual,* [ed. Barros Arana], 169, 171, 175.

trabajoso viaje que padecimos" [And in this way we ate and drank to our satisfaction, making up for the fast that we suffered on the difficult voyage].[43]

The arrival of women signifies the return to divisive pronouns and to the captive's nonparticipation: "Llegaban [las muchachas] a brindarme con mucho amor y agasajo diciéndome, que bailase también con ellas, cosa que no pude hacer de ninguna manera" [The girls arrived to drink a toast to me with much love and hospitality, telling me that I should also dance with them, something which I could in no way do]. Alvarito is granted permission to retire to bed on this and other such occasions. On the night of the extravagant celebration hosted by Ancanamón—the journey to and description of which Pineda narrates over several chapters (discurso 2, chapters 7–14)—Alvarito is particularly thankful that he is allowed to retire early. However, he is also curiously able to describe a substantial portion of these festivities—chapter 13 is dedicated to the "entretenimiento y deleitable festejo de estos naturales" [entertainment and delightful festivities of these natives]—suggesting that he perhaps witnessed more of them than his narrative claims. Not suprisingly, the inclusive "we" does not appear when Pineda describes activities involving "embriaguez" [drunkenness], "el torpe vicio de la deshonestidad" [the lewd vice of immodesty], "danzantes redículos *[sic]*" [ridiculous dancers], and "desnudez y vergüenza" [nudity and shame]. Like many other Spanish chroniclers who morally condemn the New World cultures they describe, Pineda barely manages to put the indigenous celebration on a scale of "civilized" practices by invoking a comparison to ancient cultures.[44]

43. Bauer, "Imperial History, Captivity, and Creole Identity," *Colonial Latin American Review,* VII (1998), 73; Pineda y Bascuñán, *Cautiverio feliz y razón individual,* [ed. Barros Arana], 50. The inclusive "we" also reappears at points where Pineda translates indigenous expressions for his reader: "Llegóse a darnos los buenos días, con repetidos *mari maris,* que son salutaciones entre nosotros" [They arrived to wish us a good day with repeated *mari maris,* which are greetings among us]; see ibid., 71, 87. Pineda's role as interpreter reveals the flexibility of his self-identification. See also discurso 1, chap. 15 for some of the most idyllic moments of his captivity, which Pineda predominantly narrates in first-person plural; see 61–66.

44. Pineda y Bascuñán, *Cautiverio feliz y razón individual,* [ed. Barros Arana], 134–135. Pineda writes, "Y esta es la fiesta más solemne que entre estos bárbaros se acostumbra, imitando a la antigüedad, que usaba en sus convites bárbaros, para la solemnidad de sus banquetes, hacer otro tanto emborrachando algunos y poniéndolos en cueros para que sirviesen de risa y entretenimiento; y este deshonesto abuso fue entre los babilonios más frecuente" [And this is the most solemn festivity that these barbarians are accustomed to, imitating antiquity, when they used to do the same

Nevertheless, Pineda more willingly admits his participation in Araucanian festivities by the third of the five discourses, which begins with the description of a fiesta celebrated in his honor at La Imperial. Alvarito is at the center, both literal and figurative, of these celebrations. A vast crowd of Araucanians has heard of the arrival of the son of the famous Álvaro Maltincampo and come to see him, which is made possible by his ascension to the top of a series of large steps. Alvarito gracefully complies with all that is asked of him, even donning an animal headpiece given to him by a beautiful young woman:

> Traía en la cabeza esta muchacha una *mañagua,* que llaman entre ellos, que es un hocico de zorra desollado, abierta la boca manifestando los dientes y colmillos, y las orejas muy tiesas y levantadas para arriba. . . . Yo traía puesto un sombrerillo viejo, y díjole al cacique la muchacha, que había de bailar conmigo de las manos asida, como lo acostumbran, y que me pusiese aquella mañagua en la cabeza; díjola el cacique: deja que suba primero a lo alto de las gradas para que lo miren todos y lo vean, que para eso lo traemos aquí.—Pues ponedle esta zorrita en la cabeza, para que me la dé después cuando se baje. Cogió el cacique la zorra o la mañagua, quitándosela a la moza, y díjome el cacique: capitán, ponte esta prenda de esta ilcha y estima el favor que te hace, que no le hace a todos. De muy buena gana, por cierto, respondí al cacique alegre y placentero, que por obedecerte haré todo lo que me mandares, y corresponderé con buenas cortesías a la voluntad y amor que me muestra esa hermosa dama.

> This girl wore on her head a *mañagua,* as they call them, which is the skinned muzzle of a fox, with the mouth open to show the teeth and fangs, and the ears very stiff and upright. . . . I had on an old hat, and the girl told the cacique that she would dance with me holding hands, as they usually do, and that I should put that mañagua on my head. The cacique said to her, "Let him first go up to the top of the steps so that everyone can see and look at him, for that is why we brought him here." "Then put this little fox on his head, and he can give it to me afterward when he comes down." The cacique took the fox, or mañagua, from the girl and told me, "Captain, put on the gift from this *ilcha* and esteem the favor that she

---

thing for the solemnity of their barbarous banquets, getting some people drunk and stripping them naked so that they serve as amusement and entertainment; and this immoral abuse was very common among the Babylonians].

> shows you, because she does not show it to everyone." "Certainly, with pleasure," I answered the cacique happily and pleasantly, "for to obey you I will do all that you command, and I will correspond with great courtesies the goodwill and love that this beautiful lady shows toward me."

Although Pineda is careful to represent this exchange with the cacique without affirming his true feelings, his pleasure is perhaps no more (or less) feigned than the affliction he affects as an excuse for not dancing: "Me rogaron que cantase con ellos y bailase; a que les respondí, que no sabía, ni podría aprender aunque quisiese, porque como cautivo me faltaba lo principal, que era el gusto: y esto fue mostrándome algo afligido" [They begged me to sing and dance with them; to which I responded that I did not know how, and I could not learn even if I wanted to, because as a captive I was missing the most important thing, which was pleasure; and this I said showing myself to be rather afflicted].[45]

As Alvarito's familiarity with Araucanian culture deepens, lack of knowledge or desire can no longer ensure his resistance to dancing and the cultural contamination that such an activity might imply to the Inquisition or to a European reader. During his stay with the cacique Tureopillan, Alvarito again instructs his hosts and particularly their children in the Christian religion. It is here, ironically enough, that Alvarito finally accepts the invitation to dance, in yet another celebration that is described in detail:

> Llegaron a mí los hijos del cacique dueño de aquel festejo, acompañados de algunas muchachonas con sus jarros de chicha, a brindarnos y a rogarme a mí que fuese a bailar con ellas . . . se levantaron los viejos y me dijieron que fuésemos a holgarnos, pues habían venido aquellas ilchas (que quería decir damas) a convidarme, y por el respecto de los viejos y sus agasajos, me levanté con ellos y fuimos a la rueda en que estaban bailando, dando vueltas a la redonda del tamboril, y a su imitación hice lo propio: que fue la primera vez que me pudieron obligar con regalos, con cortesías y agrados, a hacer lo que no sabía.
>
> The sons of the cacique who organized that festivity came to me, accompanied by some girls with their pitchers of chicha, to drink a toast and beg me to go dance with them; . . . the old men got up and told me to go and

45. Ibid., 202–203.

have fun with them, since those *ilchas* (which means ladies) had come to invite me, and out of respect for the old men and their kindnesses, I got up with them and we went to the ring of dancers going in circles around a small drum, and imitating them I did the same: which was the first time they managed with gifts, courtesies, and kindnesses to oblige me to do what I did not know how to do.

Pineda goes on to affirm, clearly with a Christian readership in mind, that "el corazón y el spíritu se hallaba repugnante a aquel ejercicio, que por urbanidad y buen respecto ejercitaba" [my heart and spirit found that practice repugnant, which out of courtesy and respect I performed]. As if to reassure those readers, the author follows this episode with a description of one of the most Christianized caciques that Alvarito encounters, Aremcheu, who had been raised among Spaniards. As in Garcilaso's tale of Pedro Serrano, Pineda seems to imply that Christian or pagan identity cannot be determined by appearances but rather should be evaluated according to an individual's actions and the results that they can achieve. In the captive's case, his participation in the dancing at the fiesta has the positive effect on intercultural relations that the creole seeks: "Quedaron muy pagados de mi acción los caciques y los demás muchachos y muchachas, porque me mostraba con ellos alegre, placentero y agradable" [The caciques and the rest of the boys and girls were very content with my action, because I showed myself to be happy, pleasant, and agreeable with them]. Pineda's valorization of the results of his actions over the means used to achieve them is perhaps a risky departure from Counter-Reformation theology, but it shows how the strategic and flexible role of the captive can effectively lessen intercultural hostilities as well as promote the reciprocal acceptance of Christian practices among Araucanians.[46]

By the end of his seven months among Araucanians, the captive has apparently absorbed the lesson of reciprocity that the author presented through the actions of his father and his indigenous hosts. Upon his return to Christian society, when he is redeemed in exchange for an Araucanian captive, Alvarito treats his captors to an abundant meal, although perhaps not on the par of the banquets he had enjoyed among them. The activities following the feast also reflect what he experienced during captivity and consist of a spectacle that would be just as alien to the Araucanian observers as

46. Ibid., 225.

their own celebrations were to Alvarito: "Los soldados tenían unos saraos, entremeses y danzas, y porque gozasen de ellos nuestros amigos huéspedes salimos afuera de los muros, y entre ellos y la contra estacada nos pusimos debajo de unas sombras que al propósito tenían dispuestas" [The soldiers celebrated with theatrical performances and dances, and so that our friendly guests could enjoy them, we went outside the walls, and between them and the counter-fence we put ourselves underneath some shade that we had arranged for the occasion]. Pineda carefully notes their indigenous guests' reaction:

> Volví a convidar a Quilalebo y a los demás caciques principales que entraron a comer dentro del fuerte; asentámoslos en medio de nosotros, adonde con comodidad y todo gusto pasaron la tarde entretenidos, y yo la tuve cierto muy alegre de haber visto a los caciques y a los demás sus compañeros, que asomados por entre las estacas, unos risueños, otros mesurados, y algunos las bocas abiertas, suspensos y elevados parecían de ver la variedad en las figuras, unas ridículas, otras bien compuestas, y algunas formidables, entre diversos bailes y entremeses.
>
> I again invited Quilalebo and the rest of the principal caciques to come inside the fort to eat; we sat them among us, where they comfortably and pleasantly spent an entertaining afternoon. I certainly had a happy one watching the caciques and the rest of their companions, who, sticking their heads between the posts, some smiling, others serious, and some with their mouths open, seemed to be amazed and transported at seeing the variety of figures, some ridiculous, others well composed, and some formidable, among the diverse dances and one-act farces.

The inversion of the roles of spectator and spectacle, which shows that the captive has perhaps gained a sense of what it means to observe his own culture from the outside, relativizes the designations of cultural superiority and inferiority that could be attributed to such festivities: both cultures can be equally "ridiculous" or engrossing. But more importantly for Pineda's purposes, his captivation of the Araucanians through this strategy achieves another desired effect. After being regaled with feasts and festivities, the Araucanians agree to wait one more day for the arrival of the ship that is carrying one of the cacique's relatives, a prisoner who will be exchanged for another Spanish captive who is hoping to be redeemed, Diego Zenteno. In other words, the ex-captive's treatment of his former captors has again mediated Spanish-Araucanian hostilities and brought about a peaceful and mutually beneficial solution to a conflict.[47]

Pineda's admitted absorption of or participation in indigenous practices and his involvement of Araucanians in those of his own culture correspond to the "second step" of his construction of creole identity. Once he has inverted, and thus destabilized, the oppositions between civilization and barbarism, or Spanish and Amerindian, there is room for another category that ostensibly absorbs the best of both cultures, whether exemplary qualities or authoritative knowledge. Certainly Pineda's preoccupation with maintaining his Christian chastity reveals some desire to portray himself as returning "untouched" from his experience in the wilderness, as Ralph Bauer argues. However, his imperviousness is at least partially belied by the transculturation that he shows himself to have undergone by participating in Araucanian customs. Of course, the signs of the creole's cultural immersion may be more unsettling than the techniques of inversion that he employs elsewhere, thus requiring the corresponding introduction of the Araucanians to Christian rituals and Spanish celebrations through the mediation of the captive. Nevertheless, Pineda depicts his own captivity, not as a static confrontation between irreconciliable cultures, but as a process involving exchange and transformation on the part of captives and captors, particularly in terms of a growing familiarity with and acceptance of foreign perspectives and cultural practices. For Pineda, captivity does not transform the "other" into the "same," nor vice versa, but rather distinguishes both Araucanian and Spaniard from a concept of creole identity that is embodied in the captive intermediary. Pineda argues that only creoles like himself have upheld the virtues of Christian culture while purging themselves of the Spanish vices of greed and inhumanity toward Amerindians. And only captives—also like himself—have the knowledge and experience necessary, as well as the trust of the indigenous people, in order to assure the peaceful establishment of Spanish rule and religion in Chile.

Pineda's presentation of the reverse captivity—Amerindians among Spaniards—contributes to his self-aggrandizement as a potentially successful mediator. Like Garcilaso, he portrays Spanish slave-taking and treat-

47. Ibid., 508. By giving as part of his ransom "más de ochocientos pesos de ropa" [clothes worth more than eight hundred pesos], which he knows the Araucanians to value for use in their celebrations, Pineda both contributes to his captors' transculturation and confirms the resemblance suggested in his account between Spanish and indigenous festivities; see 103, 515.

ment of captives as almost invariably cruel and unjust. Many Araucanians relate their experiences of Spanish abuses to the captive, including the kidnapping of their wives and children, which according to Pineda has justly inspired their pursuit of revenge. The cacique Quilalebo incisively contrasts the egalitarian treatment of captives among the Mapuche with the Spanish mistreatment of indigenous captives:

> Veis aquí, capitán, los más cauptivos *[sic]* españoles que andan entre nosotros, el tratamiento que tienen: comen con nosotros, beben con nosotros, visten de lo que nosotros, y si trabajan, es en compañía nuestra. . . . ¿Por qué los españoles, pregunto ahora, nos tienen por tan malos como dicen que somos? pues, en las acciones y en sus tratos se reconoce que son ellos de peores naturales y crueles condiciones, pues a los cautivos los tratan como a perros, los tienen con cormas, con cadenas y grillos, metidos en una mazmorra, y en un continuo trabajo, mal comidos y peor vestidos, y como a caballos los hierran en las caras quemándolas con fuego.
>
> You see here, captain, the treatment of most of the Spanish captives among us: they eat with us, drink with us, dress like us, and if they work, it is in our company. . . . Why then, I ask you, do the Spaniards take us for as bad as they say we are? Since in their actions and behavior one can see that they are of a worse nature and more cruel condition, for they treat their captives like dogs, they keep them fettered in shackles and chains, in a dungeon and in continual hardship, poorly fed and worse dressed, and they brand them on the face like horses, burning them with fire.

Such indictments of Spanish behavior do not appear only in the reported speeches of caciques, for Pineda himself presents the capture and enslavement of Araucanians as a principal cause of the interminable wars: "En esta esclavitud injusta se funda mi opinión y mi discurso para la perpetuidad de esta sangrienta guerra, y para la poca estabilidad en las paces que ha tenido y tendrá en adelante este reino" [My opinion and discourse about the reason for the continuation of this bloody war, and for the little stability that our peace treaties have had and will have in this kingdom, is founded on this unjust slavery]. Pineda decries how Spaniards have exceeded the terms of the 1608 *cédula real* [royal order], which permitted the enslavement of those captured in battle, by taking captive innocent Amerindian allies and those who have offered no resistance. However, he also challenges the legitimacy of all enslavement of Araucanians, arguing that the Chilean conflict does not constitute a "just war." Elsewhere, Pineda categorically affirms that "mientras no se quitare la esclavitud de esta nación . . . es imposible que haya paz firme en este reino; antes tengo por muy cierto que ha de consumirse muy breve y acabarse, porque los que vienen a gobernarle forasteros, son siempre sus mayores enemigos, alborotando la guerra y destruyendo la paz" [as long as the enslavement of this nation does not end . . . it is impossible for peace to be secured in this realm; rather I am certain that it will be consumed and destroyed, because those that come to govern it as foreigners are always its greatest enemies, stirring up war and destroying the peace]. Here, Pineda's condemnation of the captivity of Amerindians is linked to his critique of "foreign" governors, who are the "greatest enemies" of both Araucanians and creoles alike.[48]

Pineda's opposition to slavery appears to have been expressed in writing more than actions. As governor of Valdivia, he issued a certificate approving the enslavement of an Araucanian captured in battle by one of his captains, citing its legality under the terms of the cédula real. But the portrayal of inhuman Spanish captors serves a strategic purpose in *Cautiverio feliz,* for it highlights the exemplary behavior of creole captors like Pineda and his father by contrast. His father's kind treatment and frequent release of captives is recognized by Lientur in the speech that saves Pineda's life and leads to his protection and liberation by Maulicán. Another cacique, Ancanamón, tells Alvarito that his father is well loved among Araucanians because "había muchos cautivos a quienes había hecho muy buen pasaje, y solicitado sus rescates y puéstoles en libertad" [there were many captives whom he had treated very well, and solicited their ransoms and freed]. Pineda also portrays himself in the role of benevolent captor when he describes his reencounter with Maulicán's daughter after returning to Spanish society. Pineda insists that the romantic involvement represented in the play performed in Lima is based on what was merely an act of reciprocal obligation:

48. Pineda y Bascuñán, *Cautiverio feliz y razón individual,* [ed. Barros Arana], 163, 330, 336; for his arguments on just war, see discurso 3, chapter 23, "En que se trata, si la guerra que está perpetrada en este reino de Chile, es justa o injusta" [In Which Is Treated, whether the War That Is Perpetrated in This Kingdom of Chile, Is Just or Unjust], 264–270. On the 1608 *cédula*'s legalizing the enslavement of Araucanian prisoners of war, see Villalobos, *La vida fronteriza en Chile,* 265–286; the cédula was suspended during the Jesuit-led period of defensive war from 1612 to 1626, and it was officially revoked in 1683, but the practice continued into the nineteenth century. See also Korth, *Spanish Policy in Colonial Chile,* on the history of slaving policies and practices in Chile.

> Sólo pudieron dar motivo el haber cautivado a esta china después de mi rescate, y en presencia del gobernador, haber hecho que llamasen Pichi Álvaro (que así me llamaban en su tierra); y habiendo yo llegado a donde estaba . . . [ella] me representó los servicios que me había hecho cuando estuve cautivo . . . diciéndome que bien sabía yo las finezas que había hecho conmigo en tiempo que sin libertad me hallaba, de aflicciones y penas combatido . . . que ahora que ella se veía sin su libertad, en poder de mis amigos y compañeros, trocadas las suertes, mostrase ser quién era y la correspondencia que le debía, rescatándola luego y sacándola del poder en que se hallaba, porque no había de estar con otra persona que conmigo.

> The only motive for it could be the fact that this woman was captured after my ransom, and in the presence of the governor she had them call for Pichi Álvaro (for that is how they called me in her land) . . . she declared the services that she had done for me while I was captive . . . telling me that I knew well the kindnesses she had bestowed on me when I found myself without liberty, combating afflictions and hardships . . . and that now that she saw herself without liberty, in the power of my friends and companions, our fortunes exchanged, that I should show who I was and what I owed to her, ransoming her immediately and taking her out of the power in which she was held, for she would not be with another person except me.

The woman's declaration of her compassionate treatment of Pineda and his consequent obligations toward her offer a rare glimpse of a native female captive not only speaking but manipulating a situation to her own benefit. Pineda was left with no choice but to pay all that was asked for her.[49]

Although essentially forced into the role of benevolent captor by his former mistress—her compelling speech suggests that the inversion in their rela-

49. Pineda y Bascuñán, *Cautiverio feliz y razón individual,* [ed. Barros Arana], 127, 150. The "Certificación de la esclavitud de un indio en la guerra dada por el gobernador de la plaza de Valdivia, don Francisco de Pineda Bascuñán al capitán Francisco Flandes Grimados" [Certification of the Slavery of an Indian in War Given by the Governor of the Fortress of Valdivia, don Francisco de Pineda Bascuñán, to the captain Francisco Flandes Grimados], dated 1674, was published by Álvaro Jara, "Pineda y Bascuñán, hombre de su tiempo (tres documentos)," *Boletín de la Academia Chilena de la Historia,* XXI (1954), 77–85, which also includes the record of Pineda's sale of a black slave in 1641.

tionship is not quite complete—Pineda reclaims his exemplary status when he recounts the woman's subsequent conversion. He asserts that, although he avoided Christianizing her because he planned to return her to her land and family, she learned to pray and begged a visiting Jesuit to baptize her. However, the day after her baptism, splendidly celebrated by Pineda, she fell ill. A few days later, Pineda buried her "con la solemnidad que su dichosa muerte merecía y mi obligación forzosa demandaba" [with the solemnity that her blessed death deserved and my unavoidable obligation demanded]. The woman's spiritual redemption takes precedence over her physical redemption from captivity, allowing Pineda to demonstrate the positive contributions of the creole ex-captive (and, now, captor) to the evangelization of Araucanians.[50]

Francisco Núñez de Pineda y Bascuñán's challenge to Spanish imperial strategies and practices in Chile does not contest its ultimate goals of pacification and conversion. Nevertheless, the woman's death, like that of his first convert, Ignacio, reveals the limits of the creole mediator's discourse of peaceful reconciliation through happy captivities and benevolent proselytism. Maulicán would surely not have accepted the Christian burial of his daugher as fulfillment of Pineda's obligations to his former captors. Pineda may present the baptisms as evidence of the triumph of his mediation, but the deaths of his principal converts disrupt the narrative of benign evangelization and lay bare the violence of its effects on the native populace. Ultimately, Pineda is more successful at rendering a self-portrait of a model Christian creole—both captive and captor—than at producing Christian Araucanians.[51]

Diogo-Caramuru would seem to be the realization of Pineda's dream: the captive who captivates his captors to the extent that he can bring about their voluntary subjugation to the Portuguese Crown and the Catholic cross, without its costing his converts' lives. If Pineda defends the valuable service and admirable qualities of the captive (and the writer of the captivity narrative), the protagonist of *Caramuru,* we will see, gains heroic status through his experience as a captive. José de Santa Rita Durão molds the epic of American conquest—a genre inaugurated, with *La Araucana,* in the Chilean context—to the structures and motifs proper to the captivity narrative.

50. Pineda y Bascuñán, *Cautiverio feliz y razón individual,* [ed. Barros Arana], 151.

51. For Ignacio's death, see ibid., 184–188.

chapter Four : WRITING HOME : THE CAPTIVE HERO IN JOSÉ DE SANTA RITA DURÃO'S *Caramuru*

DURÃO'S HOMELESSNESS, *Caramuru*'S HOMES

A century after Francisco Núñez de Pineda y Bascuñán left his Chilean patria for the final time, the Augustinian friar José de Santa Rita Durão (1722–1784) published, in Lisbon, an epic poem about the history of his distant Brazilian homeland. The year was 1781, the same year that el Inca Garcilaso's history of Peru was withdrawn from circulation by the Spanish Crown in response to the Tupac Amaru uprising. Like Durão, Garcilaso had enjoyed both a personal and an editorial relationship with Lisbon. The Portuguese capital was not only the place of publication of two of his books but also the city that, as he claims in the dedication of *La Florida del Inca,* welcomed him as a "native son" when he first disembarked on European soil. Durão himself would arrive in the capital of the Portuguese Empire in 1731, having left his American patria to receive an education, a practice common among Brazilian elites throughout the colonial period. Years later, Durão would be forced to uproot once again and abandon his adopted homeland as the victim of an archbishop's persecution; he would return to Portugal only after an agitated migration through several European countries and a protracted stay in Rome. The publication of *Caramuru: Poema épico do descobrimento da Bahia* in Lisbon in 1781, fifty years after his first arrival there, thus marks a homecoming of sorts for this other "natural son" of Lisbon.[1]

1. Garcilaso affirms both his "afición" [fondness] for and "obligación" [obligation] to the Portuguese nation in the dedication to dom Teodosio, the duke of Bragança: "La primera tierra que vi cuando vine de la mía, que es el Perú, fue la de Portugal, la isla del Fayal y la Tercera, y la real ciudad de Lisbona, en las cuales, como gente tan religiosa y caritativa, me hicieron los ministros reales y los ciudadanos y los de las islas toda buena acogida, como si yo fuera hijo natural de alguna de ellas" ["On

However, Durão opens his work with an affirmation of love for another, more distant patria, one that is broader than the place of origin announced on the title page (where he declares himself to be "natural da Cara-Preta nas Minas Gerais" [native of Cara-Preta in Minas Gerais]). In the *reflexões prévias* to the poem, he writes, "Os sucessos do Brasil não mereciam menos um Poema que os da Índia. Incitou-me a escrever êste o amor da Pátria" [The events of Brazil are no less deserving of a poem than those of India. Love for my homeland incited me to write this one]. Modeled on *Os Lusíadas* (1572), Luis de Camões's epic of Portuguese expansion in the East, *Caramuru* pays homage to the discovery and colonization of Brazil. The poem centers on the legendary adventures of the historical figure Diogo Álvares, a Portuguese sailor shipwrecked in Bahia in the early sixteenth century. Álvares is presented as the heroic founder of the Portuguese colony, but only after he has experienced captivity among and integration with the Tupinambá Indians, taking both an Amerindian wife (Paraguaçu) and name (Caramuru). *Caramuru* also relates the couple's voyage to France, where they are married and Paraguaçu is baptized before the French court. By tracing their displacement to Europe and back to Brazil, Durão redefines the colony as home and inscribes the origins of Brazilian culture in the transculturated characters of a Portuguese ex-captive and a converted Amerindian noblewoman. Durão

---

coming to Spain from my native Peru, the first places I visited were the Portuguese islands of Fayal and Terceira, and the imperial city of Lisbon. The royal ministers and inhabitants of that city as well as the people of the islands were most kind and charitable, offering me the finest reception and welcoming me as if I had been a native son"]; see Inca Garcilaso de la Vega, *La Florida del Inca,* ed. Sylvia Lynn Hilton (Madrid, 1982 [orig. publ. Lisbon, 1605]), 61; [Garcilaso], *The Florida of the Inca,* ed. and trans. John Grier Varner and Jeannette Johnson Varner (Austin, Tex., 1951), xxxv. In "¿Por qué Inca Garcilaso de la Vega se hizo editar en Lisboa?" *Norte: Revista hispano-americana,* CCLXIV (1975), 75–76, Joaquim Montezuma de Carvalho suggestively speculates that Garcilaso's decision to publish in Lisbon and dedicate both *La Florida del Inca* and *Comentarios reales de los Incas* to members of the House of Bragança (which assumed the Portuguese throne in 1640, ending the sixty-year period known as the "Spanish captivity") arose from solidarity with another powerful empire then subject to the Spanish Crown, like that of his Inca ancestors. On Brazilian intellectuals' close ties with Portugal because of the lack of printing presses and universities in the colony, in contrast to Spanish America, see David T. Haberly, "Colonial Brazilian Literature," in Roberto González Echevarría and Enrique Pupo-Walker, eds., *The Cambridge History of Latin American Literature,* III (Cambridge, 1996), 47–68, esp. 61.

thus reacts to his own migratory, "homeless" experience in much the same way as both the displaced Peruvian mestizo and the ex-captive Chilean creole, by turning to writing in an attempt to invent—in both senses of the Latin root *invenire,* to find as well as to create—a home.[2]

Brazilian literary historians' unanimous inclusion of *Caramuru* among the accomplishments of the Escola Mineira attests to Durão's successful invention of a home for his work. The so-called Escola Mineira, a rather disparate group of Arcadian poets active in Durão's homeland of Minas Gerais, is credited with founding a national literature in its neoclassical poetry celebrating Brazilian nature. Because of the involvement of some of its members in the attempted rebellion known as the Inconfidência Mineira of 1789, the group is also associated with early political aspirations to national independence. Durão, in fact, left Brazil at the age of nine and does not appear to have corresponded with the members of literary or political society in Minas Gerais. Nevertheless, his affirmations of patriotism and his favorable depiction of Brazil and its native inhabitants have secured him a place as one of the founders in the national literary canon and a precursor to the Indianist tendency of Brazilian Romanticism. One early-twentieth-century critic would even praise Durão's "unconscious" transmission of his ideas about Brazilian independence into the poem.[3]

More modern critics have taken the opposite tack and criticized Durão's European allegiances, colonialist agenda, and negative portrayal of Amerindians in *Caramuru.* Flávio R. Kothe's examination of the "colonial canon," for example, summarily describes Durão's project as "Portuguese, colonialist, francophile, and contrary to Brazilian autonomy." Kothe pays particular

2. José de Santa Rita Durão, *Caramuru: Poema épico do descobrimento da Bahia* (São Paulo, 1945 [orig. publ. Lisbon, 1781]), 13.

3. See Arthur Viegas, *O poeta Santa Rita Durão: Revelações históricas da sua vida e do seu século* (Brussels, 1914), lxv–lxvi: "In effect, the aspiration to a new Patria—a Brazilian Patria consisting in an autonomous Nationality—was already the invincible desire, although still latent, of the best colonial poets. . . . The friar-poet was not exempt from that sentiment. . . . Durão instinctively—perhaps unconsciously—transmitted his own sentiments through the thrilling strophes of liberty that he put in the mouth of the indigenous warrior." See also José Veríssimo, *História da literatura brasileira: De Bento Teixeira (1601) a Machado de Assis (1908)* (Rio de Janeiro, 1969), 104. On the protonationalist role ascribed to Durão and his poem during the Romantic period, see Antônio Cândido, "Estrutura e função do *Caramuru,*" *Revista de letras,* II (1961), 47–66, esp. 47.

attention to the protagonists' trip to France, a journey that the critic erroneously suggests to be of Durão's invention. After criticizing the Romantics' reading of Diogo and Paraguaçu as "'the origin of Brazilianness' or 'the Brazilian Adam and Eve,'" Kothe proceeds with an inverse allegorical interpretation by reading the trip to Paris as a metaphor for the Brazilian elite's inauthentic desire to imitate, and thus gain acceptance at, the center of culture and civilization: "Durão expresses the francocentrism of the Luso-Brazilian 'elite.'" Like the Romantic and nationalist interpretations, Kothe's reading privileges a single space (the "exile" in France over the captivity in Brazil) and grants the cultural exchange that occurs there unidirectional significance (Luso-Brazilian absorption of French culture).[4]

Such a reading allows Kothe to sustain his interpretation of colonial Brazilian literature as a mere copy of metropolitan models, solely reproductive of Eurocentric discourse. In so doing, his reading reduces the plurality of spaces and movements in *Caramuru,* which reflect the more complex and interactive process of transculturation that we have seen at work in other treatments of captivity. In *Caramuru,* intercultural contact occurs on both sides of the Atlantic and is not limited to an opposition between Portuguese and Amerindian. Indeed, alliances and conflicts emerge both within and across the various indigenous and European groups represented in the poem. *Caramuru* resists the categories involved in a reading of Durão's loyalties as exclusively French, Portuguese, or Amerindian. We here will explore the ambiguous representation of the sites of home and exile in *Caramuru* in order to underscore, rather than resolve, the contradictions involved in Durão's—and Diogo Álvares's—multiple allegiances.

THE FUGITIVE FRIAR

Durão's own travels, both across the Atlantic and within Europe, reflect the migratory experience of such illustrious predecessors of Iberian letters as Father Antonio Vieira and el Inca Garcilaso. Durão recounts his journey through Europe in the *Retractação,* a statement written upon his arrival in Rome in 1764 and presented to Pope Clement XIII. Officially, the text is a retraction of some anti-Jesuit sermons that the friar had penned in Portugal. It is also an almost picaresque autobiography, narrating the identities and loyalties that Durão adopted while seeking protection and financial support

4. Flávio R. Kothe, *O cânone colonial* (Brasília, 1997), 358, 360.

during his travels through Spain, France, and Italy. As the *Retractação* suggests, Durão's written work may be the primary source of his misadventures. Although he claims to have written an anti-Jesuit *carta pastoral* for the bishop of Leiria in the effort to advance his career and serve his benefactor ("tratei somente de servir a minha ambição e o bem-estar do bispo" [I tried only to serve my ambition and the well-being of the bishop]), his writings earn him only the bishop's ungrateful condemnation. Once promoted to archbishop of Évora, Durão's former patron describes him thus: "Lá talentoso é elle, mas creio que em pouco mais deve ser empregado que em coisas galhofeiras, como são poesias e assumptos de igual jaez. De facto eu nunca lhe utilizei os serviços em coisa de maior monta" [He's quite talented, but I think that he should be employed in little more than silly things, like poetry and similar subjects. In fact, I never used his services in matters of greater importance]. According to Durão, the archbishop's statements precipitated the friction between them, which forced Durão into exile. Nevertheless, in the tradition of both the picaresque novel and the relación de servicios, Durão continued to use narration as a record of service and form of self-defense. If writing the *Retractação* represents an attempt to vindicate his actions regarding the Jesuits, perhaps *Caramuru* may also be read as Durão's affirmation of the poetic vocation that the archbishop had disparaged.[5]

5. José de Santa Rita Durão, *Retractação,* in Viegas, *O poeta Santa Rita Durão,* 3–69, esp. 20, 43. The text appeared as the preface to a work in Latin entitled *Epitome rerum in Lusitania gestarum adversus venerabilem Jesu Societotem* (written 1764). Durão narrates how, during his exile, he had to defend himself against accusations of being a Portuguese spy (while in Spain, during the 1762 war with Portugal) as well as alternately present himself as a friend or an enemy of the Jesuits, depending on the affiliations of his interlocutor. For example, Durão writes that, at an Augustinian convent in Spain, "infelizmente aquelles bons religiosos, sabendo que eu era apologista dos Jesuitas, perseguiram-me tão rudemente que não sei como não dei em doido" [unfortunately those good friars, knowing that I was an apologist for the Jesuits, persecuted me so rudely that I don't know how I didn't go crazy]. Durão apparently learned his lesson, and thenceforth presented himself as pro- or anti-Jesuit according to the biases of his potential benefactors during the rest of his journey to Rome. Thus during a particularly arduous winter in France, "vendo-me absolutamente falto de dinheiro, fui aconselhado por um amigo a quem contara as minhas desventuras, a que procurasse os Jesuitas e lhes narrasse a minha história" [finding myself absolutely out of money, I was advised by a friend to whom I told my misadventures that I should seek out the Jesuits and tell them my story] (55–56). On the connections between the picaresque and the relación de servicios, see Roberto González Echevarría, "The Law

Durão's migrations, as well as his use of writing to evoke his Brazilian homeland, actually link him to the members of the religious order that he once so vigorously condemned. Following the expulsion of the Jesuits from the Portuguese Empire in 1759, and eventually from Spain and its colonies as well, Europe would provide fertile terrain for many exiled members of the order to write about their American homelands. Perhaps because of his own forced dislocations, Durão's *Retractação* reveals a heartfelt, if belated, solidarity with the Jesuits, defending them against the accusations that had led to their expulsion. Durão might have identified particularly with the patriotic nostalgia that infused the writings of American-born Jesuits who, like him, would take refuge in Rome. David Brading describes how Jesuit writers such as the Ecuadorian Juan de Velasco, the Chilean Juan Ignacio Molina, and the Mexican Francisco Javier Clavijero took up the literary praise and philosophical defense of the New World and, in particular, of its creole and indigenous inhabitants after being forced to abandon their American homelands. Despite his origin in a different empire as well as religious order, Durão coincides on many points with the tradition of "creole patriotism" demonstrated by the exiled Jesuits. In fact, the association that can be established between Durão's exile and his affirmation of patriotism by writing his homeland's history is a thread linking him not only to his Jesuit contemporaries but also to the tradition of authorial self-fashioning among American-born writers like Garcilaso and Pineda. In *Caramuru,* as in the work of these authors, tales of captivity play a decisive role in redefining the space in which the writing subject feels "at home."[6]

---

of the Letter: Garcilaso's *Comentarios,"* in González Echevarría, *Myth and Archive: A Theory of Latin American Narrative* (Durham, N.C., 1998), 43–92.

6. The ten "reflexões" at the end of Durão's *Retractação* criticize in particular José I's powerful minister, the marquis of Pombal (Sebastião José de Carvalho e Mello), for his anti-Jesuit policies. Durão also defends the Jesuits on the basis of their scholarship and writing, affirming that "fora coisa superflua gastar tempo a defender o valor litterário da Companhia. A quem tiver dúvidas, bastar-lhe-ha examinar as livrarias" [it would be superfluous to waste time defending the literary value of the Company. Whoever is in doubt need just examine their libraries]; see Viegas, *O poeta Santa Rita Durão,* 188. Durão's defense of the Jesuit order in his writings has led some critics to mistakenly identify him as a Jesuit himself; see Kothe, *O cânone colonial,* 345. On the creole patriotism of the exiled Jesuits, see D. A. Brading, *The First America: The Spanish Monarchy, Creole Patriots, and the Liberal State, 1492–1867* (Cambridge, 1991), 447–464; the authors mentioned all produced works in the

Caramuru's construction of home is also no less complex and contradictory than that of *La Florida* or *Cautiverio feliz*. Antônio Cândido points out that, of all the members of the Escola Mineira, Durão is the only one to consign his place of origin to the title page of his work. Perhaps his very distance from Brazil makes it more urgent for him to do so, in order to explain his declaration of "amor da Pátria" [love of patria] in the preface. Although the poem's hero associates patria with a very different location, he invokes it from a corresponding point of distance. After saving a group of shipwrecked Spaniards from captivity and certain death by cannibalism, the former castaway and captive Diogo Álvares sends them off to Spain with the following words:

> Felizes vós, diz Diogo, afortunados,
> A quem da cara pátria é concedido
> Tornar hoje aos abraços desejados,
> Depois de tanto tempo a ter perdido,
> Enquanto eu nestes climas apartados
> Me vejo de seguir-vos impedido;
> Que fiar temo de tão débil lenho
> Outra vida que em mais que a própria tenho.
>
> Happy and fortunate are you, said Diogo,
> Whose return today has been granted
> To the beloved patria's desired embrace,
> After it has been so long missed.
> Meanwhile I in these distant climes
> Find myself impeded from following you,
> For trusting to such a weak plank I fear
> Another life that more than my own I hold dear.

Diogo here identifies his patria as Iberian and his current location in the Americas as one of loss and separation ("in these distant climes"). He may no longer be impeded by physical captivity, but his emotional captivation by an indigenous woman—the "life that more than my own I hold dear"—prevents him from embarking with her on a risky transatlantic voyage to his "beloved patria." In other words, Diogo's ties to the captors' culture may

---

1780s defending their homelands from accusations of "creole degeneracy" made by Enlightenment philosophers such as Buffon and De Pauw.

interfere with his ability to go home, but they have not stripped him of his Portuguese identity. Conversely, Durão's distance from his Brazilian origins as an adult in Europe has not mitigated his own sense of patria.[7]

Diogo will eventually make the journey to Europe with Paraguaçu, albeit to Paris rather than to Portugal. The dislocation is significant, since the return trip "home," for both of the protagonists, will be to Brazil rather than Portugal. *Caramuru* thus reinscribes the circular movement characteristic of captivity, shipwreck, and even conquest narratives, wherein European society is the site of departure as well as of the intended return. Unlike *Cautiverio feliz,* the events and characters of *Caramuru* belong to the period of initial contact, before different regions of the New World had become the homelands of American-born inhabitants of European descent. *Caramuru's* theme and setting as well as its genre thus more closely resemble *La Araucana* (1569), the classic epic of American conquest by Pineda's precursor in Chilean letters, Alonso de Ercilla y Zúñiga (1533–1594). Yet unlike Ercilla, Durão's site of writing is distant from the time and place of his poem's subject matter, sixteenth-century Bahia, which stands for his own origins as well as those of his Brazilian patria.

Nevertheless, the ambiguity of the locations of "beloved patria" and "distant climes" is not entirely resolved by the felicitous fusion of the two terms. The poem maintains the double inscription of Brazil as both a home and a distant colony throughout, allowing the conflicting readings among nineteenth- and twentieth-century critics indicated above. Cândido notes, "Durão's work can be seen as expressing the Portuguese triumph in America, as much as that of the particularist positions of the Americans; and in principle, it could serve either to symbolize the Lusitanization of the country, or to accentuate its nativism." In "Estrutura e função de *Caramuru,"* Cândido explores the structural and generic aspects of the poem that enable such a double reading. What follows below will approach the poem's ambivalence and the contradictory construction of both "home" and "self," first through Durão's manipulation of diverse sources and discourses and then through his invocation of motifs proper to the captivity narrative, such as inversion and reciprocity, displacement and transculturation.[8]

7. Durão, *Caramuru,* 13, 147; Antônio Cândido, *Formação da literatura brasileira (Momentos decisivos),* I, *1750–1836,* 8th ed. (Belo Horizonte, Brazil, 1996 [orig. publ. São Paulo, 1959]), 297. Cândido reads Durão as the "most isolated" member of the group that would form the Escola Mineira (170).

8. Cândido, "Estrutura e função do *Caramuru," Revista de letras,* II (1961), 60.

Caramuru's captives and exiles appear as exemplary figures when they choose to serve as mediators between the two cultures with which they can claim familiarity. Moreover, the potentially empowering nature of the disabling experience of captivity is reflected, on a formal level, in the author's ability to mediate between traditions and discourses. In effect, Durão's use of a captivity narrative to compose an epic of national origins authorizes his own intermediary position. The poem's diverse sources and generic influences demonstrate the author's familiarity with both the margins and the center of a literary tradition as well as of an empire.

Durão overtly acknowledges these sources and influences in the prologue. First, by suggesting that the "events of Brazil" are no less deserving of memorialization in poetry than those of Vasco da Gama in India, Durão aligns his project with Camões's *Os Lusíadas,* which recounts the heroic history of the Portuguese nation up to the moment of writing. Durão's historical frame is similarly ambitious. The indigenous protagonist Paraguaçu recounts a prophetic dream in cantos 8 and 9, which, together with the other interpolated narrations, provides a comprehensive history of colonial Brazil from Pedro Álvares Cabral's landing to Durão's era. Durão follows Camões by subordinating the spatial and temporal diversity of events narrated in *Caramuru* to the epic precept of unity of action. Like *Os Lusíadas,* as well, the action is structured around a voyage by sea. However, Durão's inspiration in an ancient literary genre is countered by the presence of ethnographic and naturalist discourses in the poem, which replace the mythological universe of *Os Lusíadas* and its classical models. Rather than enchanted isles and heathen gods—the "machinery" of *Os Lusíadas* criticized by Voltaire in his "Essay on Epick Poetry"—*Caramuru* follows the example of Ercilla's *La Araucana* by incorporating detailed descriptions of indigenous practices and of Brazilian flora and fauna.[9]

9. [François-Marie Arouet] Voltaire, "Essay on Epick Poetry," in Stuart Curran, ed., *Le Bossu and Voltaire on the Epic* (Gainesville, Fla., 1970 [orig. publ. London, 1727]), 37–130, esp. 74–75. In the essay, Voltaire approvingly describes Ercilla's incorporation of ethnography and geography into *La Araucana* as "necessary, and not unpleasant in a Subject where the Scene lies under the other Tropick" (94). On the structural and stylistic correspondences between *Os Lusíadas* and *Caramuru,* see Carlos de Assis Pereira, *Fontes do "Caramuru" de Santa Rita Durão* (Assis, Brazil, 1971), 58–84. Sergio Buarque de Holanda points out the continuing relevance of *Os*

The attention to nature and ethnography in the poem reflects both Diogo Álvares's sixteenth-century context and Durão's eighteenth-century one. Mary Louise Pratt describes the intellectual preoccupations of mid-eighteenth-century Europe as the convergence of "natural history as a structure of knowledge, and the momentum toward interior, as opposed to maritime, exploration." While modeling itself after the navigational paradigm of *Os Lusíadas, Caramuru's* descriptions of Brazilian flora and fauna manifest the interest in cataloguing nature that characterizes eighteenth-century narratives of interior exploration of the American continent. Yet Durão's contemporaries were hardly the first to concern themselves with the description of New World nature as well as the history and customs of its inhabitants. In Diogo Álvares's time, scholars, missionaries, and royal officials collected information from travelers and indigenous informants about the diverse arenas of Iberian exploration, in the effort to produce knowledge that would allow them to explain discrepancies with classical sources, to glorify God's handiwork, to exploit natural resources, and to promote colonization. Sixteenth-century Portuguese works of natural history often focused on the East Indies, such as Garcia da Orta's *Coloquios dos simples e drogas he cousas medicinais da India* (1563) and Cristóvão da Costa's *Tractado de las drogas y medicinas de las Indias Orientales* (1578), both of which were subsequently translated and published by the eminent Flemish botanist Carolus Clusius. But the geography, plants, animals, and indigenous cultures of Brazil were also the object of systematic description in late-sixteenth-century works, such as the scholar and royal official Pero de Magalhães Gândavo's *Tratado da terra do Brasil* (ca. 1570) and *História da província de Santa Cruz* (1576), the Jesuit father Fernão Cardim's *Tratados da terra e do gente do Brasil* (ca. 1584), and the explorer and sugar planter Gabriel Soares de Sousa's *Tratado descriptivo do Brasil em 1587*. And it was not only Portuguese scholars, officers, and ecclesiastics who contributed to the circulation of knowledge about Brazilian nature and peoples; as we have seen, the foreign-born captives Hans Staden and Peter Carder also presented reports about Brazil to royal audiences and managed to see their accounts in print.[10]

Lusíadas to eighteenth-century writers in Holanda, *Capítulos de literatura colonial,* ed. Antônio Cândido (São Paulo, 1991), 86.

10. Mary Louise Pratt, *Imperial Eyes: Travel Writing and Transculturation* (London, 1992), 9; and see Garcia da Orta, *Coloquios dos simples e drogas he cousas medicinais da India* (Goa, 1563); Cristóbal Acosta (Cristóvão da Costa), *Tractado de las drogas y medicinas de las Indias Orientales* (Burgos, 1578). On Clusius's evaluations

Participating in the tradition of Brazilian historiography initiated by Gândavo, Sousa, and Cardim are the three sources that Durão resourced for his work, which he identifies in the prologue: Simão de Vasconcelos's *Chrônica da Companhia de Jesu do estado do Brasil* (1663), Francisco de Brito Freyre's *Nova Lusitânia, história da guerra brasílica* (1675), and Sebastião da Rocha Pitta's *História da América portugueza* (1730), the first attempt at a comprehensive history of Portuguese America. These writers had themselves drawn on the oft-chronicled and already legendary story of Diogo Álvares. Durão's double gesture in the prologue to colonial historiographic sources and the European literary model of the Camonian epic thus aligns his approach with the authorial strategies of Garcilaso and Pineda. The discursive ambiguity of *Caramuru* has sometimes led to its disparagement as "rhymed chronicle," a prose history awkwardly rendered in epic verse. Nevertheless, the convergence of different discourses also reveals the author's effort to secure his authority by demonstrating a familiarity with a historiographic as well as a poetic tradition, both of which had already been transformed by the task of representing a New World.[11]

---

and annotated editions of their texts, see Brian W. Ogilvie, *The Science of Describing: Natural History in Renaissance Europe* (Chicago, 2006), 244–254. Pero de Magalhães Gândavo's *História da província de Santa Cruz* was published in Lisbon in 1576, but his *Tratado da terra do Brasil* was first published in the *Collecção de notícias para a história e geografia das nações ultramarinas,* IV (Lisbon, 1826). Gabriel Soares de Sousa's *Tratado descriptivo do Brasil em 1587* was also first published in the *Collecção de notícias para a história e geografia das nações ultramarinas,* III (Lisbon, 1825); see Gabriel Soares de Sousa, *Tratado descriptivo do Brasil em 1587,* ed. Francisco Adolpho de Varnhagen, 3d ed. (São Paulo, 1938). Fernão Cardim's *Do principio e origem dos índios do Brasil e de seus costumes, adoração e cerimonias* and *Do clima e terra do Brasil e de algumas cousas notáveis* were first published as *Tratados da terra e do gente do Brasil . . .* (Rio de Janeiro, 1925), although (as I discuss in Chapter 5) Samuel Purchas published a translation of both treatises, which had been captured by a pirate, in *Hakluytus Posthumus; or, Purchas His Pilgrimes, Contayning a History of the World in Sea Voyages and Lande Travells by Englishmen and Others* (Glasgow, 1905–1907 [orig. publ. London, 1625]), XVI, 417–517. On the influence of natural history on Durão's *Caramuru*—including a comparison of specific passages describing the pineapple, passion fruit, and whale fishing—see Pereira, *Fontes do "Caramuru,"* 27–57. On sixteenth-century natural history in the Spanish Empire, see Antonio Barrera-Osorio, *Experiencing Nature: The Spanish American Empire and the Early Scientific Revolution* (Austin, Tex., 2006), 81–127.

11. See Simão de Vasconcelos, *Crônica da Companhia de Jesus,* 3d ed. (Petrópolis,

If, in Garcilaso and Pineda, the focus on the captive figure is an attempt to vindicate the forgotten contribution of a peripheral participant to the work of conquest, Durão goes even further by making a castaway and captive—and, according to some of his eighteenth-century contemporaries, a "fugitive" or treasonous "coward"—the hero of an epic of discovery and conquest. In general, representations of the colonial period in Brazilian historiography and literature would come to focus on marginal or transculturated figures like Diogo-Caramuru only in the period following independence. Durão's portrayal of the relationship between Diogo and Paraguaçu predates, for example, the cross-cultural romances that nineteenth-century authors like José de Alencar would popularize in their novels. Alencar's *O Guaraní* (1857) and *Iracema* (1865), alternately recognized as the national novel of Brazil, both depict the love between a Portuguese settler and an Amerindian

---

Brazil, 1977 [orig. publ. Lisbon, 1663]); Francisco de Brito Freyre, *Nova Lusitânia, história da guerra brasílica* ([Lisbon, 1675]); Sebastião da Rocha Pitta, *História da América portugueza* (Lisbon, 1730). On *Caramuru* as a "chronicle in verse," see Massaud Moíses, *História da literatura brasileira* (São Paulo, 1983), I, 304; see also Cândido, *Formação da literatura brasileira,* I, 171. For overviews of the narratives of the Diogo Álvares / Caramuru legend, see Janaína Amado, "Mythic Origins: Caramuru and the Founding of Brazil," trans. Elizabeth Jackson, *Hispanic American Historical Review,* LXXX (2000), 783–811; and David Treece, "Caramuru the Myth: Conquest and Conciliation," *Ibero-Amerikanisches Archiv N.F.,* X (1984), 139–173. Treece and Amado study most of the same early modern sources, but Treece also discusses several nineteenth-century Romantic versions: Daniel Gavet and Philippe Boucher's *Jakaré-Ouassou; ou, Les Tupinambás, chronique brésilienne* (Paris, 1830), José Nogueira Jaguaribe Filho's *Os herdeiros de Caramurú* (São Paulo, 1880); Francisco Adolfo de Varnhagen's *O Caramurú: Romance histórico brasileiro* (Rio de Janeiro, 1861). Treece argues that these works represent a revision of the Caramuru myth of Brazilian origins by highlighting the negative and tragic aspects of the tale and paying more attention to its female characters. More recent versions of the tale have similarly focused on the female indigenous characters in lieu of a heroic presentation of Diogo Álvares while continuing to propound the myth of peaceful conquest and racial integration; see Assis Brasil, *Paraguaçu e Caramuru: Paixão e morte da nação tupinambá* (Rio de Janeiro, 1995); Jorge Furtado and Guel Arraes, *A invenção do Brasil* (Rio de Janeiro, 2000), which is the screenplay of a television miniseries and film, Guel Arraes's *Caramuru: A invenção do Brasil* (2001); and Tasso Franco, *Catarina Paraguaçu: A mãe do Brasil* (Rio de Janeiro, 2001).

noble in their representations of the colonial encounter. Adaptations of the Paraguaçu-Caramuru legend can also be found in novels and visual media produced around the quincentennial of the "discovery" of Brazil, suggesting the continued popularity of the notion that the paradigm for Brazilian origins can be found in the nonviolent sexual union of a Portuguese and an Amerindian.[12]

In Durão's eighteenth-century context, by contrast, the choice of Diogo Álvares to protagonize an epic of Brazilian origins was quite controversial, and his liaison with the indigenous Paraguaçu was only part of the problem. By the time *Caramuru* was published, the academic societies of Bahia and Rio had already demonstrated great interest in the creation of an epic poem to commemorate the Portuguese discovery and colonization of Brazil. Differences of opinion as to who the hero of this epic might be, however, had stalled its realization. In his study of *Caramuru*'s sources, Carlos de Assis Pereira describes several texts written by members of the Academia Brasílica dos Renascidos, founded in 1759, that discuss Diogo Álvares in the context of Brazil's early exploration. These works categorically reject his primacy as a potential representative of the discovery of Brazil.[13]

The first author mentioned by Pereira, José de Oliveira Beça, negates in two separate studies Diogo Álvares's priority in the discovery of Bahia. Pointing to Diogo Álvares's legendary trip to Paris, rather than Lisbon, as well as to his liaison with the indigenous group that murdered Bahia's first donatary captain, Francisco Pereira Coutinho, Beça affirms, "Os que dão a preferencia do tempo ao Caramuru, como primeiro povoador da Villa Velha, são obrigados a admitir ou que foi muy fraco e cobarde ou pouco leal ao seu Rei" [Those who give precedence to Caramuru as the first settler of Villa Velha are obliged to admit that either he was very weak and cowardly or not very loyal to his king]. Indeed, he would perhaps even be guilty of treason for inciting an indigenous rebellion against a court-appointed governor.[14]

12. Doris Sommer analyzes José de Alencar's *O Guaraní: Romance brasileiro* (Rio Grande, 1857) and *Iracema: Lenda do Ceará* (São Paulo, 1865) as "foundational fictions" of Brazilian national identity in *Foundational Fictions: The National Romances of Latin America* (Berkeley, Calif., 1991), 138–171. On the late-twentieth and early-twenty-first-century novels, television miniseries, and film based on the legend of Caramuru, see the previous footnote.

13. Pereira, *Fontes do "Caramuru,"* 1–9.

14. José de Oliveira Beça's essay, "Dos primeiros descobridores e povoadores da cidade da Bahia," is cited at length in Alberto Lamego, *A Academia Brazílica dos*

Domingos da Silva Teles, a supernumerary member of the Academia dos Renascidos, took up the same issue when proposing to write an epic poem entitled *Brasileida.* Teles sent an outline of the poem and a letter expressing doubts about its composition and choice of hero to the founder and director of the academy, José Mascarenhas Pacheco Pereira Coelho de Melo. In the letter, Teles argues against Diogo Álvares as the possible hero of the poem for two reasons: first, his captivity—"Como poderá conservar o carácter de Heróe Diogo Álvares, quando é sem dúvida, que se vio escravo, e servindo aos Índios?" [How can Diogo Álvares preserve the character of a hero when it is certain that he was a slave and serving the Indians?]—and second, his voyage to France, "como fugitivo, circunstância, que totalmente se oppõem ao carácter de Heróe" [as a fugitive, a circumstance that totally opposes the character of a hero]. For Teles, Pedro Álvares Cabral's primacy as "discoverer" of Brazil in 1500 merits him the role of epic hero because he took possession in the name of the Portuguese Crown, kept the natives dependent on his "dádivas" [gifts], and introduced the Christian faith. Durão, on the other hand, uses the very circumstances criticized by Teles and Beça not only to structure his poem but also to elevate Diogo to the role of epic hero. Despite the suspect loyalties that some eighteenth-century Brazilian intellectuals attributed to Diogo, *Caramuru* demonstrates the persistence of a view of him as a valuable mediator working in the service of imperial

---

Renascidos: Sua fundação e trabalhos inéditos (Paris, 1923), 68–90, esp. 76. Beça in fact reorders the dates surrounding the discovery and settlement of Bahia in order to avoid such a negative reading of Caramuru. Beça argues for Cristovão Jaques as its discoverer (in 1519 or 1520), Francisco Pereira Coutinho as its first settler in 1522, and Diogo Álvares as its "restaurador" [restorer] following his shipwreck, which Beça mistakenly claims to have occurred in 1531; see 68–69. Domingos da Silva Teles is even further off the mark, postponing the date to 1549; see his "Carta para o director perpetuo," in João Lúcio de Azevedo, "Academia dos Renascidos: A história. 'Desaggravos do Brasil' e o poema 'Brasileida,'" *Revista de língua portuguesa,* XIX (1922), 85–95, esp. 89–94. Santa Rita Durão also errs in this sense, proclaiming in the prologue that the discovery of Bahia takes place "quase no meio do século XVI" [near the middle of the sixteenth century] (*Caramuru,* 13). As Francisco Adolfo de Varnhagen demonstrates by referring to various sixteenth-century navigational accounts that mention the encounter of a Christian castaway in Bahia, Diogo Álvares's shipwreck must have occurred much earlier, probably around 1510; see Varnhagen, "O *Caramuru* perante a historia," *Revista trimensal de historia e geographia; ou, Jornal do Instituto Histórico e Geográphico Brasileiro,* III (1848), 129–152, esp. 132.

expansion, a role ascribed to him by the Portuguese king João III himself in a 1548 letter.[15]

FROM CASTAWAY TO CAPTIVE

Durão uses the protagonist's *naufrágios*—shipwrecks as well as other misadventures—to prove Diogo Álvares's status as a hero. In this sense, he reproduces some of the strategies employed by another sixteenth-century captive known for his *Naufragios,* Álvar Núñez Cabeza de Vaca. Durão presents Diogo's adventures through a series of inversions that not only turn his misfortunes into good fortune but also allow him to initiate peaceful relations between distinct nations. As Durão announces in the opening lines of the first canto, "De um varão em mil casos agitados / . . . / O valor cantarei na adversa sorte, / Pois só conheço herói quem nela é forte" [I will sing of the valor of a man / . . . / challenged by a thousand calamities / for I only know a hero by his strength in adversities]. The first example of Diogo's misfortune is his shipwreck off the Bahian coast. Durão diverges from the typical shipwreck narrative by beginning with the very event that usually marks the climactic interruption of the journey, whether it occurs on the voyage outward or the return home.[16]

Diogo's arrival in Bahia as a victim of shipwreck is certainly consistent with Durão's historiographic sources as well as the legend surrounding

15. Teles, "Carta para o director perpetuo," in Azevedo, "Academia dos Renascidos," *Revista de língua portuguesa,* XIX (1922), 89–94; "King João III to Diogo Álvares, 19 November 1548," in "Cartas regias sobre Tomé de Sousa, 1548–1551," Arquivo Público do Estado da Bahia, cópias 627 (see my introduction for a discussion of this letter). On the role of captives, castaways, and other mediating figures in colonial Brazil, see Alida C. Metcalf, *Go-betweens and the Colonization of Brazil, 1500–1600* (Austin, Tex., 2005); and, in a history written for a general public, Eduardo Bueno's *Naúfragos, traficantes e degredados: As primeiras expedições ao Brasil, 1500–1531* (Rio de Janeiro, 1998). One of Durão's contemporaries, Frei Gaspar da Madre de Deus, did portray another sixteenth-century castaway, João Ramalho, thus: "Cativou a vontade dos naturais da terra, defendendo a sua liberdade, e perpetuou, com atenções, a fidelidade dos bárbaros" [He captured the will of the natives of the land, defending their liberty, and perpetuating, through kindnesses, the fidelity of the barbarians]; see Frei Gaspar da Madre de Deus, *Memórias para a história da capitania de S. Vicente, hoje chamada de S. Paulo . . .* (São Paulo, 1953 [orig. publ. Lisbon, 1797]), 52, 55–56.

16. Durão, *Caramuru,* 19.

Caramuru. However, the inclusion of the incident also reflects the enormous popularity of shipwreck narratives in sixteenth- and seventeenth-century Portugal as well as Spain. Giulia Lanciani identifies "Antecedents" and "Departure" as the opening sequences in the model that structures most of the relações de naufrágio, preceding the pivotal "Storm" and "Shipwreck." As she points out (and as we have seen above in Mascarenhas's *Memoravel relaçam*), these narratives often include episodes of captivity among pirates, Africans, or Turks. Even without an actual capture by enemies, shipwreck accounts resemble captivity narratives by concluding with the return to the civilized or familiar world. Durão rewrites the traditional plot of the relações de naufrágio not only by situating the shipwreck at the poem's point of departure but also by making the site of shipwreck the place of return at the end of the poem.[17]

In the events immediately following the shipwreck, Durão deviates significantly from his historiographic sources. Rather than presenting the immediate submission of the natives who encounter the European survivors, *Caramuru* depicts the castaways' deception and captivity by the Amerindians. The poem first describes how the survivors are helped ashore by a group of natives described as a "benfeitor fingido" [feigned benefactor]. We have already encountered the motif of the deceptiveness of appearances at the scene of encounter in other captivity narratives. As we saw in *Cautiverio feliz,* Alvarito's initial perception of his captors' threatening barbarism is overturned with his recognition as the son of a respected creole captain, which results in his benevolent treatment as a captive. Mutual recognition thus initiates relations based on reciprocal respect and identification, to the extent that creoles and Araucanians may be allied against another "other," the Spanish "foreigners." *Caramuru,* on the other hand, focuses initially on the lack of either party's ability to recognize the other. If the scene displays a certain amount of relativism by presenting the mutual perception of otherness, the description goes on to betray a Eurocentric perspective:

E uns aos outros não crêem da espécie humana:
Os cabelos, a côr, barba e semblante
Faziam crer aquela gente insana
Que alguma espécie de animal seria
Dêsses que no seu seio o mar trazia.

17. Giulia Lanciani, *Os relatos de naufrágios na literatura portuguesa dos séculos XVI e XVII* (Lisboa, 1979), 59–60, 128.

And they don't believe each other to belong to the human species:
their hair, skin color, faces, and beards
make that insane people believe
that they must be some sort of beast
that lives in the depths of the sea.

As "that insane people," the Amerindians are at first circumscribed in *Caramuru* to the role of barbarous "other." However, by suggesting the Amerindian perspective (ironically, of Europeans as brutish creatures), the scene of encounter begins to destabilize the opposition between rational self and irrational other. Later in the poem, mutual knowledge and capacity for recognition—gained by the Portuguese protagonist and his indigenous consort in their respective captivities and transculturations—will continue to problematize, if not invert, the opposition.[18]

The depiction of the Amerindians' perception of the castaways as animals emerging from the sea challenges the categories of "beastly" natives and rational Europeans. It also points to the true meaning of *caramuru,* the indigenous word that the Tupinambá eventually use to rename him. Although many explanations of the name associate it with thunder and fire, *caramuru* actually refers to the moray eel. Durão's translation—"um dragão dos mares vomitado" [a dragon vomited from the seas], a more poetic version of Sebastião da Rocha Pitta's "dragaõ que sahe do mar" [dragon that comes out of the sea]—invokes both meanings. Durão's other sources, Vasconcelos and Freyre, offer "man of fire" as the translation of *caramuru,* tying it exclusively to his use of firearms salvaged from the wreckage, which shocks his presumed captors into submission in a flash, as it were. In his *Chrônica da Companhia de Jesu,* Vasconcelos describes the godlike reputation that Diogo's weapons earn him even among his captor's enemies:

> No ponto que tiveram notícia aqueles selvagens, que ia contra eles o homem de fogo (que assim lhe chamavam) que de longe feria, e matava, quais se viram a fúria de um vulcano, ficaram desmaiados, e deram a fugir pelos matos; ficando assim provado o valor, e arte mais que humana (na opinião desta gente) de Diogo Álvares, cuja fama correu em breve por todos os sertões, e foi tido por homem portentoso, contra quem não eram capazes seus arcos; e aqui lhe acrescentaram o nome, chamando-se o grande Caramuru. . . . Em contendas de guerra que se ofereciam, Diogo

18. Durão, *Caramuru,* 22.

Álvares era o árbitro de todas elas: foi de maneira, que *em breve tempo subiu de cativo a senhor, que tudo governava.*

> As soon as those savages learned that the man of fire (as they called him) was coming against them, and that from far away he hurt and killed, they fainted as if they had seen the fury of a volcano and fled into the forest, thus proving the valor and superhuman art (in the opinion of those people) of Diogo Álvares, whose fame soon spread throughout the backlands. He was taken for a powerful man, against whom their bows were of no use. And here they gave him the name, calling him the great Caramuru. . . . In all of the disputes of war that came about, Diogo Álvares was the arbiter: such that *in a brief time he rose from captive to lord, who governed everything.*

The "brief time" becomes even more abbreviated in Freyre's and Pitta's histories, which barely allude to a period of captivity and portray the natives as almost immediately venerating Diogo because of their fear of his firearms. Pitta writes, "O fogo, o ecco, e a queda dos passaros causou tal horror aos Gentios, que fugindo huns, e ficando estupidos outros, se renderaõ todos ao temor, tendo a Diogo Álvares por homem mais que humano, e o tratavaõ com grande veneraçaõ" [The fire, echo, and falling of the birds caused such horror among the natives that, some fleeing and others remaining senseless, they all gave themselves up to fear, considering Diogo Álvares to be superhuman, and treated him with great veneration].[19]

19. Ibid., 56; Pitta, *História da América portugueza,* 58; Vasconcelos, *Crônica da Companhia de Jesus,* 192, 193 (emphasis added). Like Pitta, Freyre shows Diogo to be spared from immediate cannibalism by helping his captors to plunder the remains of the wreck, where he finds the weapons: "Acharaõ-se entre outros, alguns barris de munições, e hum arcabuz, com que Diogo Álvarez matou hum pássaro. A novidade nunca vista daquelles bárbaros, pôz todos em fugida, com temerosa admiração do fogo, do estrondo, e do effeito. . . . Chamaraõ-lhe o Homem do fogo, grande Caramuru. E de escravo, o fizeraõ senhor, e árbitro da paz, e da guerra, entre as Nações confinantes" [Among other things, they found some barrels of munitions and a harquebus, with which Diogo Álvares killed a bird. The novelty, never before seen by those barbarians, put them all in flight, with fearful admiration of the fire, the thundering noise, and the effect. . . . They called him the Man of Fire, great Caramuru. And from a slave they made him a lord and arbiter of the peace and war between the neighboring nations]; see *Nova Lusitânia,* 71–72. Diogo Álvares's descendants were apparently aware of the true meaning of the term, since many of them signed

These passages recall European depictions of the encounter that, since Columbus, so often present the native perception of the conquistadors as superior beings owing to their weaponry. The portrayal of voluntary Amerindian subjugation to Europeans conveniently both erases the act of forcible conquest and confirms the inferiority of native intelligence. *Caramuru* is not exempt from these stereotypes, and the Tupinambá eventually respond to Diogo's firepower with similar fear and deference. Nevertheless, in contrast to the accounts in which Diogo's superior weaponry allows him to conquer the natives right after his arrival, Durão's poem includes a period of captivity that suggests his subordination is a necessary step in the formation of the hero. As Diogo is led away with the other six survivors, however, he does remember to grab a musket and a rifle from the wreckage, apparently anticipating their future usefulness. Diogo's foresight is an early example of the astuteness and adaptability that will continue to characterize him throughout the poem.

ENLIGHTENMENT HEROICS: ART AND REASON

The inclusion of the captivity episode thus allows Durão to reinvent the qualities that define Diogo's heroic status, and these are often features that reflect upon Durão's own position as a Brazilian-born writer. Diogo distinguishes himself from the other captives, who appear to be oblivious to their fate, by recognizing that the good treatment and ample food they are given is merely a preparation for their eventual sacrifice and consumption. The observation marks Diogo's difference from his fellow captives and, of course, from his captors. Yet Durão describes their cannibalism—that traditional marker of barbarism—as an effect of "corrupt reason," a reason that reveals the common humanity of "our souls": "Feras! mas feras não, que mais monstruosos / São da nossa alma os bárbaros efeitos, / E em corruta razão mais furor cabe, / Que tanto um bruto imaginar não sabe" [Beasts! But not beasts, because more monstrous / are the barbarous effects of our souls / and in corrupt reason more fury lies / than a brutish imagination can conceptualize]. A true hero of the Enlightenment, Diogo does not merely threaten or intimidate the Tupinambá into submission with his use of firearms but rather

their names with the Portuguese equivalent, "Moreia"; see Frei Vicente do Salvador, *História do Brasil, 1500–1627,* ed. Capistrano de Abreu, Rodolfo Garcia, and Venâncio Willeke, 5th ed. (São Paulo, 1965 [orig. publ. São Paulo, 1918]), 108; and Pedro Calmon, *História da fundação da Bahia* ([Salvador, Brazil], 1949), 28.

persuades them to abandon their cannibalism, explaining, "O lume da razão condena a emprêsa" [The light of reason condemns the practice]. Here and elsewhere, Diogo's skillful and successful use of language and reason is one of the qualities that establishes his exceptionality.[20]

In contrast, the usual qualifications of an epic hero—brute strength, intrepidity, a larger-than-life appearance—are nearly absent from Diogo's characterization. After the shipwreck, Diogo is described as particularly weak: "Forte sim, mas de têmpera delicada / Aguda febre traz desde a tormenta; / Pálido o rosto, e a côr tôda mudada, / A carne sôbre os ossos macilenta" [He is strong, but of a delicate temperament, / suffering from an acute fever since the storm; / his face is pale, his color altered, / his flesh over his bones lies withered]. He is thus unable to contemplate resisting his captors: "Enfermo e só, não vale a nada" [Sick and alone, he is worth nothing]. In this sense, Diogo's characterization reflects the "demythification" of the conquistador in what Beatriz Pastor calls the "discourse of failure" in chronicles of unsuccessful conquest. As in Cabeza de Vaca's *Relación,* Durão distinguishes the protagonist by his misfortune, attributing greater value to his words than to his actions. However, he also refashions Diogo's unheroic circumstances into an unexpected benefit, since his weakness prevents him from being chosen as one of the victims destined for cannibalistic sacrifice: "Mas foi-

20. Durão, *Caramuru,* 25, 50. Durão corroborates his point about the shared humanity of Europeans and Amerindians through a footnote with examples of anthropophagy among ancient Italians, "Lestrigões" and "Liparitanos," Phoenicians, Carthaginians, and Romans: "São espécies vulgares na história" [They are common types in history] (42n. 4). The sixteenth-century French explorer Jean de Léry and essayist Michel de Montaigne famously characterized Brazilian cannibalism as superior to its European forms; see Léry, *History of a Voyage to the Land of Brazil,* trans. Janet Whatley (Berkeley, Calif., 1990), 131–132; Michel de Montaigne, "On the Cannibals," in M. A. Screech, trans. and ed., *The Essays: A Selection* (New York, 1993), 79–92, esp. 86–87. On the claims of the abandonment of cannibalism after the arrival of civilizing European influence in early modern travel accounts and modern ethnographic texts, see Peter Hulme, "Introduction: The Cannibal Scene," and William Arens, "Rethinking Anthropophagy," both in Francis Barker, Peter Hulme, and Margaret Iverson, eds., *Cannibalism and the Colonial World* (Cambridge, 1998), 1–38, 39–62. Durão does allow for the existence of Amerindians who, through the use of reason, oppose cannibalism before the arrival of Europeans: in canto 1, stanzas 36–46, a dying Amerindian tells a saint who has been miraculously transported from the Old World, "Matar não quis, nem morto algum comia" [I did not want to kill, nor did I eat the dead] (33).

lhe aquela doença afortunada, / Porque a gente cruel guardá-lo intenta, / Até que, sendo a si restituído / Como os mais vão comer, seja comido" [But that illness was fortunate for him / because the cruel people intend to keep him / until, restored to himself, / he will be eaten just like the rest]. Diogo's misfortune once again rebounds in good fortune.[21]

Even when Diogo does gain superiority over his captors, appearing before them in full armor and frightening them with a display of European weapons, he still trusts the power of his communicative abilities more than brute force. Significantly, and perhaps self-reflexively, Durão here identifies Diogo's efforts to communicate as an "art":

> Esperança concebe de amansá-los
> Uma vez com terror, outra com arte
> A viseira levanta e vai buscá-los,
> Mostrando-se risonho em tôda a parte:
> . . .
> "Não temas (disse afável), cobra alento."
> E, suprindo-lhe acenos o idioma,
> Dá-lhe a entender que todo êsse armamento
> Protege amigos, se inimigos doma.
>
> He conceives of a hope to tame them
> Partly with terror, partly with art.
> He raises his visor and goes to look for them,
> Always smiling in every part.
> . . .
> "Don't fear," he said affably, "take heart."
> And supplementing language with signs,
> He makes him [the cacique Gupeva] understand that all that armor
> Protects friends, while vanquishing foes.

Although Diogo must rely on sign language at this point, his linguistic skills apparently include the ability to comprehend his captors' tongue. His

21. Durão, *Caramuru,* 26, 45. See also Maria José Paredes Meira's analysis of the demythification of the "hero of the sea" in Portuguese shipwreck narratives, in "Uma leitura da *Relação do naufrágio da nau Santa Maria da Barca, no ano de 1559,*" in Maria Alzira Seixo and Alberto Carvalho, eds., *A História trágico-marítima: Análises e perspectivas* (Lisbon, 1996), 149–160, esp. 158.

apprenticeship in a foreign language is perhaps a further testament to the role of captivity in the development of the hero, who is described, not as intrepid, but as "o prudente Diogo, que entendia / Não pouca parte do idioma escuro, / Por alguns meses em que atento o ouvia" [the prudent Diogo, who understood / not a little of the obscure language / by listening to it attentively for some months]. Diogo's contrast with Robinson Crusoe, another famous literary castaway of the eighteenth century (and who also suffers shipwreck on the Brazilian coast), could not be greater. In Daniel Defoe's novel, Crusoe not only bestows an English name upon the indigenous man that he saves from cannibalism (rather than the reverse) but also claims to teach him to speak, as if "Friday" had previously been deprived of language. Diogo continues to be shown speaking the native language in the concluding stanzas of the poem, as he explains Portuguese rule to the Tupinambá.[22]

The positive revalorization of the familiarity with the other that can be gained through intercultural contact is evident in the curiosity that Diogo demonstrates with respect to the natives' culture as well as their language. In canto 2, stanzas 69–76, Diogo attentively observes the activities that surround his welcome into the indigenous village, no longer as their captive but as a potential ally and savior from their enemies. Just before this scene, the author reveals an interest in demonstrating his own knowledge of indigenous customs by indulging in a lengthy ethnographic description of the Tupinambá. Unlike Pineda, Durão has evidently acquired this information from books rather than direct experience. However, in canto 4, note 4, he glosses over a reference to his hometown in Minas Gerais (Nossa Senhora de Nazareth, commonly known as "Inficionado" [tainted]), "povo importante das Minas do Mato dentro chamado assim, porque o ouro, que tinha mui subido, perdeu os quilates mais altos, e ficou chamando-se ouro inficionado. Assim o soube o poeta dos antigos daquela paróquia, de que êle é natural" [important town of the mines of the interior, called thus because the gold, which used to be of elevated quality, lost its highest carats and ended up being called tainted gold. The poet learned this from the elderly of that parish, of which he is a native]. As on the title page, Durão here invokes his

22. Durão, *Caramuru,* 47, 49, 244. Crusoe states, "I was greatly delighted with him, and made it my Business to teach him every Thing, that was proper to make him useful, handy, and helpful; but especially to make him speak, and understand me when I spake"; see Daniel Defoe, *The Life and Strange Surprizing Adventures of Robinson Crusoe, of York, Mariner . . .* (London, 1719), 249.

authority as a "natural," or native born, in similar terms to Pineda, even if he relies on the testimony of "ancient men."[23]

CAPTIVATING WOMEN: PARAGUAÇU AND MOEMA

Diogo's captivity may place him in contact with another culture, but it does not ensure his ability to interpret it. Just as Durão relies on other sources, Diogo is also forced to depend on an intermediary in order to fully communicate with the Tupinambá. Unable to decipher the meaning of a ceremonial fire, Diogo is pleased to learn of the imminent arrival of "certa dama gentil brasiliana; / Que em Taparica um dia comprendera / Boa parte da língua lusitana / Que português escravo ali tratara, / De quem a língua, pelo ouvir, tomara" [a certain Brazilian lady; / who in Taparica had once learned / a good part of the Lusitanian tongue / for there she knew a Portuguese slave / from whom, through listening, she acquired the language]. Like Diogo, although evidently with more success, the "Brazilian lady" Paraguaçu has learned another language through attentive listening. Significantly, Durão poses the hero's desire to meet the native woman in terms of her linguistic abilities: "Deseja vê-[la] o forte lusitano, / Por que interprete a língua que entendia / E toma por mercê do céu sob'rano / Ter como entenda o idioma da Bahia" [The brave Lusitanian desires to see her / so that she can interpret the tongue she understands / and he considers it a gift of heaven / to have a way to understand the language of Bahia].[24]

At the sight of Paraguaçu's prodigious beauty, however, Diogo is nearly overwhelmed with emotion, which is described in terms usually associated with the Tupinambá: "fúrias da paixão, que acende estranhas / Essa de insano amor doce faísca" [furies of passion, which strangely light / that sweet spark of insane love]. As in *Cautiverio feliz,* carnal temptation, even more than ritual cannibalism, poses the greatest danger to the captive: "Que houvera de perder-se naquela hora, / Se não fôra cristão, se herói não fôra" [He would have lost himself in that instant / if he were not a Christian, nor a hero]. Diogo demonstrates the same self-control as Alvarito, but the passage's religious overtones are infused with Enlightenment ideals, according

23. Durão, *Caramuru,* 117n. 4. Durão indicates his sources for the "ritos e costumes do Brasil" [rites and customs of Brazil] in his footnotes to the poem and is careful to point out when his information can be verified by firsthand testimony, as in the case of Bruzen de la Martinière, "testemunha ocular" [eyewitness]; see 68n. 10.

24. Ibid., 64–65.

to which "a razão pode mais que a ardente flama" [reason is more powerful than the burning flame].

Entanto Diogo refletiu consigo
Ser para a língua um cômodo instrumento
Do céu mandado na donzela amigo;
E, por ser necessário ao santo intento,
Estuda no remédio do perigo.
Que pode ser? sou fraco; ela é formosa . . .
Eu livre . . . ela donzela . . . será espôsa.

Meanwhile, Diogo, lost in reflection,
Thought that the damsel, graciously sent by heaven,
Was a comfortable instrument of interpretation;
And, since it is necessary to his holy intention,
He studies the remedy for the danger.
What can it be? I am weak; she is beautiful . . .
I'm free . . . she's a maid . . . I'll marry her.

Despite his exemplary demonstration of reason and missionary zeal, the hero's "weakness" continues to surface in his vacillation between prudence and "pasmo" [bewilderment] before the native woman. A few stanzas later, we read: "E [Paraguaçu] ficou do sossobro tão formosa / Quanto êle ficou cego; e, em tal porfia / Nem um, nem outro então de si sabia" [And Paraguaçu, perturbed, was as beautiful / as he was blinded; and, in such a struggle / they neither one could come to their senses]. Durão's humanization of the hero through his relationship with Paraguaçu suggests the ambiguity of his attitude toward the natives, which alternates between attraction and repulsion. Even if the "prudent hero" virtuously determines that he must baptize Paraguaçu before consummating his love, his passion and pasmo—and later, Paraguaçu's own pious reason and discourse—problematize a simple dichotomy between irrational Amerindian and rational European.[25]

Paraguaçu's exceptional beauty is described according to European standards, as she is effectively drained of any sign of being a person of color: "Bem diversa de gente tão nojosa / De côr tão alva como a branca neve" [Very different from such sordid people / of a color as white as the whitest snow]. Nevertheless, Durão does not limit her role to that of a speechless

25. Ibid., 65–67.

object of desire. Rather, he depicts her serving as a mediator between Diogo and his former captors: "Só com Gupeva a dama e com Diogo / Gostosa aos dois de intérprete servia" [The lady, alone with Gupeva and Diogo, / happily served as interpreter between the two]. Through her, Caramuru and the indigenous leader Gupeva share a wealth of information about their respective cultures in canto 3, stanzas 3–87. The European hero certainly profits more from this exchange than the Amerindian leader. Yet Paraguaçu's mediation is also presented in terms of her people's interest, when she effectively assuages Diogo's enraged response to witnessing cannibalism after he has expressed his disapproval of it. At this point, she realizes that his horrifying display of firearms may frighten her people not only into abandoning their feast but into deserting their land and giving it up to their enemies: "Mas o novo pavor na gente impresso / Mitiga Paraguassu, que o dano avista, / Se, como teme, o povo de espantado, / O terreno deixasse abandonado" [But Paraguaçu, foreseeing the damage, / mitigates the new dread impressed on the people, / in case, as she fears, the people in fright / would leave the land abandoned]. Paraguaçu's presence compensates for Diogo's, and the Tupinambás', temporary loss of reason, underscoring the fact that the hero's strength lies in his use of rhetoric rather than force.[26]

Durão's presentation of Paraguaçu in at least the nominally active role of interpreter and mediator also represents a departure from his historiographic sources and antecedents. Absent from the earliest references to a Portuguese castaway in Bahia, like Pero Lopes de Sousa's *Diario da navegação* (written 1530–1532) and Gabriel Soares de Sousa's *Tratado descriptivo do Brasil em 1587,* her figure appears for perhaps the first time in Frei Vicente do Salvador's *História do Brasil* (finished 1627). Although Salvador claims to have met Diogo Álvares's widow personally, he mistakenly identifies her

26. Ibid., 64, 69, 126. According to Tzvetan Todorov's typology of relations to the other, Diogo's interest is "praxeological" as well as "epistemic": he seeks not only knowledge of his captors' culture but the identification of common beliefs (i.e., monotheism, the flood legend, certain moral principles), which will lead to their assimilation to his cultural standards and the elimination of that which makes them different (i.e., cannibalism); see Tzvetan Todorov, *The Conquest of America: The Question of the Other,* trans. Richard Howard (New York, 1984), 185. On Durão's representation of the Tupinambá in this episode according to eighteenth-century philosophical and theological conceptions of the "noble savage," see Claude L. Hulet, "The Noble Savage in *Caramuru,*" in Raquel Chang-Rodríguez and Donald A. Yates, eds., *Homage to Irving A. Leonard: Essays on Hispanic Art, History, and Literature* ([Ann Arbor, Mich.], 1977), 123–130.

Christian name as Luísa and portrays her in the rather standardized role of the enamored indigenous princess and captor's daughter. Salvador credits her with Diogo's salvation from the Tupinambá who devour the survivors of Francisco Pereira Coutinho's shipwreck: "Foi livre da morte pela filha de um índio principal que dêle se namorou" [He was saved from death by an Indian chief's daughter who fell in love with him]. Of course, the motif of the captor's daughter who falls in love with and redeems or rescues the European captive is a salient feature of New as well as Old World narratives of captivity, such as those of Juan Ortiz, John Smith, and the "Captive's Tale" of *Don Quijote.*[27]

In contrast to Salvador, the historiographic sources that Durão consulted credit Diogo alone with his salvation and rise to power. Although Pitta introduces the Caramuru-Paraguaçu tale by stating his desire not to pass over in silence "a noticia de huma notavel Matrona deste Paiz . . . que foi instrumento de que mais facilmente se dominasse a Bahia" [the news of a notable matron of this country . . . who was the instrument through which Bahia was more easily dominated], her first intervention in the story, as in Vascon-

27. Pero Lopes de Sousa, *Diario da navegação (1530–1532),* ed. Paulo Prado (Rio de Janeiro, 1927), I, 152–153; Sousa, *Tratado descriptivo do Brasil em 1587,* ed. Varnhagen, 52, 127; Salvador, *História do Brasil,* ed. Abreu, Garcia, and Willeke, 160–161 (and see 127 for another account of this episode). Gonzalo Fernández de Oviedo y Valdés describes "Diego Álvarez" as a Portuguese who had resided in Bahia since 1510 but mentions only that "tenía consigo su mujer, que era india" [he had with him his wife, who was Indian]; see *Historia general y natural de las Indias,* ed. Juan Pérez de Tudela Bueso (Madrid, 1959 [orig. publ. Madrid, 1535]), II, 350. Salvador does not describe Diogo's indigenous lover as an interpreter or mediator, but elsewhere he includes a tale of a native woman who is captured by one of Caramuru's descendants and who comes to serve in this role. After learning Portuguese and, like Paraguaçu, being baptized and given a Christian name, she is sent to "desenganar os seus, como fêz, mostrando-lhes que aquêle era o vinho que bebíamos, e não o seu sangue, como êles cuidavam, e a carne que comíamos era de vaca e outros animais e não humana" [undeceive her people, as she did, showing them that we drank wine and not their blood, as they feared, and that the flesh we ate was of cows and other animals, and not human]; see *História do Brasil,* 334. The passage suggests the degree to which Amerindians might have associated cannibalism with their own "others." Álvar Núñez Cabeza de Vaca also records a case of European cannibalism that shocked and outraged Amerindians; see *Naufragios y comentarios,* ed. Roberto Ferrando (Madrid, 1984 [orig. publ. Zamora, 1542]), 75; Cabeza de Vaca, *Castaways,* ed. Enrique Pupo-Walker and trans. Frances M. López-Morillas (Berkeley, Calif., 1993), 46.

celos's and Freyre's accounts, occurs only when Caramuru leaves for France. At this point, she appears either as "the most beloved" that he decides to take along with him or as the intrepid lover who cannot bear separation from her soul mate, swimming after the departing French ship to join him on the journey.[28]

Durão reworks the latter episode with the invented character of Moema, one of the many Brazilian maidens who seek Diogo's affections. In *Caramuru,* it is she and not Paraguaçu who demonstrates such devotion to Diogo that she swims after him to her death. Moema has been read as a symbol of Western male fantasies of the passionate, self-abasing indigenous woman as well as an emblem of Brazil's "incapacity to elaborate . . . a rejection of the metropolis and to assume an American destiny." But since the poem suggests Diogo's romantic involvement with Moema, she may also be read as a sign of his own physical incorporation into Amerindian society, substituting for the actual ingestion that was probably suffered by his fellow captives. Readers are assured of Diogo's essential chastity with respect to the many women that are offered, or offer themselves, to him ("A todas êle deu mostras humanas / Sem a fé lhe obrigar que pretendiam" [To all of them he showed affection, / without his faith obliging him to give what they asked]). Nevertheless, some sort of relationship is clearly insinuated in Moema's dying lament to her beloved: "Bem puderas, cruel, ter sido esquivo, / Quando eu a fé rendia ao teu engano" [You could have, o cruel one, been aloof, / when I willingly surrendered myself to your deceit]; she protests, "Nem o passado amor teu peito incita / A um ai somente com que aos meus respondas!" [Past love doesn't even incite in your heart / a single sigh in response to mine!]. The hero's reaction seems to corroborate the existence of a "past love": "Nem mais lhe lembra o nome de Moema, / Sem que amante a chore, ou grato gema" [Never again will he remember the name of Moema / without lovingly lamenting, or gratefully sighing]. Cândido points out Durão's "curious" sanitization of the historical Caramuru, who is known to have fathered an extensive

28. Pitta, *História da América portugueza,* 56–57, esp. 59; Vasconcelos, *Crônica da Companhia de Jesus,* 193; Freyre, *Nova Lusitânia,* 72. Vasconcelos is apparently the first to use the name "Paraguaçu." Alberto Silva affirms that the only names that appear in contemporary documents are "Catarina Álvares" or "Catarina Álvares Caramuru" and that the headstone bearing the name "Catarina Álvares Paraguaçu" was apparently altered in the eighteenth century by one of her descendants; it originally read only "Catarina Álvares" (Silva, "Catarina Caramurú perante a lenda e a história," *Anais do IV Congresso de História Nacional, 21–28 abril de 1949* [Rio de Janeiro, 1951], X, 108–161, esp. 115).

mestizo progeny. Despite Diogo's apparent faithfulness to Paraguaçu in the poem, Moema and the other "Brazilian maidens" attest to his integration into indigenous society, for in response to their affection, Diogo "trata os pais e os irmãos como parentes" [treats their fathers and brothers as relatives]. Durão is clearly uncomfortable with affirming Diogo's assimilation into Amerindian culture outright; Moema is too much of a threat to Diogo's Portuguese and Christian identity to be allowed to survive. Nevertheless, her presence and voice, albeit limited, challenge the supposed incorruptibility of the epic hero.[29]

INVERSIONS: FROM CAPTIVE TO CAPTOR / SAVIOR

Diogo's relationship with Moema also underscores the inversion that has taken place with respect to his status at the beginning of the poem. The ex-captive is now himself a captor, albeit on a smaller scale, for Moema accuses him of leaving her "coração cativo" [heart a captive]. As a further inversion, the departure of the former castaway reflects his inauspicious arrival by causing another's "shipwreck," Moema's death by drowning:

Com mão já sem vigor, soltando o leme,
Entre as salsas escumas desce ao fundo.
Mas na onda do mar, que irado freme,
Tornando a aparecer desde o profundo:
"Ah Diogo cruel!" disse com mágoa,
E, sem mais vista ser, sorveu-se nágua.

With an already lifeless hand, letting go of the rudder,
She sinks to the bottom amidst the salty foam.

29. Kothe, *O cânone colonial,* 350; Durão, *Caramuru,* 140, 149; Cândido, "Estrutura e função do *Caramuru," Revista de letras,* II (1961), 52. See also Treece, who reads Moema as a symbol of "the dangerous, dark sensuality of the Indian woman," in contrast to Paraguaçu, "a pure white European in disguise," in "Caramuru the Myth," *Ibero-Amerikanisches Archiv N.F.,* X (1984), 156. The miniseries and film, *Caramuru: A invenção do Brasil,* replaces the rivalry between Paraguaçu and Moema with a sisterhood in which they happily share Diogo's affections. Despite the film's sexual and textual liberty in relation to its sources, the objective is still to offer a myth of Brazilian origins cleansed of violence; see Lisa Voigt, "Colonial Captivations: Textual and Cinematic Representations of Captivity in Brazil and Chile," *MLN,* CXXI (2006), 1148–1168.

But on a wave of the sea, which roars with anger,
She rises again from the deep:
"Ah, cruel Diogo!" she cries with sorrow,
And, swallowed by the water, she disappears forever.

The object of love appears here as the captor of the lover's heart, able to inspire the subject's loss of moorings, literally and figuratively.[30]

Durão also introduces the motif of inversion in relation to Paraguaçu, who is herself held captive by a "cruel bárbaro" [cruel barbarian], the same terms that Moema uses to describe Diogo. Under the gaze of her captors, Paraguaçu "descobre a todos a presença bela, / E fica quem a prende ainda mais prêso" [reveals her beautiful presence to all / and those who hold her captive are even more captivated]. Diogo appears similarly to captivate his captors during the celebration following the victory over their enemies:

Tinham disposto entanto no terreiro
As nações do sertão pompa festiva,
Criando Diogo principal primeiro
Com aplauso geral da comitiva.
Vê-se ornado de plumas o guerreiro;
E como em triunfo a multidão cativa,
E sôbre os mais num trono levantado
Cingem de pluma o vencedor ćroado.

Meanwhile, the nations of the interior had prepared
A pompous festivity in the public space,
Where they make Diogo a principal chief
To the general applause of the assembly.
The warrior finds himself with feathers adorned,
And as he triumphantly captivates the crowd
While being, above them all, enthroned,
With plumes he is crowned a victor.

Diogo's physical, as well as metaphorical, elevation recalls Alvarito's treatment by his captors during the Araucanian festivities. As in *Cautiverio feliz,* Diogo-Caramuru's cultural cross-dressing as he is adorned with feathers

30. Durão, *Caramuru,* 148–149.

serves as visual evidence that spectacles are particularly propitious sites of transculturation.[31]

Another form of inversion of roles that recurs throughout the poem and marks Diogo's transformation from captive to hero appears in the motif of reciprocity. The shipwreck survivor, who has escaped captivity and death by cannibalism, proves his heroic status by rescuing other potential victims from the same fates. As we have seen in the previous chapters, captivity narratives written from an American perspective often present reciprocal acts of kindness and generosity as an alternative, if idealized, model of intercultural relations. Garcilaso presents the Juan Ortiz–Mucozo relationship in this way, and Pineda y Bascuñán largely credits his own happy captivity to his father's benevolent treatment of Araucanian captives. As discussed in the previous chapter, the Chilean creole also portrays himself as the redeemer of a cacique's daughter who had kindly administered to him during his captivity and was later taken captive by the Spaniards. However, Pineda only hesitatingly purchases the indigenous girl as his slave and apparently does so upon her insistence.[32]

By contrast, the protagonist of *Caramuru* more heroically liberates the indigenous noblewoman from her aforementioned captivity, which otherwise might have led to her own cannibalist consumption. Like *Cautiverio feliz,* of course, *Caramuru* assures the European male's superiority over a potentially captivating indigenous female by inverting the terms of their relationship, so that the male figure is in control of her fate as a captive. Thus Paraguaçu only regains consciousness as Diogo's meek lover in his arms, in spite of the valor that she has demonstrated in battle and despite her Amazon warrior allies' attempts to save her ("Acordou num suspiro, e sôlta viu-se, / E, conhecendo

31. Ibid., 113, 135. See, in Francisco Núñez de Pineda y Bascuñán, *Cautiverio feliz y razón individual de las guerras dilatadas del reino de Chile,* [ed. Diego Barros Arana], Colección de historiadores de Chile, III (Santiago de Chile, 1863), 202–205, a chapter entitled "En que se da principio al festejo, y de como, para verme mas a su salvo toda la muchedumbre del concurso, me pidieron encarecidamente subiese al último andamio y más alto, adonde estaban todos bailando, y de otras cosas que sucedieron, fundadas en mi agasajo" [In Which the Festival is Begun, and How, to See Me More Easily among the Multitude of the Crowd, They Begged Me to Go Up on the Last and Highest Scaffold, Where Everyone Was Dancing, and of Other Things That Happened, for the Purpose of Regaling Me].

32. Pineda y Bascuñán, *Cautiverio feliz y razón individual,* [ed. Barros Arana], 150.

Diogo, olhou-o e riu-se" [She woke up with a sigh, and found herself free; / and recognizing Diogo, she looked at him and smiled]). Apparently, the hero must intervene with his "espingarda" [gun] if he wants to show who wears the pants in the relationship.[33]

Interaction between captives appears to be more reciprocal when initiated between Diogo and other European males, even when of different, and historically hostile, nationalities. For example, Diogo encounters a group of Spaniards while "penetrating" another Paraguaçu, or "great river," as the name signifies in Tupi. Surely recalling his own arrival, Diogo witnesses the Spaniards' shipwreck and the approach of presumably cannibalistic savages: "E, temendo que cedam enganados / Ao bárbaro cruel os naufragantes, / Ou que fiquem sem armas cativados / . . . / Faz-lhes sinais e deixa-os avisados" [And, fearing that the castaways, deceived, / may surrender to the cruel barbarian, / or that without arms they may be captured, / . . . / he makes signs to them in warning]. However, Caramuru's intervention saves their lives and circumvents their captivity. His reputation evidently precedes him, for a single shot of a cannon disperses the Amerindians, who, "o grão-Caramuru já divisando, / Correm todos humildes ao seu mando" [the great Caramuru already recognizing, / to his command all humbly come running]. While Paraguaçu performs the actual labor of providing the Spaniards with clothes and sustenance, Diogo reassures them verbally: "Não duvideis, responde o herói clemente, / De achar em mim socorro poderoso; / Que achais quem como vós do mar fremente / Aprendeu na desgraça a ser piedoso" [Don't doubt, responds the merciful hero, / that you can count on me for powerful relief; / for you have found someone who, like yourselves, in tribulation / learned from the roaring sea to show compassion]. Like Alvarito, this hero has absorbed the lesson of compassion that the trials of shipwreck and captivity can teach.[34]

The rescued Spaniards, as well, demonstrate their understanding of the lesson of reciprocity later in the poem. When Caramuru reencounters a member of the Spanish party upon his return to Bahia from France, he not only receives a message of gratitude from Charles V, king of Spain, but also learns that Spaniards have just saved some Portuguese castaways from their

33. Durão, *Caramuru,* 115–116.

34. Ibid., 141, 144, 146; "Na margem se entranhou do vasto rio" [He penetrated the bank of the great river] echoes the typical gendered and sexualized representations of the European discovery and conquest of the Americas.

own captivity among the Tupinambá. One of the Portuguese survivors informs Caramuru of the shipwreck and cannibalism of Bahia's first donatary captain, Francisco Pereira Coutinho—an event that the historical Diogo Álvares witnessed, although he was spared the same fate. As Gonzales, one of the Spaniards previously succored by Diogo, explains,

E por que possa em caso equivalente
Retribuir-te aquela ação piedosa,
Salva aqui te ofereço a infausta gente,
Perdida nessa praia desditosa,
De cativeiro bárbaro e inclemente
Vivia na opressão laboriosa,
Até que destas armas protegida
Remiu na liberdade a infausta vida.

And so that, in a case of equivalence,
I can reciprocate your benevolence,
I present to you the unlucky people, now rescued,
Who were lost on that unfortunate beach.
In barbarous and cruel captivity
They lived under laborious tyranny,
Until, by these arms protected,
Their unhappy lives were redeemed in liberty.

Diogo consoles the Portuguese survivors by reinforcing the lesson of compassion: "Não sou (diz) insensível, que sei quanto / Acerbo o caso é, cruel o artigo, / E a piedade aprendi no meu perigo" [I am not unmoved (he said), for I know / how bitter and cruel is your quandary, / and I learned compassion through my own jeopardy]. Like the cacique Mucozo in *La Florida* or Pineda's father in *Cautiverio feliz,* Diogo's liberation of others from an onerous captivity and cruel death initiates a chain of reciprocal actions, thus establishing friendly relations between distinct nations that would otherwise be in conflict. Portugal and Spain were, in fact, competing for sovereignty in Brazilian territory throughout the colonial period, and the site of the Spaniards' shipwreck and near-captivity could be a conflation of the two other "great rivers"—the Amazon and the Río de la Plata—that were under contention in the sixteenth century. *Caramuru* valorizes the actions of the "Americanized" ex-captive more than the European explorers, whether

Spanish or Portuguese, who have little experience in Brazil. Once again, captivity is a potentially empowering experience that allows the ex-captive to mediate not only between indigenous groups and his own people but also between rival European nations.[35]

Durão surely based the episode of the Spanish shipwreck on the historiographic sources mentioned in his prologue, which allude to Caramuru's rescue of the castaways of a Spanish ship and his receipt of a grateful letter from Charles V. Gonzalo Fernández de Oviedo includes a more detailed account of the event, describing two ships from a Spanish expedition led by Simón de Alcabaza that were shipwrecked near the settlement of "Diego Álvarez" in 1535. There, the castaways were succored with supplies and sustenance until they were able to continue to their destination. According to the survivors of this journey, with whom Oviedo claims to have spoken directly,

> [Diego Álvarez] dió a entender que residía en aquella costa y soledad para salvar y socorrer a los cristianos que por allí pasasen; y dijo que había salvado franceses, portugueses, castellanos que por aquella costa se habían perdido, y si él no estuviera allí, que los indios hobieran muerto a estos que quedaban de la armada de Simón de Alcazaba.

> [Diego Álvarez] gave them to understand that he resided on that solitary coast to save and succor the Christians who passed by there; and he said that he had saved Frenchmen, Portuguese, and Castilians who had got lost on that coast, and if he had not been there, that the Indians would have killed those that remained from the fleet of Simón de Alcazaba.

Durão thus recuperates the positive contribution that, according to Oviedo and other chroniclers, Diogo's presence on the Brazilian coast meant to other explorers and colonizers, as a savior of castaways and a mediator between otherwise hostile strangers.[36]

35. Ibid., 231, 236. Originally "discovered" by a Spanish expedition—that of Vicente Yáñez Pinzón, in January 1500—the Amazon continued to be explored sporadically by Spaniards who descended the river from the Peruvian highlands, lured by legends of El Dorado. On the early Spanish and Portuguese exploration of the Amazon, see John Hemming, *Red Gold: The Conquest of the Brazilian Indians* (Cambridge, Mass., 1978), 183–197. Río de la Plata, on the other hand, continued to be a hotly contested region between the Spanish and Portuguese Crowns until the borderlines were settled by the Treaty of Madrid in 1750.

36. Vasconcelos, *Crônica da Companhia de Jesus,* 194; Freyre, *Nova Lusitânia,*

However, Durão's text diverges significantly from his historiographic sources in the order of these events. In the poem, the rescue of the Spaniards occurs just before Caramuru and Paraguaçu's voyage to Paris. Vasconcelos, Freyre, and Pitta, on the other hand, all describe it as occurring after the protagonists' return to Bahia. The sequence in *Caramuru* accomplishes a twofold task. First, it absolves Diogo of any failure to live up to his heroic status in light of the infamous shipwreck, captivity, and murder of the donatary captain Francisco Pereira Coutinho. In *Caramuru,* Diogo is far away in Paris when the tragedy occurs, whereas some early historiographic texts—such as Gabriel Soares de Sousa's *Tratado descriptivo do Brasil* and Vicente de Salvador's *História do Brasil*—actually include him as one of the few survivors of the ordeal. Despite his absence from the scene in the poem, Diogo still manages to have a positive effect on the disaster, since it is as a result of his previous kindness toward the shipwrecked Spaniards that they, in turn, come to the aid of the Portuguese survivors. Second, *Caramuru*'s revised order of events reinforces the poem's unity of action and its parallelistic structure. Analogous shipwrecks, captivities, and rescues frame the couple's journey to France. The repetition of episodes and the inversion of roles drive home, as it were, the lesson of reciprocity. The complete elaboration of the poem's moral lesson depends on the couple's return to Brazil, Paraguaçu's patria as well as Caramuru's adopted homeland.[37]

73; Pitta, *História da América portugueza,* 60; Oviedo, *Historia general y natural,* ed. Tudela Bueso, II, 350.

37. Gabriel Soares de Sousa attributes Diogo's salvation following the shipwreck of Francisco Pereira Coutinho to his linguistic ability: "Salvou-se a gente toda d'este naufrágio, mas não das mãos dos Tupinambás, que viviam n'esta ilha, os quaes se ajuntaram, e á traição mataram a Francisco Pereira e a gente do seu caravelão, do que escapou Diogo Alvares com os seus, com boa linguagem" [The people were all saved from this shipwreck, but not from the hands of the Tupinambá who lived on this island, who joined together and treacherously killed Francisco Pereira and the people of his caravel, from which Diogo Álvares escaped with his people through good language]; see Sousa, *Tratado descriptivo do Brasil em 1587,* ed. Varnhagen, 32–33. Salvador gives the same reason for Diogo's survival—"porque lhe sabia falar a língua" [because he knew how to speak their language]—but he expresses doubt that it would have been sufficient if the chief's daughter had not fallen in love with him and come to his defense; see *História do Brasil,* ed. Abreu, Garcia, and Wílleke, 127.

Relationships of trust and tolerance between Europeans are more easily negotiated at the margins than at the center of empire, as we see when Diogo self-consciously defends his loyalty to the Portuguese Crown before the French king. Rather than being collapsed with Portugal into a single category of "Europe," France represents a third term of comparison that unravels the opposition between Portuguese and Brazilian identities. When he arrives at the French court, Diogo pays the necessary respect due the monarch but rejects the invitation to participate in the "civilizing" of Brazilian natives by bringing them to France in order to make "francesa pelo trato a gente bruta" [the rude people French through treatment]. Diogo, "leal a amada pátria" [loyal to his beloved patria], firmly defends Portuguese sovereignty in Brazil. A moment later, however, he claims, "Durando eu na pátria obediença, / Serei francês na obrigação e agência" [Staying obedient to my patria, / I will be French in obligation and agency] and offers to establish a profitable trade relationship with France once he returns to Brazil. The flexibility of Diogo's European allegiances suggests that his nascent Brazilian identity, reinforced during his stay in France, is perhaps already more important than his ties to Portugal. The strategic adoption of different loyalties while traveling in Europe attests to their constructed nature and recalls Durão's own vacillation between pro- and anti-Jesuit positions during his travels through Europe. In Caramuru's case, as in Durão's, this posturing is perhaps justified by the fact that it is motivated by the goal to return home.[38]

The ultimate identification of Caramuru with Brazil, the American land to which he returns at the poem's end but that already bears the signs of Portuguese colonization, is reinforced through the hero's parallelism to the Brazilian native Paraguaçu. As we have seen, Paraguaçu complements Diogo-Caramuru by transculturating in the reverse direction, not only through her acquisition of the "other's" language but also through her adoption of their marriage practices and religion. Like Diogo, she embraces a new name as a result of her travels abroad, for she is baptized as Catarina Álvares in Paris. Similar to Caramuru, as well, her new identity does not require her to sever ties to the old one. Cândido observes that the fundamental ambiguity of the hero is reflected in that of Paraguaçu. The protagonists' parallelism is also evident in their passage through the liminal spaces of captivity and exile. If Diogo and Paraguaçu undergo analogous experiences as captives in the first

38. Durão, *Caramuru,* 182–183.

part of the poem, they are later both cast as "exiles" from their homeland. Diogo introduces himself and his wife to Henry II as two "peregrinos" [pilgrims] who "buscam asilo" [seek refuge].[39]

The voyage to France not only reinforces Paraguaçu's transculturation but also provides Diogo with an opportunity to demonstrate the heroic qualities that he has developed in captivity: persuasive discourse, reasoned observation, and cross-cultural comparison. In fact, Diogo's experience as a captive, which acquainted him with the native language and culture, allows him to take Paraguaçu's place as the interpreter of Brazilian culture and history once in Europe. The party awaiting the interpretation is the French king, who tells him, "Sabendo que os sertões tens visitado, / E o centro do Brasil reconhecido, / Quero das terras, dos viventes, plantas, / Que a história contes de províncias tantas" [Knowing that the backlands you have visited / and the center of Brazil reconnoitered, / I would like you to tell me the histories / of the lands, plants, and peoples of so many territories]. Despite the king's query regarding the history of the inhabitants, Diogo does not repeat the ethnographic details that he has gleaned in Bahia and that the reader has encountered in the first four cantos. Instead, canto 7 focuses on the description of Brazilian flora and fauna. On a formal level, the captivity in Brazil and the exile in France allow the author to frame his ethnographic and naturalistic commentaries.[40]

Diogo's report to the king invokes the tropes of the marvelous and monstrous that so often characterize sixteenth- and seventeenth-century depictions of American nature. Diogo begins by affirming the fallibility of any attempt to articulate the wonders of the New World:

Se esperas de mim, sire, que componha
Exata narração da cópia ingente,
Emprêsa tanta é, quando obedeça,
Que faz que o tempo falte e a voz faleça.

39. Ibid., 163, 165; Cândido, "Estrutura e função do *Caramuru,*" *Revista de letras,* II (1961), 58. Although, according to the poem, she was named after Catherine de Médicis, a baptismal record dated July 30, 1528, indicates that Paraguaçu's godmother and namesake was actually Catherine des Granches, the wife of French explorer Jacques Cartier; see Calmon, *História da fundação da Bahia,* 49; Silva, "Catarina Caramurú perante a lenda e a história," *Anais do IV Congresso de História Nacional,* X, 135.

40. Durão, *Caramuru,* 166.

If you expect me, Sire, to create
An exact narration of a cornucopia so great,
It is an enterprise that, if obeyed,
Would make time run out and my voice fail.

Diogo then describes "montes de grandeza desmedida" [mountains of great immensity], "vastos rios e altas alagoas" [vast rivers and high lagoons], "ervas medicinais [de] cópia tão rara" [medicinal herbs of unusual copiousness], and "ótimo arroz em cópia prodigiosa" [excellent rice in prodigious abundance]. The infinite variety of Brazilian fruits, plants, and animals are so different from their European counterparts that they "enchem a vista da maior surprêsa" [fill the eyes with the greatest surprise]. Yet Diogo's gaze is also utilitarian and practical:

Tece-se a roupa do algodão mais fina,
Que em cópia abundantíssima se colhe;
Que, se a abundância à indústria se combina,
. . .
Houvera no algodão, que ali se topa,
Roupa com que vestir-se tôda a Europa.

The clothes are woven from the finest cotton,
Harvested in such abundant quantity
That if abundance were combined with industry,
. . .
The clothes from the cotton found there
Would be enough for all of Europe to wear.

Diogo's interest in visual marvels is complemented by a mercantilist optic, which envisions the commodities that the Brazilian colony could abundantly provide for Europe.[41]

41. Ibid., 166–169, 173–174. Although Sérgio Buarque de Holanda describes the earliest chroniclers of Brazil as comparatively more sober and "realistic" than their Spanish counterparts, by the second half of the sixteenth century, the Brazilian tradition known as "ufanismo," the literary glorification of the native land, had been inaugurated in the works of Pero de Magalhães Gândavo and Gabriel Soares de Sousa, among others. For a comparison of Spanish and Portuguese representations of American nature, see Holanda, *Visão do Paraíso: Os motivos edênicos no descobri-*

Paraguaçu's reaction to Europe reflects that of Diogo to Brazil, as expressed in his claim that a full narration of its wonders would make "time run out and my voice fail." As strange to her as any New World, the sight of Paris also renders her speechless:

Paraguassu, porém, que jamais vira
Espetáculo igual, suspensa pára:
Nem fala, nem se volta, nem respira,
Imóvel a pestana e fixa a cara;
E cheia a fantasia do que admira,
Causa lhe tanto pasmo a visão rara,
Que estúpida parece ter perdido
O discurso, a memória, a voz e o ouvido.

Yet Paraguassu, who for the first time sees
Such a spectacle, stops as if suspended;
She neither speaks, nor moves, nor breathes;
Her eyelids are immobile and her face rigid.
Admiring the sight, her imagination is replete,
And the rare vision is so astonishing
That, stupefied, she seems bereft
Of discourse, memory, voice, and hearing.

Paraguaçu is evidently more debilitated than Caramuru as a result of her reaction, but her bewilderment in fact mirrors his own amazement with respect to the wondrous visions that he encountered in Brazil. The sights of exile, be they in the Old or New World, necessarily create textual sites of discursive struggle that illustrate the difficulty of apprehending the unknown or rendering what is foreign in familiar language. Paraguaçu's reaction recalls Caramuru's "pasmo" in response not only to her startling beauty but also to the native beliefs, culture, and history that she interpreted for him in Bahia: "Pasmava o lusitano da eloqüência / Com tão alto pensar numa alma rude" [The Lusitanian was astonished at the eloquence / of such lofty thoughts in such an uncultivated soul]; "Pasmado Diogo do que atento escuta / não crê que a singular filosofia / Possa ser da invenção da gente bruta" [Amazed at

---

mento e colonização do Brasil, 2d ed. (São Paulo, 1969 [orig. publ. Rio de Janeiro, 1959]), 1–14, 304–323.

what he listens to attentively, / Diogo cannot believe that such a remarkable philosophy / could be the invention of the brutish people].[42]

Although Durão's Eurocentrism is evident in his insistence on qualifying the indigenous people as "uncivilized" and "brutish," the poem's inclusion of Paraguaçu's perception of the metropolis helps to relativize imperialist notions of European centrality. In contrast to the highlighting of Paraguaçu's perspective in the poem, most records of reverse transatlantic crossings emphasize, not how this New World appeared to Amerindians, but how they themselves were displayed to Europeans as exotic representatives of a strange and barbaric land. For example, Vasconcelos focuses only on the reaction of the French sovereigns to Diogo's tale and the sight of Paraguaçu: "Foi ouvida sua história do rei, e rainha com satisfação, como cousa tão nova: folgavam de ver a esposa, indivíduo estranho de um novo mundo" [His story was heard by the king and queen with satisfaction, as such a new thing: they were amused at seeing his wife, a strange individual from a new world]. Earlier, Vasconcelos had similarly described the Portuguese king and his subjects' untiring fascination with a native Brazilian sent by Pedro Álvares Cabral. Taken to be a "novo indivíduo da geração humana" [new individual of the human race] or even a monstrous half-human, he attracts all the attention of Cervantes's "Barbaric Isle" family before they discard their peregrine attire for that of peregrinos.[43]

Despite the stupefaction that Paraguaçu experiences at the sight of Paris, she soon recovers her speech. She may then resume, after Diogo's interlude, her position as the "voice" of Brazil. In contraposition to Diogo's narration of Brazil's colonial past to the French commander of the ship on the way to France (canto 4), on the return trip home Paraguaçu narrates Brazil's future as it has been revealed to her in a vision. Diogo himself begs her to recount

42. Durão, *Caramuru,* 66, 71, 73, 161.

43. Vasconcelos, *Crônica da Companhia de Jesus,* 55–56, 193. Affonso Arinos de Mello Franco outlines the different reasons for voyages of indigenous Brazilians to Europe, most frequently as slaves but also as objects of curiosity. He describes several sixteenth-century spectacles that featured Amerindians, including the one that welcomed Henry II and Catherine de Médicis (the royal couple that serves as godparents in *Caramuru*) to Rouen in 1550. The spectacle consisted of a *tableau vivant* of transplanted Amerindians, alongside naked French sailors to increase their ranks, in an artificial setting complete with imported plants, animals, and reconstructed villages; see Mello Franco, *O índio brasileiro e a revolução francesa: As origens brasileiras da theoria da bondade natural* (Rio de Janeiro, 1937), 52–99, esp. 76–79; see also Ferdinand Denis, ed., *Une fête brésilienne célébrée à Rouen en 1550 . . .* (Paris, 1850).

what she has seen. He thus assumes the role that the French monarch had previously held with respect to the "marvelous visions":

Narra-nos, feliz alma, a visão bela!
. . .
Não nos cales entanto o que revela
Por nosso lume, o excelso Paraíso,
E a nossos rogos com memória pronta,
Dizendo quanto viste, tudo conta.

Narrate to us, o happy soul, the beautiful vision!
. . .
Do not, meanwhile, keep from us
What lofty Paradise illuminates for us,
And as a willing memory in response to our pleas,
Tell it all, describing everything you have seen.

By intimating the fallibility of language, Paraguaçu's response also echoes Diogo's to the king:

Mandais-me (a dama disse) que o portento
Haja de expor-vos da impressão divina:
Quem poderá contar coisa tão alta,
Quando o lume cessou, a ciência falta?

You order me (said the lady) to express
A marvel of divine impression:
Who could tell something so imposing,
When the light has ceased and science is lacking?

Despite this disclaimer, Paraguaçu does recount the vision at considerable length, making up for her previous silence. In the eighth and ninth cantos, she narrates the Portuguese colony's military successes against French Calvinists in Rio de Janeiro and the Dutch in Bahia and Pernambuco. It is against these European nationalities, and their respective indigenous allies, that a Luso-Brazilian identity is drawn. This identity appears not to be racially exclusive, for we read of the heroic participation in battle of "Henrique Dias, / Capitão dos etíopes valente" [Henrique Dias, valiant captain of the Ethiopians] as well as of an indigenous captain, "o forte Camarão, que em guerra tanta / Com os seus carijós o belga espanta" [the strong Camarão, who in so many battles / terrified the Belgians [the Dutch] with his Carijó warriors], both of whom help to secure the victory of the Portuguese in Brazil.[44]

Unlike the extremely detailed prognostications that could only be the product of Durão's eighteenth-century perspective, the episode of Paraguaçu's final vision, narrated in canto 10, actually has a precedent in the author's historiographic sources. Vasconcelos, Freyre, and Pitta all recount Paraguaçu's dream of a "captive" female, an image of the Virgin that was robbed from the Spanish shipwreck. Freyre writes,

> Quando voltou Diogo Álvarez da marinha, com os novos hospedes, lhe disse sua Esposa: *Ficara uma Molher vinda também em a mesma nao, desacomodada entre aquelles bárbaros, e a havia de ir buscar, porque lho pedira affectuosamente, na clara visaõ, de um sonho extraordinario.*
>
> When Diogo Álvares returned from the shore with the new guests, his wife said to him: *There is a woman who came on board that same ship, out of place among those barbarians. I have to go look for her, because she kindly requested it in the clear vision of an extraordinary dream.*

Vasconcelos indicates that the Virgin appeared to Paraguaçu not only so that she would rescue her image from captivity in the hands of "those barbarians" but also so that the transculturated indigenous woman would build her a home. This house, according to Vasconcelos as well as other historiographic sources, is the church known as Nossa Senhora da Graça, which the "devout matron" donated upon her death to the Benedictine order.[45]

Caramuru relates the Virgin's appearance and request to Paraguaçu in similar terms, appending only a prediction of Paraguaçu's return to her homeland:

> Catarina (me diz), verás ditosa
> Outra vez do Brasil a terra amada;
> Faze que a imagem minha gloriosa
> Se restitua de vil mão roubada!

44. Durão, *Caramuru,* 185, 215, 222–223.

45. Freyre, *Nova Lusitânia,* 73 (emphasis added); Vasconcelos, *Crônica da Companhia de Jesus,* 194.

Catarina (she told me), you will happily behold
Your beloved land of Brazil once more;
Permit my glorious image to be restored
From the vile hand that stole it!

Paraguaçu later recognizes the image of the Virgin in an indigenous hut: "*Esta é (disse), é esta a grã-senhora* / . . . / Este era aquêle roubo, entendo agora" [*This is her (she said), this is the great lady.* / . . . / This was the theft, now I understand]. She thus becomes, like Diogo, the rescuer of another "captive" woman. As in Caramuru's case, Paraguaçu's transformation from captive to savior, following her return from abroad, does not suggest a recuperation of an original state but rather underscores the native woman's transculturation. As Paraguaçu explains in a statement that highlights Durão's confidence in the civilizing power of Christianity: "Aqui vos venho achar, Mãe piedosa, / No meio (disse) desta gente infanda! / Infanda como eu fui, se o vosso lume / Não me emendara o bárbaro costume" [Here, pious Mother, I come to find you / in the midst of these wicked people! (she cried) / Wicked as I would be, if your light / had not emended my barbarous way of life].[46]

In the poem, then, Paraguaçu plays a significant role in the construction of a new "house" in her homeland, the first church in the colony and a symbol of the Christian Brazil that is Durão's professed patria. Her function is religious as well as political: it is Paraguaçu, not Diogo, who in an extensive speech cedes her authority over the Tupinambá to the Portuguese throne represented by Brazil's first governor, Tomé de Sousa, appointed in 1549. As we have seen, Paraguaçu's transculturation both parallels and complements Diogo's. She reveals a desire to go to Europe even before he does, when she learns of the plot to kill her that is being hatched by her jealous rivals:

Mas ela, que o projeto alcança horrendo
Deixar pretende a pátria aborrecida;
E, na viagem de Europa discorrendo,
Deseia renascer à melhor vida:
Impulso santo, que com justa idéia
Move Diogo a deixar aquela arena.

But she, horrified, learns of the plans,
Annoyed with her homeland, she wants to leave,

46. Durão, *Caramuru,* 230, 237, 238 (emphasis added).

And in the voyage to Europe she desires
To be reborn into a better life:
A holy impulse that rightly inspires
Diogo to abandon those sands.

In the hope of starting a new and "better life" within a culture that practices monogamy and Christianity—aspects of the "other's" culture that she adopts—Paraguaçu incites Diogo to take her to Europe. Moreover, she is the one who will later inspire his desire to return to Brazil:

Mas da mísera gente na lembrança,
Que lhe excita da espôsa a cara imagem,
Meditava deixar a amiga França,
Repetindo a brasílica viagem.

But with the miserable people in his memory,
Inspired by the dear image of his spouse,
He considers leaving friendly France
And repeating the Brazilian journey.

If indigenous women represent the captivation that Brazil holds for Diogo, Paraguaçu actually impels his movements to and from her homeland. She mirrors the protagonist in her decision to cross the Atlantic, as well as in her adoption of a name and aspects of the culture that she has observed on the other shore.[47]

Paraguaçu's agency in the decision to leave, as well as the very fact that she undertakes these journeys, distinguish her from other legendary indigenous women associated with European conquistadors. Unlike La Malinche, another translator-lover of a powerful conquistador, Paraguaçu accompanies her consort to Europe, and her survival of the return voyage home differentiates her from Pocahontas, as well. Although La Malinche and Pocahontas have traditionally been represented as traitors, victims, or symbols of reconciliation, they have more recently been reinterpreted as women who made decisions in the interest of surviving, and even achieving some degree of power, within a rigidly patriarchal and colonial society. *Caramuru* encourages a similar assessment of Paraguaçu.[48]

47. Ibid., 140, 181.

48. For reassessments of La Malinche as historical figure and cultural symbol, see

Indeed, the increasing prominence of Paraguaçu in the legend of Diogo-Caramuru, to which Durão's work contributes, allowed her image to be appropriated for an explicitly anticolonial and anti-Portuguese message in the nineteenth century. With a title that surely responds to that of Durão's work, Ladislau dos Santos Titára's *Paraguassú: Epopéia da guerra da independência na Bahia (1835–1837)* offers an epic account of the 1823 victory of Bahian forces over Portuguese troops attempting to suppress dom Pedro I's formation of an independent Brazilian empire. When the hero invokes the name of his "grandmother" Paraguaçu in a speech declaring Brazilian independence, a footnote explains:

> D. Catharina Alves Paraguassu, que, vendo quanto o impolítico, e deshumano Donatário Francisco Pereira Coutinho, não só espezinhava os Índios, sendo até desapiedadamente assassinados, como tambem se arrojava a, menos-cabando sua Gerarchia, deprimi-la, e a seo Esposo, a quem fazendo prender, sem motivo, recolhera a um navio, graçando logo a notícia de o terem assassinado; fez de repente reunir os seos conterrâneos, e a testa delles, dos Tamoyos, e d'outras tribus, que chamara do Recôncavo, sitiou a Cidade e depois de sanguinolentas acções, e forte resistência de Coutinho, que perdera nellas um filho, o poseram em fugida com todos os seos, que abrigando-se a bordo dos navios, escaparam-se para os Ilhéos, ficando a Bahia livre de taes verdugos.

> D. Catharina Alves Paraguassu, who saw how the imprudent and inhuman donatary Francisco Pereira Coutinho not only crushed and impiously assassinated the Indians but also—scorning their hierarchy—dared to destroy her and her husband, whom Coutinho arrested for no reason and took to his ship, spreading the news that he had been mur-

---

Frances Karttunen, "Rethinking Malinche," in Susan Schroeder, Stephanie Wood, and Robert Haskett, eds., *Indian Women of Early Mexico* (Norman, Okla., 1997), 291–312; Mary Louise Pratt, "'Yo Soy la Malinche': Chicana Writers and the Poetics of Ethnonationalism," in Peter Verdonk, ed., *Twentieth-Century Poetry: From Text to Context* (London, 1993), 171–187. On "decolonizing" revisions of the symbol and legend of Pocahontas, see Rebecca Blevins Faery, *Cartographies of Desire: Captivity, Race, and Sex in the Shaping of an American Nation* (Norman, Okla., 1999), 131–141. Pauline Turner Strong also discusses the agency of North American Indian captives, like Pocahontas, who manage to "derive considerable power from a formally subordinate position"; see Strong, *Captive Selves, Captivating Others: The Politics and Poetics of Colonial American Captivity Narratives* (Boulder, Colo., 1999), 23, 63–71.

> dered. Catharina quickly united her compatriots and, at the head of her own people, the Tamoyos, and the other tribes she had summoned from the bay, she put the city under siege. After much bloodshed and strong resistance from Coutinho, who lost a son in the battle, Catharina's troops finally forced Coutinho to flee with all his people to their ships, whereby they escaped to Ilhéos, leaving Bahia free from such assassins.

Titara turns on its head Salvador's image of the indigenous princess who saves the Portuguese castaway. Here she rescues him, through an act of violent resistance to colonial oppression, from the captivity of his own compatriots. The nineteenth-century epic image of a vengeful female warrior is, of course, no closer to the real Paraguaçu than that of Durão's poem. But unlike so many versions of the Caramuru-Paraguaçu legend, it forces us to recall the violence committed in the conquest of Brazil as well as in the war of Brazilian independence (1822–1824). Much like the conquest itself, the latter has been imagined, not as a war at all, but as a peaceful transition of power.[49]

INVENTING "HOME"

Sérgio Buarque de Holanda writes that the hero of Durão's poem is not a discoverer or conquistador but one who, "wandering from his own people among the natives of Bahia and mingling with them, . . . belonged to the colony as much as to the metropolis, and to the former more than the latter." For an eighteenth-century epic by a nomadic friar, captivity and exile may be metaphors of cultural contact more apt than heroic battles of conquest. Like the other captives studied in this book, Diogo-Caramuru is transformed by his "adversa sorte" [bad luck], even to the point of adopting the site of his misfortune as a new homeland. Unlike Juan Ortiz or Francisco Núñez de Pineda, however, Caramuru embraces a new name and wife as well as a new patria. Durão also introduces an indigenous figure, Paraguaçu, whose

49. Ladislau dos Santos Titára, *Paraguassú: Epopéia da guerra da independência na Bahia* (São Paulo, 1973 [orig. publ. Bahia, 1835, 1837]), 227–228. Francisco M. P. Teixeira calls the notion of peaceful independence "one of the most resistant images embedded in [Brazilian] historical memory," comparable to that of peaceful conquest. Brazilian independence from Portugal involved, Teixeira recalls, both military violence (campaigns, popular insurrection, foreign intervention) and political violence (persecution, exile, censorship); see Teixeira, *História concisa do Brasil* (São Paulo, 1993), 135.

own agency and transculturation help to challenge the opposition between omnipotent European colonizers and passive, colonized natives. Both characters come to represent the intercultural mediators that we have observed in the figures of Juan Ortiz and Alvarito and in the self-representations of el Inca Garcilaso and Francisco Núñez de Pineda.[50]

Garcilaso and Pineda may be comparatively closer in time to the stories of captivity that they relate than Durão is to the sixteenth-century adventures of Diogo Álvares. In all cases, however, we have seen how the representation of captivity is inevitably molded by personal, ideological, and authorial concerns at the moment of writing. Durão's personal investment in the retelling of a captivity tale may be less obvious than it is in the authors who explicitly identify themselves with the captives they write about, but his appropriation of the story of Diogo Álvares is similarly informed by concerns of self-authorization and -aggrandizement. Durão demonstrates his ability, like Caramuru and Paraguaçu, to move between and manipulate cultural and discursive traditions. Despite the humble, self-incriminating tone of the *Retractação,* Durão perhaps also means to portray himself, as Cândido suggests, as "um varão em mil casos agitados" [a man challenged by a thousand difficulties], one who demonstrates "valor . . . na adversa sorte" [valor in misfortune]. If writing had originally been responsible for Durão's political troubles and forced dislocations, he also turns to it in order to "invent" the patria to which he, unlike his protagonists, would never return. In so doing, Durão partakes of the tradition of self-fashioning that other exiled American-born authors of his day would demonstrate in the historical, geographical, and naturalistic descriptions of their homelands.[51]

Yet the home invented in *Caramuru* is unquestionably part of the Portuguese Empire, not the forerunner of an independent nation-state. However much Diogo Álvares has been affected by his physical and emotional captivation by the Tupinambá, his heroic status depends on his ability to bring about successfully the Portuguese colonization and Christian evangelization of Brazil. *Caramuru*'s portrayal of the transculturated castaway Diogo-Caramuru as the ideal colonizer is a more explicit demonstration of a tendency also evident in *La Florida del Inca* and *Cautiverio feliz:* these texts posit the captive-mediator as a more effective colonizer, not a figure of anticolonial resistance. Nevertheless, the contradictory and ambivalent figures

50. Holanda, *Capítulos de literatura colonial,* ed. Cândido, 88; Durão, *Caramuru,* 19.

51. Cândido, *Formação da literatura brasileira,* I, 178; Durão, *Caramuru,* 19.

and spaces in these works also display the tensions of empire, challenging the notion that colonial relations as well as representations were limited to the opposition of fixed identities.[52]

The final chapter turns from the tensions within to the tensions between empires. For Diogo Álvares's contemporaries, European national identities were no more stable or inflexible than those of Iberians in the New World, and captivity was just as liable to reveal their tenuous nature.

52. Ann Laura Stoler and Frederick Cooper use the term "tensions of empire" to call attention to the "contestation over the very categories of ruler and ruled at the heart of colonial politics"; although their focus is on nineteenth-century "bourgeois" empires, their argument that "the history of colonies is not simply about implacable opposition against monolithic power; it is just as much a story of multifaceted engagements with cultures of rule as of efforts to negate them" is just as applicable to the early modern imperial world; see Stoler and Cooper, "Between Metropole and Colony: Rethinking a Research Agenda," in Cooper and Stoler, eds., *Tensions of Empire: Colonial Cultures in a Bourgeois World* (Berkeley, Calif., 1997), 1–56, esp. 6, 7, 36.

chapter Five : "AN ENGLISH HARVEST OF SPANISH & PORTUGALL SEEDE" : CAPTIVES & CAPTURED TEXTS IN ENGLISH NEW WORLD WRITING

NAVIGATING ANGLO-IBERIAN RELATIONS

As a youth, the sixteenth-century Portuguese pilot Nuno da Silva traveled the inverse route of the adolescent José de Santa Rita Durão: as we read in a sworn deposition before the tribunal of the Inquisition of Mexico, at the age of eight, he relocated from his native Portugal to Brazil in the company of a seafaring uncle. Silva's voyages between Portugal and Brazil continued as he worked his way from the position of sailor to pilot and finally captain; in another deposition, to the viceroy of New Spain, he is identified both as a "native of Lisbon, citizen of Oporto, and resident of Gaia" and as someone who has "resided" in Brazil "for a long time." Nuno da Silva's multiple homes, journeys, and international contacts resemble those of another sixteenth-century mariner: Durão's epic protagonist, Diogo Álvares "Caramuru." Yet Silva's capture by Francis Drake en route to Brazil in 1578 thrust him into an interimperial sphere of rivalry and intrigue that diverged dramatically from *Caramuru*'s idealized depiction of Spanish, French, and Portuguese cooperation. Whereas Diogo Álvares politely declined, for reasons of national loyalty, the French king's offer to establish trade with Brazil, Silva apparently did not shun the powerful role that, as a knowledgeable captive, he was granted on Drake's expedition. Although Silva himself claimed that it was only his familiarity with the Brazilian coastline and sources for fresh water that made him valuable to Drake, the viceroy and others suspected that the Portuguese pilot had offered essential guidance through the Straits of Magellan. Nuno da Silva's captivity among the English, rather than Amerindians, rendered him even more suspect for his contemporaries than Diogo Álvares "Caramuru" was for eighteenth-century Brazilian academicians in search of an epic hero.[1]

1. See the "Relation of the Voyage of the English Corsair Given by the Pilot Nuño

Silva's deposition before the Inquisition attests to the fact that Drake treasured the information he acquired from captured ships in the form of navigation charts, maps, and other texts: "In one particular instance he seized all the papers and dispatches which were being carried by Colchero, the said pilot of the Viceroy of New Spain. He prized these greatly and rejoiced over them, saying he was going to take them to his native kingdom." In Silva's case, his services as a translator might have made his capture doubly useful. The deposition summary states that Drake took Silva's astrolabe, *libro de regimiento,* and chart of the Brazilian coast as well as his "merchandise and provisions";

> what is more, after taking the chart, which was in the Portuguese language, [Drake] had it translated into English and, as he navigated along the coast of Brazil, he went on verifying it. . . . In point of fact, Francis Drake wrote down all he had learnt and had heard related concerning the routes of the Portuguese, to the Island of Cape Verde, the coast of Guinea, and Santa Maria and the Indies, as well as of the ports and the land and sea forces of the Portuguese Indies.

As the editor's footnote points out, Nuno da Silva's fluency in English, corroborated by other captives, makes him the likely translator of the chart, even if he left out that bit of compromising information. Silva not only disseminates his own work through translation but plants the seeds of additional textual production, for Drake himself writes down "all he had learnt and had heard concerning the routes of the Portuguese"—presumably information acquired from his Portuguese captive(s). The famous English corsair pirates texts as much as ships, and his relationship to the captured pilot and chart points up the different ways in which the English enterprise in the Americas followed those of Spain and Portugal: not only in time but

---

da Silva in the Presence of His Lordship [the Viceroy of New Spain] on the 20th of May, 1579 . . . ," and the "Sworn Deposition III of the Portuguese Pilot Nuño da Silva, Given on May 23rd, 1579, before the Tribunal of the Inquisition of Mexico, Immediately after His Arrest," in Zelia Nuttall, ed. and trans., *New Light on Drake: A Collection of Documents relating to His Voyage of Circumnavigation, 1577–1580,* Works Issued by the Hakluyt Society, 2d Ser., no. 34 (London, 1914), 256–271, 295–319 (quotation on 269–270). "Nuño," the Hispanicized version of "Nuno," appears in most documents; I will render names in their original Portuguese spelling throughout this chapter, however they may appear in English and Spanish sources.

also in being dependent upon Iberian sources of information, individuals as well as texts.[2]

After Drake released him on the coast of New Spain, Silva was tried and condemned by the Inquisition for heretical participation in his captors' religious practices. Several witnesses—other Spanish and Portuguese captives—claimed to have seen him read a book during the Englishmen's "ceremonies," attend sermons, pray, and eat meat during Lent. Silva himself confessed to taking communion twice but affirmed that he only did so under compulsion. The Inquisition trial indicates the currency of the belief in the religious adulteration of returning captives, but according to Silva, it was his knowledge and service to Drake—not his unorthodox behavior—that provoked the allegations. Silva imputed his accusers' statements "to the great hatred they had conceived against him, because, seeing him in the company of the Englishman they had inferred that he had acted as a guide to Drake." The viceroy and inquisitors even suspected that he had been left in Mexico as a spy, implying that the knowledge he could continue to provide to the English was as much a threat as, if not more than, his questionable religious leanings. Nuno da Silva was condemned to public abjuration and perpetual exile from the Indies in an auto-da-fé of 1582. However, the Portuguese pilot must have managed to captivate his new captors, as well, surely owing to the information about Drake and his voyage that he was now able to provide. After "duly examin[ing]" him upon his arrival in Spain, Philip II set him free, made him a gift of one hundred reales, granted him safe-conduct to visit his family in Portugal, and employed him as the bearer of a royal dispatch. Nuno da Silva, in other words, earned the favorable reception and rewards granted to ex-captives and ex-castaways like Álvar Núñez Cabeza de Vaca and el Inca Garcilaso de la Vega's Pedro Serrano.[3]

The English, of course, were even more grateful for his assistance, and

2. "Sworn Deposition III," ibid., 308–309.

3. See the "Examination of Juan Pascual," "Deposition of Juan Pascual," and "Documents relating to Nuño da Silva after His Release from the Inquisition and Return to Spain," ibid., 323–327, 332–339, 393–399 (quotations on 326, 394, and 398). Among the documents translated by Nuttall is an unsigned letter dated July 30, 1583, addressed to the Royal Council in Madrid, which states, "His Majesty, having received notice that a Portuguese pilot, who navigated with Francis Drake in the South Sea, was in Seville, ordered the President and Judges of the House of Trade to send him here, as His Majesty particularly wished to know what manner of navigation he had made and all that had happened to him" (397).

Francis Drake credited him publicly with the success of the journey. Lopes Vaz, another Portuguese who was taken captive—along with his text—by an English pirate, also refers to Nuno da Silva as someone who provided "great helpe and furtherance unto Francis Drake." Through his account of his captor's voyage Silva also furthered textual production about the New World, in multiple languages and for different publics. Lopes Vaz would himself rely on Silva's work in his "Discourse of the West Indies and the South Sea" (ca. 1587): "And this which I shall here say," Vaz writes of the passages dedicated to Drake's voyage, "I had in writing of the Portugall pilot himselfe." Silva's navigational accounts were thus captured—and reproduced—at least four times over: by the English corsair Drake, by the Spanish Inquisition and the viceroy in New Spain, by the Portuguese navigator Lopes Vaz, and finally by the English propagandist and anthologizer Richard Hakluyt, who acquired both Silva's and Vaz's texts from their pirate captors and published them in his landmark collection, *Principal Navigations of the English Nation* (1589 and 1598–1600). Hakluyt's self-proclaimed successor Samuel Purchas further revised Lopes Vaz's text for publication in his 1625 *Hakluytus Posthumus; or, Purchas His Pilgrimes.* Hakluyt and Purchas clearly valued captured texts at least as much as Drake. Whereas the corsair read, verified, and copied his captive's navigation chart throughout his journey, the stay-at-home compilers acquired many such documents from the pirate captors and published them, along with other Iberian accounts, for the purpose of recording and fostering English imperial expansion.[4]

4. Lopes Vaz, "A Discourse of the West Indies and the South Sea, Written by Lopez Vaz a Portugall," in Richard Hakluyt, *The Principal Navigations, Voyages, Traffiques, and Discoveries of the English Nation Made by Sea or Over-land to the Remote and Farthest Distant Quarters of the Earth at Any Time within the Compasse of These 1600 Yeeres,* 12 vols. (Glasgow, 1903–1905 [orig. publ. London, 1589, 1598–1600]), XI, 227–290, esp. 260. Nuttall refers to Drake's public acknowledgment of his debt to Nuno da Silva, in *New Light on Drake,* 395. Samuel Purchas includes an abridged version of Lopes Vaz's text in "The Historie of Lopez Vaz a Portugall (Taken by Captaine Withrington at the River of Plate, Anno 1586. with This Discourse about Him) Touching American Places, Discoveries, and Occurents; Abridged," in Purchas, *Hakluytus Posthumus; or, Purchas His Pilgrimes, Contayning a History of the World in Sea Voyages and Lande Travells by Englishmen and Others,* 20 vols. (Glasgow, 1905–1907 [orig. publ. London, 1625]), XVII, 247–292. On Drake's dependence on the "specialised knowledge and local sea-charts" of captured Iberian pilots, see Kenneth R. Andrews, *Drake's Voyages: A Re-assessment of Their Place in Elizabethan Maritime Expansion* (London, 1967), 60. Drake's liberation of Nuno da

Although Hakluyt frequently resorted to foreign texts in the absence of English primary materials, he made clear in his title that he was mainly concerned with documenting the voyages of the "English nation." Ever since historian James A. Froude pronounced *Principal Navigations* the "Prose Epic of the modern English nation" in 1853, Hakluyt's name has been linked with national identity formation. Indeed, Elizabethan and Jacobean travel writing in general has been associated with the construction of an English and Protestant identity defined through its imperial endeavors, whether these are understood as examples of heroic mastery or, in later accounts, of toilsome failure. In this context, the translation and incorporation of Iberian texts in the volumes of Hakluyt and Purchas have been viewed as an appropriation of the knowledge that they contain while "discrediting the authority of their authors." Yet English navigators and writers are also dependent on the authority of their "captives" and are thus often eager to credit that authority. Drake's and Hakluyt's use of Silva suggests that English dependence on Iberian sources of information was not a matter to be suppressed, even in a period of open Anglo-Spanish hostility under Elizabeth I.[5]

Silva on the coast of New Spain was apparently well known and was one of the few actions on his voyage of circumnavigation to be condemned in England; see William Camden, *The History of the Most Renowned and Victorious Princess Elizabeth, Late Queen of England . . .*, 4th ed. (London, 1688 [orig. publ. London, 1625]), 253–254, who relates how Drake arrived England "to the great Admiration of all men, and without any Crime laid to his Charge by his Adversaries, but onely that he had put *Doughtey* to death, that he had left a Portugueeze whom he had taken upon the Coast of *Africa* to the Cruelty of the *Spaniards* at *Aquatulco,* and had inhumanely set that *Negro*-Maid before mentioned on Shoar in an Island, after she was gotten with Child in his Ship." On Camden's derisive view of Drake, whom he elsewhere calls a "Pirate," see William S. Maltby, *The Black Legend in England: The Development of Anti-Spanish Sentiment, 1558-1660* (Durham, N.C., 1971), 73–74.

5. James A. Froude, "England's Forgotten Worthies," in Froude, *Essays in Literature and History* (London, 1906), 34–80, esp. 36, orig. publ. in *Westminster Review,* no. 2 (July–October 1852), 32–67; Ralph Bauer, *The Cultural Geography of Colonial American Literatures: Empire, Travel, Modernity* (Cambridge, 2003), 91–92. Bauer is here characterizing arguments made by "modern Spanish and Spanish American historians and philosophers of history who have detected a distinctly anti-Catholic geo-political agenda at the root of modern historical epistemologies, originating with Britain's early modern geo-political struggle against Spain for imperial hegemony in the New World." Louis Montrose similarly argues that Sir Walter Ralegh must "ground his own credibility upon the credibility of the very people whom he wishes

The dependence on foreign sources like Silva complicates the way in which critics have characterized the emergence of an English imperial identity in sixteenth- and seventeenth-century travel writing and this identity's relationship to other imperial powers, particularly Spain. Many scholars have noted how the Spanish Empire served as a model and/or a countermodel for English imperial ideology. Yet the emphasis on imitation or contradistinction, envy or enmity, assumes too rigid a conception of national boundaries and obscures relationships of interdependence and collaboration between imperial subjects. Drake may imitate Silva by writing an account of the "routes of the Portuguese," but he must rely on Silva's information and cooperation to do so. And the malleable loyalties of Silva himself challenge the way in which captivity narratives, specifically, are thought to contribute to the formation of an English national identity.[6]

---

to discredit"; see Montrose, "The Work of Gender in the Discourse of Discovery," in Stephen Greenblatt, ed., *New World Encounters* (Berkeley, Calif., 1993), 177–217, esp. 192. For a reading of Hakluyt as part of a generation of writers engaged in national identity formation, see Richard Helgerson, *Forms of Nationhood: The Elizabethan Writing of England* (Chicago, 1992), 149–191. On the critical reception of Hakluyt's volumes as a national epic, inaugurated by Froude, see Mary C. Fuller, *Voyages in Print: English Travel to America, 1576–1624* (Cambridge, 1995), 141–174. Fuller emphasizes the rhetoric of failure in sixteenth- and seventeenth-century English travel writing, including Hakluyt's editorial discourse. J. N. Hillgarth offers examples of the dependence of English geographers on their Spanish, Portuguese, and Italian predecessors in Hillgarth, *The Mirror of Spain, 1500–1700: The Formation of a Myth* (Ann Arbor, Mich., 2000), 370–379. Hillgarth reviews the historical process through which Spain usurped France's place as the traditional enemy of England, beginning under the reign of Mary I and her unpopular marriage to Philip II and culminating in the period of open Anglo-Spanish war (1585–1604) as a result of the Spanish embargo on English trade under Elizabeth I (351–395).

6. Anthony Pagden elucidates England's development of a distinct imperial ideology from that of Spain in Pagden, *Lords of All the World: Ideologies of Empire in Spain, Britain, and France, c. 1500–c. 1800* (New Haven, Conn., 1995). For examples of literary scholars who trace a shift from a rhetoric of imitation to one of opposition to Spain—characterizing English imperialism in terms of mercantile rather than "universal" aspirations and posing the English as "liberators" of the natives from Spanish oppression—see Helgerson, *Forms of Nationhood,* 149–191; Bauer, *Cultural Geography of Colonial American Literatures,* 77–117; Thomas Scanlan, *Colonial Writing and the New World, 1583–1671: Allegories of Desire* (Cambridge, 1999). Other scholars have observed not a shift but rather an enduring ambivalence in English attitudes toward the Spanish Empire, a competing but sometimes simultaneous, contradic-

To be sure, many tales of the captivity of Englishmen among Iberians—most often as prisoners of the Inquisition—could be said to serve a nationalist agenda by opposing innocent English Protestants and tyrannical Iberian Catholics. Job Hortop's account of captivity among Spaniards—after being stranded by John Hawkins and Francis Drake on the coast of New Spain in 1568, about a decade before Nuno da Silva would suffer the same fate—stresses the protagonist's national identity in the titles of both editions published in 1591, *The Travailes of an English Man* and *The Rare Travailes of Job Hortop, an Englishman.* The "rare travailes" refer less to Hortop's hostile yet brief encounter with "wilde and savage people" than to his Inquisition trial and "slaverie and bondage in the Spanish Galley," as announced on one edition's title page. The title of another account of an Englishman left in New Spain by Hawkins, first published in Hakluyt's *Principal Navigations,* offers an even more overtly nationalistic perspective: "A Discourse Written by One Miles Philips Englishman . . . Conteining Many Special Things of That Countrey and of the Spanish Government, but Specially of Their Cruelties Used to Our Englishmen, and amongst the Rest to Him Selfe for the Space of 15. or 16. Yeres Together, until by Good and Happy Meanes He Was Delivered from Their Bloody Hands, and Returned into His Owne Countrey." The cruelty and treachery with which Hortop and Philips represent Spaniards are typical of narratives of inquisitorial captivity, which depict

---

tory appeal to both imitation and differentiation; see, for example, Jonathan Hart, *Representing the New World: English and French Uses of the Example of Spain* (New York, 2000); and Barbara Fuchs, who usefully recovers the strategic dimensions of imitation in the relations between Spain, England, their American colonies, and the Ottoman Empire in Fuchs, *Mimesis and Empire: The New World, Islam, and European Identities* (Cambridge, 2001). On the nationalist agenda of the earliest English captivity narratives—those written by captives of Muslims and Iberian Catholics in the sixteenth century—see Joe Snader, *Caught between Worlds: British Captivity Narratives in Fact and Fiction* (Lexington, Ky., 2000), 66–68; for an interpretation stressing the ways in which captives not only reinforce but also trouble notions of British national superiority and cultural oppositions, see Linda Colley, *Captives: Britain, Empire, and the World, 1600–1850* (London, 2002). Both Snader and Colley explore the diverse international arenas in which Britons were held captive in the early modern period, disputing the notion of an exclusively (Anglo-)American phenomenon or genre. Captivity narratives written in other languages also form a part of the global context within which accounts of English captivity should be read, given the interimperial circulation of both captives and captives' tales that I trace in this chapter.

the "shocking Barbarities" of the Spanish and Portuguese Inquisitions in order to assert the moral and cultural superiority of English Protestantism. Notions of English liberty and humanity can thus emerge in opposition to Spanish (and Portuguese) tyranny not only when the captives are Amerindian, as in English uses of Bartolomé de Las Casas and other sources of the Black Legend of Spanish atrocities in the New World, but also when the captives are Englishmen.[7]

Nevertheless, as the case of Nuno da Silva demonstrates, relationships of captivity between Iberians and Englishmen can also problematize narratives of national difference and civilizational hierarchy. The notion of implacable religious and national opposition cannot adequately account for Drake's, Hakluyt's, and Purchas's uses of Silva and his texts, as well as for Silva's own uses of his captivity. On one hand, tracing the circulation of captives

7. [Job Hortop], *The Rare Travailes of Job Hortop, an Englishman, Who Was Not Heard of in Three and Twentie Yeeres Space. Wherein Is Declared the Dangers He Escaped in His Voyage to Gynnie, Where after Hee Was Set on Shoare in a Wilderness Neere to Mexico, Hee Endured Much Slaverie and Bondage in the Spanish Galley. Wherein Also He Discovereth Many Strange and Wonderfull Things Seene in the Time of His Travaile, as well concerning Wilde and Savage People, as Also of Sundrie Monstrous Beasts, Fishes, and Foules, and Also Trees of Wonderfull Forme and Qualitie* (London, 1591). As the title indicates, Hortop's captivity is among Spaniards, and his text is thus not "the first story of the Indian captivity of an Englishman," as some scholars have claimed, such as R. W. G. Vail, *The Voice of the Old Frontier* (Philadelphia, 1949), 30. For Hawkins, see Hakluyt, *Principal Navigations,* IX, 398. The reference to the "shocking Barbarities" of the Spanish Inquisition is from the editor's introduction to John Coustos's *Sufferings of John Coustos, for Free-Masonry, and for His Refusing to Turn Roman Catholic, in the Inquisition at Lisbon; Where He Was Sentenc'd, during Four Years, to the Galley; and Afterwards Releas'd from Thence by the Gracious Interposition of His Present Majesty King George II* (London, 1746), xxvi. Seventeenth-century antecedents to Coustos's narrative of inquisitorial captivity include James Wadsworth, *The English Spanish Pilgrime; or, A New Discoverie of Spanish Popery, and Jesuiticall Stratagems . . .* (London, 1630); William Lithgow, *The Totall Discourse of the Rare Adventures and Painefull Peregrinations of Long Nineteene Yeares Travayles from Scotland to the Most Famous Kingdomes in Europe, Asia, and Affrica* (London, 1632). On inquisitorial captivity narratives as Protestant propaganda, see Snader, *Caught between Worlds,* 19; on the development of the Black Legend in England, see Maltby, *Black Legend in England;* Hillgarth, *Mirror of Spain,* 309–327. Portugal's Catholicism, Inquisition, and association with the Spanish Crown during the 1580–1640 period of Habsburg rule made it an occasional target of English Protestant propaganda (as in Coustos's narrative), overriding

and captured texts between the Iberian and English worlds, and the valuable knowledge that they provide, can challenge notions of Iberian intellectual backwardness and to recover a moment when, as Jorge Cañizares-Esguerra suggests with respect to the sixteenth and early seventeenth century, Spanish (and Portuguese) scholarship "far surpassed anything then available in English." On the other hand, the trajectories of the captives—their own responses to their captivities—call into question whether a stable sense of national identity either successfully emerged from or contributed to the imperial competition of the sixteenth and seventeenth centuries. English expansion was not just a national project that arose in opposition to Spain, whether in a relationship of imitation, competition, or differentiation, but a project that was intimately dependent on—captive to, if you will—Spanish and Portuguese subjects, texts, and discourses.[8]

TRAVEL AND TRAVAIL: THE WORK OF PIRACY

"I meddle in this worke with the Navigations onely of our owne nation," Hakluyt declares in the preface of his *Principal Navigations of the English Nation* (1589), while also confessing that, "as the matter and occasion required," he has called on the testimony of "strangers as witnesses of the things done." He goes on to acknowledge his dependence on this testimony, in light of the lack of English accounts of their own travels: "They [are] none

---

the fourteenth-century Anglo-Portuguese Alliance and English support for the Portuguese pretender to the throne, dom Antonio, prior de Crato.

8. Jorge Cañizares-Esguerra, *How to Write the History of the New World: Histories, Epistemologies, and Identities in the Eighteenth-Century Atlantic World* (Stanford, Calif., 2001), 363n. 134; see also his "Iberian Science in the Renaissance: Ignored How Much Longer?" *Perspectives on Science,* XII (2004), 86–124. A revised version of the essay appears in Cañizares-Esguerra, *Nature, Empire, and Nation: Explorations of the History of Science in the Iberian World* (Stanford, Calif., 2006), 14–45. Cañizares-Esguerra discusses Spanish and Portuguese technical superiority with respect to navigation, cosmography, cartography, military technology, metallurgy, and a host of other fields and points out how this superiority was recognized by the English themselves, as when Hakluyt writes in his preface to the first volume of the second edition of *Principal Navigations,* "These two worthy Nations had those bright lampes of learning (I meane the most ancient and best Philosophers, Historiographers and Geographers) to shewe them light; and the load-starre of experience (to wit those great exploits and voyages layed up in store and recorded) whereby to shape their course"; see *Principal Navigations,* I, xlii.

but such as either faythfully remember, or sufficiently confirme the travels of our owne people: of whom (to speake trueth) I have received more light in some respects, then all our owne Historians could afford me in this case, Bale, Foxe, and Eden onely excepted." By the time he wrote the epistle dedicatory to Sir Robert Cecil, included in the third volume of the second edition (1600), Hakluyt was even more willing to admit the importance of foreign sources not only to corroborate but also to supplement English experience abroad: "And albeit my worke do carry the title of The English voyages . . . and that my travaile was chiefly undertaken for preservation of their memorable actions, yet where our owne mens experience is defective, there I have bene careful to supply the same with the best and chiefest relations of strangers." Hakluyt frequently describes his editorial efforts as involving both travel and "travaile" ("huge toile," "troublesome and painfull action"), thus substituting voyages to foreign lands with domestic travel to different libraries and textual exploration of foreign histories:

> What restlesse nights, what painefull dayes, what heat, what cold I have indured; how many long and chargeable journeys I have traveiled; how many famous libraries I have searched into; what varietie of ancient and moderne writers I have perused; what a number of old records, patents, privileges, letters, etc. I have redeemed from obscuritie and perishing; into how manifold acquaintance I have entred; what expenses I have not spared; and yet what faire opportunites of private gaine, preferment, and ease I have neglected.

"Travel" and "travail" were employed interchangeably in Hakluyt's time, as his use of "traveil" suggests. Although Hakluyt omits from this list of labors the task of translation itself, his "extreeme travaile in the histories of the Spanyards" certainly involved it. The "histories of the Spanyards" included in *Principal Navigations* range from firsthand exploration accounts (for example, narratives of expeditions to New Mexico by Fray Marcos de Niza, Francisco Vázquez de Coronado, Augustín Ruiz, and Antonio de Espejo) to authoritative, published histories by Francisco López de Gómara and Gonzalo Fernández de Oviedo y Valdés.[9]

9. Hakluyt, *Principal Navigations,* I, xix, xxiv, xxix, xxxi, xxxix–xl, lxxvi. According to the *Oxford English Dictionary, travel* ("the action of travelling or journeying") was originally "the same word . . . (in a specialized sense and form)" as *travail* ("bodily or mental labour or toil"). *Travail,* in turn, derives from the Latin *trepalium*

Mary Fuller has astutely described how Hakluyt appropriates the rhetoric of travel and travail to describe his own work of compiling and editing as a means of constructing and defending his authority without undertaking voyages of exploration himself. But Hakluyt also links voyaging and work in a larger sense, as part of his arguments for English imperial expansion. In the private document known as the *Discourse of Western Planting* (1584), written for Elizabeth I, one reason he gives for "this westerne voyadge" is that it will provide employment for England's idle men. Although the document generally vilifies the Spaniards and their "moste *outragious* and more then Turkish cruelties," in this chapter the Spanish and Portuguese provide models of honest employment, in contrast to English piracy and vagabondage: "Bothe wch Realmes being of themselves poore and barren and hardly able to susteine their inhabitaunts by their discoveries have founde such occasion of employmente, that these many yeres wee have not herde scarcely of any pirate of those twoo nations: whereas wee and the frenche are moste infamous for our *outeragious,* common, and daily piracies." With respect to piracy, Hakluyt's outrage points inward. In contrast, the Iberian example shows how colonization breeds virtue and industriousness by providing work for those who go abroad ("artificers, husbandmen, seamen, marchauntes, souldiers, capitaines, phisitions, lawyers, devines, Cosmographers, hidrographers, Astronomers, historiographers, yea olde folkes, lame persons, women, and younge children . . . shalbe kepte from idlenes, and

---

(an instrument of torture) via the Romance languages, including the Spanish *trabajo* and the Portuguese *trabalho;* see *OED,* 2d ed., s.v. "travel," "travail." In the epistle dedicatory to Sir Robert Cecil of his revised translation of Antonio Galvão's *Tratado* (Lisbon, 1563), published in English in Hakluyt, *The Discoveries of the World . . . Corrected, Quoted, and Now Published in English by Richard Hakluyt . . .* (London, 1601), Hakluyt emphasizes the travail involved in correcting the "manifold errours" of the anonymous translator, which required the consultation of "originall histories (. . . many of them exceeding rare and hard to come by)"; the prologue is reprinted in E. G. R. Taylor, ed., *The Original Writings and Correspondence of the Two Richard Hakluyts* (London, 1935), II, 483–486 (hereafter cited as Hakluyt, *Original Writings and Correspondence*). Purchas similarly describes the "great paines" involved in correcting translations in *Hakluytus Posthumus,* XIV, 428. For a list of translations with which Hakluyt was involved, either as translator or sponsor, see F. M. Rogers, "Hakluyt as Translator," in D. B. Quinn, ed., *The Hakluyt Handbook,* 2 vols., Works Issued by the Hakluyt Society, nos. 144–145 (London, 1974), I, 37–47; on the Spanish and Portuguese sources used by Hakluyt, see K. R. Andrews, "Latin America," ibid., 234–243.

made able by their owne honest and easie labour to finde themselves wthoute surchardginge others") as well as those who do not, whether by producing English goods to sell in this newfound market or working the "unwrought" commodities imported back home. This mercantilist model can also describe the economy of knowledge production represented by Hakluyt's and Purchas's travel collections—a geographical division of labor whereby a metropolitan historian appropriates and reworks the "raw materials" of travelers' accounts—even though, as Ralph Bauer argues, only Purchas explicitly theorizes his method this way.[10]

To be sure, the trade-based expansion recommended by Hakluyt eventually replaced, under James I, the aristocratic model of conquest and Elizabethan privateering, as many scholars have argued. Yet Hakluyt's formulation suggests that Spain and Portugal provided examples of "honest labour" and trade, not just models of conquest and pillage with which English mercantilism could be contrasted. At the same time, the collections of Hakluyt and Purchas depend on piracy, however much they disavow the practice and

10. Fuller, *Voyages in Print,* 156; Richard Hakluyt, *Discourse of Western Planting,* in Hakluyt, *Original Writings and Correspondence,* II, 211–326, esp. 211, 233–239, 257 (emphasis added); Bauer, *Cultural Geography of Colonial American Literatures,* 80. Bauer cites Purchas's preface in *Hakluytus Posthumus:* "What a World of Travellers have by their owne eyes observed in this kinde, is here (for the most part in their owne words transcribed or translated) delivered . . . as Pioners are employed by Enginers, and Labourers serve Masons, and Bricklayers, and these the best Surveyers and Architects: so here Purchas and his Pilgrimes minister individuall and sensible materials (as it were with Stones, Brickes and Mortar) to those universall Speculators for their Theoricall structures. And well may the Author be ranked with such Labourers (howsoever here a Master builder also) for that he hath beene forced as much to the Hod, Barrow and Trowel, as to contemplative survaying: neither in so many . . . Circumnavigations about the World in this and his other Workes, was ever enabled to maintaine a Vicarian or Subordinate Scribe, but his own hands to worke, aswell as his head to contrive these voluminous Buildings" (*Hakluytus Posthumus,* I, xl–xli). Bauer explains Purchas's equivocation between identifying himself as a "laborer" or a "master builder" as indicative of the "opening of an epistemological gap between the empirical traveler and the philosophical historian" and a corresponding division of labor between the "circumference" and the "center" in Purchas's metaphors; see *Cultural Geography of Colonial American Literatures,* 86–88. Yet Purchas's emphasis on his own labor as involving not just "contemplative surveying" but the "Hod, Barrow and Trowel," the work of his "own hands" as well as his "head," also follows Hakluyt's characterization of his editorial efforts as involving physical exertion.

insist on an empire built on trade. Hakluyt incorporated dozens of captured letters, relations, and rutters as well as depositions of Iberian captives, particularly in the third volume of *Principal Navigations.* He presents the work involved in the collection and dissemination of captured texts as labor that supersedes the illegitimacy of piratical acquisition. In the epistle dedicatory to the third volume of *Principal Navigations,* he presents the accumulation, translation, and publication of such booty as a worthy "endeavor" unto itself:

> Moreover, because since our warres with Spaine, by the taking of their ships, and sacking of their townes and cities, most of all their secrets of the West Indies, and every part thereof are fallen into our peoples hands (which in former time were for the most part unknowen unto us,) I have used the uttermost of my best endevour, to get, and having gotten, to translate out of Spanish, and here in this present volume to publish such secrets of theirs, as may any way availe us or annoy them.

Hakluyt in effect defends both literal and literary piracy. Both function as a laborious form of national defense and international aggression, a way to "availe us or annoy them." But the privileged place granted to the spoils of piracy entails a redefinition of Hakluyt's editorial labors—including, as he specifies in this passage, the previously unmentioned "travaile" of translation—and underscores English dependence on the "secrets" of its imperial rivals.[11]

11. Hakluyt, *Principal Navigations,* I, lxxvii; Pagden, *Lords of All the World,* 66–73; Helgerson, *Forms of Nationhood,* 149–191; Bauer, *Cultural Geography of Colonial American Literatures,* 89–105. The 2006 online revision of the *Oxford English Dictionary* antedates the figurative definition of *piracy* ("The appropriation and reproduction of an invention or work of another for one's own profit, without authority; infringement of the rights conferred by a patent or copyright") to 1654, more than a century earlier than the date given for its appearance (1771) in the second edition of the *OED.* However, "entrance" into the Stationers' Register—the direct antecedent of copyright—dates from the late sixteenth century, contributing to the development of the notion of unauthorized publication; see Joseph Loewenstein, *The Author's Due: Printing and the Prehistory of Copyright* (Chicago, 2002), 4–5. See also Bauer's discussion of the "piracy of knowledge" in *Cultural Geography of Colonial American Literatures,* 169. The captured texts and captives' reports published by Hakluyt relate not only to the New World but also to other areas of Spanish and Portuguese expansion; see A. M. Quinn and D. B. Quinn's "Contents and Sources of the Three Major

Hakluyt's dependence on Iberian texts to do the work of "availing" his homeland complicates his apparently unrelenting criticism of Spain in the *Discourse of Western Planting,* a posture that has been characterized as "uninflected anti-hispanism." At the end of the *Discourse,* in fact, Hakluyt even encourages English voyagers to take with them "the bookes of the discoveries and conquests" of both the East and the West Indies—surely of Portuguese and Spanish authorship, respectively—"to kepe men occupied from worse cogitations, and to raise their myndes to courage and highe enterprizes." Furthermore, "it is wisshed that it were learned oute what course bothe the Spaniardes and Portingales tooke in their discoveries for government, and that the same were delivered to learned men, that had perused most of the lawes of thempire and of other princes Lawes." Even Hakluyt finds Iberian texts to be indispensable to English voyaging; for sailors, they provide distraction as well as inspiration, whereas for the queen and her council, they offer a model for English governance overseas. As we will see, explorers and would-be colonizers like Sir Walter Ralegh and John Smith read and emulated Iberian histories of the conquest at least in part owing to Hakluyt's editorial efforts and encouragement. And Iberian texts represent not just a model for inspiration but a source of information and authority. Hakluyt's extensive citation of Spanish and Portuguese works in chapter 3, entitled "That This Westerne Voyadge Will Yelde unto Us All the Commodities of Europe, Affrica and Asia, as Farr as Wee Were Wonte to Travell, and Supplye the Wantes of All Our Decayed Trades," demonstrates how much he trades in Iberian sources in order to describe New World resources and defend the trading potential of "this westerne voyadge."[12]

Works," in Quinn, ed., *Hakluyt Handbook,* II, 335–360, which identifies the letters and documents that were captured from Iberian ships as well as the depositions taken from Iberian captives.

12. Hakluyt, *Original Writings and Correspondence,* II, 222, 324–325. David Armitage distinguishes the "uninflected anti-hispanism of Hakluyt" with Hakluyt's successor, Samuel Purchas, and the complexity of foreign policy and public opinion toward Spain under James I; Purchas's publications are "consistently anti-papal and only incidentally anti-Spanish" (Armitage, *The Ideological Origins of the British Empire* [Cambridge, 2000], 87, 89). In an earlier study, Maltby presents the "anti-hispanism" of Hakluyt and Purchas (and their contributors) as even less inflected: "They are discouragingly uniform in their portrayal of a malignant and ill-favored race without a single saving virtue" *(Black Legend in England,* 71). Among the Iberian authors cited in chapter 3 of the *Discourse of Western Planting* are Nicolás Monardes, Gonzalo Fernández de Oviedo y Valdés, Francisco Vázquez de Coro-

Hakluyt's self-proclaimed successor Samuel Purchas also does not hesitate to credit the "best and chiefest relations of strangers," many of which he acquired from Hakluyt himself. Among these is an anonymous description of Brazil, captured at sea in 1601, which we now know to be the work of the Portuguese Jesuit friar Fernão Cardim. Purchas's lack of knowledge of the author—one of the chief guarantees of credibility in the seventeenth century, according to Steven Shapin—does not interfere with his unqualified praise of the work's veracity:

> Reader, I here present thee the exactest Treatise of Brasil which I have seene written by any man, especially in the Historie of the multiplied and diversified Nations and customes of men; as also in the naturall Historie of Beasts, Serpents, Fowles, Fishes, Trees, Plants, with divers other remarkeable rarities of those Regions. It was written (it seemeth) by a Portugall Frier (or Jesuite) which had lived thirtie yeares in those parts, from whom (much against his will) the written Booke was taken by one Frances Cooke of Dartmouth in a Voyage outward bound for Brasil, An. 1601. who sold the same to Master Hacket for twenty shillings; by whose procurement it was translated out of Portugall into English: which translation I have compared with the written Originall, and in many places supplied defects, amended errours, illustrated with notes, and thus finished and furnished to the publike view. Great losse had the Author of his worke, and it not a little of his name, which I should as willingly have inserted as worthy much honour for his industrie, by which the great and admirable workes of the Creator are made knowne; the visible and various testimonies of his invisible power, and manifold wisedome. Sic vos non vobis. In this and other written tractates the Spaniards and the Portugals have taken paines, and (which was denied to Spaine and Portugall) England is here entred into their labours, and hath reaped an English harvest of

---

nado, Francisco López de Gómara, and Gaspar Corte Real, the latter four through Giovanni Battista Ramusio's translation into Italian; see Hakluyt, *Original Writings and Correspondence,* II, 223–231. Hakluyt concludes, "Thus, *having alleaged many printed testymonies of these credible persons* wch were personally betwene 30. and 63. degrees in America . . . I may well and truly conclude *with reason and aucthoritie* that all the commodities of all our olde decayed and daungerous trades in all Europe, Africa, and Asia haunted by us may in shorte space for little or nothinge and many for the very workemanshippe in a manner be had in that parte of America" (233 [emphasis added]).

Spanish and Portugall seede. . . . I may well adde this Jesuite to the English Voyages, as being an English prize and captive.

English translators frequently used the figure of captivity to characterize their relationship with the original work and author—with, as Massimiliano Morini explains, a transition toward identifying themselves as "conquerors" rather than "slaves" of the source text by the end of the sixteenth century—but Purchas's description of the Jesuit treatise as an "English prize and captive" is, in this instance, both literal and figurative.[13]

Although Purchas refers to his efforts in improving the translation, the text remains a harvest of another's "labours"; the "pains" and "industrie" that Hakluyt and Purchas often use to describe their own editorial activities are here attributed to the "Spaniards and the Portugals." Purchas acknowl-

13. Purchas, *Hakluytus Posthumus,* XVI, 417–418. On the use of figurative language to describe translation in sixteenth-century England, see Massimiliano Morini, *Tudor Translation in Theory and Practice* (Aldershot, Eng., 2006), 35–61; he focuses on the motif of "submission and conquest" on 51–55. Colin Steele identifies the "Master Hacket" of this passage with Hakluyt in Steele, *English Interpreters of the Iberian New World from Purchas to Stevens: A Bibliographical Study, 1603–1726* (Valencia, Spain, 1975), 45; see Steele's "From Hakluyt to Purchas," in Quinn, ed., *Hakluyt Handbook,* I, 74–96, for a list of the 121 items in *Hakluytus Posthumus* that belonged to Hakluyt. Steven Shapin describes the constitutive role of trust—of knowledge about people as sources of testimony—in the production of knowledge about things in Shapin, *A Social History of Truth: Civility and Science in Seventeenth-Century England* (Chicago, 1994). Purchas's side note reveals his attempt to identify the author of the treatise: "I finde at the end of the Booke some medicinall receipts, and the name subscribed Ir. Manoel Tristaon Emfermeiro do Colegio da Baya: whom I imagine to have beene the Author of this Treatise. Cooke reported that he had it of a Friar: but the name Jesus divers times on the top of the page, and often mention of the Fathers and societie maketh me thinke him a brother of that order, besides the state-tractate following" (*Hakluytus Posthumus,* XVI, 417). In 1881, João Capistrano de Abreu convincingly attributed the work published by Purchas to Fernão Cardim (an important Jesuit in colonial Brazil who held the rectorship of the Jesuit college in Bahia and Rio de Janeiro, among other posts), based on a comparison with another known text by Cardim as well as on the fact that Cardim was captured by Englishmen on his way back to Brazil in 1601 after a trip to Rome; see Cardim, *Do princípio e origem dos índios do Brasil e de seus costumes, adoração, e cerimónias,* ed. João Capistrano de Abreu (Rio de Janeiro, 1881). Cardim's *Do princípio e origem dos índios do Brasil* was first published together with his *Do clima e terra do Brasil e de algumas cousas notáveis* and the two letters known as the *Narrativa epistolar de uma viagem e missão jesuítica*

edges the unauthorized nature of his publication of the treatise and even portrays himself as a plagiarizer by invoking Virgil's famous poetic challenge to another poet who had claimed a Virgilian distich as his own: "Sic vos non vobis" [Thus do ye, but not for yourselves]. He also presents his acquisition of foreign texts in territorial terms—the *Oxford English Dictionary* dates the legal definition of "enter into" ("To make entry [into lands] as a formal assertion of ownership; to take possession") to the sixteenth century—as if his editorial work effectively colonized Iberian representations of the New World, to compensate for the lack of English success in actual "plantations." Indeed, Purchas's mixing of agricultural and juridical metaphors suggests the conquest and usurpation involved in "plantation," the common English term for "colony" in the res nullius justification of imperial expansion that was used to contrast with the Spanish model of "conquest."[14]

Yet rather than emphasize religious opposition or national rivalry, Purchas's comments suggest a shared sense of purpose between the Jesuit and the Anglican writer. Purchas praises the Jesuit's "industrie" in making known "the great and admirable workes of the Creator," the "visible and various testimonies of his invisible power, and manifold wisedome." The description of natural and cultural diversity as a testament to divine magnificence indeed motivated Jesuit authors like Fernão Cardim and the Spaniard

. . . *desde o anno de 1583 ao de 1590* under the title by which his work is generally known today, *Tratados da terra e gente do Brasil* . . . in Rio de Janeiro in 1925; for a more modern scholarly edition, see Cardim, *Tratados da terra e gente do Brasil,* ed. Ana Maria de Azevedo (Lisbon, 1997). While a captive in the Gatehouse in London, Cardim wrote several letters to Sir Robert Cecil in the effort to secure his and other Jesuits' release in exchange for English prisoners in Spain (in one of these letters, he complains about the confiscation of his written work). He succeeded in these efforts and earned his release sometime in 1603; see W. H. Grattan Flood, "Portuguese Jesuits in England in Penal Times," *The Month,* CXLIII (1924), 157–159; J. Manuel Espinosa, "Fernão Cardim, Jesuit Humanist of Colonial Brazil," *Mid-America,* XXIV (1942), 252–271.

14. *OED,* 2d ed., s.v. "enter." On the use of "plantation" as a synonym for "colony" in English imperial discourse and its association with the English use of the Roman law res nullius, or "agriculturalist" argument to justify colonization, see Pagden, *Lords of All the World,* 79. Virgil proved his authorship of a distich celebrating Augustus, which had been claimed by another poet, by affixing it together with four unfinished lines beginning with "Sic vos non vobis" to the palace gate; only Virgil was able to complete the lines. See J. G. Cooper, ed., *Publii Virgilii Maronis Opera; or, The Works of Virgil* (New York, 1829 [orig. publ. New York, 1827]), xii.

José de Acosta. Acosta prefaces his *Historia natural y moral de las Indias* (1590), published in English as *The Naturall and Morall Historie of the East and West Indies* in 1604 and extracted heavily by Purchas in volume III, book 5 (15 of the modern edition) with the claim that the goal of his work is "que por la noticia de las obras naturales que el Autor tan sabio de toda naturaleza ha hecho, se le dé alabanza y gloria al Altísimo Dios, que es maravilloso en todas partes" ["that having knowledge of the workes of nature, which the wise Author of all nature made, we may praise and glorifie the high God, who is wonderfull in all things and all places"]. Similarly, Purchas clarifies in his own preface that "Divine things are . . . not the peculiar argument of this Worke. . . . Naturall things are the more proper Object, namely the ordinary Workes of God in the Creatures, preserving and disposing by Providence that which his Goodnesse and Power had created, and dispersed in the divers parts of the World." The common project of revealing the "Workes of God" legitimizes Purchas's efforts in publishing the Jesuit treatise, even if that work was seized "much against [the author's] will."[15]

Indeed, Purchas's metaphor of "Spanish and Portugall seede" in English soil suggests hybridization—in the botanical origins of the term—rather than the demarcation of imperial boundaries and differences. Purchas in effect recasts as productive generation the threat of contamination that Iberian texts might have posed for some readers in seventeenth-century England, according to James Mabbe's preface to his translation of Cristóbal de Fonseca's *Discursos para todos los evangelios de la quaresma* (1614; trans. 1629). Mabbe acknowledges, "Some peradventure may dislike it, because it was first composed by a Spaniard," but he goes on to cite biblical and historical examples of the profitable appropriation of foreign fruits: "Shall not the corne be reaped because there's cockle in the field? Shal not the rose be pluckt because it grows on a Brier?" Yet Mabbe insists that his translation also purifies the text of its Spanish and Catholic origins:

15. José de Acosta, *Historia natural y moral de las Indias,* ed. Edmundo O'Gorman (Mexico City, 1940 [orig. publ. Seville, 1590]), 8; Acosta, *The Naturall and Morall Historie of the East and West Indies . . . ,* [trans. Edward Grimeston] (London, 1604), [iv]; Purchas, *Hakluytus Posthumus,* I, xxxix. On the different approaches to natural diversity by Acosta and his predecessor in the writing of New World natural history, Gonzalo Fernández de Oviedo y Valdés, see Antonio Barrera-Osorio, *Experiencing Nature: The Spanish American Empire and the Early Scientific Revolution* (Austin, Tex., 2006), 104–120, who points out that both share the understanding that one of the main purposes of empirical knowledge is to "know God more fully."

> And yet let me tell thee, to hearten thy adventure against all needlesse and imaginarie fears, The captive here hath her head shorn, and may well be admitted for a true Israelite. Thou shalt not cry out, *Mors in olla, Death is in the pot;* that little leafe of *Coloquintida* which was in it, is taken out, and the children of the Prophets may tast of the broth without danger.

If Purchas calls the treatise on Brazil an "English prize and captive," Mabbe goes one step further by likening the text to a captive who reneges, thus posing no threat of contamination to an English reader.[16]

Purchas, like Mabbe, asserts the profitability of foreign texts for an English public, but he is less interested in converting or purifying his "captive" than in using it to condemn the inhumanity of Portuguese practices in the New World. Appended to the "Treatise of Brasil, Written by a Portugall Which Had Long Lived There" is the translation of another treatise captured at the same time and apparently written by the same hand, entitled "Articles Touching the Dutie of the Kings Majestie Our Lord, and to the Common Good of All the Estate of Brasill." The articles describe and censure the unjust and illegal enslavement of the Brazilian Indians by the Portuguese. In the same spirit as English translations of Las Casas, Purchas explains that he included the treatise "for better knowledge both of the civill uncivill dealings of the Portugals with the Indians; and of the unchristian christianitie in their owne practise and conversion of the Indians, and that by Jesuiticall testimonie." Yet Purchas's translation belies a convergence rather

16. Cristóbal de Fonseca, *Discursos para todos los evangelios de la quaresma* (Madrid, 1614); Fonseca, *Devout Contemplations Expressed in Two and Fortie Sermons upon All Ye Quadragesimall Gospells,* trans. J[ames] M[abbe] (London, 1629), [ii]–[iii]. On the botanical and biological origins of the term "hybridity," see Robert J. C. Young, *Colonial Desire: Hybridity in Theory, Culture, and Race* (London, 1995), 6. A similar metaphor of botanical hybridization was invoked by exiled English Catholics in their reception of Philip II at the English Jesuit college in Valladolid in 1592. Robert Parsons's account describes how one of the hieroglyphs displayed on the walls depicted white pigeons taking wheat from a pile guarded by a Spanish eagle, which they carried "into an other coũtrie, and sowed it where it sprung up and prospered wonderfullie"; the accompanying text declares (in Parsons's translation), "This wheat of Spaine in Ingland yet will growe"; see Parsons, *A Relation of the King of Spaines Receiving in Valliodolid* [sic], *and in the Inglish College of the Same Towne* . . . ([Antwerp], 1592), 55–56. On this text and the English Jesuit colleges in Spain more generally, see Hillgarth, *Mirror of Spain,* 405–414.

than a divergence of perspectives on New World conquest; the hybridization implied by his metaphor seems already to be in effect and embodied in the captor-translator as much as in the captive-text. A comparison with the original work evinces several suggestive changes in the translation that could be the result of a misreading of the manuscript or a faulty knowledge of Portuguese but in any case speak volumes about the translator's expectations. Purchas's translation begins the section dedicated to the flora and fauna that have been transplanted from Portugal to Brazil: "This Brasill is alreadie another Portugall, and not speaking of China, which is much more temperate and healthful." The original was not, in fact, "speaking of China" but of the climate ("no clima"); Purchas's privileging of China reflects not only English mercantile interests but Portugal's own imperial priorities at the time. More to the point, Purchas's translation drastically alters Cardim's portrait of Amerindian customs when he renders "São muito maviosos" as "They are verie wicked," perhaps mistaking *mavioso* (tender or affectionate) for *malvado* (perverse, criminal, or evil). The new epithet inevitably conditions the interpretation of the subsequent description of how the Amerindians mourn their dead by embracing the corpse, sometimes prematurely ("when any one dieth, the Kindred doe cast themselves upon him in the Net, and so suddenly that sometimes they choake him before he dieth, seeming to them he is dead"; "Lamentations to be lamented," reads Purchas's marginal note). Rather than evidence of Amerindian humanity and compassion, as in the original Portuguese, in the translation the custom would seem to corroborate the "brutishness" that Purchas emphasizes (typographically, and through marginal comments) in the ensuing account of the cannibalistic sacrifice of captives. Purchas's translation, in other words, does not display a particularly sympathetic perspective toward Amerindians that would contrast with the incivility and unchristianlike behavior of the Portuguese toward them. On the contrary, the deviations from the original text in Purchas's translation evince the same attitudes toward Amerindians that he condemns in the Portuguese, suggesting that Purchas may actually be less critical of Portuguese practices than the Portuguese Jesuit himself.[17]

17. Purchas, *Hakluytus Posthumus,* XVI, 418, 428, 499; Cardim, *Tratados da terra e gente do Brasil,* ed. Azevedo, 157. Purchas inserts a sentence and paragraph break in the midst of the account of how captives are killed with a single stroke to the nape of the neck, so that he can begin a new paragraph with "And their brutishnesse is so much"; the entire passage is marked with the marginal comment "Butchery rites"; see *Hakluytus Posthumus,* XVI, 437. Purchas compares Bartolomé de Las Casas

Some of the "English prizes and captives" in Hakluyt's and Purchas's collections did, in fact—unlike Cardim—"speak of China," to the great interest of Englishmen invested in overseas trade. Hakluyt included in the second edition of *Principal Navigations* a "most exact" treatise on China, which had been published in Latin in the Portuguese colony of Macao in 1590; in the epistle dedicatory to Sir Robert Cecil, Hakluyt describes how it "was intercepted in the great Carack called Madre de Dios two yeeres after, inclosed in a case of sweete Cedar wood, and lapped up almost an hundred fold in fine calicut-cloth, as though it had beene some incomparable jewell." Hakluyt includes the treatise because he believes that Northern China will offer "ample vent of our wollen cloth" and later adds that it helps to shed the "broad light of full and perfect knowledge" on the "secret trades and Indian riches" of the far East. The captured treatise could thus both instigate and facilitate English commercial expansion in China: "Whereby it should seeme that the will of God for our good is (if our weaknesse could apprehend it) to have us communicate with them in those East Indian treasures, and by the erection of a lawfull traffike to better our meanes to advance true religion and his holy service." Theodore Leinwand has argued that Hakluyt's valorization of the treatise marks the passage from "the spoils of privateering to the profits of commerce" in English maritime endeavors. Richard Helgerson has similarly argued that Hakluyt's work reveals the emergence of a mercantile imperial ideology—one based on trading between nations—in contrast to an earlier, aristocratic one based on conquest and pillage, exemplified by Elizabethan privateers like Drake. Yet Hakluyt's and Purchas's use and treatment of plundered sources suggests that this transition is not quite complete or that the opposition does not hold, since the development of the "profits of commerce" are dependent on the "spoils of privateering." For the author that

---

explicitly to Cardim in his introduction to the former: "The like abuses of Savages in Brasill, you have seene by Portugals, complained of by Jesuites"; see *Hakluytus Posthumus,* XVIII, 81. On Purchas's perpetuation of the Black Legend through his inclusion of excerpts from Las Casas, Girolamo Benzoni, and other critical Spanish and Portuguese authors, see Maltby, *Black Legend in England,* 26–27. However, Purchas claims that he does not publish the extracts from Las Casas out of anti-Spanish bias: "If any thinke that I publish this in disgrace of that Nation; I answere, Every Nation (We see it at home) hath many evill men, many Devill-men. Againe, I aske whether the Author (himselfe a Spaniard and a Divine) intended not the honour and good of his Countrie thereby: which also was effected, evill manners producing good Lawes"; see *Hakluytus Posthumus,* XVIII, 81.

we will turn to next, Sir Walter Ralegh, the Portuguese carrack's bullion was in fact its most precious booty, for it earned his release from captivity in the Tower of London. If Hakluyt and Purchas demonstrate the value of captured texts to collectors, editors, and readers in England, Ralegh reveals how captured texts and individuals were even more valuable to the actual explorers whose survival and success—as well as the subsequent promotion of their efforts—depended on such information.[18]

SPANISH CAPTORS AND CAPTIVES IN RALEGH'S *Discoverie*

Less than a decade after Nuno da Silva's participation on Drake's voyage through the Straits of Magellan, another Portuguese pilot, Simão Fernandes, served on the 1587 expedition to the Chesapeake Bay led by John White and sponsored by Sir Walter Ralegh, a colonizing venture intended to establish a "Citie of Ralegh in Virginia." If Ralegh depended on the assistance of a Portuguese pilot—and perhaps not only for his navigational skills, for Fernandes is also described by a contemporary as "the author and promoter of the venture"—Richard Hakluyt acknowledged the importance of Spanish

18. Hakluyt, *Principal Navigations,* I, lxxii, VII, 116; Theodore B. Leinwand, *Theatre, Finance, and Society in Early Modern England* (Cambridge, 1999), 127; Helgerson, *Forms of Nationhood,* 149–191. Fuchs also complicates Helgerson's argument about the transition from aristocratic to mercantile ideology in *Mimesis and Empire,* 118–138. On Ralegh's release from the Tower of London after the capture of the *Madre de Deus,* see Raleigh Trevelyan, *Sir Walter Raleigh* (London, 2002), 184–187. Similar to Hakluyt, Purchas refers to one of the captured texts that he published as "the choisest of my Jewels": the Codex Mendoza, a Nahua pictographic manuscript commissioned by the viceroy of New Spain that was captured by French pirates, acquired by the royal cosmographer André Thevet, purchased by Richard Hakluyt in 1587, and translated under the sponsorship of Sir Walter Ralegh in 1591; see Purchas, *Hakluytus Posthumus,* XV, 412; Steele, *English Interpreters of the Iberian New World,* 43. Like the Jesuit treatise on Brazil, this captured text provides ethnographic rather than mercantile knowledge; on its capture and publication by Purchas, see Cañizares-Esguerra, *How to Write the History of the New World,* 94–95, 362n. 34; Bauer, *Cultural Geography of Colonial American Literatures,* 169. Purchas also refers to his abridged translation of el Inca Garcilaso de la Vega's *Comentarios reales de los Incas* (Lisbon, 1609) and *Historia general del Perú* (Córdoba, 1617) as a "jewell, such as no other Peru Merchant hath set to sale"; see Purchas, *Hakluytus Posthumus,* XVII, 412.

and Portuguese precedents as a model and inspiration for Ralegh's project. In the dedication to Ralegh in his translation of Peter Martyr's *De orbe novo decades,* published earlier that year, Hakluyt praises Ralegh's investment not only in the fleet but also in navigational knowledge, having employed Thomas Harriot to train him and his pilots in the "mathematical sciences" and thus link "theory with practice." Hakluyt surely had in mind the example of Iberian nautical instruction, which the English had begun to access in the late 1540s through the defection of navigators who had served the Spanish and Portuguese Crowns like Sebastian Cabot and Diogo Homem. In 1586, a captured pilot from the Canary Islands named Pedro Díaz provided Hakluyt with a description of the training and examination of Spanish pilots in Seville's Casa de Contratación, an account that Hakluyt published, along with other regulations concerning Spanish navigation that he might have acquired from Díaz, in the final pages of *Principal Navigations.* Hakluyt elsewhere argues for the creation of a "Lecture of the Art of Navigation" in "imitation of Spaine," referring to the institution described by Díaz. "This one thing I know," Hakluyt continues in his dedication to Ralegh, "and that is that you are entering upon the one and only method by which first the Portuguese and then the Spaniards at last carried out to their own satisfaction what they had previously attempted so often at no slight sacrifice." Hakluyt attributes Portugal's and Spain's imperial advantage to superior navigational knowledge acquired in the classroom as well as on the seas. His hope to sidestep these nations' "no slight sacrifice" would not, however, be borne out by the Roanoke or Virginia colonies for several decades, nor by Ralegh's voyage in search of El Dorado in South America, a voyage even more explicitly inspired by Spanish precedents.[19]

19. Hakluyt, *Principal Navigations,* VIII, 386 (first quotation), I, xxxvi (fourth quotation); Pedro Diaz, "The Relation of Pedro Diaz," in David Beers Quinn, ed., *The Roanoke Voyages, 1584–1590: Documents to Illustrate the English Voyages to North America under the Patent Granted to Walter Raleigh in 1584,* Works Issued by the Hakluyt Society, 2d Ser., nos. 104–105 (London, 1955), 786–795, esp. 793 (second quotation); Hakluyt, *Original Writings and Correspondence,* II, 366–367 (third and fifth quotations). Purchas offers a favorable depiction of Simão Fernandes, "a Pilot of Lisbone," but Hakluyt and John Smith accuse him of attempting to lead White's voyage astray; see Purchas, *Hakluytus Posthumus,* XVII, 246–247; Hakluyt, *Principal Navigations,* VIII, 392; Philip L. Barbour, ed., *The Complete Works of Captain John Smith (1580–1631),* 3 vols. (Chapel Hill, N.C., 1986), II, 83 (hereafter cited as Smith, *Complete Works*). On the defection of Cabot, Homem, and others to

Hakluyt also presents his own objective in translating Martyr's work as that of fostering English imitation of Spain: "I took this burden upon myself," he explains, so "that other maritime races, and in particular our own island race, perceiving how the Spaniards began and how they progressed, might be inspired to a like emulation of courage." He concludes by exhorting Ralegh to "follow the path on which you have already set foot . . . , spurn not the immortal fame which is here offered you, but let the doughty deeds of Ferdinand Cortes, the Castilian, the stout conqueror of New Spain, here beautifully described, resound ever in your ears and let them make your nights not less sleepless than did those of Themistocles the glorious triumphs of Miltiades." Hakluyt's translation vows to further incite Ralegh in his imitation of Spanish conquistadors, if only to gain the immortality already granted to Cortés when "some happy genius" (presumably Hakluyt himself) rescues Ralegh's own "heroic enterprises from the vasty maw of oblivion." Mary Fuller has described the circular process evident here—in which Hakluyt publishes voyage accounts in order to stimulate more voyages about which to write—as "a process of *textual* generation and accumulation with which Hakluyt is identified." Yet as the work of both Hakluyt and Purchas suggests, such "generation" often springs from "Spanish and Portugall seede." In Ralegh's case, both his voyage and his defense of it in *The Discoverie of the Large, Rich, and Bewtiful Empyre of Guiana* (1596) spring from Iberian seed, for Ralegh depends on Spanish captives and captured texts for inspiration and information as well as legitimation.[20]

Hakluyt need not have feared that the "doughty deeds" of Hernán Cortés would fail to resound in Ralegh's ears, although Ralegh would set his sights on emulating them in South America rather than North. His 1595 voyage to Guiana—in search of a gold-rich empire supposedly established by emigrating Incas from Peru—did not prove him to be a very successful imitator, but it at least allowed him to "discover" a way to rival and surpass Cortesian feats in the future:

England, see David W. Waters, *The Art of Navigation in England in Elizabethan and Early Stuart Times* (London, 1958), 83–90. Waters includes in an appendix Stephen Borough's 1562 petition for the creation of the office of "Pilott Major" in England, modeled on the Spanish and Portuguese institution (513–514).

20. Hakluyt, *Original Writings and Correspondence,* II, 365, 368–369; Fuller, *Voyages in Print,* 149; Purchas, *Hakluytus Posthumus,* XVI, 417–418; Sir Walter Raleigh, *The Discoverie of the Large, Rich, and Bewtiful Empyre of Guiana,* ed. Neil L. Whitehead (Manchester, 1997 [orig. publ. London, 1596]).

> It pleased not God so much to favour me at this time; if it shalbe my lot to prosecute the same, I shall willingly spend my life therein, and if any else shalbe enabled thereunto, and conquere the same, I assure him thus much, he shall performe more then ever was done in *Mexico* by *Cortez,* or in *Peru* by *Pacaro [sic],* whereof one conquered the Empire of *Mutezuma,* the other of *Guascar,* and *Atabalipa,* and whatsoever Prince shall possesse it, that Prince shalbe Lorde of more Gold, and of a more beautifull Empire, and of more Cities and people, then eyther the king of Spayne, or the great Turke.

Ralegh's promise of future success is characteristic of *The Discoverie of the Large, Rich and Bewtiful Empyre of Guiana,* an apologetic text that draws on a rhetoric of deferral, as Fuller has analyzed, to compensate for Ralegh's lack of actual discovery and conquest. As many critics have argued, Ralegh undertook both of his voyages to Guiana with a great deal of political self-interest in mind: with the 1595 voyage, he hoped to restore his reputation and relationship with Queen Elizabeth after being imprisoned for a clandestine marriage with one of her maids of honor, Elizabeth Throckmorton; with the 1617 expedition, he sought—rather unsuccessfully—James I's favor and exoneration from his 1603 conviction for conspiracy in the Main Plot. Given the paltry results of the 1595 expedition, from which he returned with only a handful of gold and no conquest to speak of, self-justification and -promotion are primary concerns in the *Discoverie.* In this sense, Ralegh perhaps unwittingly followed not the imperial but the textual feats of writers like Columbus, Cabeza de Vaca, and even Cortés, whose *Segunda carta de relación* was written from a similarly precarious position before his sovereign.[21]

21. Raleigh, *Discoverie,* ed. Whitehead, 136; Fuller, *Voyages in Print,* 57. On the Main Plot (which purportedly conspired to foster a dissident uprising and a Spanish invasion to install Lady Arabella Stuart on the throne), and Ralegh's suspected Spanish leanings, see Karen Cunningham, "'A Spanish Heart in an English Body': The Ralegh Treason Trial and the Poetics of Proof," *Journal of Medieval and Renaissance Studies,* XXII (1992), 327–351. Ironically, Ralegh's execution in 1618 was instigated by accusations of just the opposite behavior toward Spain, after one of his ships in the second Guiana expedition attacked the Spanish fort of San Tomé, thus violating the peace between the two nations. In the introduction to his Spanish translation of Ralegh's *Discoverie,* Demetrio Ramos Pérez points out its similarity to the Spanish genre of the relación de servicios; see Ramos, *El mito de El Dorado* (Madrid, 1988), 481. In his *Segunda carta de relación* (Seville, 1522), Hernán Cortés had to finesse or justify his rebellion against a superior (the governor of Cuba, Diego Velázquez), his

Like Cabeza de Vaca, in particular, Ralegh presents not success but rather his own misfortunes and suffering as evidence of the services he has performed for his sovereign. Defending himself against accusations that the gold he presented to Elizabeth was not gold after all or that it had been bought on the Barbary Coast, he writes, "I am not so much in love with these long voiages, as to devise, thereby to cozen my selfe, to lie hard, to fare worse, to be subjected to perils, to diseases, to ill savours, to be parched and withered, and withall to sustaine the care and labour of such an enterprize, excepte the same had more comfort, then the fetching of *Marcasite* in *Guiana,* or bying of gold oare in Barbery." Ralegh's "parched and withered body" authenticates both his narrative and his gold, testifying to labor performed in imperial service in much the same way as Pedro Serrano's and the Soto expeditioners' furry and fur-clad bodies, as we have seen in previous chapters. In the epistle dedicatory, Ralegh similarly portrays himself as a "beggar, and withered" for pursuing his sovereign's interests rather than seeking to improve his "poore estate" through "journeys of picorie": "It had sorted ill with the offices of Honor, which by her Majesties grace, I hold this day in England, to run from Cape to Cape, and from place to place, for the pillage of ordinarie prizes." Unable to identify his unproductive voyage to Guiana with the Spanish conquests that serve as his model, Ralegh distinguishes his "travail" from piracy, ironically but perhaps intentionally invoked through a term of possible Spanish origins.[22]

---

unauthorized imprisonment of the emperor Moctezuma, the massacre initiated by Pedro de Alvarado, and the resulting expulsion of the Spaniards from Tenochtitlan. Ralegh's *Discoverie* conforms to Stephanie Merrim's characterization of Cortés and other early Spanish explorers: "Many of the earliest historiographical writings from the New World were motivated not only by the desire to recount victories but to an important degree by the need to seek pardon, legitimation, power, and reward, which needs would lend special urgency to their writings. Special urgency and narrative interest—for out of necessity the actor-chroniclers of the New World contrived complex verbal strategies in mounting their self-defenses and petitions." See Merrim, "The First Fifty Years of Hispanic New World Historiography: The Caribbean, Mexico, and Central America," in Roberto González Echevarría and Enrique Pupo-Walker, eds., *The Cambridge History of Latin American Literature* (Cambridge, 1996), I, 58–100, esp. 58–59.

22. Raleigh, *Discoverie,* ed. Whitehead, 121, 127. In his edition, Whitehead annotates *picorie* as "Apparently derived from the Spanish *picaro,* 'villainous,' and so implying pillage and plunder" (121n. 2). However, the *OED* (March 2006 online draft revision) relates *picorie* ("plunder or pillage by force; marauding, looting, piracy")

Of course, Ralegh had already profited from piratical ventures, such as that of the capture of the *Madre de Deus,* the Portuguese carrack seized in 1592. Even in these enterprises, however, Ralegh portrayed his involvement in terms of an "ethos of toil and self-sacrifice," as Leinwand has argued in a discussion of Ralegh's role in the capture. As we have seen, Hakluyt and Purchas invoke a similar ethos in their self-figurations as toiling editors. Nevertheless, Ralegh's care to distinguish his own efforts from "journeys of picorie" or the "pillage of ordinarie prizes" cannot conceal his dependence—like that of Hakluyt and Purchas—on the spoils of piracy, and in his case the capture of not only texts but individuals.[23]

Ralegh assures the success of English attempts to rival Spain in Guiana by stressing the difference of these attempts from the unsuccessful Spanish predecessors in the region—a distinction that appears most clearly in the practice of captive-taking, on one hand, and in the use of indigenous testimony, on the other. Taking up the discourse of the Black Legend, Ralegh presents the Spaniards as tyrannical captors of the Guianian natives, recounting tales of the Spanish governor Antonio del Berrío's imprisonment and torture of caciques and of the Spaniards' kidnapping and rape of native "wives, and daughters." In contrast, the men of his company "by violence or otherwise, [n]ever knew any of their women" nor stole as much as a pineapple or a potato without due compensation by Ralegh. The difference in the treatment of natives, according to Ralegh, earns the English better results in the region than anything the Spaniards have achieved so far: "[This] course, so contrarie to the Spaniards (who tyrannize over them in all things) drew them to admire hir Majestie, whose commandement I told them it was, and also woonderfully to honour our nation." The actions of Ralegh and his men (but principally Ralegh) thus corroborate his initial speech to the captive

---

to the Middle French *picorée* (1573, 1571 as *pecorée*), the Dutch *picorei* (c. 1600), and the Spanish *pecorea* (1602). The latter is defined in the 1737 *Diccionario de autoridades* as "el hurto o pillaje que salen a hacer los soldados" [the stealing or pillage that soldiers go out to do] and notes its derivation from the Latin *pecus* [cattle], "por ser el que regularmente salen a pillar" [since that is what they usually go out to steal]. See *Diccionario de la lengua castellana, en que se explica el verdadero sentido de las voces* . . . (Madrid, 1737), s.v. *pecorea.*

23. Leinwand, *Theatre, Finance, and Society,* 126. Fuller describes how, in the early Jacobean period, Ralegh came to represent an "outdated and discredited" colonial project, "the search for a windfall profit." However, this association "contrasts sharply with Ralegh's representation of himself in the *Discoverie:* a self characterized by strenuous and abstemious self-sacrifice" (*Voyages in Print,* 85–86).

caciques, whom he informed "that [Elizabeth] was an enemy to the Castellani in respect of their tyrannie and oppression, and that she delivered all such nations about her, as were by them oppressed, and having freed all the coast of the northern world from their servitude had sent me to free them also, and with al to defend the countrey of *Guiana* from their invasion and conquest." Ralegh clearly recognizes the rhetorical effectiveness of the opposition between Spanish tyranny and English liberty in dealing with the Amerindians—or, perhaps more accurately, in dealing with Elizabeth and her court.[24]

The *Discoverie*'s moral distinction between Spaniards and Englishmen allows Ralegh not only to assure English victory where so many previous Spanish attempts have failed—as he demonstrates in his extensive catalogue of earlier, unsuccessful Spanish expeditions—but also to assert the necessity of deferring this victory. The aged cacique Topiawari, who as a captive of Spaniards had been "ledde . . . like a dogge from place to place, until hee had paide 100. plates of Golde, and divers chanes of spleene stones for his raunsome," begs Ralegh to "deferre it till the next yeare," since he fears Spanish retribution for his "conference with the English" and needs time to gather allies among bordering tribes. As Ralegh reflects on the old man's advice, he reassures readers that the natives will submit to England rather than Spain precisely because of the English repudiation of Spanish captive-taking: "If I had either laid handes on the borderers, or ransomed the Lordes as [the Spanish governor] *Berreo* did, or invaded the subjects of *Inga,* I knowe all had been lost for hereafter." Ralegh does not appear to disavow these strategies either in principle or for use on future occasions, when he may arrive at a more seasonal time of year and with a stronger expeditionary force. He merely gives up "the sacke of one or two townes" rather than "to have defaced or endaungered the future hope of so many millions, and the great good, and rich trade which England maie bee possessed off thereby." Ralegh's success—in capturing loyalty, if not gold—is owed to native belief

24. Raleigh, *Discoverie,* ed. Whitehead, 133, 134, 165. Montrose pursues the effects of what he calls a "subversive irony" in the *Discoverie*—that Ralegh grounds his own credibility "upon the credibility of the very people whom he wishes to discredit"—in Ralegh's exaggerated distinction between English and Spanish sexual conduct in the New World, which, he argues, emerges as a way to obfuscate his "dependency upon and identification with the enemy"; see "Work of Gender in the Discourse of Discovery," in Greenblatt, ed., *New World Encounters,* 192. As we will see, the differences that Ralegh draws with respect to captive-taking and testimony do not obfuscate, but rather underscore, this dependence.

in English difference from Spaniards, not to any actual distinction. English delays, suffering, and toil are favorably contrasted with Spanish "sacking and spoiling," the labor of the liberator with the ill-gotten gains of the captor. Nevertheless, Ralegh need not hide from readers the identity of Spanish and English purposes in Guiana; indeed, he uses the Spanish "desire for" (and testimony of) gold to corroborate his claims about the land's potential wealth.[25]

The portrait of Spaniards as cruel, treacherous captors not only helps to conceal Ralegh's own deceit of the Guianians and the identity of English and Spanish objectives, as Louis Montrose has argued; it also obscures the role of English captive-taking throughout the account. In fact, the Spanish acquire more visibility and importance as valuable captives than malevolent captors in the *Discoverie,* from the governor Antonio del Berrío, whom Ralegh captured on Trinidad and plied for information throughout the expedition, to the Spanish "Letters Taken at Sea by Captaine George Popham" included as an appendix to Ralegh's account. Spanish as well as Amerindian captives become not only Ralegh's collaborators in the exploration of Guiana but also the guarantors of his veracity and of the expedition's legitimacy.[26]

Beyond the models of Cortés and Pizarro, Ralegh's journey was inspired by information gathered from Spanish sources before his journey. In the

25. Raleigh, *Discoverie,* ed. Whitehead, 183–185. Ralegh himself acknowledges that, if he had proceeded with the conquest of Guiana, the natives would have "proved that we came both for one errant, and that both sought but to sacke and spoyle them, but as yet our desier of gold, or our purpose of invasion is not known unto those of the Empire."

26. Montrose, "Work of Gender in the Discourse of Discovery," in Greenblatt, ed., *New World Encounters,* 177–217. In *Social History of Truth,* Shapin describes the ineradicable role of the testimony of others in knowledge production, even in scientific cultures (like that of seventeenth-century England) that assert the primacy of direct individual experience. Shapin focuses on how early modern English culture granted gentlemen the status of reliable truth-tellers and rendered nongentlemanly sources of knowledge (servants, technicians) invisible, despite their indispensable participation in the making of scientific knowledge. Here, I extend Shapin's argument by examining how English travelers, writers, and anthologizers negotiated trust in foreign (whether gentlemanly or nongentlemanly) sources of testimony. Shapin discusses the constitutive role of travelers in scientific knowledge in chapter 6, but he relegates the consideration of non-English travelers' testimony to a footnote, simply pointing out, "Special disabilities arising from imputations of national unreliability . . . might come into play" (245n. 3).

epistle dedicatory, Ralegh refers to the "knowledge by relation" that he had acquired "many yeares since . . . of that mighty, rich, and beawtifull Empire of *Guiana,*" which may refer to information acquired almost a decade earlier from the renowned navigator Pedro Sarmiento de Gamboa, who had been captured by two of Ralegh's ships. Although Ralegh does not mention Sarmiento de Gamboa by name, he cites as well as transcribes several Spanish textual sources to make his assertions about Guiana's wealth "seeme more then credible." If Ralegh's success as an explorer depends on his ability to convince natives of the difference between English and Spanish objectives, his success as a writer derives from his ability to persuade readers of the similarity (or, in fact, the identity) of Guiana to the Inca Empire conquered by the Spaniards. Ralegh draws on Spanish sources to claim that Guiana, conquered by one of the younger sons of Inca emperor Huayna Capac after he fled the Spaniards, "is governed by the same lawes, and the Emperour and people observe the same religion, and the same forme and pollicies in government as was used in Peru, not differing in any part." Ralegh thus follows Hakluyt's injunction to emulate Spanish methods of conquest by imitating the object of conquest itself. If Guiana is another Peru (indeed, an extension or derivation of the Inca Empire), then textual evidence of Inca gold—such as Francisco López de Gómara's description of Huayna Capac's opulent court in chapter 120 of his *Historia general de las Indias* (1552)—can serve as proof of Guiana's riches as well, "because we may judge of the one by the other."[27]

Ralegh complements his textual evidence of the Inca presence in Guiana with the oral report of his captive Antonio del Berrío, according to whom the Incas had prophesied "that from *Inglatierra* those *Ingas* shoulde be againe

27. Raleigh, *Discoverie,* ed. Whitehead, 121–122, 136–137, and see also 193; Francisco López de Gómara, *Historia general de las Indias* (Zaragoza, Spain, 1552). Sarmiento de Gamboa was captured by Ralegh's pinnaces, the *Serpent* and the *Mary Spark,* off the Azores Islands in 1586. A renowned navigator, cosmographer, and author, Sarmiento wrote a *Historia de los Incas* that was presented to Philip II in 1572 but not published in his lifetime. Ralegh liberated Sarmiento in England and allowed him to return to Spain, but he was once again captured by Protestants in France before he could cross the border. In a letter to Ralegh, Hakluyt ascribes Sarmiento's recapture "to the juste plage of God for his ingratitude to my lord admiral and yor self the authors of his undeserved libertie. There was a packet founde aboute hym contayninge great tresons of Peter Sibures agynst England"; see Hakluyt, *Original Writings and Correspondence,* II, 354–355. Perhaps resentment toward his ungrateful captive kept Ralegh from mentioning him in the *Discoverie.*

in time to come restored, and delivered from the servitude of the said Conquerors." The Incas themselves thus corroborate Ralegh's representation of the English as liberators of the empire of Guiana from Spanish captivity. Several decades later, the Peruvian creole Antonio de la Calancha would mock the linguistic manipulation that allows Ralegh to make such a claim:

> Es para reír lo que dice Gualtero Raleg, y alega testigos Españoles, que se halló en el Tenplo del Sol en el Cuzco, un pronóstico, que decía, que los Reyes de Ingalaterra habían de restituir en su Reyno a estos Indios, sacándoles de servidunbre y volviéndolos a su Inperio; debió de soñarlo, o pronosticó su deseo, debió de usar de la figura Anagrama, que partiendo silabas y trocando razones, hace diferentes sentidos el vocablo; Ingalaterra dividida la palabra, dirá Inga, y luego dirá la tierra, y de aqui debió de formar el pronóstico, diciendo, la tierra del Inga será de Ingalaterra, con esta irrisión se hace burla de Gualtero.

> It is laughable what Walter Ralegh says—and he cites Spanish testimony—that there was found in the Temple of the Sun in Cuzco a prophecy that said that the kings of England would restore this kingdom to these Indians, liberating them from servitude and returning their empire. He must have dreamt it, or he prophesied his desire, and he must have used the figure of anagram, which, dividing syllables and exchanging senses, gives different meanings to the word; the word Ingalaterra divided would say Inga, and then would say *la tierra* [land], and from here he must have formed the prophecy, saying, that the Inga's land would be England's, and with this mockery they make fun of Walter.

Calancha corroborates Ralegh's claim, which Ralegh "protest[s] before the Majesty of God to be true," that he learned of the prophecy through his Spanish captive, Berrío, although Calancha implies that the Spanish informants were actually making fun of Ralegh's gullibility. But Ralegh's reliance on Spanish testimony is mirrored in Calancha's own use of Ralegh's text, which he cites in his account of the flight of the son of Huayna Capac and a thousand Inca warriors to the land between the Amazon and the Orinoco. Calancha's response to Ralegh, however derisive, reciprocates Ralegh's original reliance on Spanish texts to assert the Inca settling of Guiana.[28]

28. Raleigh, *Discoverie,* ed. Whitehead, 199; Antonio de la Calancha, *Coronica moralizada del orden de San Augustin en el Peru, con sucesos egemplares vistos en esta*

The information acquired from Spaniards like Berrío during Ralegh's own expedition serves the same corroborating and legitimizing purpose as the extracts of Spanish histories cited in the *Discoverie*. In case readers harbor any doubt that identical laws, religion, and government entail identical mineral wealth, Ralegh includes eyewitness (rather than syllogistic) evidence: "I have beene assured by such of the *Spanyardes* as have seene *Manoa* the emperiall Citie of *Guiana*, which the Spanyardes cal *el Dorado*, that for the greatnes, for the riches, and for the excellent seate, it farre exceedeth any of the world." One of these Spaniards is undoubtedly "Johannes Martines," a participant on the Diego Ordaz expedition, whom Ralegh credits with the discovery of Manoa. Condemned to exile among the natives by Ordaz, Martínez was brought, captive and blindfolded, by the Guianians to Manoa, where he lived for seven months before being allowed to return to Spanish society. Most of his gold was robbed on the way back, but more valuable to subsequent expeditioners was the "relation of his travels" that Ralegh claims can be found at the "Chauncery of *Saint Juan de puerto rico*." Ralegh acquires this captive's tale—like the Inca prophecy—through his own captive, Antonio del Berrío, for whom it "appeared to be the greatest incouragement as well . . . as to others that formerly attempted the discovery and conquest." Through Ralegh's use of his account, Martínez may now encourage English voyages of discovery and conquest, as well. The eyewitness testimony offered by the report apparently outweighs its indirect manner of acquisition.[29]

Ralegh also appends to his narrative a translation of portions of several captured Spanish reports and letters, affirming, "Seeing they confirme in

---

Monarquia (Barcelona, 1638), 115–116. José Antonio Mazzotti reads Calancha's text as a response to Ralegh's publication in "The Legend of El Dorado in Seventeenth-Century Peru: A Creole Agenda," MS, to be published in an upcoming collection.

29. Raleigh, *Discoverie*, ed. Whitehead, 136, 139. A similar lack of immediacy pertains to Ralegh's description of the ritual in which caciques are covered with gold dust, the practice that gave rise to the legend of El Dorado, "The Gilded Man." Ralegh's account of the ritual is derived from "that tract which I have seen" and is further "confirmed by a letter written into *Spaine* which was intercepted, which master *Robert Dudley* told me he had seen" (141). Ralegh's claim to eyewitness testimony is reduced to seeing a text and to talking to someone who had seen a text. Ralegh here overlooks one of the maxims that, according to Shapin, were used in seventeenth-century England to evaluate testimony, that of "immediacy": "The length of a testifying chain might be taken as an indication of the uncertainty of what was claimed" (Shapin, *Social History of Truth*, 217).

some parte the substance, I meane, the riches of that Countrey: it hath beene thought fitte that they shoulde be thereunto adjoyned." Even in an autobiographical account of his own voyage, Ralegh—like Hakluyt and Purchas—relies on captured Iberian texts. And although the inclusion of these documents would seem to offer readers more immediate access to eyewitness testimony, Ralegh's translation of them betrays a significant amount of mediation. Unlike the extended citations from Gómara, which are offered in both Spanish and English and thus allow the reader to evaluate the fidelity of the translation, the letters and reports are presented in English only. However, a comparison of Ralegh's version with the Spanish original of one of the documents—the *Actas de las tomas de posesión* of Domingo de Vera Ybarguen, held at the Archivo General de Indias in Seville—reveals that Ralegh deviated significantly from his Spanish source-text. The *Actas* record the Spanish expedition's erection of a cross and declaration of possession, as well as rather fanciful Amerindian offers of submission, in successive villages on the Orinoco from the April 23 to May 13, 1593. Ralegh, however, follows the Spanish text only until the entry for May 4. Here, a first-person plural subject ("we came to a province") substitutes the third-person plural of the *Actas* ("they prosecuted the said possession and discovery"), and detailed encounters and conversations with two Amerindian caciques replace the formulaic rituals of conquest. The information provided by these caciques in their conversations with the Spaniards substantiates, as Neil Whitehead points out in his introduction to the text, some of the most controversial elements of Ralegh's account, including the prevalence of gold objects, the existence of headless men, and the ritual anointment with gold that gave rise to the legend of El Dorado. Aside from supporting his more tenuous claims, Ralegh's depiction of the behavior of the Spaniards in their interaction with the caciques suggests a convergence of English and Spanish imperial practices—like Purchas's translation of Cardim, but with the reverse implication. When the cacique Arataco offers Domingo de Vera golden eagles for hatchets, Vera only gives him one; "He would give him no more because they should not understand we went to seeke Gold." And when Vera is given a twenty-seven-pound eagle of "good Gold," he merely "tooke it, and shewed it to the soldiers, and then threwe it from him *making shew not to regard it.*" By showing the Spaniards to engage in the same strategies that Ralegh has deployed in his dealings with Amerindians, Ralegh either undermines his portrait of Spanish tyranny and insatiable lust for gold or reveals the identical—and far from innocent—objectives of those strategies, whether used by

Englishmen or Spaniards. In either case, the "we" of Ralegh's translation seems to extend beyond the Spaniards to include Ralegh himself.[30]

Another distinction that Ralegh emphasizes between Spanish and English imperial behavior—their uses of indigenous testimony—further reveals Ralegh's willingness to engage in the "Spanish" practice of captive-taking while confirming his reliance on foreign testimony, and not just on that of fellow Europeans. Ralegh lays out this difference most pointedly in his portrayal of his prized captive, the governor of Trinidad Antonio del Berrío, one of the two Spaniards that Ralegh kept with him after he sacked the capital, San José de Oruña. Berrío's ten years of experience in the region and three voyages in search of El Dorado make him Ralegh's principal source of information about Guiana. Ralegh frequently portrays him in this capacity and characterizes him as a "Gent. of great assurednes." Yet Ralegh must also explain why Berrío has been unsuccessful at finding Guiana while defending his own prospects for success. Ralegh asserts, "He had also neither friendship among the people, nor any interpreter to perswade or treate with them." These factors not only inhibit the progress of Berrío's expedition but preclude his access to important information: "*Berreo* affirmed that there fell an hundred rivers into *Orenoque* from the north and south . . . But he knew not the names of any of these, but *Caroli* only, neither from what nations they descended, neither to what Provinces they led, for he had no meanes to discourse with the inhabitants at any time: neither was he curious in these things, being utterlie unlearned, and not knowing the east from the west." Ralegh outlines, in contrast, his own process of information gathering, by which he learns the names of the numerous rivers as well as the status of relations between different indigenous groups:

> But of al these I got som knowledg, and of manie more, partly by mine own travel, and the rest by conference: of som one I lerned one, of others the rest, having with me an Indian that spake many languages, and that of

30. Raleigh, *Discoverie,* ed. Whitehead, 200, 204–205 (emphasis added). Demetrio Ramos includes the Spanish version of the *Actas* in his translation of the *Discoverie* and comments on the discrepancies with Ralegh's version in the footnotes; see Ramos, *El mito de El Dorado,* 651–652. Whitehead suggests that Ralegh might not have invented this information but rather acquired it orally from Berrío or other informants, but even so, his placement of it within a Spanish text suggests the "greater 'authority' of the Spanish sources"; see Whitehead, introduction, in Raleigh, *Discoverie,* ed. Whitehead, 3–116, esp. 43.

> *Guiana* naturally. I sought out al the aged men, and such as were greatest travelers, and by the one and the other I came to understand the situations, the rivers, the kingdoms from the east sea to the borders of *Peru* . . . and of all the kings of Provinces and captains of townes and villages, how they stood in tearms of peace or war.

Ralegh's assertion of Berrío's refusal to use indigenous guides, informants, and interpreters is contradicted elsewhere in the narrative and belied in Spanish sources, including the captured documents appended to the *Discoverie,* which again suggests that Ralegh's strategies did not differ from those of the Spaniards any more than did his goals. In any case, Ralegh acknowledges the limited extent to which his information is acquired through direct personal experience (travel/travail) and how much he relies on the testimony of others ("the rest by conference"). He must, of course, also depend on interpreters in order to have access to the testimony of these "others."[31]

Acutely aware of the importance of linguistic and cultural intermediaries for the work of colonial expansion, Ralegh sponsored the voyages to England of many Amerindian natives—both captured and not—for instruction and interrogation, as Alden T. Vaughan has described. About a dozen were from Guiana and Trinidad, including four who were brought to England on Jacob Whiddon's reconnaissance voyage of 1594 and returned to Trinidad

31. Raleigh, *Discoverie,* ed. Whitehead, 135, 148–149, 152, 164, 204. Ralegh's description of Berrío—"This *Berreo is* a gent. well descended, and had long served the Spanish king in *Millain, Naples,* the lowe Countries and else where, very valiant and liberall, and a Gent. of great assurednes, and of a great heart"—corroborates Shapin's argument about the importance of gentlemanly status to assure credibility in early modern England; see *Social History of Truth,* 65–125. Ralegh identifies other Spanish captive-informants as gentlemen, as well. An unnamed Spanish "gentleman prisoner" (of Captain Preston) attests to Guiana's riches (although not directly to Ralegh), and another unnamed Spanish gentleman corroborates reports of headless men. Ralegh's description of Berrío also assures his own gentlemanly status: "I used him according to his estate and worth in all things I could, according to the small meanes I had"; see Raleigh, *Discoverie,* ed. Whitehead, 135, 143, 178. It takes one to "use" one, so to speak. Whitehead points out: "It was not just [the] better-publicised, full-scale *entradas* that were the effective source of Spanish knowledge of the uncolonised interior. In point of fact many of these expeditionaries, like Ralegh, relied on the local contacts that were already established with the native population for the initial logistics and intelligence required to lead an armed force into native territories" (40).

by Ralegh on his voyage the following year. Ralegh depends on "my Indian interpreter, which I caried out of England" to communicate with the caciques held captive by the Spaniards in Trinidad. And once in the Orinoco, Ralegh interrogates "the most ancient and best traveled" about geography and navigation as well as legends of Amazon women and headless men. He also relies on indigenous pilots "of great experience and travel," affirming in one instance that "it shall be requisite for any man that passeth it to have such a Pilot." Although sometimes Ralegh claims that the pilot was "given" to him by a friendly cacique, he also does not hesitate to take captives for this purpose.[32]

Although Ralegh insists on the Spanish failure to use indigenous testimony, he generally presents native and Spanish informants as supplementing rather than supplanting one another, both substituting for his lack of personal experience:

> Because I have not my selfe seene the cities of *Inga,* I cannot avow on my credit what I have heard, although it be very likely, that the Emperour Inga hath built and erected as magnificent pallaces in *Guiana,* as his auncestors did in *Peru,* which were for their riches and rarenes most marveilous and exceding al in *Europe,* and I think of the world, *China* excepted, which also the Spanyards (which I had) assured me to be of trueth, as also the nations of the borderers, who being but *Salvaios,* to those of the Inland, do cause much treasure to be buried with them, for I was enformed of one of the *Cassiqui* of the valley of *Amariocapana.* . . .

Ralegh's substitution of the labor of conquest with the labor of compiling reliable information reveals his dependence on the very sources that are assumed to be the rivals (Spaniards) and potential subjects (Amerindians) of the English nation.[33]

Ralegh's valorization of the information and material support of Spaniards and Amerindians to his enterprise is evident in the extent to which he jealously guards English knowledge from similar use by foreign nations. When he finally finds out, through captured Arwacan pilots, "where and in what countries the Spaniards had labored for gold," he "made not the same

32. Alden T. Vaughan, "Sir Walter Ralegh's Indian Interpreters, 1584–1618," *William and Mary Quarterly,* LIX (2002), 341–376; Raleigh, *Discoverie,* ed. Whitehead, 134, 146, 158, 164, 168, 178.

33. Raleigh, *Discoverie,* ed. Whitehead, 193–194.

knowen to all." Asserting his need for more time, men, and instruments, Ralegh "thought it best not to hover thereabouts, least if the same had been perceived by the company, there would have bin by this time many barks and ships set out, *and perchance other nations would also have gotten of ours for Pilots,* so as both our selves might have been prevented, and all our care taken for good usage of the people been utterly lost, by those that onely respect present profit." Ralegh redefines the goal of his voyage from the acquisition of gold to the acquisition of information—information, however, that must be safeguarded just as much as gold. Indeed, Ralegh argues that having information precludes acquiring gold: knowing where the gold is means not exploiting it, in case others try to take advantage of that knowledge (as he has taken advantage of theirs).[34]

FRANCIS SPARREY, "DESIROUS TO TARRY, AND COULDE DESCRIBE A CUNTREY WITH HIS PEN"

Ralegh's preoccupation with the Spanish acquisition of English knowledge about Guiana was not, in fact, unwarranted, as demonstrated by the case of an Englishman who stayed in Guiana after Ralegh's departure. Ralegh left one Francis Sparrey, "a servant of captaine *Gifford,* (who was desirous to tarry, and coulde describe a cuntrey with his pen)," as one of two hostages in exchange for the cacique Topiawari's son, whom he brought back to England. Sparrey (or "Sparrow," in Ralegh's text) was instructed to learn the language and the "secrets of the land" until Ralegh's return the following year—a return that Ralegh was prohibited from undertaking until 1617. Nevertheless, Sparrey's description of the "cuntrey" would eventually reach an English public, when Purchas acquired his relation from Hakluyt and published it in *Hakluytus Posthumus* under the title "Description of the Ile of Trinidad, the Rich Countrie of Guiana, and the Mightie River of Orenoco Written by Francis Sparrey Left There by Sir Walter Raleigh, 1595. and in the End Taken by the Spaniards and Sent Prisoner into Spaine, and after Long Captivitie Got into England by Great Sute." Like many captives' accounts, this text showcases both the exploits of the narrator and the ethnographic and geographic "secrets" that, just as Ralegh hoped, he had acquired in Guiana.[35]

34. Ibid., 164 (emphasis added).

35. Ibid., 185; Purchas, *Hakluytus Posthumus,* XVI, 301–308. Sparrey also describes his instructions to "saber los secretos de la tierra" [discover the secrets of

Sparrey's "Description" does not include any information about his "long captivitie" in Spain or his "great sute" to return to England: presumably these brief verbal cues would be enough to conjure up a narrative of suffering at the hands of tyrannical papists in the minds of English readers. However, we do know a bit more about Sparrey's time in Spain from contemporary documents, including a "Memorial del servicio" that Sparrey dictated to a scribe and that is now found in the Archivo General de Indias. In the memoir, Sparrey offers his services to Philip II in terms of his knowledge of Guiana, as well as the gold that he left buried there, which he promises to recover and give to the king if allowed to make the voyage back. Sparrey states in his memoir that, after traveling widely in Guiana and acquiring much gold and precious stones, he began to have doubts about Ralegh's return: "Enfadado de vivir entre aquellos salvaxes, descendió el rrio avaxo por ver si en la boca del pasavan yngleses . . . o españoles, que por menos inconvenientes tenía ser preso dellos que estar con los indios" [Tired of living among those savages, he went down the river to see if at the mouth there were any Englishmen . . . or Spaniards, for he held it to be less inconvenient to be a prisoner of them than to be with the Indians]. Indeed, once he encounters Berrío's soldiers, they take him prisoner, relieve him of sixty thousand *ducados* worth of valuables, and send him to Spain. The memoir insists that Sparrey initially withheld his "secrets" from his captors "con el natural amor que a su reyna y naturales tenía . . . por rreservar la diconquista y thesoro para la dicha rreyna" [with the natural love that he had to his queen and compatriots . . . to reserve the said conquest and treasure for the said queen]. But Sparrey was apparently more captivated by his Spanish captors than by his Guianian hosts, for while a prisoner in Spain, he converted to Catholicism and married a native of Madrid, with whom he had a son. In the memoir, Sparrey presents his marriage and paternity as signs of his newly adopted religious faith and national loyalty.[36]

---

the land] in a "Memorial del servicio" written while a prisoner in Spain. Sparrey states that his companion, Hugh Goodwin, was devoured by beasts; Ralegh, however, apparently encountered Goodwin on his return trip of 1617. See Francis Sparrey, "Memorial del servicio que haze el capitán Francisco Sparri, Inglés, preso en la cárcel desta villia de Madrid, a su Magestad," in Ramos, *El mito de El Dorado,* 671–675, esp. 672.

36. Sparrey, "Memorial del servicio," in Ramos, *El mito de El Dorado,* 674–675. Sparrey apparently offered his information about Guiana's wealth to a fellow Englishman as well: in his edition of the *Discoverie,* V. T. Harlow cites a petition written by one Capt. Jo. Stanley to Sir Robert Cecil in 1598, in which he claims that his prison-

Unlike the Portuguese pilot Nuno da Silva, Sparrey does not appear to have achieved success with his plea to Philip II, whether this was sincerely stated in the memoir or not. However, Sparrey did make it back to his homeland, where he presumably gave his manuscript to Hakluyt and perhaps even met John Smith, as we will see. Demetrio Ramos, who published the "Memorial" as an appendix to his Spanish translation of the *Discoverie,* affirms that Sparrey was exchanged in 1603 for Jesuit missionaries in Brazil who had been captured by the English. Sparrey might even have been traded for, among others, the author of the treatise on Brazil that was Purchas's "English prize and captive," Fernão Cardim. Purchas confirms the exchange value of their texts, if not of the captives themselves, for they are published together in the fourth volume of *Hakluytus Posthumus,* dedicated to the Americas. Nevertheless, the greater length and praise that Purchas dedicates to the Jesuit work suggests that Cardim's more extensive time in Brazil (thirty years) and his religious vocation—and thus his interest, shared with Purchas, in revealing God's handiwork through an account of natural and human diversity—outweigh any concern over religious and national differences.[37]

Sparrey's offer to serve the Spanish king suggests that the willingness to provide valuable information to a rival nation was not an exclusive characteristic of treacherous Iberians. Recognizing the value of their firsthand

---

mate Francis Sparrey "gave me reason how and a mapt where to find" the gold mines of Guiana, "which the Spaniard knoweth not"; see Harlow, introduction, in Sir Walter Ralegh, *The Discoverie of the Large and Bewtiful Empire of Guiana,* ed. Harlow (London, 1928), xv–cvi, xcn. 2. Harlow also includes in an appendix a translation of a Spanish account of Sparrey's capture, which shows him to be a source of information about Ralegh's voyage for the Spanish. In a report from 1596, Pedro de Liaño relates how, of the two Englishmen left behind, one "when sailing one day down the river, was seized by four Spaniards, who brought him to the Island of Margarita on the 25th of Februrary of this year, where his declaration was taken. He related most of what has been narrated"; see "Extract from a Report by the Licenciate Pedro de Liaño to the King," ibid., 120–125, esp. 122–123.

37. Ramos specifies that Sparrey was traded for Spanish Jesuit missionaries in Brazil but does not offer the source of his information; see *El mito de El Dorado,* 619–620n. 257. According to Flood, Cardim was held captive in England between December 5, 1601, and at least January 7, 1603. Flood affirms that the date of Cardim's release is unknown, but it probably occurred shortly after one of his companions was released in early 1603; see Flood, "Portuguese Jesuits in England in Penal Times," *The Month,* CXLIII (1924), 157–159, esp. 159.

knowledge of New World routes and riches, captives like Francis Sparrey and Nuno da Silva packaged and presented their knowledge to patrons or princes regardless of nationality. In fact, in order to increase his authority in this respect, Sparrey antedates Ralegh's voyage in the memoir to 1592 so that he appears to have spent almost four years in Guiana rather than one. Even more than the Spanish sovereign to whom both Silva and Sparrey directed their appeals for recompense and reward, Englishmen like Ralegh, Hakluyt, and Purchas viewed such captives—as well as captured texts like Cardim's—as valuable resources in the promotion of English imperial expansion and the propagation of knowledge about the New World, whether for religious or political purposes. But Sparrey's and Silva's own responses to their captivities reveal the porous nature of national and religious boundaries, despite the animosity that infused Anglo-Hispanic and Catholic-Protestant relations in the sixteenth and seventeenth centuries.[38]

WORTHY PAGES: PETER CARDER'S AND ANTHONY KNIVET'S TALES OF CAPTIVITY IN BRAZIL

Francis Sparrey is not the only English captive whose narrative merited inclusion in the fourth volume of *Hakluytus Posthumus.* His "Description of the Ile of Trinidad" is preceded and followed by numerous accounts that depict Englishmen taken captive by (occasionally benevolent) Spaniards and Portuguese. Purchas summarizes several accounts of English captives in New Spain—including the well-known narratives of Miles Philips and Job Hortop—that Hakluyt had published in *Principal Navigations.* For Hakluyt, the publication of these captives' accounts, much like captured Iberian texts, revealed the "secrets of the West Indies": in the preface, he describes these sources as "sixe verie excellent discourses of our men, whereof some for 15. or 16. whole yeeres inhabited in New Spaine, and ranged the whole Countrie, wherein are disclosed the cheefest secretes of the west India, which may in time turne to our no smal advantage." Purchas's brief summary of these sources displays less of the imperial rivalry and utilitarian purposes motivating Hakluyt's publication of them. Purchas does recount some of the "Spanish indignities and treacheries" experienced by Hawkins and Drake as well as by the captives Philips and Hortop—in particular, the Inquisition's "Martyrdome" of Philips's companions. However, his synopsis of Hortop's "23. yeeres misery" focuses almost exclusively on various objects sent to the

38. Sparrey, "Memorial del servicio," in Ramos, *El mito de El Dorado,* 671.

king of Spain in the ship that carried Hortop as a prisoner: "the Anatomie of a Giant, sent from China to Mexico," "two chists ful of earth with Ginger growing in them," and the written certification of the sighting of a "Monster in the Sea . . . proportioned like a man." These hardly seem to be the secrets that Hakluyt thought would increase England's imperial competitiveness. Rather, Purchas's interest lies more on the border between wonder and curiosity at the secrets of the natural world. As the preface to *Hakluytus Posthumus* and the introduction to Cardim's treatise on Brazil make clear, Purchas regarded natural and cultural diversity as a testament to divine design, a perspective that mirrors the Jesuits' own approach to New World nature.[39]

The captives' accounts that Purchas edits and publishes (rather than summarizes) suggest motivations that similarly transcend national and religious borders. Purchas prominently features two captives' relations that he acquired from Hakluyt, for he uses them to complement accounts of Drake's and Thomas Cavendish's voyages, respectively. As Purchas explains,

> That as both served under them in their Discoveries, so they may in this our Discoverie of those Discoveries, as Pages to those Worthies; the one a Mariner wayting on a Mariner; the other a Gentleman following a Gentleman; both unmatchable by any English for the rare adventures, disadventures, and manifold successions of miseries in those wilde Countries, and with those wilder Countrimen of Brasilia.

39. Hakluyt, *Principal Navigations,* I, xxvii, lxxvii; Purchas, *Hakluytus Posthumus,* XVI, 111. Susan Scott Parrish describes the transition from "*wonder* at the preternatural and a belief in magic, demonism, and providential monsters" to "*curiosity* about God's stable and orderly creation" between the sixteenth and eighteenth centuries in Parrish, *American Curiosity: Cultures of Natural History in the Colonial British Atlantic World* (Chapel Hill, N.C., 2006), 25. Purchas's interest in natural anomalies like the giant's skeleton and the "sea monster" is akin to that of Iberian Jesuits like Juan Eusebio Nieremberg, whose *Historia naturae, maxime peregrinae* (Antwerp, 1635) and *Curiosa y oculta filosofia: Primera y segunda parte de las maravillas de la naturaleza, examinadas en varias questiones naturales* (Madrid, 1643) sought to reveal the "secrets and problems of nature" (as the full title reads) by interpreting them as evidence of divine purposes and moral lessons; see Domingo Ledezma, "Una legitimación imaginativa del Nuevo Mundo: La *Historia naturae, maxime peregrinae* del jesuita Juan Eusebio Nieremberg," in Luis Millones Figueroa and Domingo Ledezma, eds., *El saber de los jesuitas, historias naturales y el Nuevo Mundo* (Madrid, 2005), 53–84, esp. 56.

These "Pages" (pun, of course, intended) are worthy of inclusion less for what they reveal about Drake's and Cavendish's "Discoveries"—both sailors are separated from their commanders early on in the expedition—than for the firsthand knowledge of American nature and Amerindian culture they acquire through their misadventures. And readers may gather not only credible information from these accounts but also gratification: in reference to the latter, more extensive account, Purchas writes, "Out of his manifold paines, thou maist gather this posie of pleasures, and learne to bee thankefull for thy native sweets at home, even delights in the multitude of peace." Purchas invokes the pleasure of reading about others' misfortunes that made "true histories" of shipwreck and captivity so appealing to Iberian audiences, as well.[40]

The "mariner waiting on a mariner" is Peter Carder, whose account Purchas apparently found in Hakluyt's papers. A participant on Drake's 1577 expedition, Carder might have met the Portuguese pilot Nuno da Silva before he and seven companions were separated from the rest of the expedition after passing the Straits of Magellan in late 1578. As the full title of Carder's narrative explains, they "were all cast away, save this one only afore named, who came into England nine yeeres after miraculously, having escaped many strange dangers, as well among divers Savages as Christians." Yet the "strange dangers" Carder suffers are almost exclusively limited to his separation from the English expedition and subsequent shipwreck; as a captive first of "Savages" and then of Christians, Carder is well treated. Carder describes a friendly encounter with the "Tuppan Basse" (Tupinambá) once his last remaining English companion dies, and later points out that he "staied among them (being well entertained) for certaine moneths, untill I had learned most part of their language." His linguistic abilities assure the credibility of his report of "their manners," which includes their treatment of captured enemies—predictably eliciting from Purchas the marginal comment "Man-eating," even though no cannibalism is in fact depicted in this passage (it is mentioned elsewhere in his account).[41]

After several months, the "King" gives Carder leave to depart and sends four people to guide and provide for him along the way. Carder apparently anticipated similarly kind treatment by the Portuguese, for as they approach Bahia, he "yeelded [himself] to a Portugall, called Michael Jonas, declaring unto him that I was an Englishman, and enquired whether there were any

40. Purchas, *Hakluytus Posthumus,* XVI, 150–151.

41. Ibid., 136, 140.

Englishmen dwelling in the towne." Like Sparrey, Carder prefers Iberian to indigenous company, but he encounters a remarkably less hostile reception than Sparrey did among the Spanish despite identifying himself immediately as an Englishman. Indeed, his English identity earns him an immediate ally, but not a compatriot: "[Michael Jonas] told me that there was one Antonio de Pava in the towne which could speake good English, and was a lover of our Nation, and brought mee directly unto his house." This Portuguese Anglophile, Antonio de Paiva (which Purchas alternately renders as "Pava" and "Payve"), serves as Carder's "Interpreter" before the governor. Yet this role is not, apparently, owing to Carder's lack of knowledge of Portuguese, for Paiva advises him not to make known "that I understood the Portugall Tongue" during his interview with the governor. The latter regards Carder as "a stranger, contrary to their Lawes," and thus deserving of imprisonment. However, Carder's argument—made on the advice of and through his interpreter—that he freely sought out the "Portugall Christians" and "peaceably . . . put [himself] into their hands"—sufficiently confounds assumptions about hostile national identities, such that the governor agrees to await specific instructions from the king. Although the king orders him to come to Portugal, Carder successfully engages in business with his "good friend" Antonio de Paiva for three years before the command is carried out.[42]

When a ship finally arrives to carry Carder to Portugal, Paiva helps him escape to Pernambuco, where he encounters a "Hulke" with a mixed crew of Englishmen and Portuguese that is on its way to England with "English and Portugall goods." The multiple linguistic abilities and national affinities of Carder as well as Paiva are reflected even in the ship that brings Carder to his homeland: the national origin of the "Hulke" remains ambiguous until we read of its capture in 1586 by "two English Ships of warre, who because the peace betweene England and Spaine was broken the yeare before, commanded us to yielde our selves to them as their lawfull prises, which we did all five accordingly without any resistance." Carder's description of his last misadventure at sea confirms his adaptable use of "we" (he employs the inclusive pronoun with his indigenous as well as Portuguese hosts) as well as his lack of "resistance" to peaceful transit between and absorption into different nations. Ironically, Carder arrives in England as an "English prize and captive," not unlike the Jesuit friar Fernão Cardim. As we saw in Chapter 1, above, the queen herself prized Carder's account of Drake's expedition as much as his delightful tale of misadventures in Brazil:

42. Ibid., 142–145.

> My strange adventures, and long living among cruell Savages being known to the right honorable the Lord Charles Howard, Lord high Admirall of England, he certified the Queenes Majesty thereof with speede, and brought me to her presence at White-hall, where it pleased her to talke with me a long houres space of my travailes and wonderfull escape, and among other things of the manner of M. Dowties execution; and afterward bestowed 22. angels on me, willing my Lord to have consideration of me.

Carder earns a similar reward from his sovereign as his Portuguese counterpart, Nuno da Silva, did for relating his capture by Drake to Philip II.[43]

The "gentleman following a gentleman," whose tale of misfortunes Purchas uses to complement Cavendish's letter describing his last voyage, is Anthony Knivet, whose journal Purchas had bought from Hakluyt "at so deere a rate," as he states in his earlier volume, *Purchas His Pilgrimage* (1613). Purchas supplemented the text with information acquired directly from Knivet, as he indicates in a marginal note, and published it in *Hakluytus Posthumus* under the title "The Admirable Adventures and Strange Fortunes of Master Anthonie Knivet, Which Went with Master Thomas Candish in His Second Voyage to the South Sea. 1591." Knivet (or as he appears in early modern documents, Knyvett) was a gentleman with important family connections but also an illegitimate son without aspirations to inherit his father's estate. He sailed with Cavendish's fleet that left Portsmouth in August 1591, but fifteen months later, after contracting frostbite in the Straits of Magellan, he was put ashore along with other sick men on the island of São Sebastião, off the southwestern coast of Brazil. When a group of Portuguese and "Savages" from Rio de Janeiro attacked the surviving Englishmen, only Knivet and one companion survived: "Henrie Barrawell, who was saved by my meanes." It is Knivet's linguistic and narrative abilities that assure his survival on this and other occasions: "I striving, cryed out in Portugall, That if they would save mee I would tell them newes, with that a Portugall passed by, and I caught hold of him, so well as I could I told him a Tale which saved my life at that time." The text is notably ambiguous about the content of this "Tale"; Richard Hitchcock has argued that it was surely that he and his friend were Catholics, and Purchas must have suppressed

43. Ibid., 141, 144–146. For other examples and fictional dramatizations of the profitable results of narrating "true histories" of shipwreck and captivity, see Chapter 1, above.

this information out of anti-Catholic bias. Whether Knivet was indeed a Catholic or successfully passed for one, the episode challenges notions of essential national and religious differences, as Barbara Fuchs has argued in her reading of the tale of Miles Philips, who also passed for a Catholic in the New World.[44]

The subsequent passage suggests that Knivet's promise of "newes"—as well as his captors' sense of humor—might also have been responsible for his survival. When the captain arrives "with a piece of bread and Marmallet in his hand," Knivet writes,

> As soone as he saw me, he asked me what newes, I answered that I was very hungry, and desired him that hee would give mee some meate, and then I would tell him all the newes that I could, with that all the Portugals brake out in a laughter, and gave me bread and fish to eate, after I had eaten that which they had given me, I told them the truth of all that they asked me, heere they killed eight and twentie of our men, and saved only my selfe, and Henrie Barrawell, who was saved by my meanes.

More than a foreigner who has simply convinced his captors that he shares their religion, Knivet is a valued informant for travelers eager for (and depen-

44. Samuel Purchas, *Purchas His Pilgrimage; or, Relations of the World and the Religions Observed in All Ages and Places Discovered, from the Creation unto This Present,* 4th ed. (London, 1626 [orig. publ. London, 1613]), 910; Purchas, *Hakluytus Posthumus,* XVI, 194, 212; Richard Hitchcock, "Samuel Purchas as Editor—a Case Study: Anthony Knyvett's Journal," *Modern Language Review,* XCIX (2004), 301–312, esp. 308. Hitchcock summarizes Knivet's biography based on available documents; his uncle Lord Thomas Knyvett was co-M.P. for Westminster with Robert Cecil, gentleman of the Privy Chamber, and warden of the Royal Mint. Miles Philips's account of misadventures in New Spain between 1568 and 1582 is included in Hakluyt, *Principal Navigations,* IX, 398–445. In "An English *Pícaro* in New Spain: Miles Philips and the Framing of National Identity," *CR: The New Centennial Review,* II, no. 1 (Summer 2002), 55–68, esp. 57, Barbara Fuchs suggests that "Miles's tale . . . casts suspicion not just on the individual narrator's national allegiance, but on the very category of Englishness," a category whose borders were apparently flexible enough to allow Philips's various disguises as well as the decision of his companions to marry Africans, a mestiza, and a Spaniard. For a response to Fuchs's reading that emphasizes instead Miles Philips's "unbendable sense of who he is and who he wishes to remain," see Richard Helgerson, "'I Miles Philips': An Elizabethan Seaman Conscripted by History," *PMLA,* CXVIII (2003), 573–580, esp. 577.

dent on) news. Unlike Carder, Knivet displays rather than hides his ability to communicate in his captors' native language, but the effect of contradicting assumptions about nationalist enmity is the same. The seemingly lighthearted camaraderie suggests a set of shared cultural codes and offers a striking contrast with the homicidal violence of the surrounding passage.[45]

Knivet's subsequent experiences among the Portuguese—as well as his several "escapes" to "cannibals" in the Brazilian interior and even across the sea to Angola—similarly alternate between distantiation and identification, between verbal and physical abuse and shared (mis)adventures among "friends." Throughout, Knivet's storytelling ability has the capacity to seduce his listeners, just as it did in his first encounter with the Portuguese. Among the "cannibals," he writes, "in publike I would rehearse somwhat unto them of my coming into their Countrie"; before the king of Congo, on the other hand, he "told him of my Countrie; what plentie of things we had." Knivet excels at both modes of relaying information obtained through travels: the personal narrative of misadventures and the catalogue of ethnographic, geographic, and naturalistic information that can prove equally captivating to listeners or readers.[46]

"The Admirable Adventures and Strange Fortunes of Master Anthonie Knivet" is itself constituted by both narrative modes, with the first three chapters focused on Knivet's travels and misadventures and the latter two devoted to ethnographic and navigational information. The length of the text makes it one of the few in this volume to rival Purchas's "English prize and captive"—Fernão Cardim's treatise on Brazil—and its structure might, in fact, have been partially modeled on the Jesuit treatise. Knivet's fourth chapter is entitled "The Divers Nations of Savages in Brasil, and the Adjoyning Regions: Their Diversities of Conditions, States, Rites, Creatures, and Other Things Remarkeable, Which the Author Observed in His Many Yeares Manifold Peregrinations," whereas the Jesuit treatise's third chapter is "Of the Diversitie of Nations and Languages, and of the Soyle and Climate." Purchas himself indicates a parallel between the works at several points in the margin of the Jesuit treatise, where he cites Knivet as an

45. Purchas, *Hakluytus Posthumus,* XVI, 194. Knivet's account of the sharing of food also reveals the linguistic sharing that resulted from close trading relations between Portugal and England since the fourteenth century. The captain's "marmallet" is surely marmalade or quince jam, derived from the Portuguese "marmelada"; see the *OED* (online draft revision March 2002), s.v. "marmalade."

46. Purchas, *Hakluytus Posthumus,* XVI, 204, 270–271.

authoritative reference ("See before in M. Knivet" and "See of these [the Tapuya] Master Knivet which lived with them"). In Knivet's account, the ethnographic and naturalistic information of the fourth chapter interrupts the narrative of the protagonist's experiences in Lisbon before his ultimate return to England, for the previous chapter concluded with Knivet's crying for help from a dungeon, "in such sort that a great many came to the window, where many pittied me, but none could helpe me, etc." Yet the narrative of Knivet's adventures also interjects and repeats itself in the informational fourth chapter. Purchas might have been more interested in the ethnographic, geographic, and naturalistic descriptions that Knivet could provide, so much so that he drastically truncated—inexcusably mangled, according to some readers—Knivet's narrative. However, the reinsinuation of the autobiographical narrative in the ethnographic chapter suggests that the credibility of the information was dependent on the authority of the captive's firsthand experience. The chapter concludes with a "short discourse in the language of the Petiwares," reminding the reader of the linguistic abilities that he acquired, like Carder and so many other captives, among his indigenous hosts.[47]

47. Purchas, *Hakluytus Posthumus,* XVI, 245, 246, 273–274, 441, 444; for the repetitions and narrative interjections in the fourth chapter of Knivet's account, see 260–264. Hitchcock affirms that Purchas modeled the informational fourth chapter on "Portuguese gazetteers" like Cardim's treatise and argues that Purchas's consequent editing resulted in a "punitive treatment" of Knivet's text, rendering "the journal at times unintelligible to the average reader." Hitchcock also characterizes Purchas's editing as "anti-Catholic" with respect to the lack of information about the "Tale" that saved Knivet and Barrawell's lives and the excision of Knivet's "escape" and return to Lisbon. Yet far from evidence of Purchas's lack of "endorsement" of the narrative, as Hitchcock claims, I would argue that Purchas's unsuccessful division of the text into "narrative" and "descriptive" chapters reveals his interest in both dimensions of Knivet's account and their inextricable nature. Whereas Hitchcock reads Purchas's introduction to Knivet as "foolish word-play which could hardly have recommended his journal to anyone," Purchas's enumeration of Knivet's "Colds, Sicknes, Famine, Wandrings, Calumnies, Desertions, Solitarines, Deserts, Woods, Mountaines, Fennes, Rivers, Seas, Flights, Fights; wilde Beasts, wilder Serpents, wildest Men, and straight passages beyond all names of wildnesse" calls attention to both the delightful and spiritual profit to be obtained from a narrative of misadventures: "God yet delivered [Master Knivet], that out of his manifold paines, thou maist gather this posie of pleasures, and learne to bee thankefull for thy native sweets at home, even delights in the multitude of peace" (XVI, 150–151). See Hitch-

At least one of the many listeners of Knivet's tales within the text recognizes him as both a delightful storyteller and a trustworthy authority: the king of Congo, whom Knivet describes as "verie favourable to all Travellers, and doth delight verie much to heare of forreigne Countries. He was in a manner amazed to heare how it was possible her Majestie had lived a Maiden Queene so long, and alwaies reigned in peace with her subjects." The king defends his informant's veracity when the Portuguese in his court interrupt and dispute the Englishman's account: "The King would shew himselfe verie angrie, and tell them that everie man was best able to speake of his Countrie, and that I had no reason but to tell him that which was true." For the Catholic Álvaro II (1587–1614)—whose kingdom had embraced Christianity after the arrival of Portuguese missionaries in the late fifteenth century and had sent numerous embassies to Rome and Iberia—England is the distant and strange nation whose novelty inspires amazement. With the English as the object rather than the recipient of the narrative, the scenario inverts not only that of Knivet's written account of Angola, Congo, and Angica but that of *Hakluytus Posthumus* as a whole. In the conclusion, Purchas describes the travel reports that comprise his volumes as "lines" that "tend to this Centre . . . that is to his Countrey. . . . All Nations dance in this Round to doe the English service, and English Travellers here enjoy the Mayne, others the By, to attend, and with their Travels to perfect the English, at lest the Knowledge of the World to the English." Purchas's frequent reliance on Iberian and other travel narratives—requiring, at one point, an apology to readers for having "so long held you in Spanish discourses"—suggests that the distinction between (English) "Mayne" and (other nations') "By" is not so clear. At the same time, Knivet's report to the king of Congo indicates how "English Travellers" were also providing "Knowledge of the World" to foreign sovereigns in an incipient era of global circulation of information.[48]

---

cock, "Samuel Purchas as Editor—a Case Study," *Modern Language Review,* XCIX (2004), 301–312, esp. 305–307, 310.

48. Purchas, *Hakluytus Posthumus,* XVI, 270–271, XVIII, 68, XX, 130. On the adoption and development of Catholicism in the kingdom of Congo, see John Thornton, "The Development of an African Catholic Church in the Kingdom of Kongo, 1491–1750," *Journal of African History,* XXV (1984), 147–167. Duarte Lopes describes many such embassies in the account that he dictated to Filippo Pigafetta, entitled *Relatione del reame di Congo et delle circonvicine contrade* (Rome, 1591), which was published in English as *A Reporte of the Kingdome of Congo, a Region of Africa, and of the Countries That Border Rounde about the Same . . . Drawen out*

When Purchas called Peter Carder and Anthony Knivet "unmatchable by any English for the rare adventures, disadventures, and manifold successions of miseries," he may not have had in mind "The Travels and Adventures of Captaine John Smith in Divers Parts of the World, Begun about the Yeere 1596," which he included in volume II of *Hakluytus Posthumus,* based on a manuscript obtained from Smith. Purchas had introduced the narrative—which Smith would publish five years later in *The True Travels, Adventures, and Observations of Captaine John Smith, in Europe, Asia, Affrica, and America, from Anno Domini 1593. to 1629.*—as a "Tragicall Comedie . . . full of Raritie and Varietie, the parents of Wonder and Delight." Purchas was capitalizing on the dimensions of Smith's travels that apparently had already captivated a theatrical audience, for in his dedication of the work, Smith himself points out that one of his reasons for publishing it is that "they have acted my fatall Tragedies upon the Stage, and racked my Relations at their pleasure. To prevent therefore all future misprisions, I have compiled this true discourse." We do not know whether these "fatall Tragedies" included a love affair with female captors like the "comedia de las cosas de Chile" that Francisco Núñez de Pineda y Bascuñán complained about in the autobiographical work intended to set the record straight about his own captivity. But Smith's successive rewritings of his adventures, especially his captivity in Virginia, surely encouraged readers' and theatergoers' interest in the "raritie and varietie" of his work. Certainly they failed to prevent "future misprisions" of an affair with Pocahontas, who has been presented as enamored of Smith, and occasionally as his lover, in numerous literary and cinematic renditions since the early nineteenth century.[49]

---

of the Writinges and Discourses of Odoardo Lopes a Portingall . . . , trans. Abraham Hartwell (London, 1597). Lopes himself was sent by Álvaro I to Spain and Rome in 1583 to request priests to "establish the Gospel in those remote regions, where the people had so lately been converted to Christianity"; see Pigafetta, *A Report of the Kingdom of Congo, and of the Surrounding Countries; Drawn Out of the Writings and Discourses of the Portuguese, Duarte Lopez,* ed. and trans. Margarite Hutchinson (London, 1881), 103.

49. John Smith, "The Travels and Adventures of Captaine John Smith in Divers Parts of the World, Begun about the Yeere 1596," in Purchas, *Hakluytus Posthumus,* VIII, 321–342, and see 320; Smith, *Complete Works,* III, 141; Francisco Núñez de Pineda y Bascuñán, *Cautiverio feliz y razón individual de las guerras dilatadas del*

Modern scholarship generally disputes the most dramatic and legendary moment of Smith's account of his captivity among Powhatan's people in December of 1607, when Pocahontas supposedly laid her head on his in order to save him from execution. Some critics have highlighted the event's lack of accord with what is known about the treatment of captives or the role of young girls like Pocahontas in Algonquian society, for Smith's story corresponds well to neither execution nor adoption rituals. Scholars have also pointed out that Smith did not include the episode in the first account of his captivity, written shortly after it occurred in a letter, which was published without his knowledge as *A True Relation of Such Occurrences and Accidents of Noate as Hath Hapned in Virginia* (1608). Although Smith mentions Powhatan's daughter Pocahontas in this text ("the only Nonpariel *[sic]* of his Country") and disputes claims of his intention to marry her in order to "make himself a king" in *The Proceedings of the English Colony* (1612), he first identifies Pocahontas as "the meanes to deliver" him in *New Englands Trials* (1622). The precise account of "How Pocahontas saved his life" first occurs in *The Generall Historie of Virginia* (1624), which also portrays Pocahontas delivering much-needed food and warning of an attack on the colony. By this time, Smith appears to have stumbled upon a way to cast all of his relations with foreign women, for in the dedication of this work to the duchess of Richmond and Lenox, Smith refers to the "honorable and vertuous Ladies" that "have offred me rescue and protection in my greatest dangers":

> The beauteous Lady Tragabigzanda, when I was a slave to the Turkes, did all she could to secure me. When I overcame the Bashaw of Nalbrits in Tartaria, the charitable Lady Callamata supplyed my necessities. In

---

reino de Chile, [ed. Diego Barros Arana], in Colección de historiadores de Chile, III (Santiago, 1863), 150. Pineda complains that the comedy "representó estos amores muy a lo poético, estrechando los afectos a lo que las obras no se desmandaron" [represented these loves very poetically, stretching the affection farther than the deeds went]. On the many historiographic, literary, and artistic representations of Pocahontas since the colonial period, see Robert S. Tilton, *Pocahontas: The Evolution of an American Narrative* (New York, 1994); Tilton suggests that John Davis's *Travels of Four Years and a Half in the United States of America during 1798, 1799, 1800, 1801, and 1802 . . .* (London, 1803) "first posited that it was her romantic love for Smith, rather than just a general feeling of benevolence or charity for all men, that prompted her heroic action"; see Tilton, *Pocahontas,* 35. More recently, Terrence Malick's film *The New World* (2005) represents a romantic relationship between Smith and Pocahontas.

the utmost of many extremities, that blessed Pokahontas, the great Kings daughter of Virginia, oft saved my life. When I escaped the crueltie of Pirats and most furious stormes, a long time alone in a small Boat at Sea, and driven ashore in France, the good Lady Madam Chanoyes, bountifully assisted me.

Camilla Townsend refers to Smith's repetition of similar incidents as the "clincher" in the debate over the authenticity of the Pocahontas rescue. Yet the repetition raises questions not only about Smith's veracity but about his motivations and sources.[50]

Smith's plotting of his encounters with foreign women surely owes more to literary vogues than to verisimilitude. The amorous adventures of shipwrecked and captured protagonists inundate ancient Greek novels like Heliodorus's *Aethiopica* and their Renaissance imitators. Stories specifically about a Muslim woman who falls in love with, converts, and flees to Christendom with her father's or husband's captive have appeared in a variety of European traditions since the Middle Ages. In the Iberian world, the theme of the enamored female captor, present in medieval ballads and folktales, surfaces in sixteenth- and seventeenth-century historical and fictional writing related to both the New World and the Mediterranean. Smith could have encountered

50. Smith, *Complete Works,* I, 93, 274, 432, II, 41–42, 152, 259; Camilla Townsend, *Pocahontas and the Powhatan Dilemma* (New York, 2004), 52. Townsend summarizes the evidence against the episode's authenticity on 52–56. See also Helen C. Rountree, *Pocahontas, Powhatan, Opechancanough: Three Indian Lives Changed by Jamestown* (Charlottesville, Va., 2005), 76–82, who points out the lack of fit between what Smith describes and what is known about adoption and initiation rituals in Algonquian society and in any case disputes the notion that an eleven-year-old girl like Pocahontas would have been present at an adoption ceremony. Although acknowledging Smith's lack of comprehension and skewed interpretation of events, other scholars have argued that he underwent some sort of adoption or incorporation ritual; see, for example, Pauline Turner Strong, *Captive Selves, Captivating Others: The Politics and Poetics of Colonial American Captivity Narratives* (Boulder, Colo., 1999), 54–60. Perhaps to lend the story greater credibility, Smith included in *The Generall Historie* a letter that he wrote to Queen Anne in 1617 (on the occasion of Pocahontas's arrival in England), which recounts the same version of events, but no other copy or original of this letter has yet been found; see Smith, *Complete Works,* II, 258–262. On Pocahontas's expanded role in the *Generall Historie* and Smith's depiction of female benevolence as another form of the "mastery" that he continually asserts over other men, see Fuller, *Voyages in Print,* 123–134.

the episode of the captive captain's escape from Algiers with the help of the Moorish princess Zoraida in the first part of Cervantes's *Don Quijote,* which was published in English in 1612. Smith's reference to how the young "Charatza Tragabigzanda" (from the Greek for "girl from Trebizond") "woulde feigne her selfe sick when she should goe to the Banians" recalls Zoraida's feigned swoon into the Christian captive's arms as well as the Spanish term, *baño,* used to describe the place where captives were confined in Algiers. In the New World context, Gonzalo Fernández de Oviedo y Valdés includes an episode of a Spaniard held captive in early-sixteenth-century Venezuela who was thrice saved from death by an "india principal" [Indian noblewoman]. Although Oviedo's work was known in England through the translation of excerpts in Richard Eden's *Decades of the New World* (1555), Richard Wille's *History of Travayle in the West and East Indies* (1577), and Purchas's *Hakluytus Posthumus,* the story of Francisco Martín's captivity is related in book 25, which was not included in the partial Spanish editions of 1535 and 1557.[51]

A far more likely source for Smith is the tale of Juan Ortiz, recounted in the anonymous Fidalgo d'Elvas's *Relaçam verdadeira dos trabalhos que o governador dom Fernando de Souto e certos fidalgos portugueses passarom no descobrimento da provincia da Frolida* [sic] (1557) and el Inca Garcilaso de la Vega's *La Florida del Inca* (1605). Although a note by Purchas indicates that Garcilaso's version was also known in England, the *Relaçam* circulated in

51. Smith, *Complete Works,* III, 187; Gonzalo Fernández de Oviedo y Valdés, *Historia general y natural de las Indias,* ed. Juan Pérez de Tudela Bueso (Madrid, 1959 [orig. publ. Seville, 1535]), III, 28. On the motif of the "enamored captor's daughter," see Mohja Kahf, *Western Representations of the Muslim Woman: From Termagant to Odalisque* (Austin, Tex., 1999), 33–38; Harriet Goldberg, "Captivity as a Central Node in Hispanic Popular Legends: There's Something about a Prisoner," in Delia V. Galván, Anita K. Stoll, and Philippa Brown Yin, eds., *Studies in Honor of Donald W. Bleznick* (Newark, N.J., 1995), 49–58. Miguel de Cervantes Saavedra, *The History of the Valorous and Wittie Knight-Errant, Don-Quixote of the Mancha,* trans. [Thomas Shelton] (London, 1612), 459, renders "baño" as "bath" ("a prison or house, which the *Turks* call Bathes, wherein they do inclose the Captive Christians"; see 477 for the episode in which Zoraida pretends to faint in the Christian captive's arms when her father finds them together in the garden. However, Smith most likely borrowed the passage from William Biddulph's letter, published in the same volume of Purchas, which identifies "Bannios" as "hot Baths," one of the few public destinations open to women; see Smith, *Complete Works,* III, 187n. 4; Purchas, *Hakluytus Posthumus,* VIII, 268.

English specifically to promote the Virginia colony. Richard Hakluyt translated and published Elvas's text as *Virginia Richly Valued, by the Description of the Maine Land of Florida, Her Next Neighbour* in 1609; he dedicated it to the Virginia Company ("the Right Honourable, the Right Worshipfull Counsellors, and others the cheerefull adventurors for the advancement of that Christian and noble plantantion in Virginia"). The work was reissued in 1611 with a new title that more fittingly emphasized the work's narrative rather than descriptive qualities, but its function as propaganda for the Virginia colony is still evident:

> *The Worthye and Famous History, of the Travailes, Discovery, and Conquest, of That Great Continent of Terra Florida, Being Lively Paraleld, with That of Our Now Inhabited* VIRGINIA. *As Also the Comodities of the Said Country, with Divers Excellent and Rich Mynes, of Golde, Silver, and Other Mettals, etc. Which Cannot but Give Us a Great and Exceeding Hope of Our* VIRGINIA, *Being So Neere of One Continent. Accomplished and Effected, by That Worthy Generall and Captaine, Don Ferdinando de Soto, and Six Hundreth Spaniards His Followers.*

Both of these publications predate Smith's account of Pocahontas's rescue in the *Generall Historie* of 1624 (and even his presumed letter to Queen Anne in 1617), and we can be reasonably assured that Smith was familiar with at least one of them. John Brereton had already drawn from Elvas's account in his *Briefe and True Relation of the Discoverie of the North Part of Virginia* (1602); Brereton credits his source as the "discovery of Florida by de Soto" and indicates Hakluyt's intention to publish it. Smith, in turn, included an abridged version of Brereton's account of a 1602 voyage in the *Generall Historie.* Furthermore, in *A Description of New England* (1616), Smith cites Soto as one of the many Spanish and Portuguese navigators and conquistadors worthy of emulation:

> Columbus, Cortez, Pitzara, Soto, Magellanes, and the rest served more then a prentiship to learne how to begin their most memorable attempts in the West Indies: which to the wonder of all ages succesfully they effected, when many hundreds of others farre above them in the worlds opinion, beeing instructed but by relation, came to shame and confusion in actions of small moment, who doubtlesse in other matters, were both wise, discreet, generous, and couragious. I say not this to detract any thing from their incomparable merits, but to answer those questionlesse questions

> that keep us back from imitating the worthinesse of their brave spirits that advanced themselves from poore Souldiers to great Captaines, their posterity to great Lords, their King to be one of the greatest Potentates on earth, and the fruites of their labours, his greatest glory, power, and renowne.

The Soto expedition can hardly be described as "successfully effected": it found no gold nor established any settlements and resulted in the death of its leader and almost half of the six hundred participants. Smith's inclusion of Soto as one of the "great Captaines" of "incomparable merits" is thus surprising, but less so when we consider that English readers knew of him through Elvas's account; that portrayal of Soto and of the expedition as a whole is more flattering than Garcilaso's or Oviedo's. If Smith did read Hakluyt's translation, he would not have failed to notice the tale of a European held captive by alternately hostile and friendly indigenous groups, not to mention the role played by the captor's daughter in preventing his death and helping him to escape—in a region close to where Smith himself had been held captive a few years before.[52]

Even more than the treatment of the captor's daughter, Smith might have

52. Fidalgo d'Elvas, *Virginia Richly Valued, by the Description of the Maine Land of Florida, Her Next Neighbour,* trans. Richard Hakluyt (London, 1609 [orig. publ. Évora, 1557]); Fidalgo d'Elvas, *The Worthye and Famous History, of the Travailes, Discovery, and Conquest, of That Great Continent of Terra Florida . . . ,* trans. Richard Hakluyt, Works Issued by the Hakluyt Society, no. 9 (London, 1611); John Brereton, *A Briefe and True Relation of the Discoverie of the North Part of Virginia* (London, 1602), 37–38, 46–48; Smith, *Complete Works,* II, 88–90, I, 327–328. I discuss the Juan Ortiz tale as related by Elvas and Garcilaso in Chapter 2, above. Purchas refers to Garcilaso's *La Florida del Inca* (Lisbon, 1605) in *Hakluytus Posthumus,* XVII, 311, and published an abbreviated version of Elvas's account on 525–550 as well as in XVIII, 1–51. Historians who have speculated that Elvas's tale of Juan Ortiz was a source for Smith include Marjory Stoneman Douglas, *The Everglades: River of Grass* (New York, 1947), 123; Strong, *Captive Selves, Captivating Others,* 73–74n. 18. Philip L. Barbour asserts that Smith "certainly knew" *Virginia Richly Valued* but offers no evidence; see Barbour, *The Three Worlds of Captain John Smith* (Boston, 1964), 296. Vianna Moog compares the Pocahontas legend with the tale of Diogo Álvares "Caramuru" and Paraguaçu and also suggests its possible influence on Smith; see Moog, *Bandeirantes and Pioneers,* trans. L. L. Barrett (New York, 1964), 70–72, 304n. 29 (originally published as *Bandeirantes e pioneros: Paralelo entre duas culturas* [Rio de Janeiro, 1956]).

been attracted to the *Relaçam*'s portrayal of the privileged role granted to Juan Ortiz as a result of his captivity. Although all of the narratives of the expedition depict Ortiz as a valued interpreter and adviser to Soto owing to the knowledge he gained through captivity, the *Relaçam*'s representation of the dire consequences of his death is unmatched in any of the other accounts:

> *John Ortiz* died in *Autiamque;* which grieved the Governor very much: because that without an Interpretour hee feared to enter farre into the land, where he might be lost. . . . The death of *John Ortiz* was so great a mischiefe for the discovering inward, or going out of the land, that to learne of the Indians, that which in foure words hee declared, they needed a whole day with the youth [their indigenous interpreter].

In the epistle dedicatory to the translation, Hakluyt also relies on the linguistic competence of the ex-captive: "I finde them here noted to be very eloquent and well spoken, as the short Orations, interpreted by *John Ortiz,* which lived twelve yeeres among them, make sufficient proofe." Ortiz's interpretive abilities, gained through captivity, authorize the text's depiction of the "qualities and conditions of the inhabitants," which Hakluyt claims to be one of the main purposes of the work. Indeed, Juan Ortiz corresponds precisely to Smith's model of someone who has learned by experience ("served more than a prentiship"), in contrast to those who have been "instructed but by relation."[53]

However much Smith's account of rescue by his captor's daughter is reminiscent of the tales of Juan Ortiz or Diogo Álvares "Caramuru," his self-promotion as a "man of experience" best suited to govern the Virginia colony even more closely resembles the author discussed in Chapter 3 (above), Francisco Núñez de Pineda y Bascuñán. Smith argues that, if he had been allowed to continue in the colonial government, he could have avoided the dissension, disorganization, and disasters that plagued Virginia in its first few decades, much as the Chilean author would later assert the ability of a "natural y experimentado hijo de [la patria]" [native and experienced son of the patria] like himself to resolve the Araucanian conflict in seventeenth-

53. Fidalgo d'Elvas, *Virginia Richly Valued, by the Description of the Maine Land of Florida, Her Next Neighbour,* in Peter Force, ed., *Tracts and Other Papers Relating Principally to the Origin, Settlement, and Progress of the Colonies in North America, from the Discovery of the Country to the Year 1776* (Washington, 1846), IV, 1–132, esp. [3], [6], 89; Smith, *Complete Works,* I, 327.

century Chile. Unlike Pineda, Smith cannot appeal to his status as "natural," but he does assert his qualifications as "experimentado." In *The Proceedings of the English Colony,* for example, Smith laments, "The 2. first years though by his adventures he had oft brought the Salvages to a tractable trade, yet you see how the envious authority ever crossed him, and frustrated his best endeavours. Yet this wrought in him that experience and estimation among the Salvages, as otherwaies it had bin impossible he had ever effected that he did." Smith's "experience and estimation among the Salvages," much like that which Pineda achieved through his own captivity, serves as the ground for his authority and offers a stark contrast to "his unlawfull successors, who onlie by living in James Towne, presumed to know more then al the world could direct them." Many scholars have highlighted the importance of the notion of experience in Smith's writing, to the extent that he has been credited with inaugurating the modern use of experiential authority as a rhetorical strategy. However, Smith's reference to the Spaniards and Portuguese who advanced through "more then a prentiship" to become "great Captaines" recalls the Iberian context within which Smith constantly evaluated and promoted English colonial endeavors. And Iberian writers had begun to affirm experiential knowledge as a source of both political and textual authority since at least the early sixteenth century. In the introduction to the 1535 publication of the first part of his *Historia general y natural de las Indias,* Oviedo modifies Pliny's claim to have derived his work from "two billion" volumes that he had read: "Yo acumulé todo lo que aquí escribo, de dos mill millones de trabajos y nescesidades e peligros en veinte e dos años e más que ha que veo y experimento por mi persona estas cosas" [I accumulated all that I write here from two billion trials and needs and dangers in the more than twenty-two years that I have experienced and seen these things in person]. The resulting work diverges from (and surpasses) not only ancient authorities like Pliny but also those who write about the Americas "sin verlo, desde España, a pie enjuto" [without seeing it, from Spain, with dry feet].[54]

54. Pineda y Bascuñán, *Cautiverio feliz y razón individual,* [ed. Barros Arana], 422; Smith, *Complete Works,* I, 267–268; Oviedo, *Historia general y natural,* ed. Tudela Bueso, I, 9, 11. Smith served as president of the Virginia colony from September 10, 1608, to roughly September 10, 1609, when he was forced to end his term and return to England not only because of a severe gunshot wound but also because of charges made against him by his political opponents; see Barbour, *Three Worlds of Captain John Smith,* 276–280. On Smith's "modern" use of experiential authority—

Oviedo is careful to point out the particularity of his American experience to those who might criticize him in Europe, Asia, or Africa: "Que adviertan a que no estó en ninguna desas tres partes . . . no me juzguen sin ver esta tierra donde estoy y de quien tracto" [Let them note that I am not in any of those three parts . . . and not judge me without seeing this land where I am and about which I write]. Smith, in contrast, appeals both to his experience in Virginia and his travels and misadventures on all four continents. In the above-cited passage from the *Proceedings,* he refers to "the many miserable yet generous and worthy adventures he had long and oft indured as wel in some parts of Africa, and America, as in the most partes of Europe and Asia by land or sea," whereas in the dedication to *A Description of New England* (1616), he describes himself as having "beene taught by lamentable experience, aswell in Europe and Asia, as Affrick, and America." It is thus not only Smith's captivity and rescue by benevolent women that unite his adventures in the New and Old World. Jim Egan has described how Smith bases his authority on all of his experiences abroad because the cumulative effect of these travels "qualifies him to know experience when he sees it" and distinguishes him as a "member of a new category—the man of experience—that presumably any number of such individuals could occupy." As Egan points out, Smith borrows liberally and frequently from the experiences of other individuals belonging to this category; Smith's manner of compiling others' accounts, especially in the *Generall Historie,* recalls the labors of Hakluyt and Purchas, whose volumes certainly aided him in his enterprise. However, Smith claims the value of his own experience even in his editorial endeavors, pointing out "how difficult a matter it is, to gather the truth from amongst so many forren and severall relations, except you have exceeding good ex-

---

derived specifically from his colonial and mediating experience—see Jim Egan, *Authorizing Experience: Refigurations of the Body Politic in Seventeenth-Century New England Writing* (Princeton, N.J., 1999), 32–46; William C. Spengemann, *A New World of Words: Redefining Early American Literature* (New Haven, Conn., 1994), 51–93; and Fuller, *Voyages in Print,* 103–140. See also Bauer, *Cultural Geography of Colonial American Literatures,* 112–117, who emphasizes the Spanish antecedents for Smith's use of experiential authority, particularly el Inca Garcilaso de la Vega. Fuller points out, "If Smith's life is the ultimate authority for his textual practice as editor, that life was itself already heavily textualized," influenced by both an English and Spanish (and Portuguese, we might add) written tradition; see *Voyages in Print,* 135. For other references to Spanish and Portuguese discoveries and conquests in Smith's work, see *Complete Works,* I, 257, 349–350, II, 206–207, 462, 474.

perience both of the Countries, people, and their conditions." But as widely traveled as he was, Smith did not have "exceeding good experience" the world over and in fact had to rely on "foreign" relations in the same way as Hakluyt and Purchas.[55]

Among the accounts compiled in the second part of Smith's *True Travels,* the "Continuation of His Generall Historie of Virginia," are those of Walter Ralegh and even Francis Sparrey. Despite the near lack of Smith's own testimony in this section, he still attempts to subordinate knowledge earned through "relations" to direct experience. In chapter 24, Smith recounts how Ralegh was informed of "twentie severall voyages . . . made by the Spanyards" to find Manoa but affirms that Ralegh "did his utmost to have found some better satisfaction than relations." Smith is clearly familiar with Ralegh's *Discoverie,* and the one detail that he chooses to relate from it is how Ralegh left his "trustie servant" Francis Sparrey in Guiana: "Who wandring up and downe those Countreyes, some foureteene or fifteene yeares, unexpectedly returned: I have heard him say, he was led blinded into this Citie by Indians . . . his body seeming as a man of an uncurable consumption, shortly dyed here after in England." The credibility of Smith's account seems to rely on his direct visual and aural contact with Sparrey. However, the information that he relates about Sparrey is derived from textual sources, and indirect ones at that. Sparrey did not, as we have seen, wander "fourteen or fifteen years" in Guiana (or even the four years he claims in his "Memorial"), but one. On the other hand, the individual led "blinded" into Manoa was, according to Ralegh, a Spaniard named Juan Martínez, whose relation Ralegh claimed could be found in Spanish archives; Ralegh had obtained

55. Oviedo, *Historia general y natural,* ed. Tudela Bueso, I, 12; Smith, *Complete Works,* I, 267, 310, III, 236, and see also II, 44; Egan, *Authorizing Experience,* 38. Egan argues that Smith incorporates the "experience of other men as if it were his own" and that what allows him to do so "is the fact that he speaks for a category of men for whom knowledge becomes common property. Such experience was not common to all, as the Aristotelians demanded. Quite the contrary, it was common only to colonial men and not necessarily to men of Classical learning." Egan does not specify the identities of these "colonial men," but it seems that he has only Englishmen in mind, given his conclusion that, before Smith, writers "invoked experience only rarely and certainly never to authorize an individual"; see Egan, *Authorizing Experience,* 39, 46. As this book has shown, Smith is certainly a participant but far from a forerunner in the process by which "knowledge becomes common property" across national and linguistic boundaries. See Everett Emerson, *Captain John Smith* (New York, 1993), 55–69, for a detailed account of Smith's use of his sources.

a copy from his captive Antonio del Berrío. If Francis Sparrey is one of the "men of experience" whom Smith can trust—having "experienced" Sparrey directly himself—his account of Sparrey's travels among the natives of Guiana is thoroughly infused with textual sources, some of which are Spanish in origin.[56]

Smith does not always dissimulate his inspiration in Iberian sources. Whereas Purchas draws from Smith's works in *Purchas His Pilgrimage* and *Hakluytus Posthumus,* Smith, in turn, borrows from Purchas in his own publication of the *True Travels,* particularly when he arrives at the portion dedicated to Africa. In his description of Barbary in chapter 18, Smith lifts from the Granadine Leo Africanus's *Geographical Historie of Africa,* translated by John Pory, published in 1600, and reprinted by Purchas in volume II of *Hakluytus Posthumus.* In the following chapter, "The Strange Discoveries and Observations of the Portugalls in Affrica," Smith fills out his account of Africa by offering a relation of Congo and Angola, realms where he—unlike Knivet—had never been. Chapter 19 is a condensed version of *A Reporte of the Kingdome of Congo, a Region of Africa . . . Drawen out of the Writinges and Discourses of Odoardo Lopez a Portingall, by Philippo Pigafetta,* which was translated from Italian by Abraham Hartwell at the instigation of Hakluyt and published in 1597. The Portuguese New Christian Duarte Lopes traveled to the Congo in 1578, became a member of Álvaro I's court, and in 1583 was sent as an ambassador to Philip II and the pope in order to request priests to aid in the reestablishment of Christianity in the country. While in Rome, Lopes shared his writings and oral information about the history, geography, and culture of the kingdom of Congo with the Italian Filippo Pigafetta, who published it in 1591. According to Philip Barbour, Smith condensed Purchas's already abridged version of the text, but Smith might have drawn from Hartwell's translation directly. Smith acknowledges

56. Smith, *Complete Works,* III, 224; Ralegh, *Discoverie,* ed. Whitehead, 138–140. The editor of Smith's *Complete Works,* Philip L. Barbour, affirms that the paragraph on Ralegh is "obviously derived" from Sparrey's relation in Purchas, but these texts bear no relation; rather, Smith is drawing on Ralegh's own *Discoverie* and even spells Sparrey's name as it appears there (Sparrow). With respect to the number of years attributed to Sparrey in Guiana, Smith could have had in mind Miles Philips's "15 or 16" years in New Spain, according to Hakluyt (actually, it was fourteen years, 1568–1582); see *Principal Navigations,* IX, 398. Ralegh's Juan Martínez was only held captive in Guiana seven months, but Smith could have drawn the reference to fourteen or fifteen years from the "14. or 15. daies" of Martínez's passage through the city of Manoa.

his need to rely on Lopes's text, since "those interiour parts of Affrica are little knowen to either English, French, or Dutch, though they use much the coast; therefore we will make a little bold with the observations of the Portugalls." The primacy of the authority of direct experience, in other words, necessitates the borrowing across national and linguistic borders that we have seen throughout this chapter—even for those as widely traveled as Smith. Indeed, Smith's valorization of direct experience as a source of authority, at the same time that he relies on the experiences of others, is not necessarily hypocritical or even contradictory. The rise of experiential authority in the sixteenth and early seventeenth century—particularly in a country like England, where efforts at maritime exploration and imperial expansion began slowly and belatedly—necessitates a dependence on "foreign" sources when "native" ones are not available.[57]

Abraham Hartwell's preface to the reader in *A Reporte of the Kingdome of*

57. Smith, *Complete Works,* III, 204n. 7, 208, 208n. 4; [Hassan ibn Muhammad al-Wazzan al-Fasi, a.k.a. Leo Africanus], *A Geographical Historie of Africa, Written in Arabicke and Italian by John Leo a More, Borne in Granada, and Brought up in Barbarie . . .*, trans. John Pory (London, 1600 [orig. publ. Venice, 1550]). On Hassan al-Wazzan, known in Europe as Leo Africanus—a Granadine Moor who was raised and traveled extensively in Africa before being captured by Christian corsairs in the Mediterranean and held captive by Pope Leo X in Rome, where he wrote a renowned history and description of Africa—see Natalie Zemon Davis, *Trickster Travels: A Sixteenth-Century Muslim between Worlds* (New York, 2006). For documents related to Duarte Lopes's embassy to Philip II and the pope, including Álvaro I's instructions, see António Brásio, ed., *Monumenta missionaria africana: África ocidental (1570–1599)* (Lisbon, 1953), III, 234–235, 238–239, 340–341, 358-364. Smith attributes his source-author with no less than having "planted there [in the Kingdom of Congo] Christian Religion, and spent most of his life to bring those Countreyes to the Crowne of Portugall" (Smith, *Complete Works,* III, 209). However, evangelization in the Congo dates to at least 1491 (when King Nzinga a Nkuwu requested baptism), and the ruling elite's embrace of Christianity deterred Portuguese domination. Lopes himself attributes the restoration of Christianity after the kingdom's defeat by the "Jaggas" to the return of Congolese natives who had been sold into slavery during the invasion: "A great number were ransomed and brought home to their own country, by whose means . . . the king was enabled to re-establish the Christian religion, which had suffered great loss, and also to employ them as valuable counsellors and ministers of state in his kingdom, *their long captivity having given them much experience of the world*" (Pigafetta, *Report of the Kingdom of Congo,* ed. and trans. Hutchinson, 100–101 [emphasis added]). Here, the Congolese king Álvaro I also recognizes the experiential authority acquired through captivity.

Congo aptly addresses the issues and concerns involved in the English use of Iberian sources examined in this chapter and can thus help to conclude it. First, Hartwell reveals England's marginality even more than Knivet's report to the king of Congo. Hartwell relates how his friends encouraged him to translate foreign works "to help our *English Nation,* that they might knowe and understand many things, which are common in other languages, but utterly concealed from this poore *Island.*" If Hakluyt similarly intended his work "for the benefit and honour of my Countrey," Hartwell reveals just what that benefit is: England is behind in the interrelated pursuits of knowledge and empire, and translations of foreign works are necessary for it to catch up. A Portuguese resident in Africa at the court of the king of Congo "knowe[s] and understand[s] many things" that are worth knowing in Italy and England.[58]

Second, Hartwell's preface demonstrates the degree to which national rivalries and concerns about the legitimacy of English imperial endeavors inflected the reading and translation of foreign works. Hartwell relates his first reaction to Lopes's text:

> Within two houres conference, I found him nibling at two most honourable Gentlemen of *England,* whome in plaine tearmes he called *Pirates:* so that I had much adoo to hold my hands from renting of him into many mo peeces, then his *Cosen Lopez* the *Doctor* was quartered. Yet . . . *My second wits* stayed me, and advised me, that I should peruse all his *Report,* before I would proceede to execution: which in deede I did. And, because I sawe that in all the rest of his behaviour hee conteyned himselfe very well and honestly, and that he used this lewd speech, not altogether *exanimo,* but rather *ex vitio gentis,* of the now-inveterate hatred, which the *Spanyard* and *Portingall* beare against our *Nation,* I was so bold as to pardon him, and so taught him to speake the *English toung.*

The "Cosen" alluded to is surely the Portuguese Jew Dr. Roderigo Lopez, Queen Elizabeth's private physician, who was hanged and quartered for allegedly trying to poison her in 1594. Yet Hartwell's initial revulsion and condemnation are rather misplaced: it is the Italian Pigafetta who refers to Drake and Cavendish as "Corsale" [pirates] in a question he puts to his informant about the Portuguese lack of fortification of the island of Saint

58. Hakluyt, *Principal Navigations,* I, xxxix; Hartwell, "The Translator to the Reader," in Pigafetta, *Reporte of the Kingdome of Congo,* trans. Hartwell.

Helena after its plunder by both men. Even if the statement were Lopes's, it need not have proceeded "ex vitio gentis," since Englishmen sometimes called Drake a "pirate" as well. Hartwell's sensitivity about the matter of English piracy is reflected in Smith's last, apparently irrelevant, chapter of the *True Travels,* "The bad life, qualities and conditions of Pyrats; and how they taught Turks and Moores to become men of warre." Here, Smith laments how unemployed and underpaid soldiers under James I have "turned Pirats" and concludes with an exhortation to them to embrace more worthy overseas enterprises: "Those titles of Sea-men and Souldiers, have beene most worthily honoured and esteemed, but now regarded for the most part, but as the scumme of the world; regain therefore your wonted reputations, and endevour rather to adventure to those faire plantations of our English Nation." The "outeragious, common, and daily piracies" of the English that preoccupied Hakluyt in 1584 had apparently not abated by the time Smith published the *True Travels* in 1630; English maritime ventures continued to be viewed at home and abroad as piratical, however much colonial promoters like Hakluyt and Smith promulgated the benefits of trade and "plantation." Hartwell's mock near-execution of the Portuguese author reveals more about the extent of English anxiety about its identity as a nation of "pirates" than about any "inveterate hatred, which the Spanyard and Portingall beare against our Nation."[59]

Lastly, however, Hartwell's preface reveals how these national rivalries were sometimes subordinated to the common imperial projects of knowledge production and religious dissemination. Hartwell devotes the rest of his preface to defending the text against potential criticisms about its form and content. Among these is the "paradox" of the habitability of the Torrid and Frigid Zones, which Lopes asserts by virtue of firsthand experience, contradicting "the opinion of the old world, and of the auncient *Philosophers.*" The issue was taken up by many authors of the Iberian empires, including el Inca Garcilaso and José de Acosta, whose *De natura novi orbis* Hartwell cites as

59. Hartwell, "Translator to the Reader," in Pigafetta, *Reporte of the Kingdome of Congo,* trans. Hartwell, [2]; Smith, *Complete Works,* III, 238–241. For Pigafetta's reference to Drake and Cavendish as "Corsale" in his questioning of Lopes, see Pigafetta, *Relatione del reame di Congo,* facs. ed. in Pigafetta, *Relação do reino de Congo e das terras circunvizinhas* (Lisbon, 1949), 4. William Camden also calls Drake a "pirate" in Camden, *History of the Most Renowned and Victorious Princess Elizabeth,* 249; see also 255. For similar uses of the metaphor of translating foreign texts as teaching them to speak the "English tongue," see Morini, *Tudor Translation in Theory and Practice,* 54–55.

an "excellent Treatise." Acosta "both by good reasons and also by his owne experience prove[s] this his position to be true," Hartwell writes,

> and therefore I protest unto you, it was one of the chiefe Motives, which moved me to translate this Report, to the end it might be more publikely knowen, that it was not the single fancie of one man, touching the temperature of these two Zones, but also of divers others that by their owne travell have tryed the certayntie thereof: among whome, this *Lopez* was one, who delivered this *Relation* in *Anno 1588,* being foure yeares after the *Treatise* made by *Josephus-a-Costa.* And I do not doubt, but that within few yeares you shall have it confirmed by many others that are and have been travellers, who have not as yet published their knowledge and trials in this behalfe.

The obligation of travelers to "publish their knowledge and trials"—and of translators and editors to publish foreign travel accounts—derives from the interest, shared across national boundaries, in offering a new and more accurate understanding of the world based on verifiable, eyewitness evidence. Hartwell does not even limit this role to European travelers: with respect to the "paradox" of the existence of Amazons, Hartwell makes an ironic nod to Ralegh's *Discoverie* when he declares his "hope that in good time, some good *Guianian* will make good proofe to our *England,* that there are at this day both *Amazones,* and *Headlesse men.*" For Hartwell, the mythical beings of an ancient textual tradition are fully reconciliable with the modern "proofe" of firsthand testimony. Hartwell's reference to the "many others" who will yet publish their accounts demonstrates the intimate link between travel, travail (and here, trial), narration, and knowledge production that we have seen throughout this chapter and book. And Hartwell confirms the link, just as intimate, between textualization and experience in "true histories" of travel, captivity, and shipwreck.

The last potential charge against which Hartwell preemptively defends his translation relates to the central node of Anglo-Iberian opposition since Elizabeth I: religion. Hartwell acknowledges that some English readers may view the work's history of the conversion of the kingdom of Congo as serving the cause of "the *Pope* and his *Adherents.*" However, his response extends beyond the affirmation that the Catholic missionaries' efforts in the Congo serve as a "notable example to the *World*" and can thus stimulate Protestant imitation of them. Despite what he calls the "pompe and solemnitie, after the *Romish* manner" used to convert the people of Congo, Hartwell defends the "good intent" of the Portuguese priests, "because they converted a great part of the *People,* not to *Poperie,* but to *Christianitie,* the true foundation of all *Religion.*" In the following paragraph, littered with biblical references, Hartwell in effect propounds a Christian universalism:

> And are we angrie, or shall we finde fault, that the *Portingall Priests* being *Papists,* should be reported to have converted the *Realme* of *Congo* to the profession of Christian Religion? Shall we envie them in their well doing? I for my part do earnestly wish with all my hart, that not onely *Papists* and *Protestants,* but also all *Sectaries,* and *Presbyter-Johns men* would joyne all together both by word and good example of life to convert the *Turkes,* the *Jewes,* the *Heathens,* the *Pagans,* and the *Infidels* that know not God, but live still in darknesse, and in the shadow of *Death.*

Hartwell's preface proceeds from outright condemnation of the text based on national pride to a call to transcend national and religious boundaries in the common objective of Christian evangelization. Just as his translation crosses national and linguistic boundaries in order to contribute to knowledge of the world, so the translator also implicitly recognizes that effective evangelization of all those who "know not God" across the globe would demand cooperation across religious boundaries. The expansion of both spiritual and natural knowledge was not only a goal shared by the different European empires but one that required sharing across borders.[60]

60. Hartwell, "Translator to the Reader," in Pigafetta, *Reporte of the Kingdome of Congo,* trans. Hartwell, [5], [6], [8–11]. David Boruchoff analyzes the shared spiritual objectives and ideals of conquest in England and Spain in "The Politics of Providence: History and Empire in the Writings of Pietro Martire, Richard Eden, and Richard Hakluyt," in Anne J. Cruz, ed., *Material and Symbolic Circulation between Spain and England, 1554–1604* (Aldershot, Eng., 2008), 103–122. Ann Laura Stoler and Frederick Cooper's questions with respect to the circulation of knowledge in the nineteenth- and twentieth-century empires and its contribution to a "consensual notion of *Homo europeaus*" are just as, if not more, relevant to the early modern imperial world: "The production of colonial knowledge occurred not only within the bounds of nation-states and in relationship to their subject colonized populations but also transnationally, across imperial centers. To what extent—and by what processes—did the knowledge of individual empires become a collective imperial knowledge, shared among colonizing powers? Was there ever a language of domination, crossing the distinct metropolitan politics and linguistic barriers of French, English, Spanish, German, and Dutch?" See Stoler and Cooper, "Between Metropole and

Hartwell demonstrates the familiar range of English sentiments toward Iberians in the Elizabethan and Jacobean age—enmity, envy, rivalry—but also one that is often overlooked: the desire for collaboration in the pursuit of a common imperial project. This chapter has highlighted instances of not only co-optation but also cooperation—whether its motives are lofty or self-interested, universalist or individualistic—at the very site where one would least expect collaboration: captivity. Whether texts or individuals, the captives of this chapter have not simply been "taught to speak" their captors' tongue, as Hartwell declares of the *Relatione del reame di Congo.* They have also taught their captors the value of the experience that crosses borders, of the ability to speak foreign tongues.

Colony: Rethinking a Research Agenda," in Cooper and Stoler, eds., *Tensions of Empire: Colonial Cultures in a Bourgeois World* (Berkeley, Calif., 1997), 1–56, esp. 13.

conclusion : comparative crossings

Throughout this book, I have highlighted common features among the texts under study. Nevertheless, these captives and authors teach us to embrace, rather than elide, distance and difference. Although many of the authors coincide in identifying, to some degree, with European or Euro-American captives, their affinities with the indigenous peoples that figure in their accounts vary much more widely. El Inca Garcilaso de la Vega is the only author to explicitly identify himself with the Amerindians of Florida, affirming that he and they belong to a single "nation." Meanwhile, the self-legitimation that Francisco Núñez de Pineda y Bascuñán and John Smith derive from their knowledge of indigenous culture is based, not on heritage, but on experience. Because of their intimate contact with Amerindians through more or less "happy captivities," they both offer favorable and individualized presentations of indigenous people—the Chilean-born Pineda to a much greater degree than the Englishman Smith, who spent only a few years in North America. In contrast to all of these authors, José de Santa Rita Durão's more standardized depiction of the Tupinambá is based on knowledge acquired through books and is conditioned by a Catholic perspective, Enlightenment ideas of the noble savage, and epic literary conventions.[1]

The authors' portrayals of Amerindian captives among Europeans are particularly illustrative of their different positions with respect to indigenous perspectives. *La Florida del Inca* frequently dramatizes the plight of Amerindian captives, who never enjoy the happy captivity granted to Juan Ortiz by Mucozo. The violence provoked by Spanish slave-raiding undermines the potential for intercultural understanding that ex-captives could otherwise promote. Similar to Garcilaso, Pineda principally blames the continuation

1. Garcilaso refers in the proem to his obligation to write about La Florida as deriving from "ambas naciones, porque soy hijo de un español y una india" [both nations, because I am the son of a Spaniard and an Indian]; he later preempts accusations that he exaggerates indigenous rhetorical abilities "por loar nuestra nación, que, aunque las regiones y tierras estén tan distantes, parece que todas son Indias" [to praise our nation, because, even though the regions and lands are so distant, it seems that they are all the Indies]. See el Inca Garcilaso de la Vega, *La Florida del Inca,* ed. Sylvia Lynn Hilton (Madrid, 1982 [orig. publ. Lisbon, 1605]), 63, 192.

of the Chilean wars on the Spanish practice of enslaving Araucanians. However, he and his father are shown to treat their captives with benevolence, suggesting that Pineda presents the "unhappy captivity" of Amerindians mainly in order to underscore differences between the peninsular Spaniards, whose misrule has devastated colonial Chile and exemplary creoles like him and his father.

Durão's depiction of the conquest and colonization of Brazil entirely elides the Portuguese enslavement of Amerindians. Paraguaçu's voyage to France requires a captivity-like immersion in a foreign culture, but her displacement and return home are presented as voluntary. Nearly a century after Paraguaçu, Pocahontas made a similar transatlantic journey to Europe, but with two significant differences: she accompanied as wife, not the man whom she presumably saved from execution, but another colonist of lesser status, and she died before she could make the return trip home. Although Pocahontas is most often remembered as the savior of an English captive, she was also taken captive herself in an effort to secure her father's submission and the release of English hostages. In his letter to Queen Anne describing Pocahontas, John Smith recounts that, through her captivity, "the Colonie . . . was relieved, peace concluded, and at last rejecting her barbarous condition, was maried to an English Gentleman; the first Christian ever of that Nation, the first Virginian ever spake English, or had a childe in mariage by an Englishman." Smith's comments reveal the extent to which he views the captivity of Amerindians as capable of producing assimilated, English-speaking Christians who can ensure the success of English colonization. In Smith's text and Durão's epic, it is not only the European ex-captive but also the captivated Amerindian women who serve the goals of conquest and evangelization.[2]

2. Philip L. Barbour, ed., *The Complete Works of John Smith (1580–1631)*, 3 vols. (Chapel Hill, N.C., 1986), II, 259 (hereafter cited as Smith, *Complete Works*). As in colonial Chile, Portuguese law generally permitted the enslavement of Amerindians captured in a "just war," although the Crown prohibited it during a few brief periods (1609–1611; 1680–1688). Amerindian slavery was banned in the mid-eighteenth century, but illegal slave-trading continued for at least a century; see Robin M. Wright, with the collaboration of Manuela Carneiro da Cunha, "Destruction, Resistance, and Transformation—Southern, Coastal, and Northern Brazil (1580–1890)," in Frank Salomon and Stuart B. Schwartz, eds., *The Cambridge History of the Native Peoples of the Americas,* III, *South America,* part 2 (Cambridge, 1999), 287–385, esp. 295, 307–308. On the disastrous effects of enslavement on indigenous populations in Bra-

Although both Paraguaçu and Pocahontas remind us of the all too frequent captivity of Amerindians among Europeans, they are more often characterized as enamored female captors, a theme that appears in all of these texts, albeit inflected in different ways. Garcilaso's version of the Juan Ortiz tale differs from that of the Fidalgo d'Elvas by asserting an amorous relationship between the cruel cacique's daughter and Mucozo, to whom she sends Ortiz in order to spare him from her father's wrath. In this way, Garcilaso underscores Mucozo's willingness to sacrifice marriage to his beloved in order to save the Christian captive. Demonstrating the noble character of both the daughter and Mucozo through their kind actions toward the captive is perhaps more important to Garcilaso than portraying a cross-cultural love affair, which he roundly condemns—despite his own mixed ancestry—in the case of the deserter Diego de Guzmán.

Like Garcilaso and the Fidalgo d'Elvas, Pineda reveals the popularity of the trope of the captor's enamored daughter for a contemporary public. He recounts how Maulicán's daughter, out of "affectionate love," repeatedly visits him alone—much to the pious captive's chagrin—in order to provide him with food while he is hiding from enemy caciques who have announced their intention to kill him. However, Pineda explicitly writes against readers' expectations of a cross-cultural love affair, something that had already been misrepresented on-stage in Lima. Pineda's account of the episode thus sets the facts straight by attesting to the virtue of the Christian captive. The girl's actions also contribute to the portrait of happy captivity that is essential to Pineda's critique of corrupt colonial administrators. She corroborates the lesson of reciprocity and model of proper evangelization proposed by Pineda, for she later becomes his own happy captive who voluntarily embraces her captor's religion. Nevertheless, her untimely death can remind us of the innumerable Amerindians, both male and female, whose captivity among Spaniards and creoles was anything but pleasant.[3]

---

zil, see John Hemming, *Red Gold: The Conquest of the Brazilian Indians* (Cambridge, Mass., 1978), 146–160, 505–521. Captain Samuel Argall took Pocahontas hostage in 1613, and her captivity among the English resulted in her conversion and marriage to John Rolfe in 1614; see Pauline Turner Strong, *Captive Selves, Captivating Others: The Politics and Poetics of Colonial American Captivity Narratives* (Boulder, Colo., 1999), 63–70.

3. Francisco Núñez de Pineda y Bascuñán, *Cautiverio feliz y razón individual de las guerras dilatadas del reino de Chile,* [ed. Diego Barros Arana], Colección de historiadores de Chile, III (Santiago, 1863), 150.

In contrast to Pineda's or Garcilaso's mere suggestions, Durão fleshes out the amorous relationship between the Portuguese captive and the captor's daughter in *Caramuru,* even though he affirms both the essential chastity of the hero and his attraction to and involvement with other native women. Still, the romance is by no means an interreligious one, for Paraguaçu, like Maulicán's daughter, fully assumes her husband's faith. Paraguaçu's central and multiple roles in the poem—as interpreter, mediator, traveling companion, consort, convert, and deliverer of Brazil to the Portuguese sovereign—represent a striking contrast to the nameless indigenous women in *La Florida* and *Cautiverio feliz.* Yet her distinctive "white" features and eager acceptance of Christianity and Portuguese rule negate the possibility of a truly cross-cultural romance.[4]

Pocahontas also appears, in the English texts and images that depict her, to have embraced wholeheartedly a Christian and English identity after her baptism as "Lady Rebecca." The disparity between Diogo Álvares's willingness to marry his indigenous savior and John Smith's reluctance to do so could easily be generalized to their respective cultures, as when Vianna Moog asserts, "Just as Diogo Álvares is very Catholic and Portuguese in marrying Paraguassú, John Smith, by not marrying Pocahontas, is very Anglo-Saxon and Protestant, perhaps more Protestant than Anglo-Saxon." For Moog and other proponents of Luso-Tropicalism—Portugal's supposedly milder brand of colonialism—Iberia's previous conquest and occupation by the Moors prepared the Portuguese to embrace sexual miscegenation with "peoples of darker skins." Nevertheless, the historical cases of Paraguaçu and Pocahontas differ less than the national myths that have been constructed retrospectively about them. Like her Brazilian counterpart, Pocahontas married and had a child with a white colonist, John Rolfe—a fact that John Smith could present to the queen in 1617 as "a matter surely . . . worthy of a Princes understanding"—but only after she converted and was baptized as Lady Rebecca.[5]

Like the rumored relationship between Alvarito and Maulicán's daughter, and between John Smith and Pocahontas or the "Lady Tragabigzanda,"

4. José de Santa Rita Durão, *Caramuru: Poema épico do descobrimento da Bahia* (São Paulo, 1945 [orig. publ. Lisbon, 1781]), 64.

5. Vianna Moog, *Bandeirantes and Pioneers,* trans. L. L. Barrett (New York, 1964), 68, 72; Moog's book was originally published as *Bandeirantes e pioneros: Paralelo entre duas culturas* (Rio de Janeiro, 1956). Smith denies the rumors that he intended to marry Pocahontas in Smith, *Complete Works,* I, 274.

the legend of Caramuru and Paraguaçu appears to have inspired theatrical representations in colonial Brazil. The second part of Nuno Marques Pereira's *Compêndio narrativo do peregrino da América,* whose first part was published in Lisbon in 1728, describes the performance of a comedy based on Diogo Álvares's shipwreck. The title, *El dichoso naufragante* [The Happy Castaway], echoes that of Pineda's work, *Cautiverio feliz* [Happy Captivity], and it is also written in the same language. The reader who annotated a 1731 edition of the first part of the *Compêndio* held at the Newberry Library might have been perturbed to encounter this episode in the second part (which remained unpublished until the twentieth century). In the Newberry's copy, several instances of Spanish verse merit marginal comments like "Era milhor que escrevesse em Português esta poesia" [It would have been better to write this poem in Portuguese] or "Devia ser [em] Português para quem escreveu, e naõ para hispanhões" [It should be in Portuguese for those for whom he is writing, and not for Spaniards]. The scornful comments point up the fact that, since the period in which Spain and Portugal shared a sovereign—frequently referred to in Portugal as the "Spanish captivity" (1580–1640)—the Castilian language has proverbially been characterized as "a língua do enemigo" [the language of the enemy]. Nevertheless, poetic composition in Spanish and performances of Spanish plays were not uncommon in Brazil long after the Golden Age currency of the Spanish language among Portuguese writers like Gil Vicente, Jorge de Montemor, and Camões. As we have seen throughout this book, linguistic and national borders between the Spanish, Portuguese, and English Empires were permeable, and the individuals as well as texts who crossed them were not always subject to suspicion or derision.[6]

6. Nuno Marques Pereira, *Compêndio narrativo do peregrino da América,* 6th ed., 2 vols. (Rio de Janeiro, 1939), II, 59, 97–99; Pereira, *Compendio narrativo do peregrino da America* (Lisbon, 1731 [orig. publ. Lisbon, 1728]), 258, 260. Two festival accounts from eighteenth-century Minas Gerais (Simão Ferreira Machado's *Triunfo eucharístico* [Lisbon, 1734]) and the anonymous *Áureo throno episcopal* [Lisbon, 1749]) refer to the performance of Spanish plays and the recitation of Spanish poetry; see Affonso Ávila, *Resíduos seiscentistas em Minas: Textos do Século do Ouro e as projeções do mundo barroco,* 2 vols. (Belo Horizonte, Brazil, 1967), I, 274, II, 489–501. Lewis Hanke points out examples of the reverse influence—the Portuguese cultural and literary presence in Spanish America—and laments the "curious fact . . . that relatively few studies have been made of the long-sustained and involved relations between the Portuguese and Spaniards in the New World" in Hanke, *The Portuguese*

Indeed, early modern readers and writers, as well as other historical actors, surely crossed these borders more easily than we traverse the national and other boundaries that delimit our fields of study today. The reference to a version of Diogo Álvares's tale as *El dichoso naufragante* can thus remind us of a comparative approach that goes beyond analyzing parallel developments of the theme of shipwreck and captivity in different contexts. Rather than contrast distinct literary traditions—usually retrospectively constructed to correspond to the modern borders of nation-states—we should interrogate the shared and interconnected histories, the explicit and implicit dialogues, that are so often obscured by modern disciplinary divisions.[7]

In relation to captivity narratives, an interconnected history has perhaps unintentionally been claimed by critics who identify the antecedents to the Anglo-American captivity narrative in sixteenth-century accounts of captivity in areas of Spanish and Portuguese expansion: Álvar Núñez Cabeza de Vaca's *Relación,* the Fidalgo d'Elvas's account of Juan Ortiz in the *Relaçam verdadeira,* Hans Staden's *Warhafftig Historia,* and Job Hortop's *Rare*

---

in Spanish America, with a Special Reference to the Villa Imperial de Potosí (n.p., 1962), rpt. from *Revista histórica de América,* LI (1961), 2.

7. In "Introduction: Cheek to Cheek," in Gustavo Pérez-Firmat, ed., *Do the Americas Have a Common Literature?* (Durham, N.C., 1990), 1–5, Pérez-Firmat outlines four approaches to comparative inter-American study: "generic," which "attempts to establish a hemispheric context by using as a point of departure a broad, abstract notion of wide applicability" (such as captivity, miscegenation, etc.); "appositional," which "involves placing works side by side without postulating causal connections"; "genetic," which "record[s] the uses to which a given author or text have been put by his or her successors"; and "mediative," which "concentrates on texts that already embed an inter-American or comparative dimensions" (3–4). For examples of what Pérez-Firmat might call the "generic" approach to the comparison of Anglo- and Latin American captivity narratives, see Ralph Bauer, *The Cultural Geography of Colonial American Literatures: Empire, Travel, Modernity* (Cambridge, 2003), 118–156; Manuel Broncano, "De cautivos y cautiverios," in María José Álvarez, Manuel Broncano, and José Luis Chamoso, eds., *La frontera: Mito y realidad del Nuevo Mundo* (León, 1994), 167–181. Whereas Broncano finds "two versions of the same process" in Álvar Núñez Cabeza de Vaca and Mary Rowlandson, Bauer's more careful contextualization allows him to point out important similarities as well as differences between Rowlandson and Francisco Núñez de Pineda y Bascuñán. Although to a certain extent my approach in this book has been similarly "generic," in Pérez-Firmat's terms, I have also sought to highlight the shared and interconnected histories that Pérez-Firmat would characterize as "genetic" and "mediative."

Travailes. The first three of these texts have been included in several early-twenty-first century anthologies of colonial "American" writing, anthologies that respond to the call within the field of American studies to widen the canon by incorporating texts in other languages and from other areas of the hemisphere. Cabeza de Vaca, in particular, has been cast as a protonational figure; one of the anthologies introduces his journey as the one "that perhaps best signifies the process of becoming an American." The Iberian imperial context of Cabeza de Vaca's rhetoric and objectives—even his career subsequent to his North American misadventures—is inevitably elided in such a reading.[8]

Such appropriations are not new: the Juan Ortiz tale has long been included in anthologies of "Indian captivity narratives," although for purposes quite different from contemporary uses of Cabeza de Vaca. A version presumably based on the Fidalgo d'Elvas's text can be found in Samuel G. Drake's *Indian Captivities: Being a Collection of the Most Remarkable Narratives of Persons Taken Captive by the North American Indians* (1839), one of the earliest and most popular of the nineteenth-century collections, as well as in James Wimer's *Events in Indian History* (1841). Far from offering the original "without the slightest abridgment," as Drake affirms in the preface, his version includes references to "European guile" and other insidious qualities of the Spaniards: "Upon the whole it is hard to say which was the predominant trait in the character of Soto and his followers, avarice or cruelty. It is as difficult to decide which was the more superstitious, the Indians or the self-styled 'Christian Spaniards.'" Even Iberian narratives of the

8. For the trans-American genealogy of captivity narratives, see R. W. G. Vail, *The Voice of the Old Frontier* (Philadelphia, 1949), 29–30; Richard VanDerBeets, ed., *Held Captive by Indians: Selected Narratives, 1642–1836* (Knoxville, Tenn., 1973), xx; Nancy Armstrong and Leonard Tennenhouse, *The Imaginary Puritan: Literature, Intellectual Labor, and the Origins of Personal Life* (Berkeley, Calif., 1992), 203. Anthologies include Gordon M. Sayre, ed., *American Captivity Narratives* (Boston, 2000); Susan Castillo and Ivy Schweitzer, eds., *The Literatures of Colonial America: An Anthology* (Malden, Mass., 2001); Paul Lauter et al., eds., *The Heath Anthology of American Literature,* 4th ed., 2 vols. (Boston, 2002); Carla Mulford, ed., *Early American Writings* (New York, 2002) (quotation in Lauter et al., eds., *Heath Anthology,* 17). I address the promises and pitfalls of the "hemispheric turn" exemplified by these anthologies in Lisa Voigt, "'Por Andarmos Todos Casy Mesturados': The Politics of Intermingling in Caminha's *Carta* and Colonial American Anthologies," *Early American Literature,* XL (2005), 407–439.

captivity of Iberians—not just Iberian denouncements of the enslavement of Amerindians, like Bartolomé de Las Casas's and Fernão Cardim's—could be used, quite contrary to the authors' intentions, to promote the Black Legend of Spanish barbarism and Papist superstition.[9]

The peregrination of captivity narratives from Portuguese and Spanish to (American) English has a transatlantic dimension, as well. In the preface to *Slaves in Algiers; or, A Struggle for Freedom* (1794), a play about United States captives on the Barbary Coast of North Africa, Susanna Rowson acknowledges Cervantes as a source for "some part of the plot." Perhaps more interesting than the various details derived from Cervantes is the play's ironic invocation of the theme of the "enamored captor's daughter." The Spanish captive Sebastian laments his captivity of more than two years:

> All that time [working] in the garden of the Alcaide, who has twelve wives, thirty concubines, and two pretty daughters; and yet not one of the insensible husseys ever took a fancy to me.—'Tis dev'lish hard—that when I go home, I can't say to my honoured father, the barber, and to my reverend mother, the laundress—this is the beautiful princess, who fell in love with me; jumped over the garden wall of his holiness her father, and ran away with your dutiful son, Sebastian—then, falling on my knees—thus.

Eighteenth-century audiences might have been familiar with not only the motif but the textual source—the "Captive's Tale" of *Don Quijote*—invoked in the soliloquy. Although not as negatively portrayed as the greedy, dishonest Jew Hassan or the "old, ugly, ill natured Turk" Muley, the Spaniard still

9. Samuel G. Drake's *Indian Captivities: Being a Collection of the Most Remarkable Narratives of Persons Taken Captive by the North American Indians . . .* (Boston, 1839) was reissued in at least ten subsequent editions under various titles, including (the one from which I cite) *Tragedies of the Wilderness; or, True and Authentic Narratives of Captives, Who Have Been Carried Away by the Indians from the Various Frontier Settlements of the United States, from the Earliest to the Present Time . . .* (Boston, 1841), iii, 17, 19. James Wimer's *Events in Indian History, Beginning with an Account of the Origin of the American Indians, and the Early Settlements in North America . . .* (Lancaster, Pa., 1841) apparently drew the tale of Juan Ortiz from Drake's collection. Gordon Sayre's more recent *American Captivity Narratives* includes Garcilaso's version of the Ortiz tale, which he juxtaposes with John Smith in a section entitled "Saved by the Chief's Daughter."

serves as a foil for the honest and virtuous American and English protagonists, who, unlike Sebastian, refuse to marry Muslims.[10]

Rowson's and Drake's appropriations and adaptations of Iberian captivity narratives are infused with the same anti-Spanish sentiment that informs Job Hortop's and other tales of captivity among Iberians. However, other Anglo-American captivity narratives evince a more complex attitude toward Spaniards and Spanish culture that is comparable to that which we have seen in English writers of the Elizabethan and Jacobean periods. A case in point is Jonathan Dickinson's journal of his shipwreck and captivity in Florida, published in 1699 under the title *God's Protecting Providence, Man's Surest Help and Defence in the Times of the Greatest Difficulty and Most Imminent Danger; Evidenced in the Remarkable Deliverance of Divers Persons, from the Devouring Waves of the Sea, amongst Which They Suffered Shipwrack. And Also from the More Cruelly Devouring Jawes of the Inhumane Canibals of Florida. Faithfully Related by One of the Persons Concerned Therein, Jonathan Dickenson* [sic]. This best-selling work, reprinted fourteen times between 1700 and 1868, recounts the shipwreck of Dickinson's family and companions off Jupiter Island on the east coast of Florida, which occurred on their way from Port Royal, Jamaica, to Philadelphia in 1696. After nearly six months of wandering along the Florida coast, they reached the Spanish fort of Saint Augustine and from there went on to Charlestown in the English colony of Carolina. Among the most remarkable features of their "remarkable deliverance," according to the editor's preface to the first edition, is the "hardship" that they were "forced to mask themselves under the name of Spaniards though few of them could speak any Spanish . . . mostly because the natives often suspected them to be English, and thereby they were continually in danger of their lives." Indeed, Dickinson and his companions survive only because of their ability to disguise themselves as Spaniards among Amerindians who constantly ask whether they are "Nickaleer" (Englishmen). Solomon Cresson, a Harlem native of French Huguenot descent, is the most valued member of the group because of his considerable fluency in

10. Susanna Haswell Rowson, *Slaves in Algiers; or, A Struggle for Freedom,* ed. Jennifer Margulis and Karen M. Poremski (Acton, Mass., 2000 [orig. publ. Philadelphia, 1794]), 6, 46, 51. I thank Diana de Armas Wilson for the reference to *Slaves in Algiers.* On the Anglo-American Barbary captivity narrative, to which Rowson's play is thematically affiliated, see Paul Baepler, introduction, in Baepler, ed., *White Slaves, African Masters: An Anthology of American Barbary Captivity Narratives* (Chicago, 1999), 1–58.

Spanish, but all the survivors are forced to avail themselves of what Spanish they know.[11]

Another of the "remarkable things" is the "courtesy of the governor of Augustine, who clothed these naked people, fed their hungry stomachs, and caused them to be conducted safely to Carolina . . . especially being a man of another nation, as well as of a different religion." Furthermore, it was a Spanish party (Sebastián López, ten soldiers, and an Amerindian interpreter) that sought out and brought the survivors to Saint Augustine: "The Spaniards were extraordinary kind unto us, so that we had occasion to rejoice, and thank the Lord for this part of our deliverance by this means." Divine intervention aside, the English shipwreck survivors' "remarkable deliverance" is a Spanish accomplishment in a double sense, for it is achieved both through the knowledge of the Spanish language and through the assistance of Spaniards. The survivors' ability to "pass" for Spaniards, as well as the Spaniards' eagerness to help the Englishmen, challenge the national and religious boundaries that the editor presents as self-evident. The Spanish governor of Saint Augustine also acknowledges the force of those borders when he bids farewell to the English party, declaring—as the imprint emphasizes in all capital letters—"WE SHOULD FORGET HIM WHEN WE GOT AMONGST OUR OWN NATION, and also added THAT IF WE FORGOT, GOD WOULD NOT FORGET HIM." Yet Dickinson did not, in fact, forget the Spaniard's kindness, as the publication of his narrative attests. Neither should we forget the importance of attending to such dialogues and collaborations in our haste to discover "national" precursors and identities. Nor, one might add, should we forget the other lesson that Dickinson learned in La Florida: the importance of knowing Spanish in this part of the Americas.[12]

Even as the English and Spanish intermingle in *God's Protecting Providence,* for the Florida Indians, the distinction between the two nations is important. The Amerindians continually interrogate their prisoners whether they are "Nickaleer" (English) or "Espania" (Spanish), and they are able to distinguish the two nationalities by hair color and language. Dickinson only provides one individual's reason for hating the English, but it surely explains more about the universal loathing of "Nickaleers." This man had

11. Evangeline Walker Andrews and Charles McLean Andrews, eds., *Jonathan Dickinson's Journal; or, God's Protecting Providence. Being the Narrative of a Journey from Port Royal in Jamaica to Philadelphia between August 23, 1696, and April 1, 1697* (New Haven, Conn., 1945 [orig. publ. Philadelphia, 1699]), 104.

12. Ibid., 63, 87, 104.

been kidnapped "by some of our English sloops" to serve as a diver, but he had managed to escape and return home. "The greatest charge this man had against the English was for taking him and their people away," Dickinson writes, while hastening to add, "not but that he was well used amongst them." The English, that is, kidnapped and enslaved natives just as the Spanish had elsewhere in La Florida more than a century earlier, and with the same results. As described in Chapter 2, it was just such a capture and removal that might have led to don Luis's revenge on the Jesuit missionaries in 1570. The same practice (perhaps even the same episode) inspired the hostility toward Spaniards that the English settlers of Jamestown encountered among the Chickahominy in 1614, according to Ralph Hamor: "The name [of Spaniards] is odious amongst them, for Powhatan's father was driven by them from the west-Indies into those parts."[13]

Apparently—and despite all the rhetoric of the Black Legend—this was one aspect of the Spanish experience that the English did choose to forget. Or, more likely, they chose to imitate it. Englishmen, Portuguese, and Spaniards not only shared the experience of being held captive in the New World (and elsewhere), and the ability to turn the knowledge gained through captivity to their own ends; they also shared the experience of being captors in the New World. And as this more insidious common ground suggests, perhaps what should replace assumptions about the coherence and stability of national identities in early modern Portugal, Spain, and England is an understanding of what the crossings between them helped to produce: a European-dominated imperial world. Even if captives and American-born authors writing in European languages succeeded in challenging the aspects of an imperial system that marginalized them, they had little effect on its legacy with respect to the indigenous populations of the Americas.

13. Ibid., 62; Ralph Hamor, *A True Discourse of the Present Estate of Virginia* (London, 1615), 13. On the connection sometimes claimed between don Luis and Hamor's "Powhatan's father," see Chapter 2, note 3.

Index